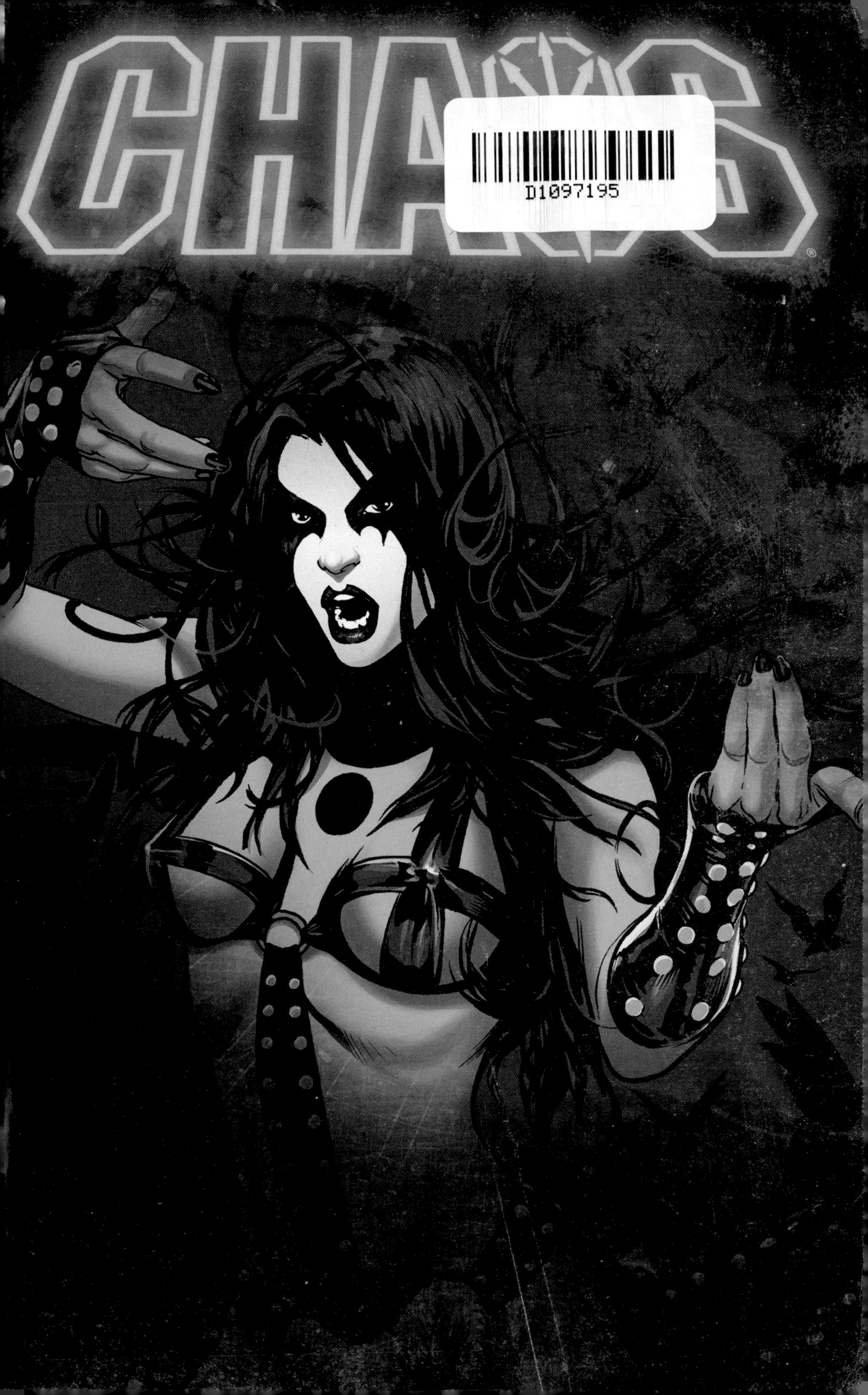
CHAOS

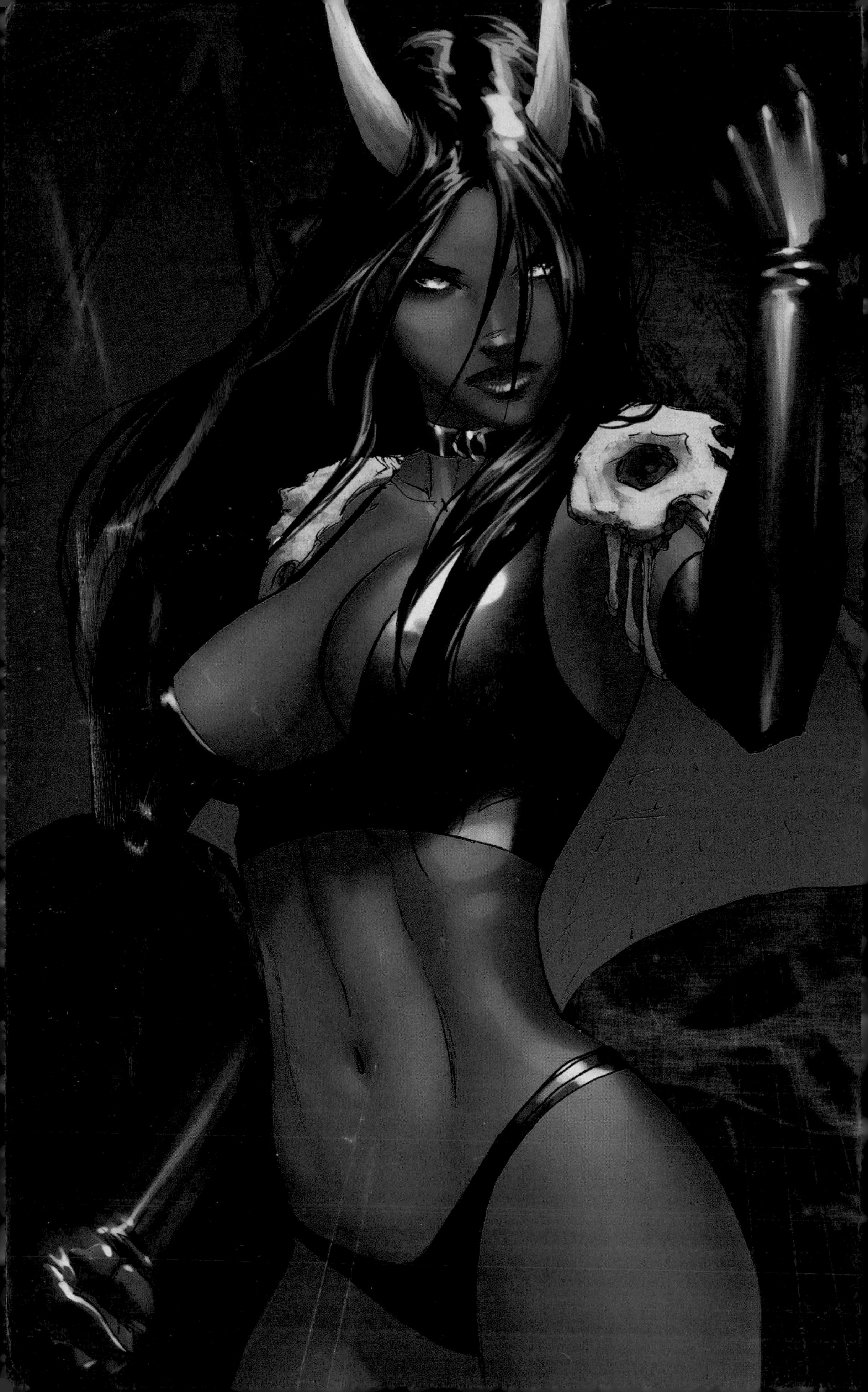

CHA☉S

HIGHWAY TO HEL

WRITTEN BY
TIM SEELEY

ART BY
MIRKA ANDOLFO

LAYOUTS BY
CLINT HILINSKI

COLORS BY
WALTER BAIAMONTE

LETTERS BY
MARSHALL DILLON

COLLECTION COVER BY
J. SCOTT CAMPBELL

COLLECTION COVER COLORS BY
NEI RUFFINO

COLLECTION DESIGN BY
KATIE HIDALGO

THIS VOLUME COLLECTS ISSUES 1-6 OF CHAOS BY DYNAMITE ENTERTAINMENT.

Nick Barrucci, CEO / Publisher
Juan Collado, President / COO
Rich Young, Director Business Development
Keith Davidsen, Marketing Manager

Joe Rybandt, Senior Editor
Hannah Elder, Associate Editor
Molly Mahan, Associate Editor

Jason Ullmeyer, Design Director
Katie Hidalgo, Graphic Designer
Chris Caniano, Digital Associate
Rachel Kilbury, Digital Assistant

Online at www.DYNAMITE.com
On Twitter @dynamitecomics
On Facebook /Dynamitecomics
On YouTube /Dynamitecomics
On Tumblr dynamitecomics.tumblr.com

ISBN-10: 1-60690-586-4   ISBN-13: 978-1-60690-586-9   First Printing   10 9 8 7 6 5 4 3 2 1

CHAOS!®, VOL. 1: HIGHWAY TO HEL. This volume collects material originally published in Chaos #1-6. Published by Dynamite Entertainment. 113 Gaither Dr., STE 205, Mt. Laurel, NJ 08054. Chaos!, Chaos Comics, Evil Ernie, Smiley, Purgatori, and Chastity are ® & © 2015 Dynamite Characters, llc. All Rights Reserved. Mistress Hel, The Chosen, The Dead Onez, Billy Zone, Brandon Green, Harvey Schwartz, Senator Abe Cruise, Serendipity, Lucifer, Asteroth, Cremator, Hell's Belles, Pagan, and Leviatha are ™ & © 2015 Dynamite Characters, llc. All Rights Reserved. DYNAMITE, DYNAMITE ENTER-TAINMENT and its logo are © & ® 2015 Dynamite. All rights reserved. All names, characters, events, and locales in this pub-lication are entirely fictional. Any resemblance to actual persons (living or dead), events or places, without satiric intent, is coincidental. No portion of this book may be reproduced by any means (digital or print) without the written permission of Dynamite Entertainment except for review purposes. The scanning, uploading and distribution of this book via the Internet or via any other means without the permission of the publisher is illegal and punishable by law. Please purchase only authorized electronic editions, and do not participate in or encourage electronic piracy of copyrighted materials. Printed in Canada

For information regarding press, media rights, foreign rights, licensing, promotions, and advertising e-mail:
marketing@dynamite.com

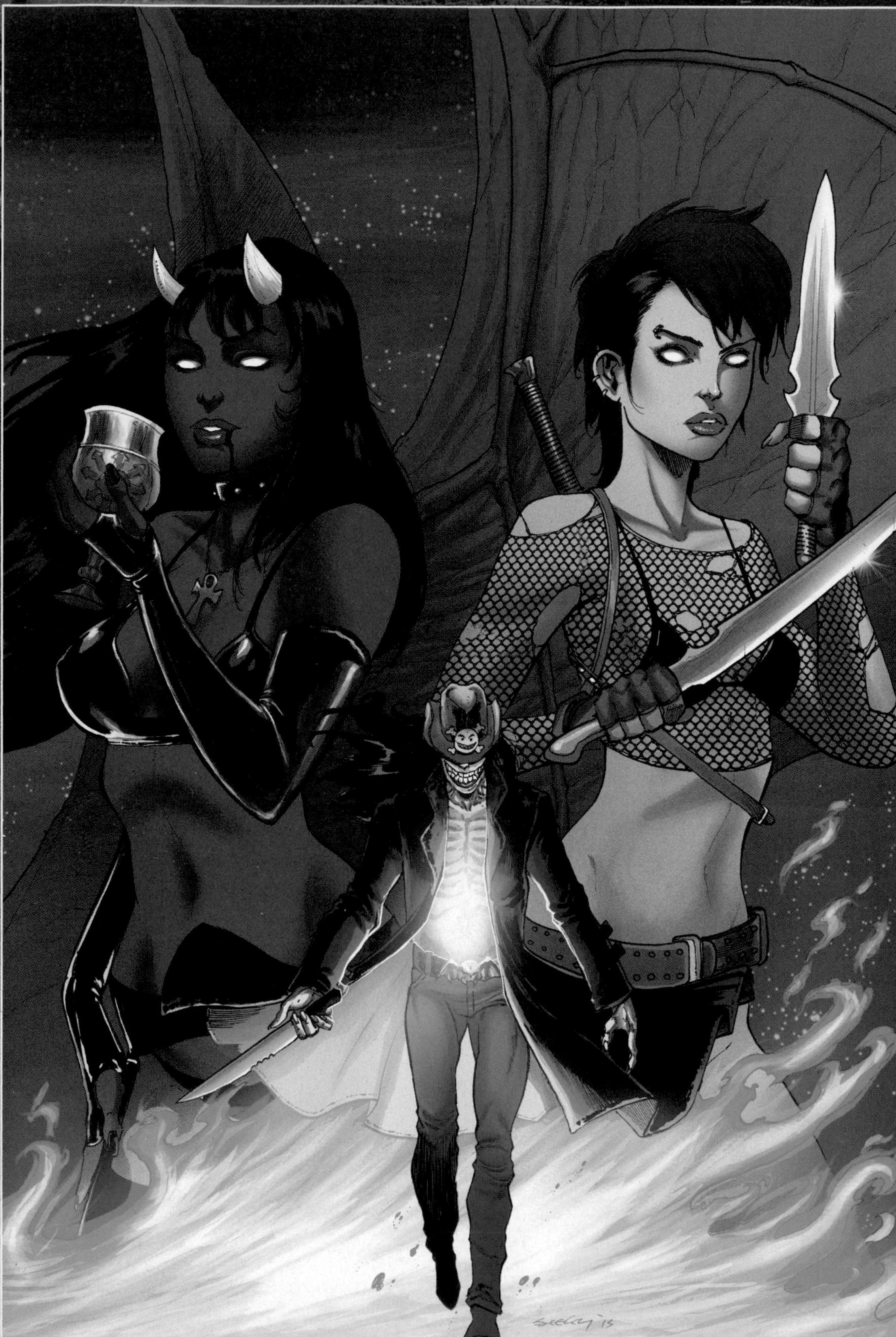

issue #1 cover by TIM SEELEY
colors by ADRIANO LUCAS

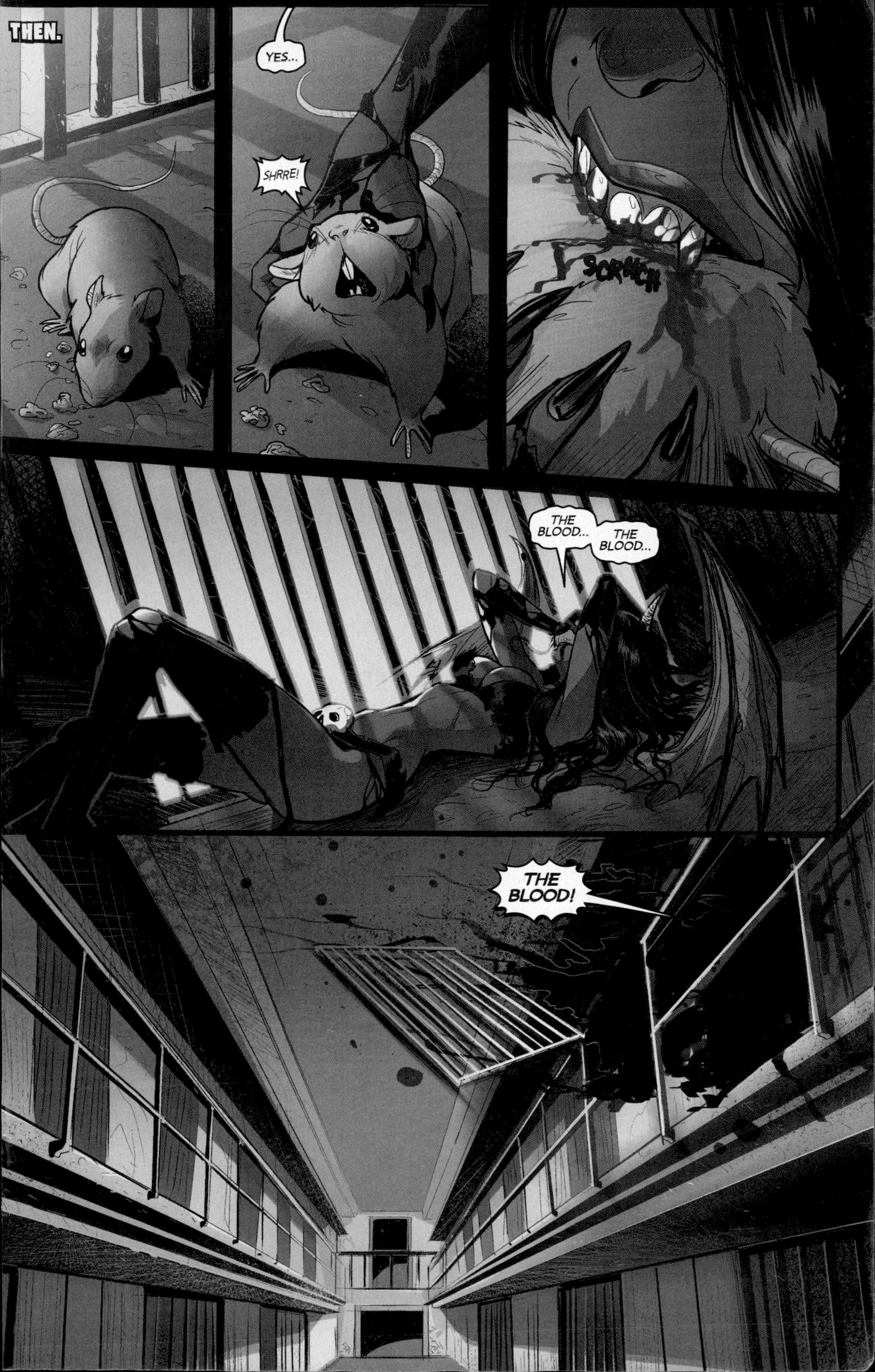
THEN.
YES...
SHRRE!
SCRUNCH
THE BLOOD...
THE BLOOD...
THE BLOOD!

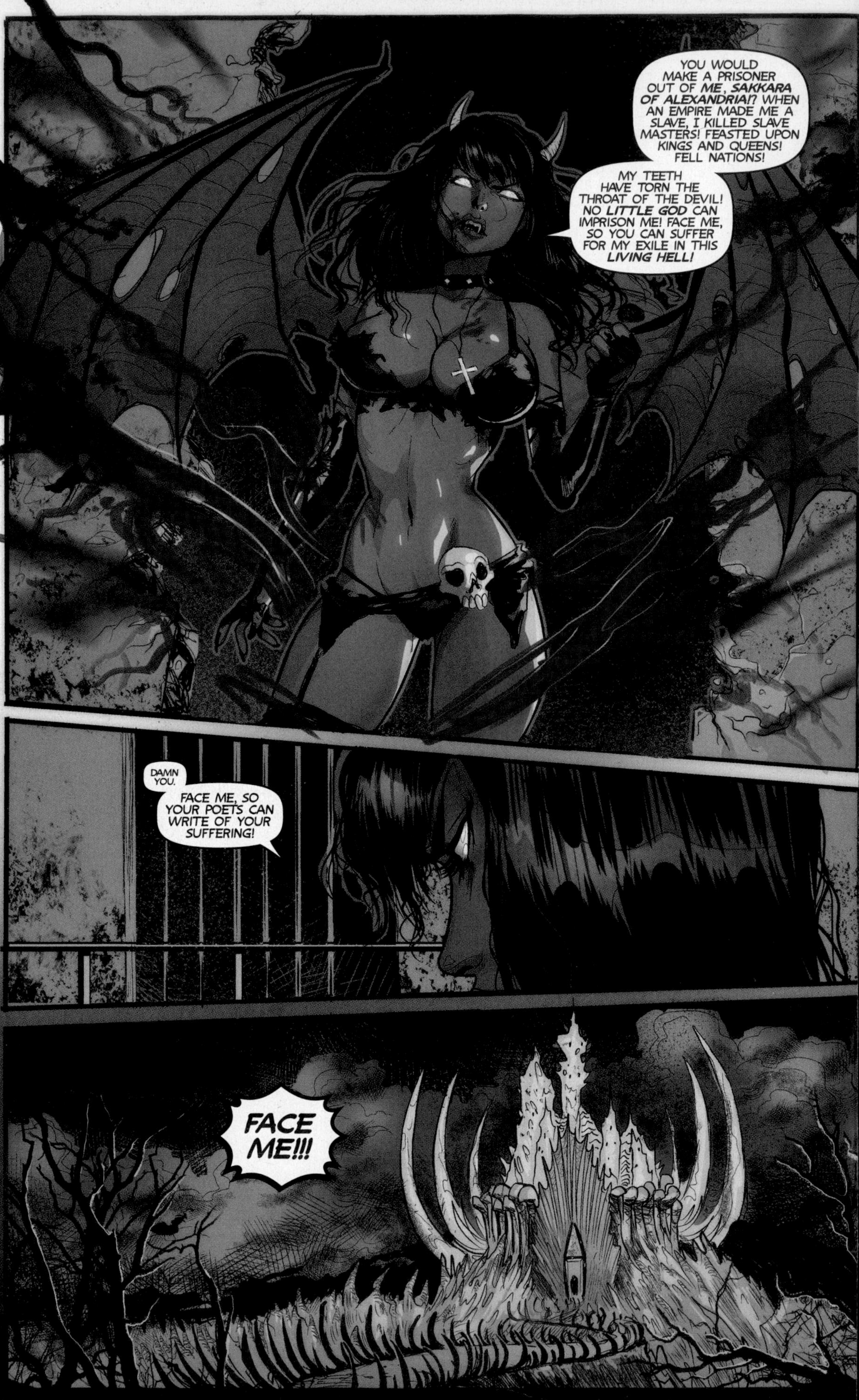

YOU WOULD MAKE A PRISONER OUT OF ME, SAKKARA OF ALEXANDRIA!? WHEN AN EMPIRE MADE ME A SLAVE, I KILLED SLAVE MASTERS! FEASTED UPON KINGS AND QUEENS! FELL NATIONS!
MY TEETH HAVE TORN THE THROAT OF THE DEVIL! NO LITTLE GOD CAN IMPRISON ME! FACE ME, SO YOU CAN SUFFER FOR MY EXILE IN THIS LIVING HELL!
DAMN YOU.
FACE ME, SO YOUR POETS CAN WRITE OF YOUR SUFFERING!
FACE ME!!!

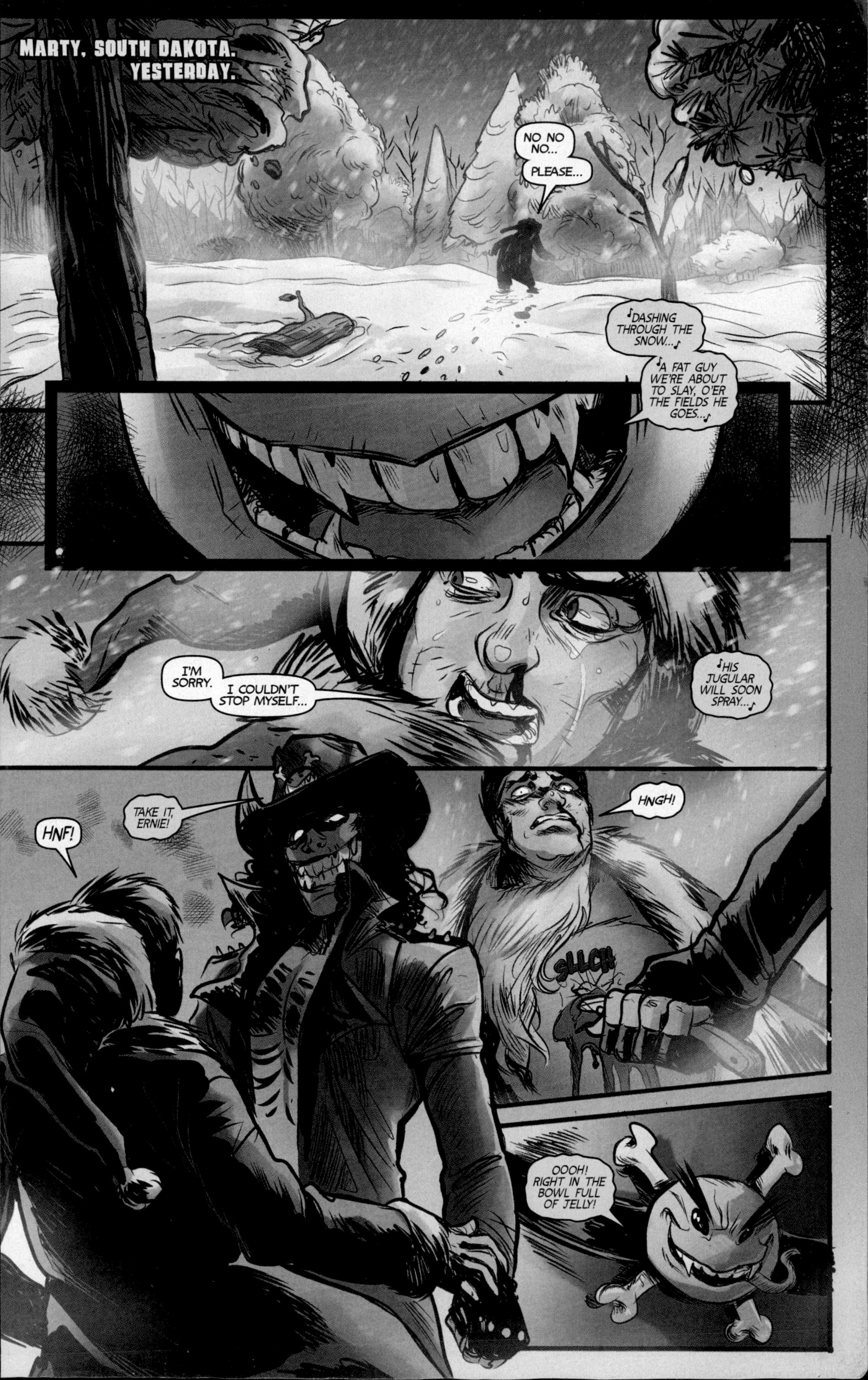
MARTY, SOUTH DAKOTA. YESTERDAY.
NO NO NO...
PLEASE...
♪DASHING THROUGH THE SNOW...♪
♪A FAT GUY WE'RE ABOUT TO SLAY, O'ER THE FIELDS HE GOES...♪
I'M SORRY.
I COULDN'T STOP MYSELF...
♪HIS JUGULAR WILL SOON SPRAY...♪
TAKE IT, ERNIE!
HNGH!
HNF!
SLLCH
OOOH! RIGHT IN THE BOWL FULL OF JELLY!

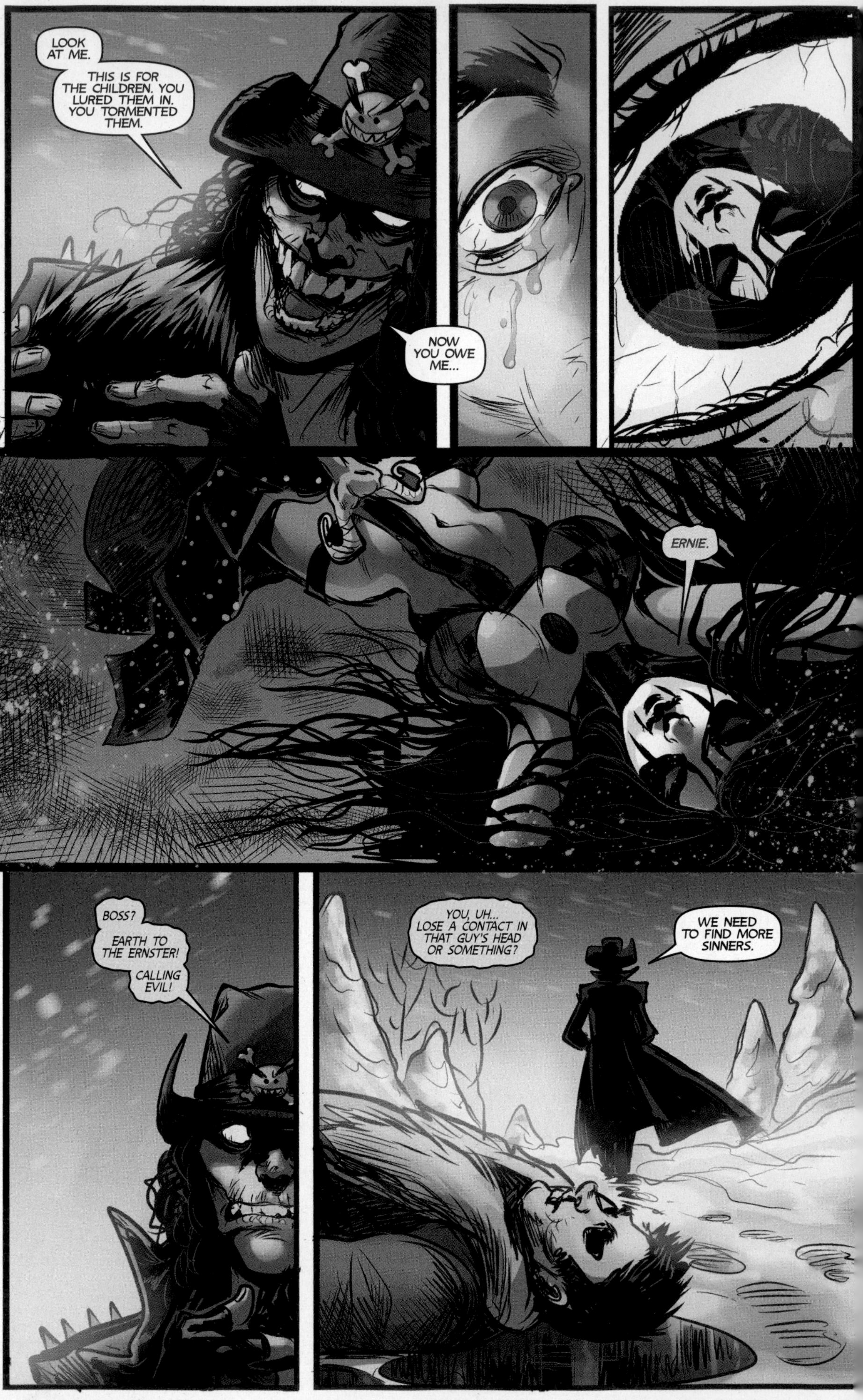
LOOK AT ME.
THIS IS FOR THE CHILDREN. YOU LURED THEM IN. YOU TORMENTED THEM.
NOW YOU OWE ME...
ERNIE.
BOSS?
EARTH TO THE ERNSTER!
CALLING EVIL!
YOU, UH... LOSE A CONTACT IN THAT GUY'S HEAD OR SOMETHING?
WE NEED TO FIND MORE SINNERS.

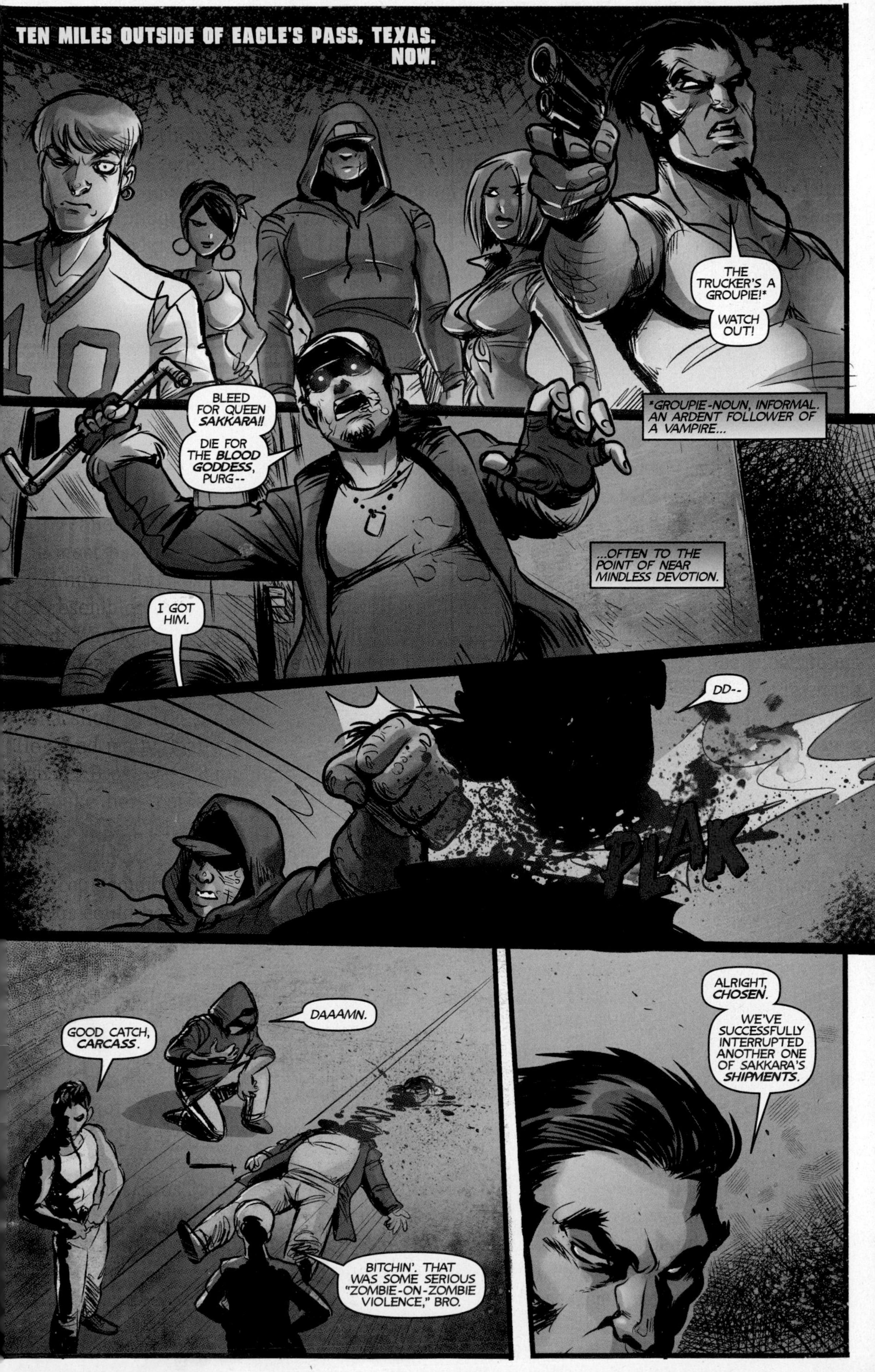
TEN MILES OUTSIDE OF EAGLE'S PASS, TEXAS. NOW.
THE TRUCKER'S A GROUPIE!*
WATCH OUT!
BLEED FOR QUEEN SAKKARA!!
DIE FOR THE BLOOD GODDESS, PURG--
*GROUPIE-NOUN, INFORMAL. AN ARDENT FOLLOWER OF A VAMPIRE...
...OFTEN TO THE POINT OF NEAR MINDLESS DEVOTION.
I GOT HIM.
DD--
PLAK
GOOD CATCH, CARCASS.
DAAAMN.
BITCHIN'. THAT WAS SOME SERIOUS "ZOMBIE-ON-ZOMBIE VIOLENCE," BRO.
ALRIGHT, CHOSEN.
WE'VE SUCCESSFULLY INTERRUPTED ANOTHER ONE OF SAKKARA'S SHIPMENTS.

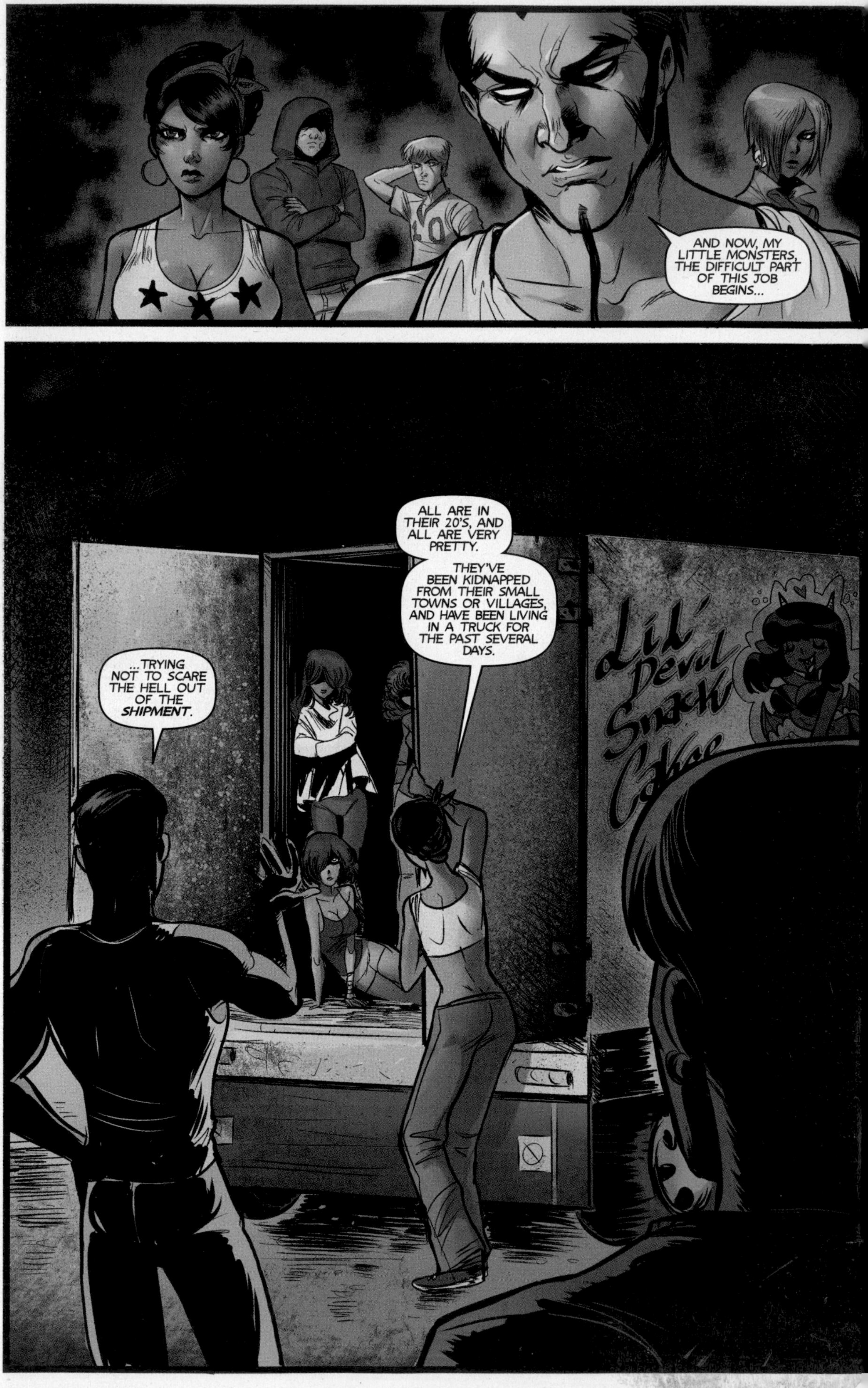
AND NOW, MY LITTLE MONSTERS, THE DIFFICULT PART OF THIS JOB BEGINS...
...TRYING NOT TO SCARE THE HELL OUT OF THE SHIPMENT.
ALL ARE IN THEIR 20'S, AND ALL ARE VERY PRETTY.
THEY'VE BEEN KIDNAPPED FROM THEIR SMALL TOWNS OR VILLAGES, AND HAVE BEEN LIVING IN A TRUCK FOR THE PAST SEVERAL DAYS.

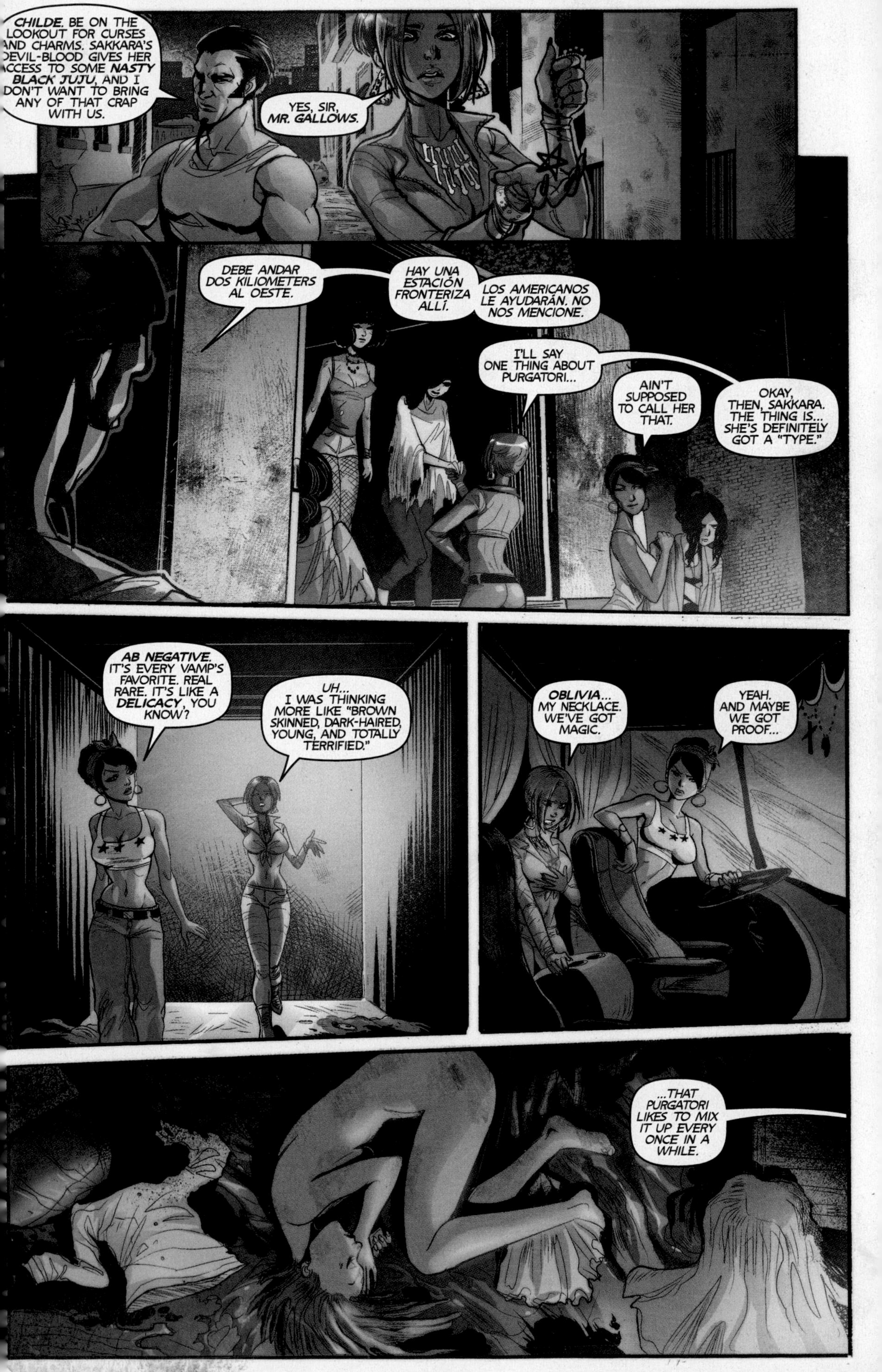
CHILDE. BE ON THE LOOKOUT FOR CURSES AND CHARMS. SAKKARA'S DEVIL-BLOOD GIVES HER ACCESS TO SOME NASTY BLACK JUJU, AND I DON'T WANT TO BRING ANY OF THAT CRAP WITH US.
YES, SIR, MR. GALLOWS.
DEBE ANDAR DOS KILIOMETERS AL OESTE.
HAY UNA ESTACIÓN FRONTERIZA ALLÍ.
LOS AMERICANOS LE AYUDARÁN. NO NOS MENCIONE.
I'LL SAY ONE THING ABOUT PURGATORI...
AIN'T SUPPOSED TO CALL HER THAT.
OKAY, THEN, SAKKARA. THE THING IS... SHE'S DEFINITELY GOT A "TYPE."
AB NEGATIVE. IT'S EVERY VAMP'S FAVORITE. REAL RARE. IT'S LIKE A DELICACY, YOU KNOW?
UH... I WAS THINKING MORE LIKE "BROWN SKINNED, DARK-HAIRED, YOUNG, AND TOTALLY TERRIFIED."
OBLIVIA... MY NECKLACE. WE'VE GOT MAGIC.
YEAH. AND MAYBE WE GOT PROOF...
...THAT PURGATORI LIKES TO MIX IT UP EVERY ONCE IN A WHILE.

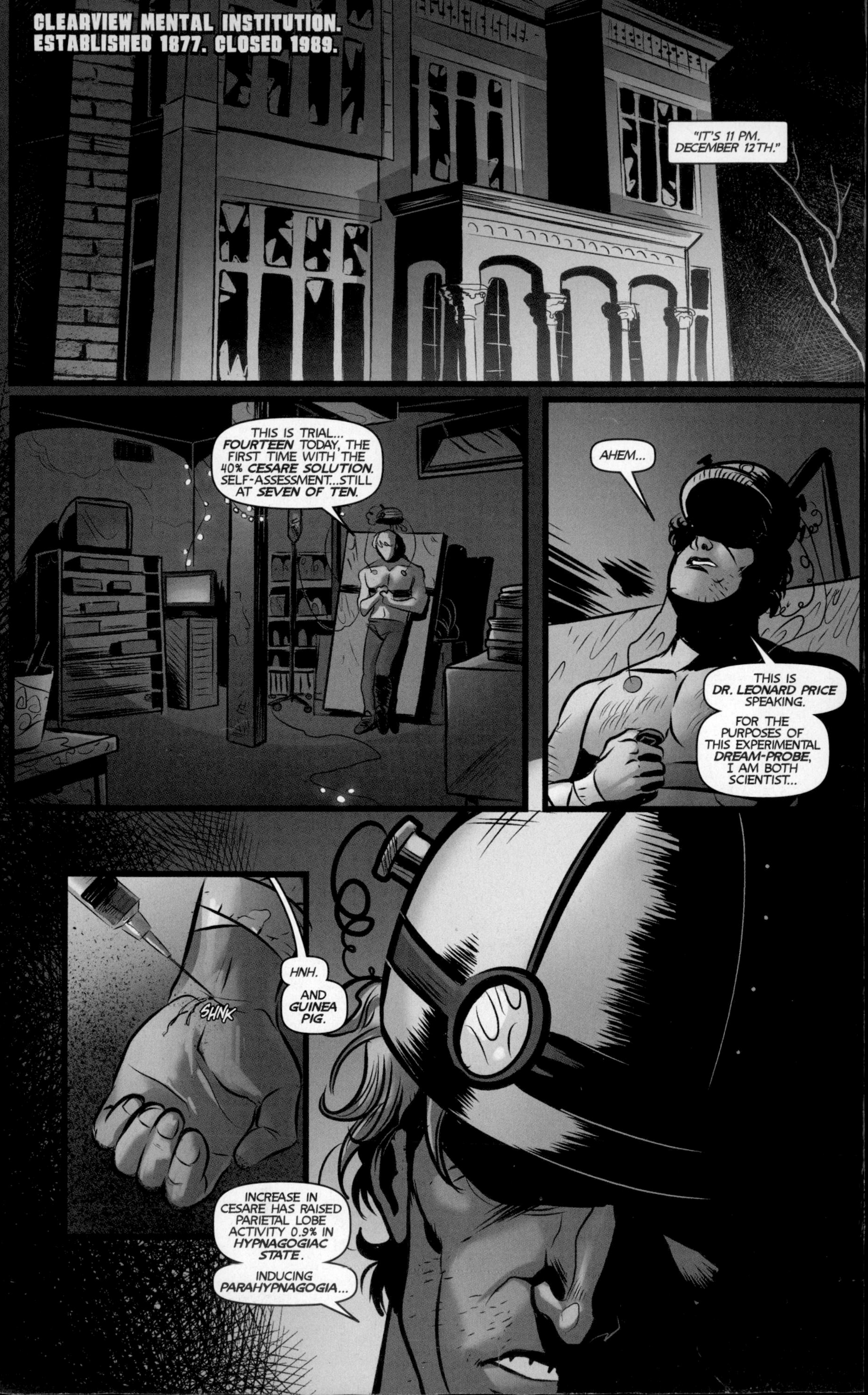
CLEARVIEW MENTAL INSTITUTION. ESTABLISHED 1877. CLOSED 1989.
"IT'S 11 PM. DECEMBER 12TH."
THIS IS TRIAL... FOURTEEN TODAY, THE FIRST TIME WITH THE 40% CESARE SOLUTION. SELF-ASSESSMENT...STILL AT SEVEN OF TEN.
AHEM...
THIS IS DR. LEONARD PRICE SPEAKING.
FOR THE PURPOSES OF THIS EXPERIMENTAL DREAM-PROBE, I AM BOTH SCIENTIST...
HNH.
AND GUINEA PIG.
SHNK
INCREASE IN CESARE HAS RAISED PARIETAL LOBE ACTIVITY 0.9% IN HYPNAGOGIAC STATE.
INDUCING PARAHYPNAGOGIA...

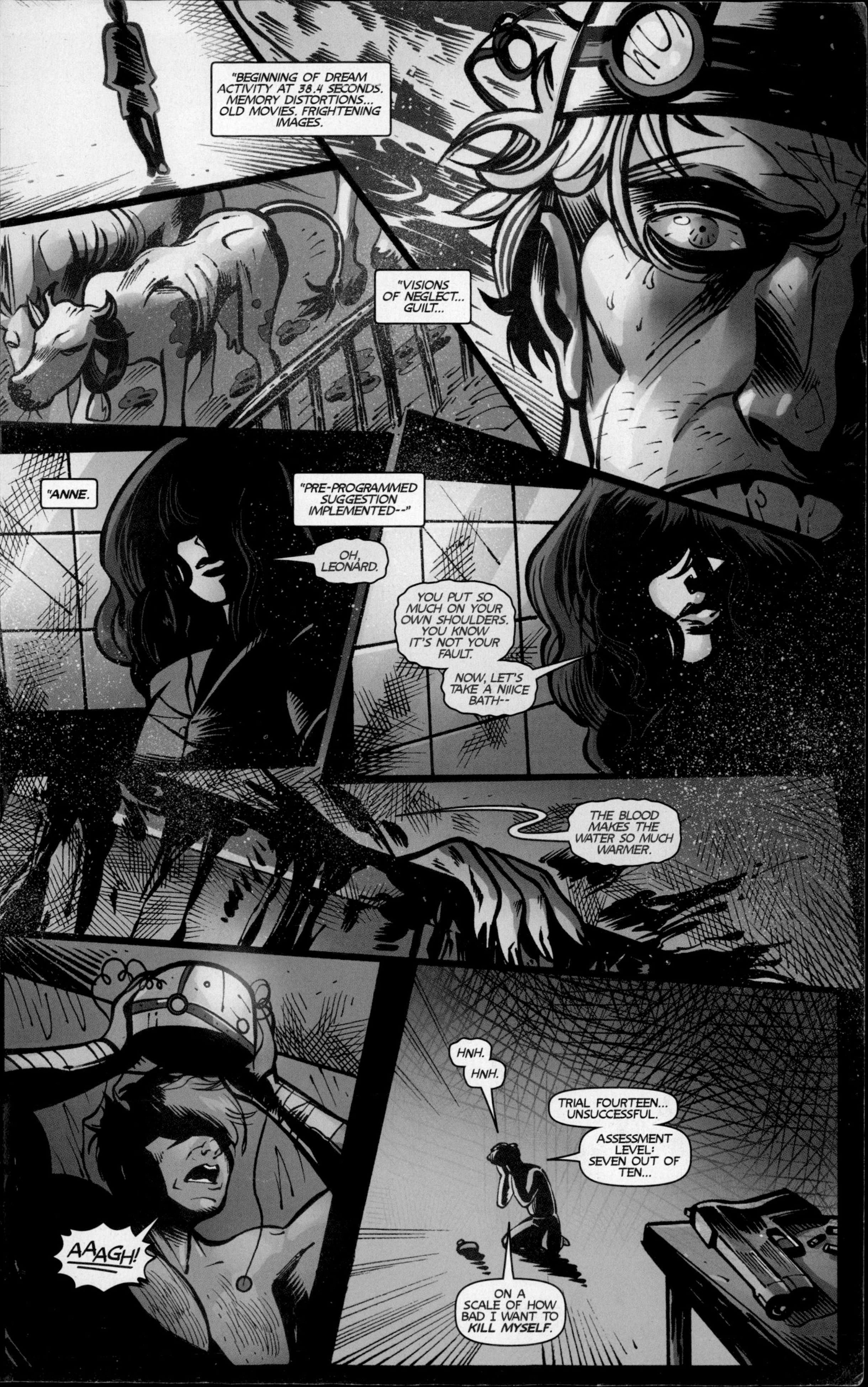
"BEGINNING OF DREAM ACTIVITY AT 38.4 SECONDS. MEMORY DISTORTIONS... OLD MOVIES. FRIGHTENING IMAGES.
"VISIONS OF NEGLECT... GUILT...
"ANNE.
"PRE-PROGRAMMED SUGGESTION IMPLEMENTED--"
OH, LEONARD.
YOU PUT SO MUCH ON YOUR OWN SHOULDERS. YOU KNOW IT'S NOT YOUR FAULT.
NOW, LET'S TAKE A NIIICE BATH--
THE BLOOD MAKES THE WATER SO MUCH WARMER.
AAAGH!
HNH.
HNH.
TRIAL FOURTEEN... UNSUCCESSFUL.
ASSESSMENT LEVEL: SEVEN OUT OF TEN...
ON A SCALE OF HOW BAD I WANT TO KILL MYSELF.

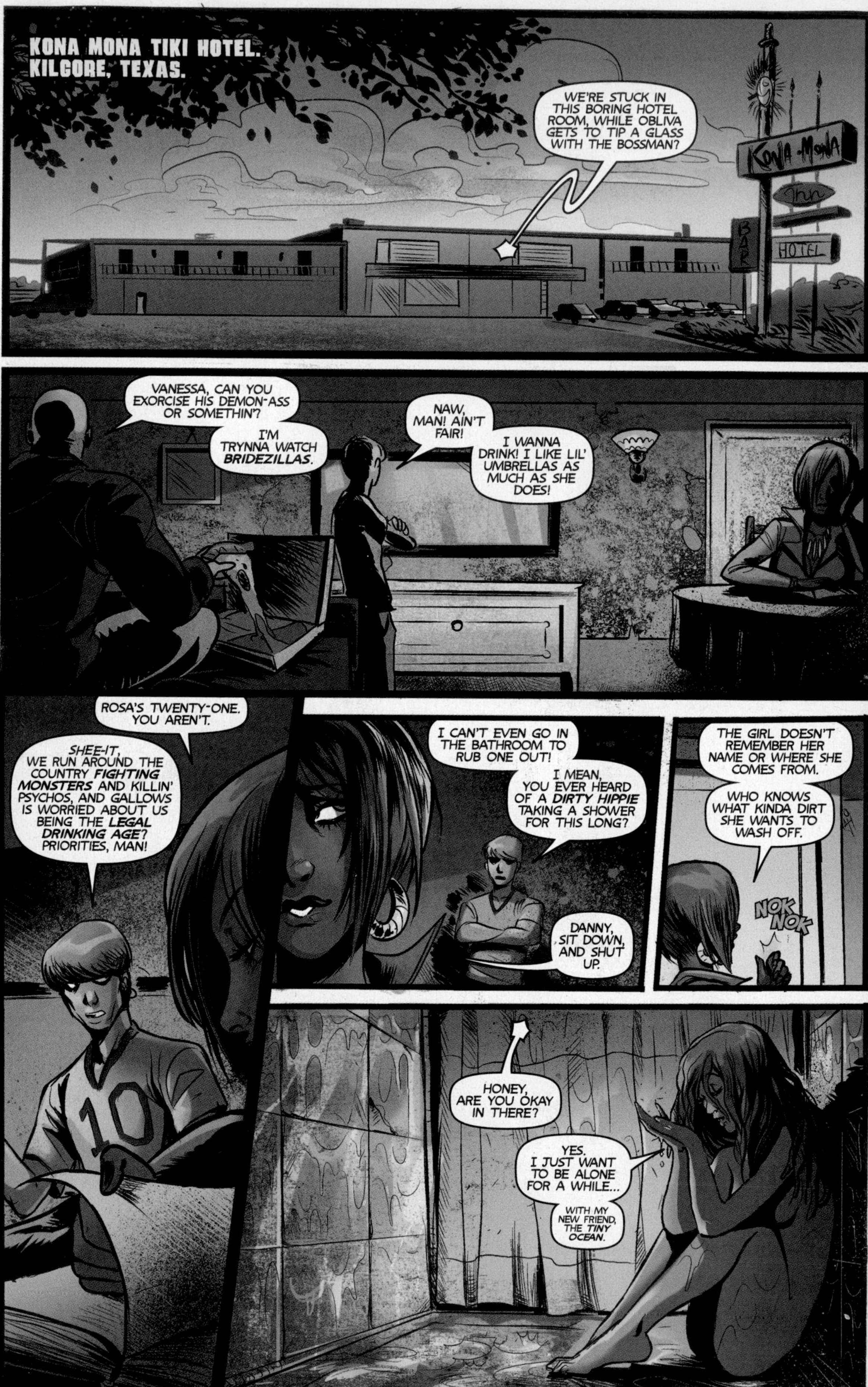
KONA MONA TIKI HOTEL. KILGORE, TEXAS.
WE'RE STUCK IN THIS BORING HOTEL ROOM, WHILE OBLIVA GETS TO TIP A GLASS WITH THE BOSSMAN?
KONA MONA
Inn
BAR
HOTEL
VANESSA, CAN YOU EXORCISE HIS DEMON-ASS OR SOMETHIN'?
I'M TRYNNA WATCH BRIDEZILLAS.
NAW, MAN! AIN'T FAIR!
I WANNA DRINK! I LIKE LIL' UMBRELLAS AS MUCH AS SHE DOES!
ROSA'S TWENTY-ONE. YOU AREN'T.
SHEE-IT, WE RUN AROUND THE COUNTRY FIGHTING MONSTERS AND KILLIN' PSYCHOS, AND GALLOWS IS WORRIED ABOUT US BEING THE LEGAL DRINKING AGE? PRIORITIES, MAN!
I CAN'T EVEN GO IN THE BATHROOM TO RUB ONE OUT!
I MEAN, YOU EVER HEARD OF A DIRTY HIPPIE TAKING A SHOWER FOR THIS LONG?
DANNY, SIT DOWN, AND SHUT UP.
THE GIRL DOESN'T REMEMBER HER NAME OR WHERE SHE COMES FROM.
WHO KNOWS WHAT KINDA DIRT SHE WANTS TO WASH OFF.
NOK NOK
HONEY, ARE YOU OKAY IN THERE?
YES. I JUST WANT TO BE ALONE FOR A WHILE...
WITH MY NEW FRIEND, THE TINY OCEAN.

THANKS FOR THE DRINK, MR. GAROU.

ANYTIME, BOB. SAY HI TO CAROL FOR ME, WOULD YOU?

HE DON'T LOOK LIKE NO SECRET AGENT.

IF HE DID, HE'D BE A PRETTY SHITTY SECRET AGENT.

TIKI BAR

HERE. ONE BLOODY MARY, NO GARLIC. THANKS FOR COVERING ME. BOB'S A GOOD GUY, BUT THINGS HAVE BEEN...TOUCHY SINCE WIDMARK.

WHAT'D HE SAY?

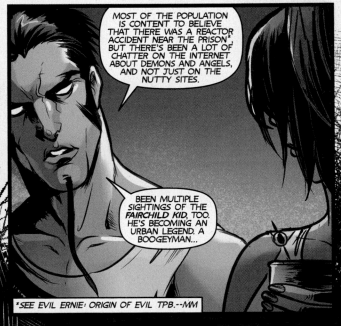

MOST OF THE POPULATION IS CONTENT TO BELIEVE THAT THERE WAS A REACTOR ACCIDENT NEAR THE PRISON*, BUT THERE'S BEEN A LOT OF CHATTER ON THE INTERNET ABOUT DEMONS AND ANGELS, AND NOT JUST ON THE NUTTY SITES.

BEEN MULTIPLE SIGHTINGS OF THE FAIRCHILD KID, TOO. HE'S BECOMING AN URBAN LEGEND. A BOOGEYMAN...

*SEE EVIL ERNIE: ORIGIN OF EVIL TPB.--MM

HE THINKS IF SHIT LIKE THAT KEEPS SCARING THE STRAIGHTS, IT COULD GET HAIRY FOR PEOPLE LIKE US. HAIRIER.

SNF

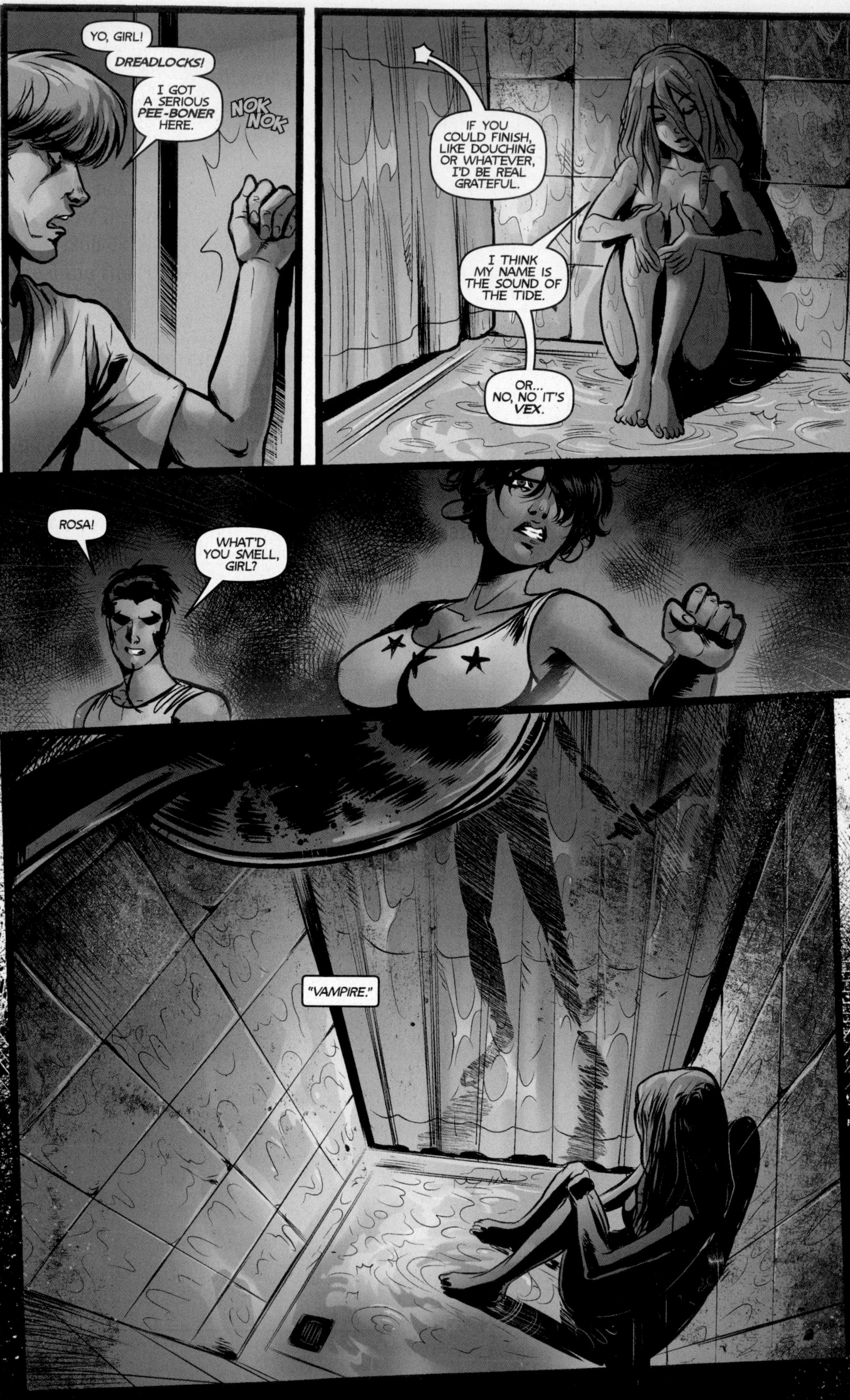

YO, GIRL!
DREADLOCKS!
I GOT A SERIOUS PEE-BONER HERE.
NOK NOK
IF YOU COULD FINISH, LIKE DOUCHING OR WHATEVER, I'D BE REAL GRATEFUL.
I THINK MY NAME IS THE SOUND OF THE TIDE.
OR... NO, NO IT'S VEX.
ROSA!
WHAT'D YOU SMELL, GIRL?
"VAMPIRE."

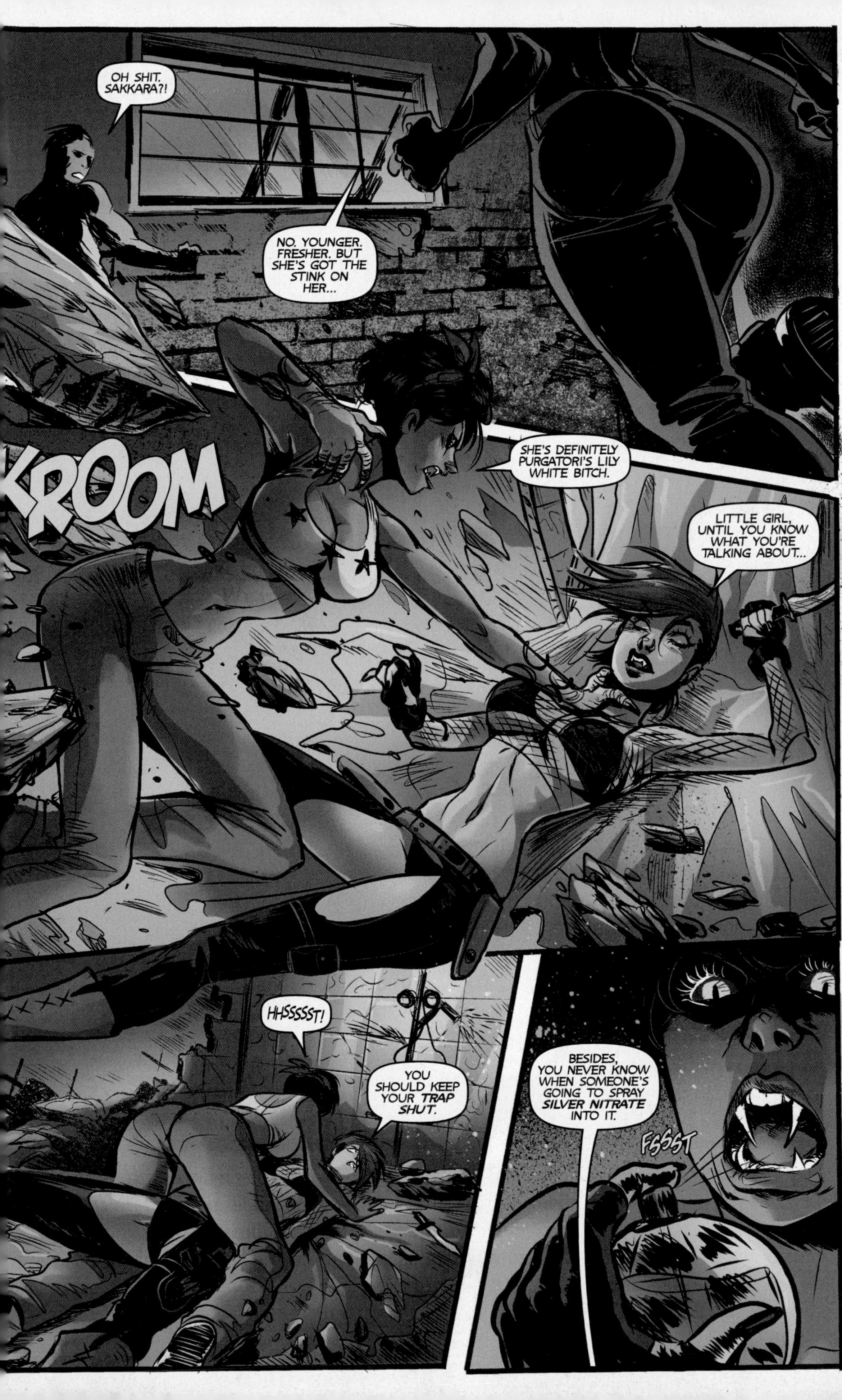
OH SHIT. SAKKARA?!
NO. YOUNGER. FRESHER. BUT SHE'S GOT THE STINK ON HER...
KROOM
SHE'S DEFINITELY PURGATORI'S LILY WHITE BITCH.
LITTLE GIRL, UNTIL YOU KNOW WHAT YOU'RE TALKING ABOUT...
HHSSSSST!
YOU SHOULD KEEP YOUR *TRAP SHUT*.
BESIDES, YOU NEVER KNOW WHEN SOMEONE'S GOING TO SPRAY *SILVER NITRATE* INTO IT.
FSSST

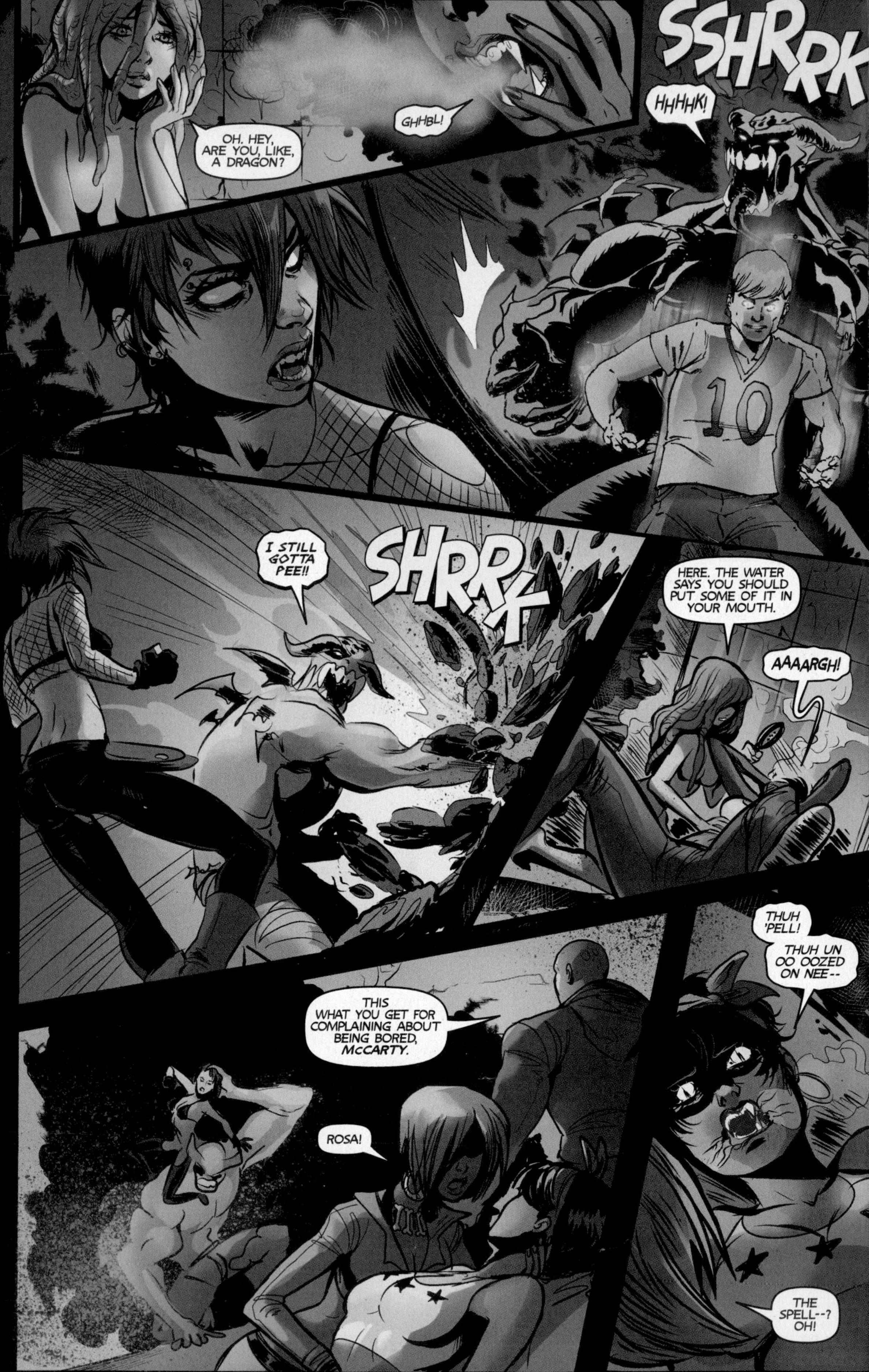
OH. HEY, ARE YOU, LIKE, A DRAGON?
GHHBL!
SSHRRK
HHHHK!
I STILL GOTTA PEE!!
SHRRK
HERE. THE WATER SAYS YOU SHOULD PUT SOME OF IT IN YOUR MOUTH.
AAAARGH!
THIS WHAT YOU GET FOR COMPLAINING ABOUT BEING BORED, McCARTY.
ROSA!
THUH 'PELL!
THUH UN OO OOZED ON NEE--
THE SPELL--? OH!

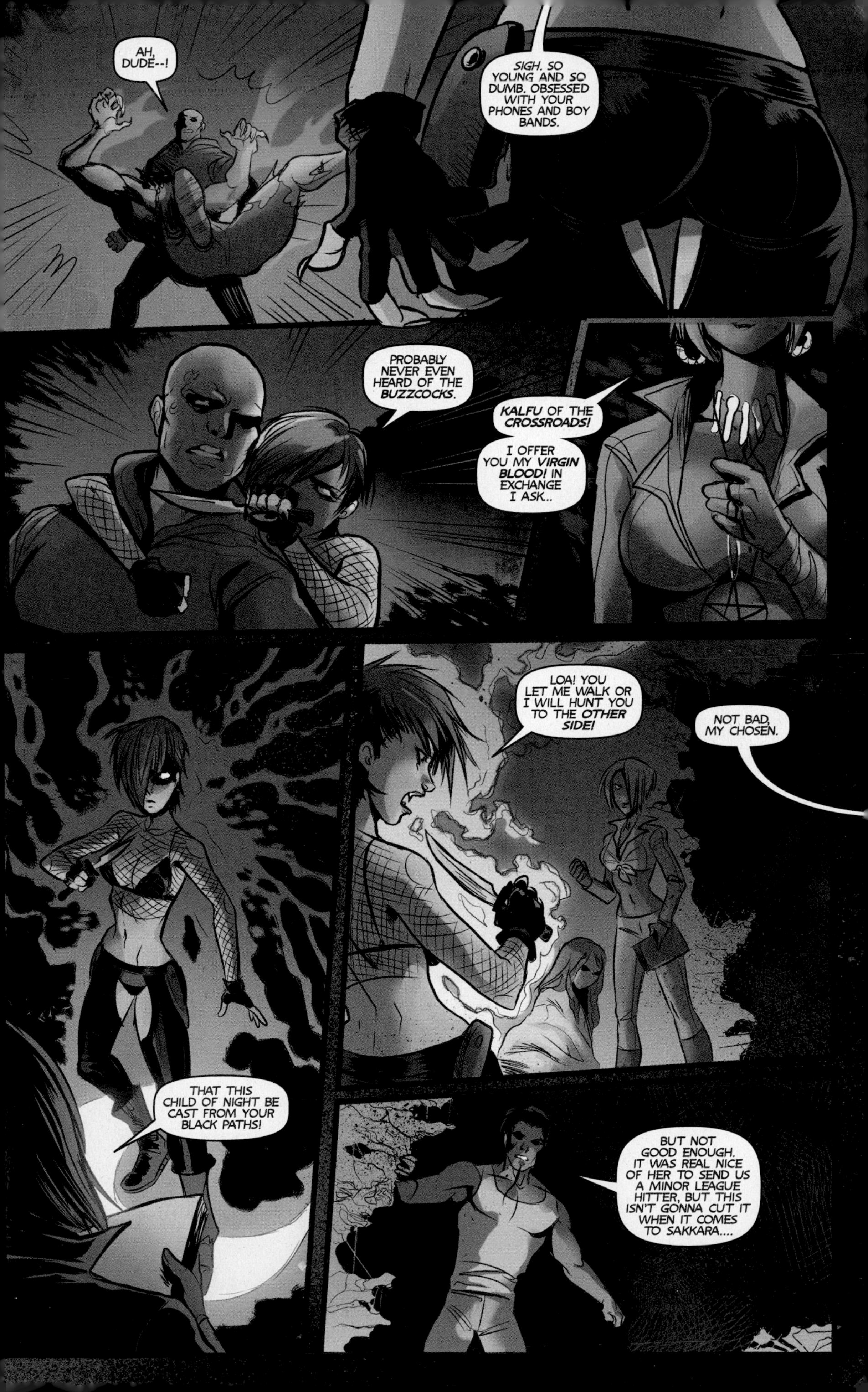
AH, DUDE--!
SIGH. SO YOUNG AND SO DUMB. OBSESSED WITH YOUR PHONES AND BOY BANDS.
PROBABLY NEVER EVEN HEARD OF THE BUZZCOCKS.
KALFU OF THE CROSSROADS!
I OFFER YOU MY VIRGIN BLOOD! IN EXCHANGE I ASK..
THAT THIS CHILD OF NIGHT BE CAST FROM YOUR BLACK PATHS!
LOA! YOU LET ME WALK OR I WILL HUNT YOU TO THE OTHER SIDE!
NOT BAD, MY CHOSEN.
BUT NOT GOOD ENOUGH. IT WAS REAL NICE OF HER TO SEND US A MINOR LEAGUE HITTER, BUT THIS ISN'T GONNA CUT IT WHEN IT COMES TO SAKKARA....

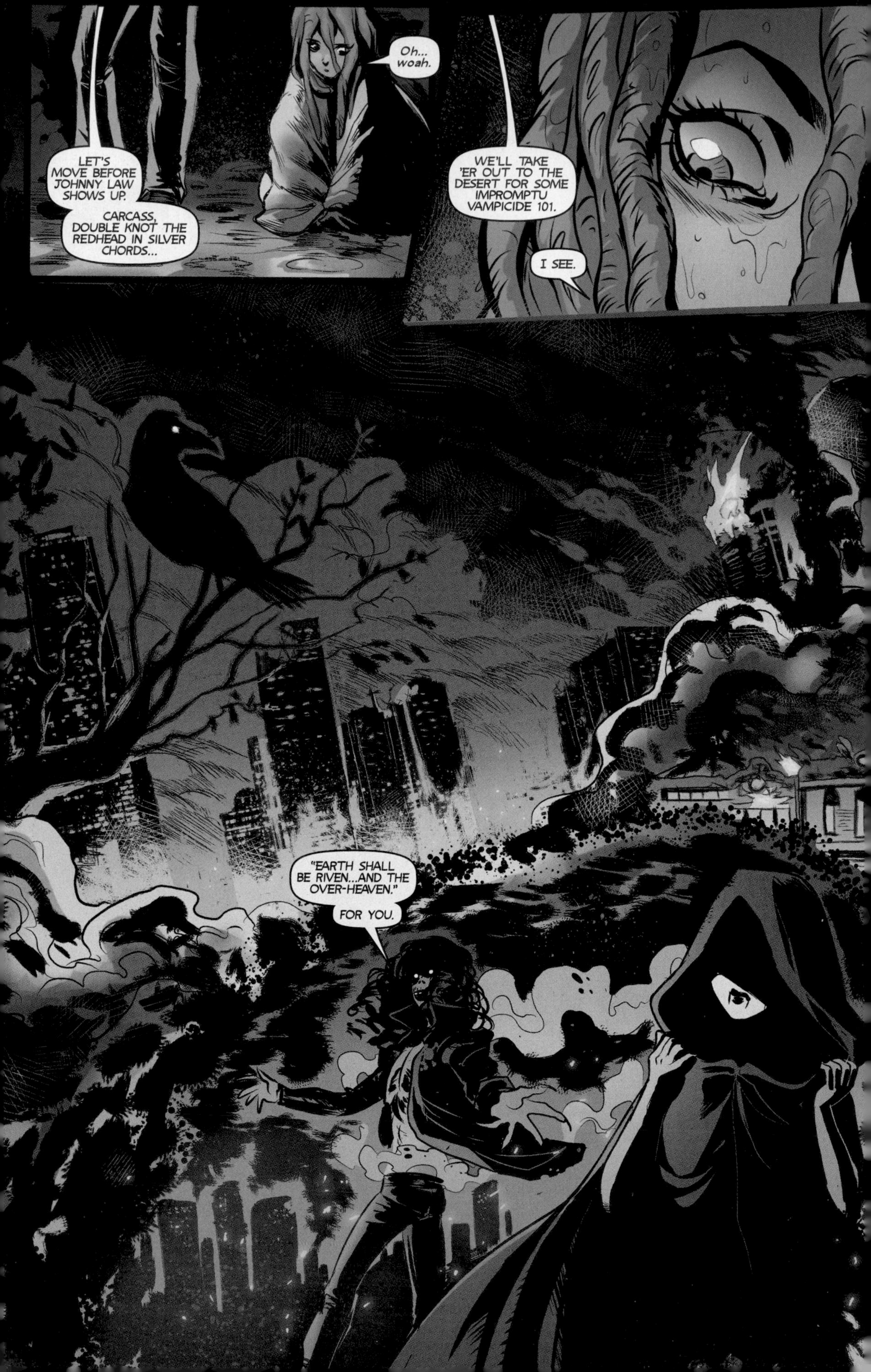
Oh... woah.
LET'S MOVE BEFORE JOHNNY LAW SHOWS UP.
CARCASS, DOUBLE KNOT THE REDHEAD IN SILVER CHORDS...
WE'LL TAKE 'ER OUT TO THE DESERT FOR SOME IMPROMPTU VAMPICIDE 101.
I SEE.
"EARTH SHALL BE RIVEN...AND THE OVER-HEAVEN."
FOR YOU.

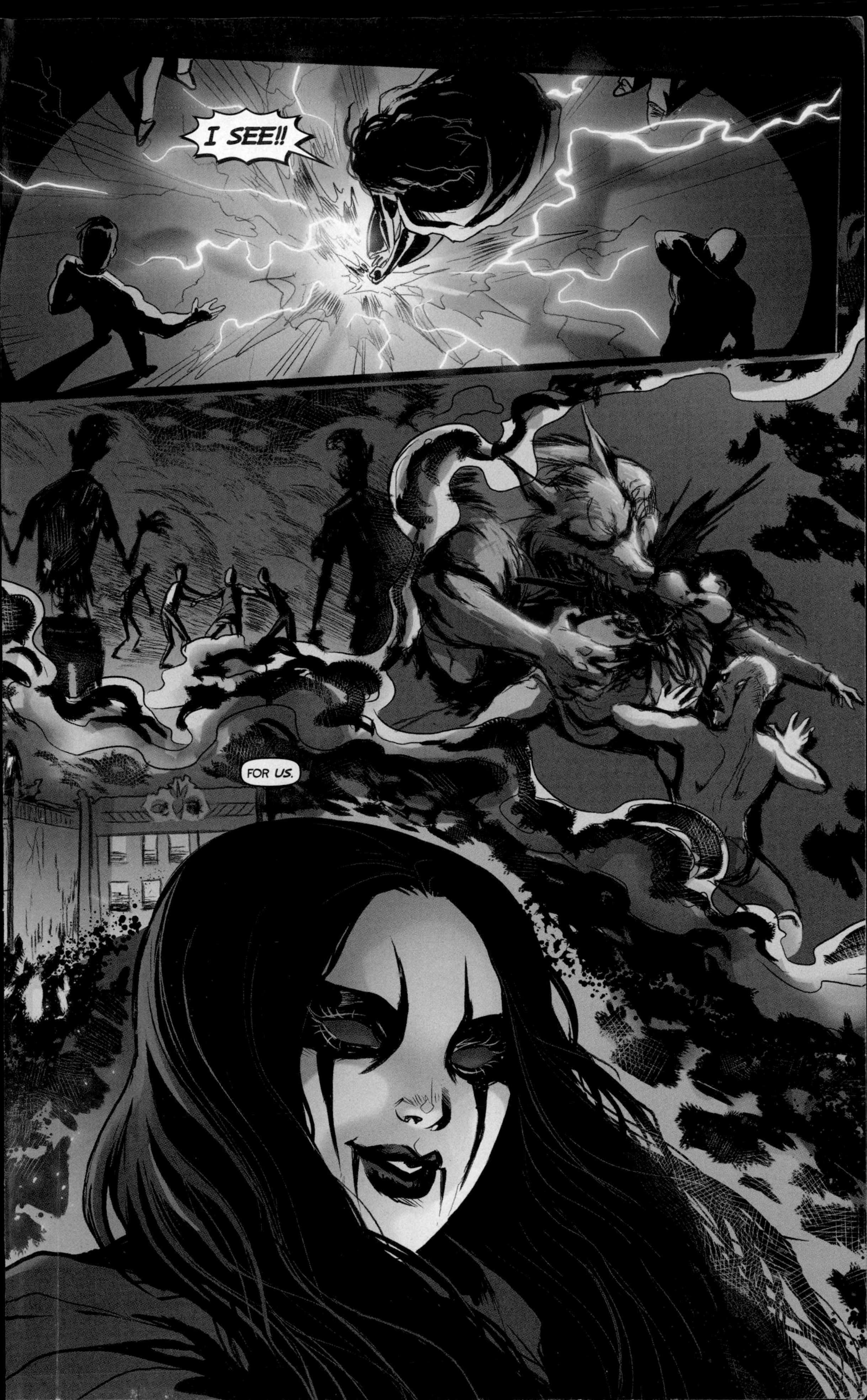
I SEE!!
FOR US.

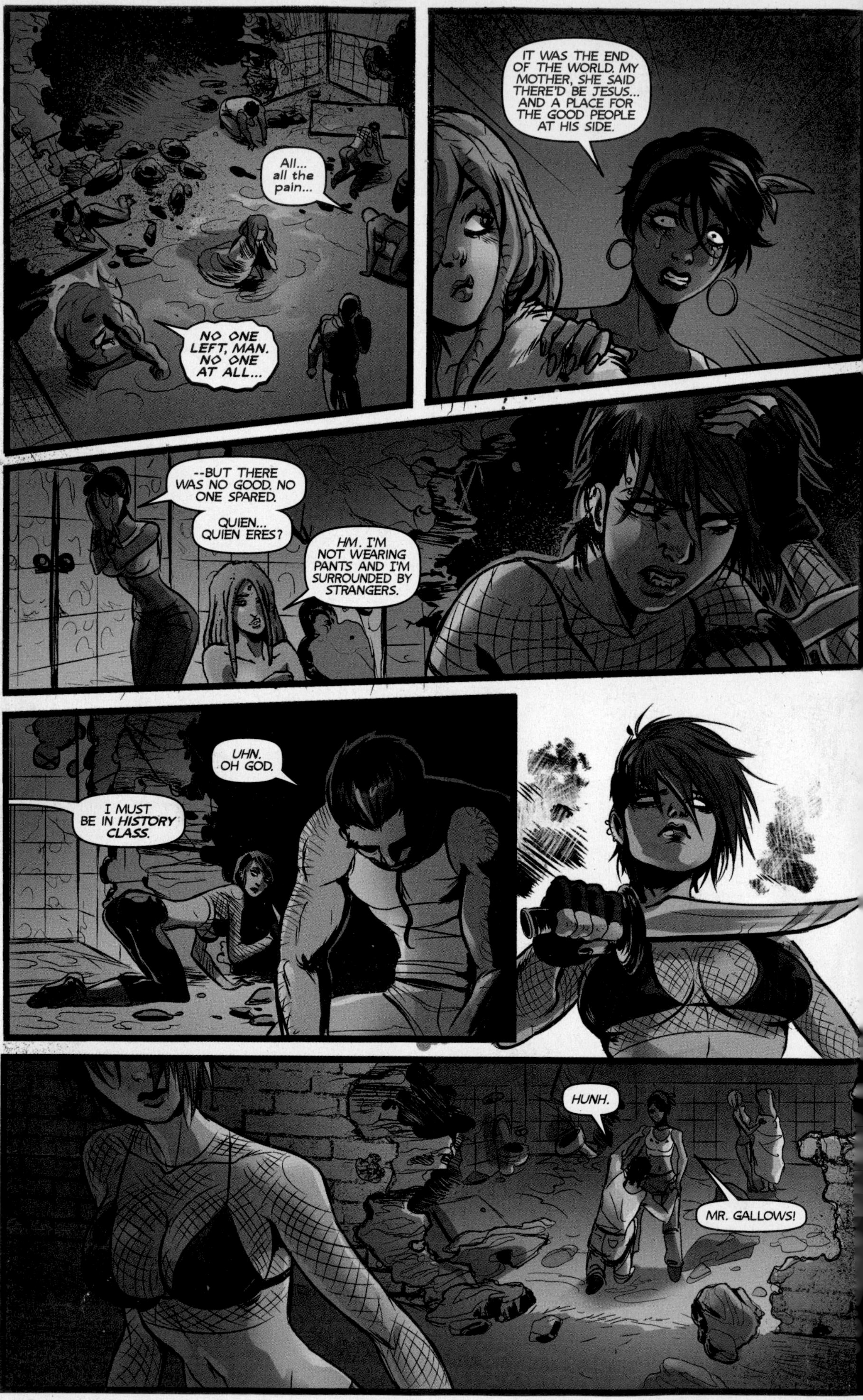
All... all the pain...
NO ONE LEFT, MAN. NO ONE AT ALL...
IT WAS THE END OF THE WORLD. MY MOTHER, SHE SAID THERE'D BE JESUS... AND A PLACE FOR THE GOOD PEOPLE AT HIS SIDE.
--BUT THERE WAS NO GOOD. NO ONE SPARED.
QUIEN... QUIEN ERES?
HM. I'M NOT WEARING PANTS AND I'M SURROUNDED BY STRANGERS.
UHN. OH GOD.
I MUST BE IN HISTORY CLASS.
HUNH.
MR. GALLOWS!

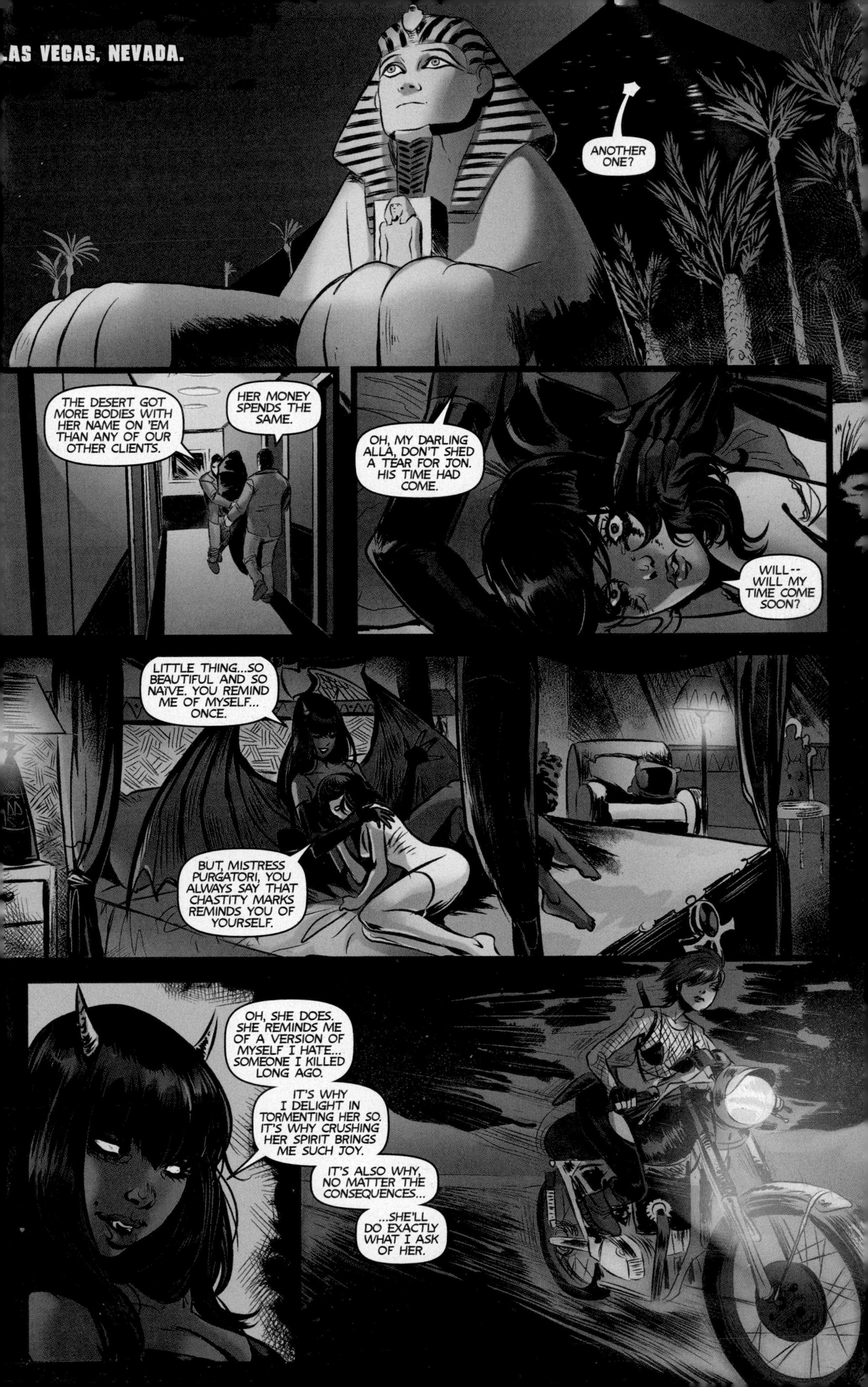
LAS VEGAS, NEVADA.
ANOTHER ONE?
THE DESERT GOT MORE BODIES WITH HER NAME ON 'EM THAN ANY OF OUR OTHER CLIENTS.
HER MONEY SPENDS THE SAME.
OH, MY DARLING ALLA, DON'T SHED A TEAR FOR JON. HIS TIME HAD COME.
WILL-- WILL MY TIME COME SOON?
LITTLE THING...SO BEAUTIFUL AND SO NAÏVE. YOU REMIND ME OF MYSELF... ONCE.
BUT, MISTRESS PURGATORI, YOU ALWAYS SAY THAT CHASTITY MARKS REMINDS YOU OF YOURSELF.
OH, SHE DOES. SHE REMINDS ME OF A VERSION OF MYSELF I HATE... SOMEONE I KILLED LONG AGO.
IT'S WHY I DELIGHT IN TORMENTING HER SO. IT'S WHY CRUSHING HER SPIRIT BRINGS ME SUCH JOY.
IT'S ALSO WHY, NO MATTER THE CONSEQUENCES...
...SHE'LL DO EXACTLY WHAT I ASK OF HER.

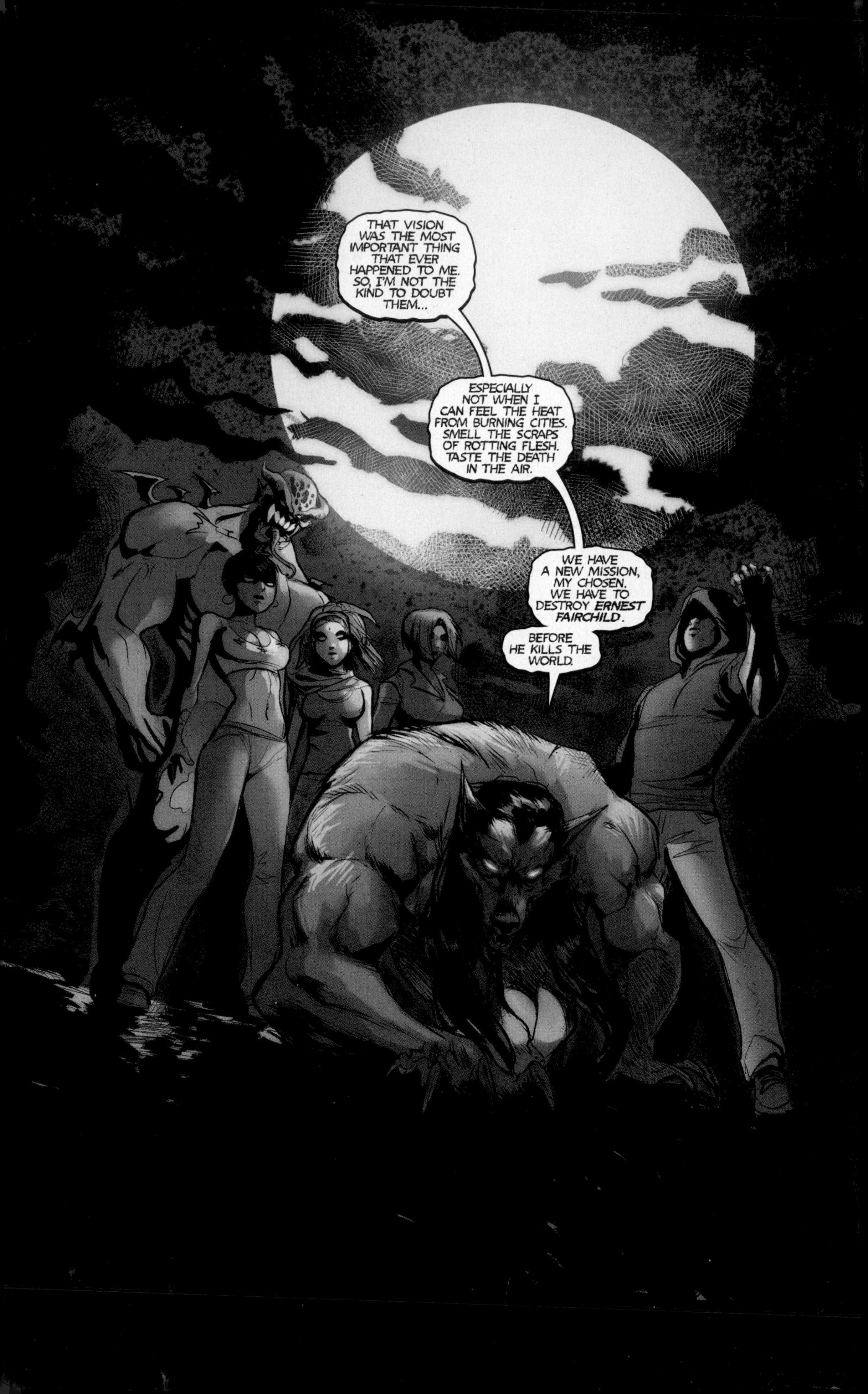

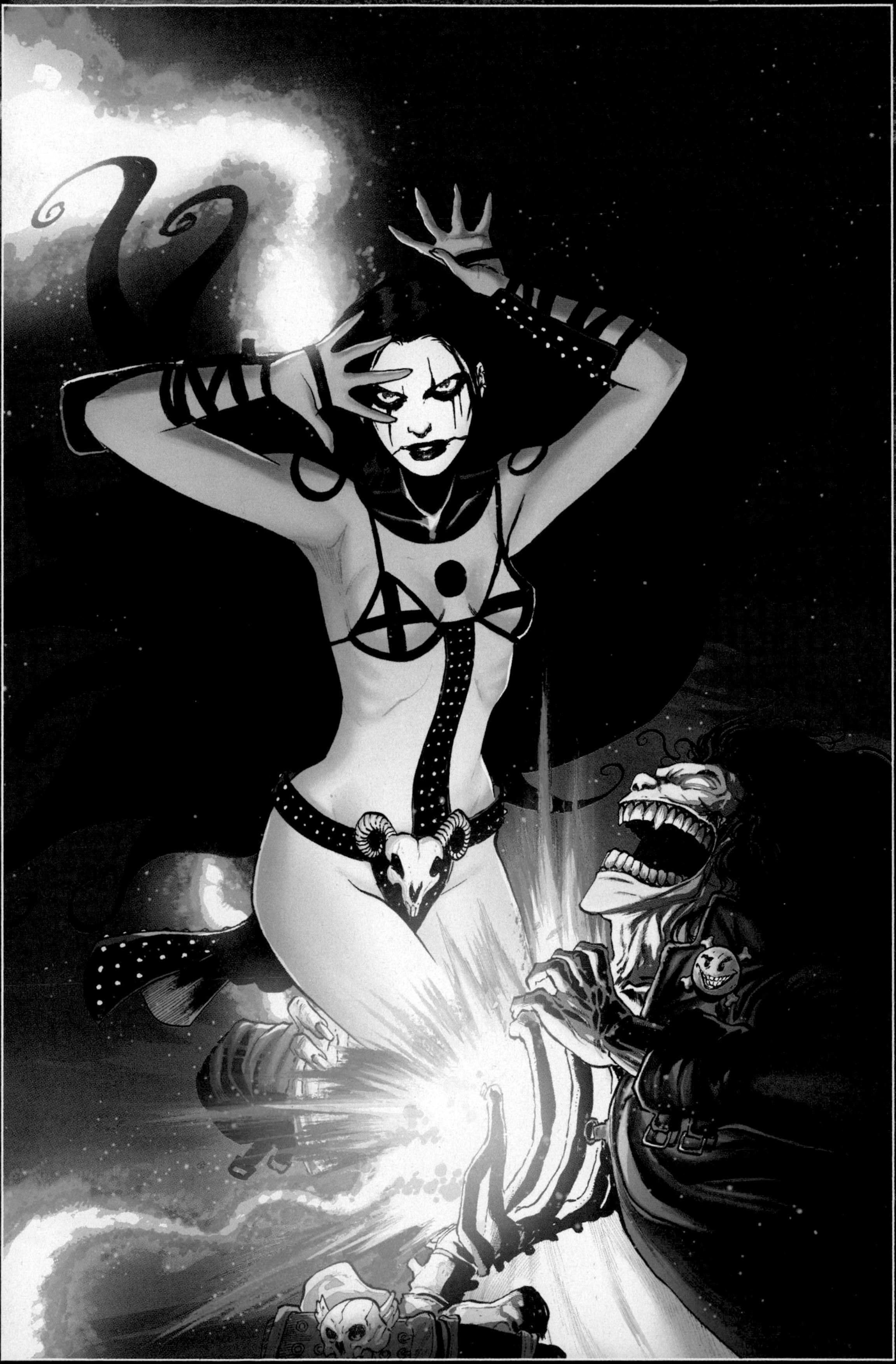

issue #2 cover by TIM SEELEY
colors by ADRIANO LUCAS

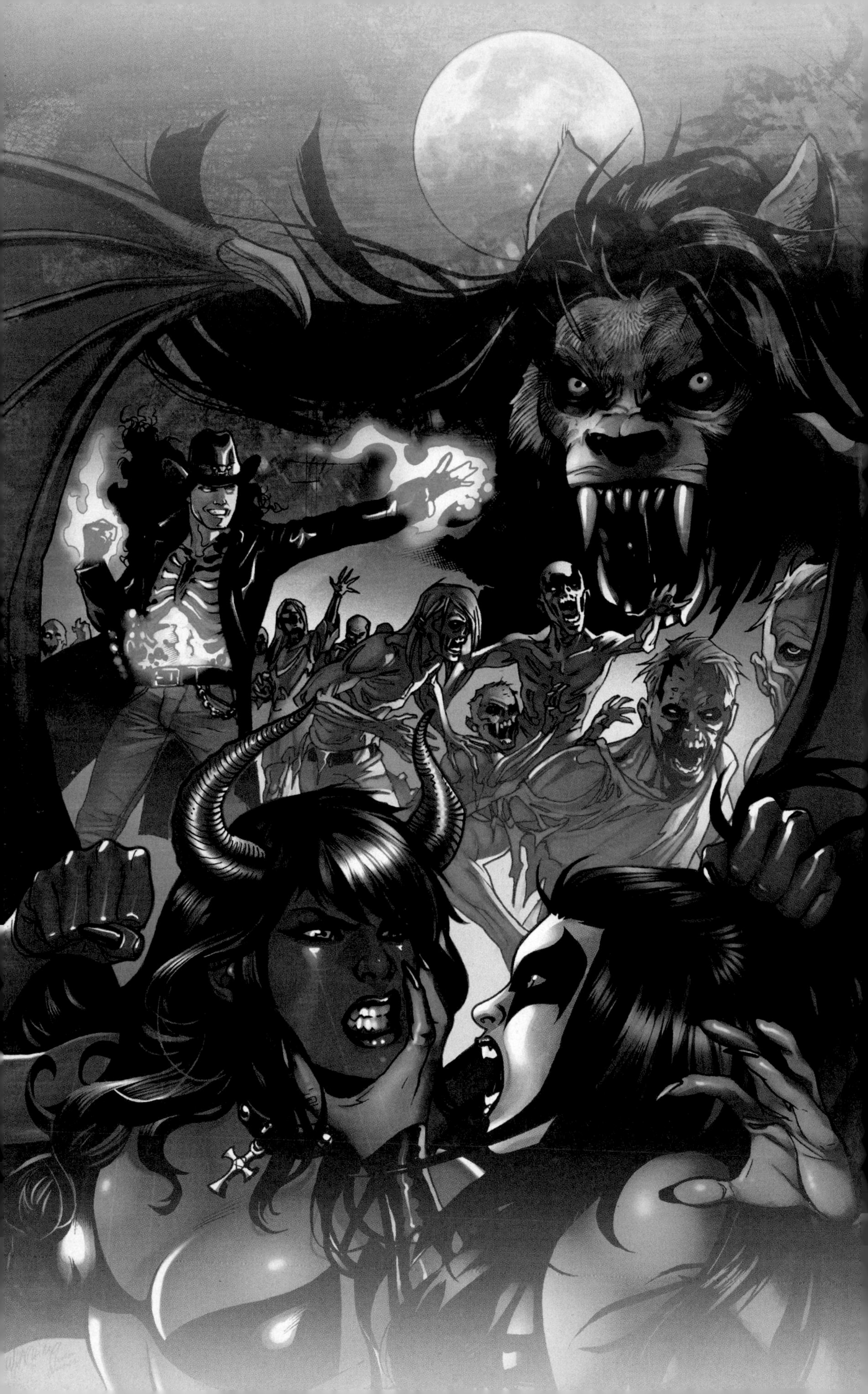

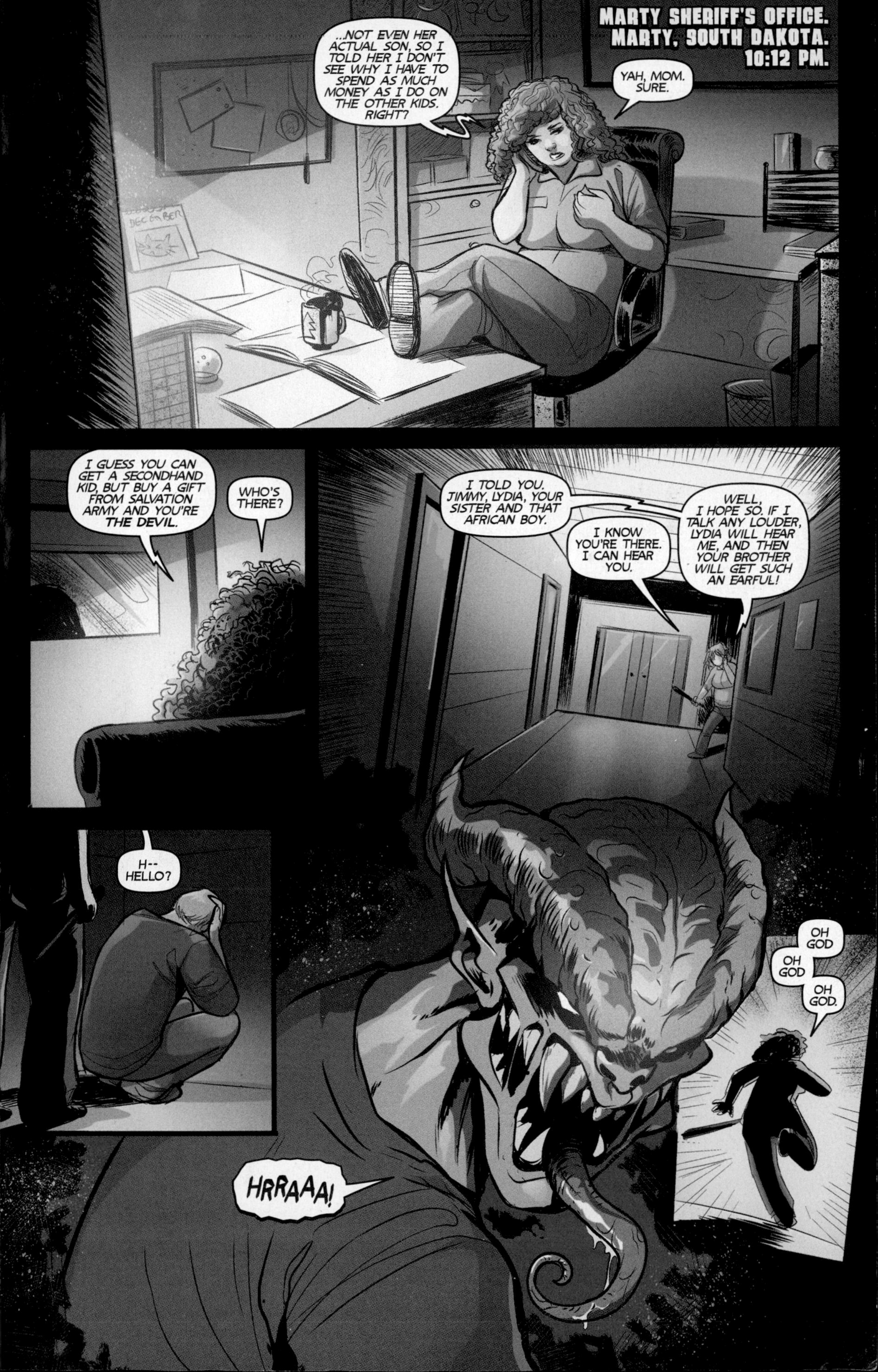
MARTY SHERIFF'S OFFICE. MARTY, SOUTH DAKOTA. 10:12 PM.
...NOT EVEN HER ACTUAL SON, SO I TOLD HER I DON'T SEE WHY I HAVE TO SPEND AS MUCH MONEY AS I DO ON THE OTHER KIDS. RIGHT?
YAH, MOM. SURE.
DECEMBER
I GUESS YOU CAN GET A SECONDHAND KID, BUT BUY A GIFT FROM SALVATION ARMY AND YOU'RE THE DEVIL.
WHO'S THERE?
I TOLD YOU. JIMMY, LYDIA, YOUR SISTER AND THAT AFRICAN BOY.
WELL, I HOPE SO. IF I TALK ANY LOUDER, LYDIA WILL HEAR ME, AND THEN YOUR BROTHER WILL GET SUCH AN EARFUL!
I KNOW YOU'RE THERE. I CAN HEAR YOU.
H-- HELLO?
HRRAAA!
OH GOD
OH GOD
OH GOD.

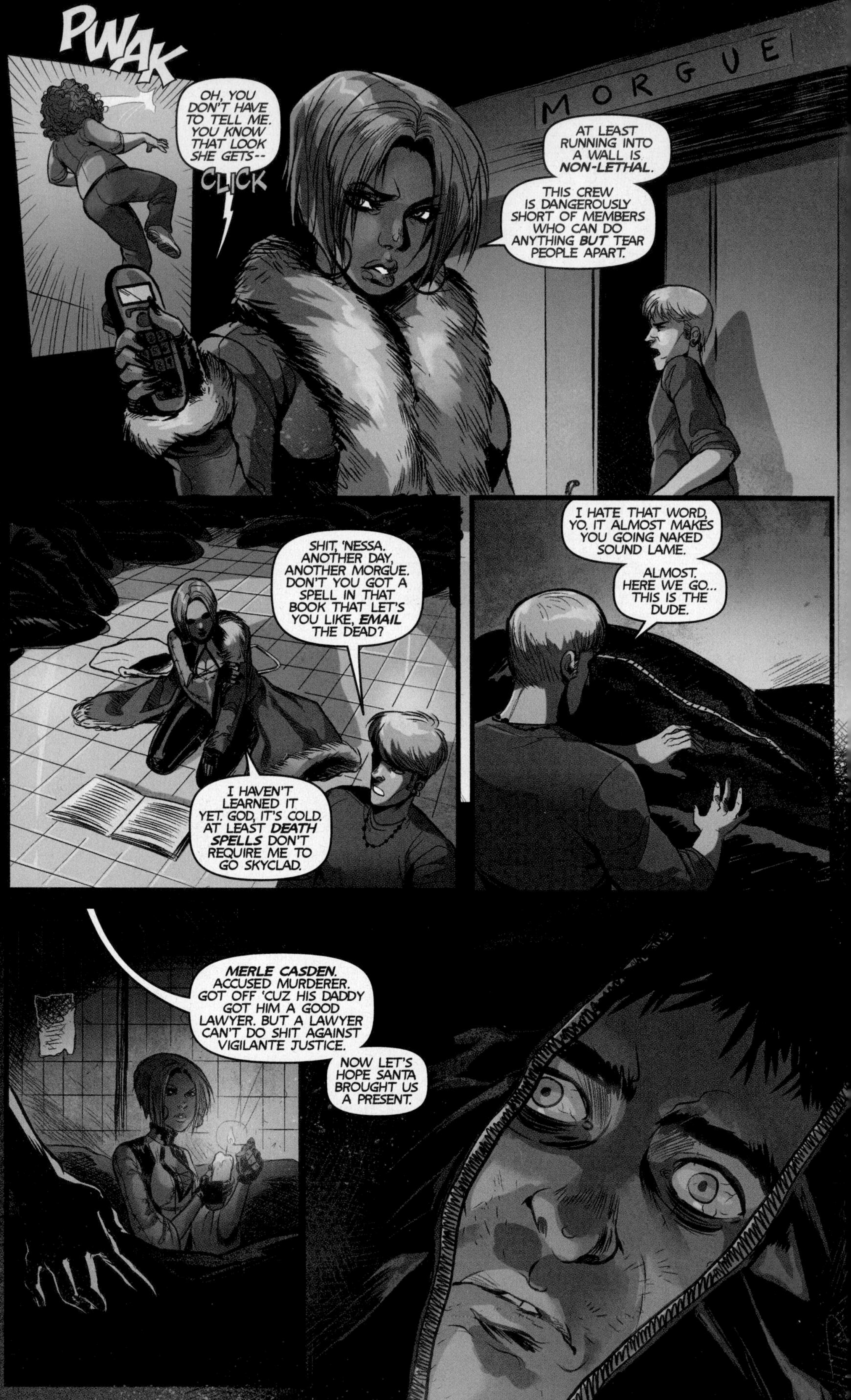
PWAK
OH, YOU DON'T HAVE TO TELL ME. YOU KNOW THAT LOOK SHE GETS--
CLICK
MORGUE
AT LEAST RUNNING INTO A WALL IS NON-LETHAL.
THIS CREW IS DANGEROUSLY SHORT OF MEMBERS WHO CAN DO ANYTHING BUT TEAR PEOPLE APART.
SHIT, 'NESSA. ANOTHER DAY, ANOTHER MORGUE. DON'T YOU GOT A SPELL IN THAT BOOK THAT LET'S YOU LIKE, EMAIL THE DEAD?
I HAVEN'T LEARNED IT YET. GOD, IT'S COLD. AT LEAST DEATH SPELLS DON'T REQUIRE ME TO GO SKYCLAD.
I HATE THAT WORD, YO. IT ALMOST MAKES YOU GOING NAKED SOUND LAME.
ALMOST. HERE WE GO... THIS IS THE DUDE.
MERLE CASDEN. ACCUSED MURDERER. GOT OFF 'CUZ HIS DADDY GOT HIM A GOOD LAWYER. BUT A LAWYER CAN'T DO SHIT AGAINST VIGILANTE JUSTICE.
NOW LET'S HOPE SANTA BROUGHT US A PRESENT.

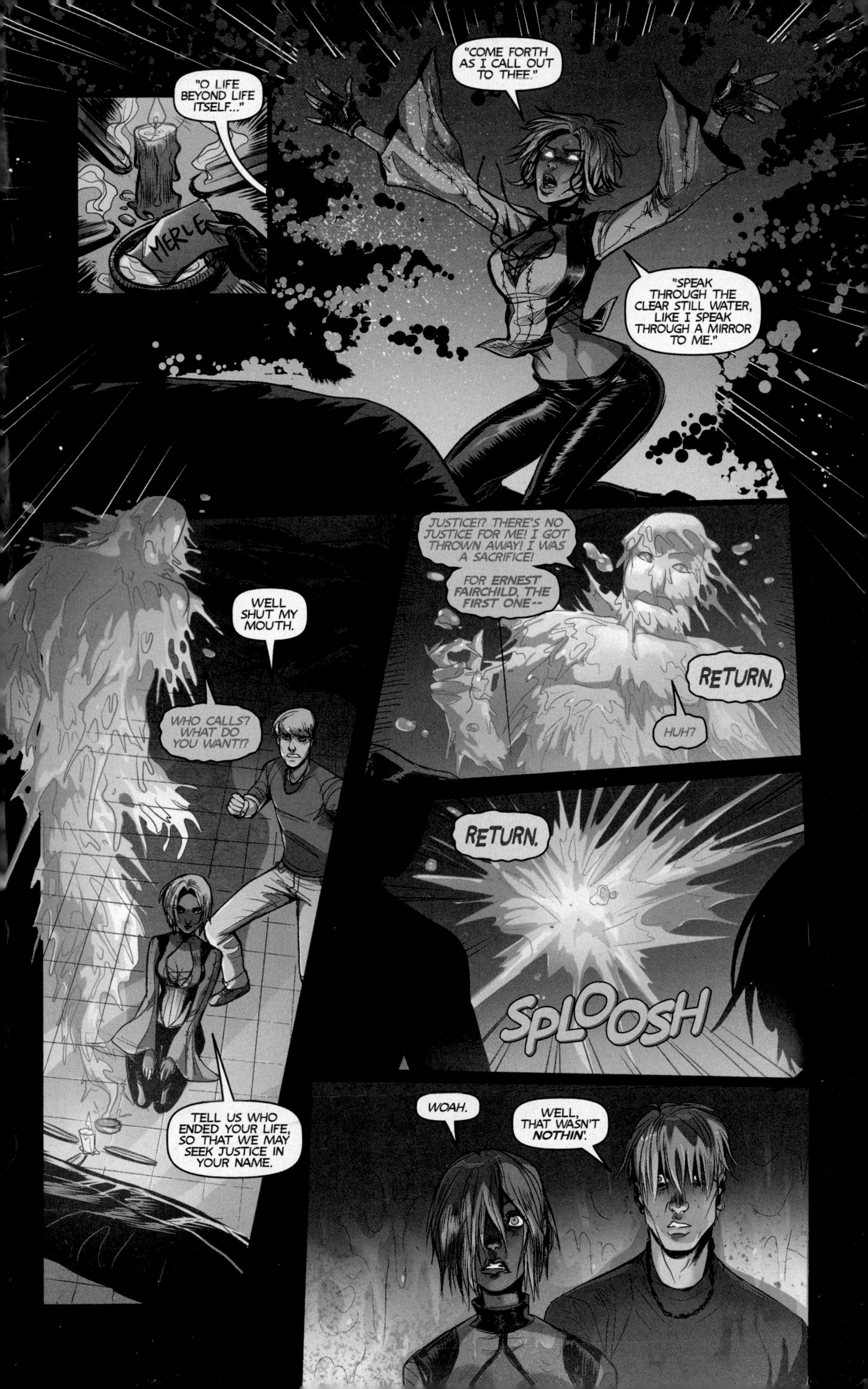
"O LIFE BEYOND LIFE ITSELF..."
MERLE
"COME FORTH AS I CALL OUT TO THEE."
"SPEAK THROUGH THE CLEAR STILL WATER, LIKE I SPEAK THROUGH A MIRROR TO ME."
WELL SHUT MY MOUTH.
WHO CALLS? WHAT DO YOU WANT!?
TELL US WHO ENDED YOUR LIFE, SO THAT WE MAY SEEK JUSTICE IN YOUR NAME.
JUSTICE!? THERE'S NO JUSTICE FOR ME! I GOT THROWN AWAY! I WAS A SACRIFICE!
FOR ERNEST FAIRCHILD, THE FIRST ONE--
RETURN.
HUH?
RETURN.
SPLOOSH
WOAH.
WELL, THAT WASN'T *NOTHIN'*.

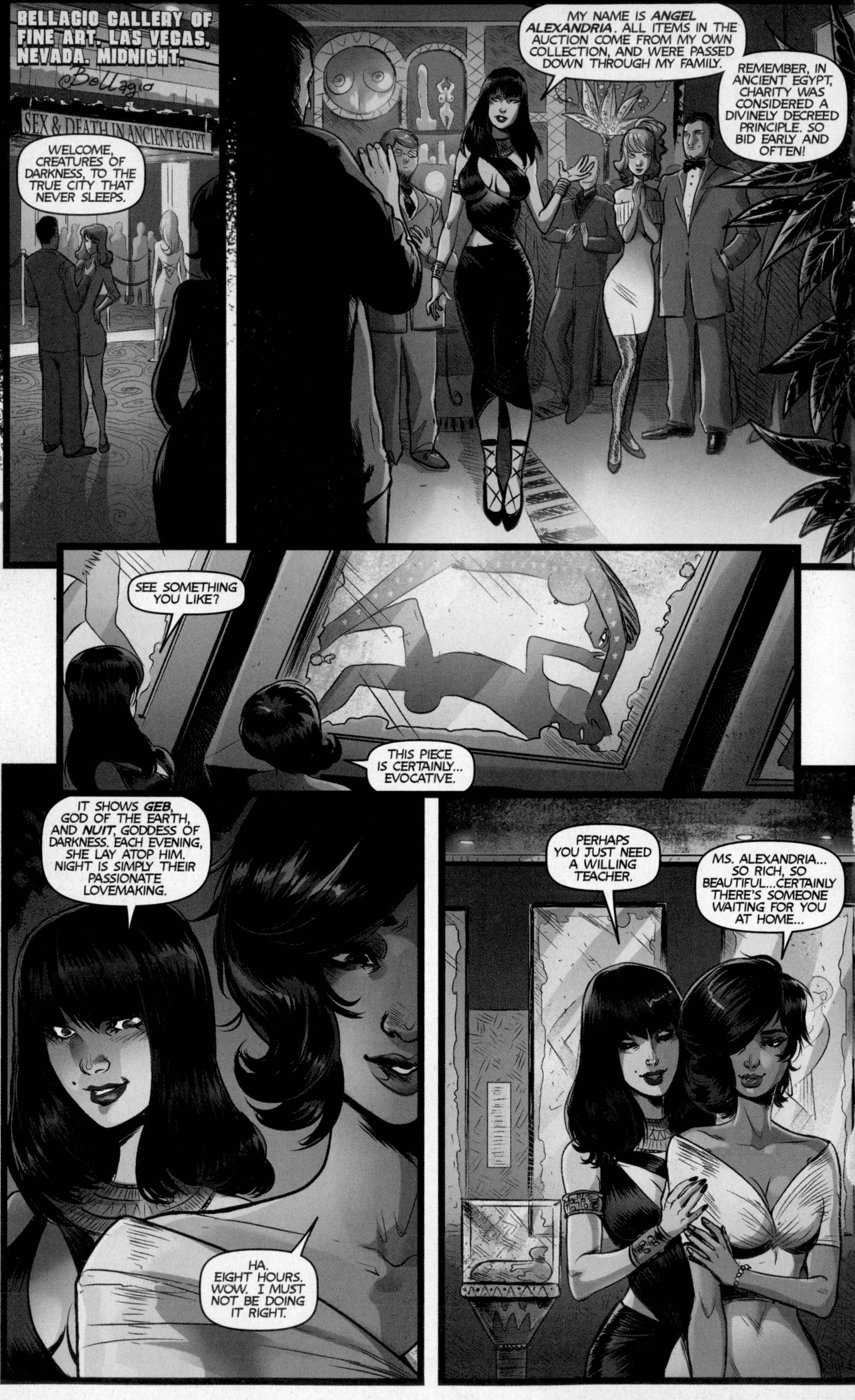
BELLAGIO GALLERY OF FINE ART. LAS VEGAS, NEVADA. MIDNIGHT.
Bellagio
SEX & DEATH IN ANCIENT EGYPT
WELCOME, CREATURES OF DARKNESS, TO THE TRUE CITY THAT NEVER SLEEPS.
MY NAME IS ANGEL ALEXANDRIA. ALL ITEMS IN THE AUCTION COME FROM MY OWN COLLECTION, AND WERE PASSED DOWN THROUGH MY FAMILY.
REMEMBER, IN ANCIENT EGYPT, CHARITY WAS CONSIDERED A DIVINELY DECREED PRINCIPLE. SO BID EARLY AND OFTEN!
SEE SOMETHING YOU LIKE?
THIS PIECE IS CERTAINLY... EVOCATIVE.
IT SHOWS GEB, GOD OF THE EARTH, AND NUIT, GODDESS OF DARKNESS. EACH EVENING, SHE LAY ATOP HIM. NIGHT IS SIMPLY THEIR PASSIONATE LOVEMAKING.
HA. EIGHT HOURS. WOW. I MUST NOT BE DOING IT RIGHT.
PERHAPS YOU JUST NEED A WILLING TEACHER.
MS. ALEXANDRIA... SO RICH, SO BEAUTIFUL...CERTAINLY THERE'S SOMEONE WAITING FOR YOU AT HOME...

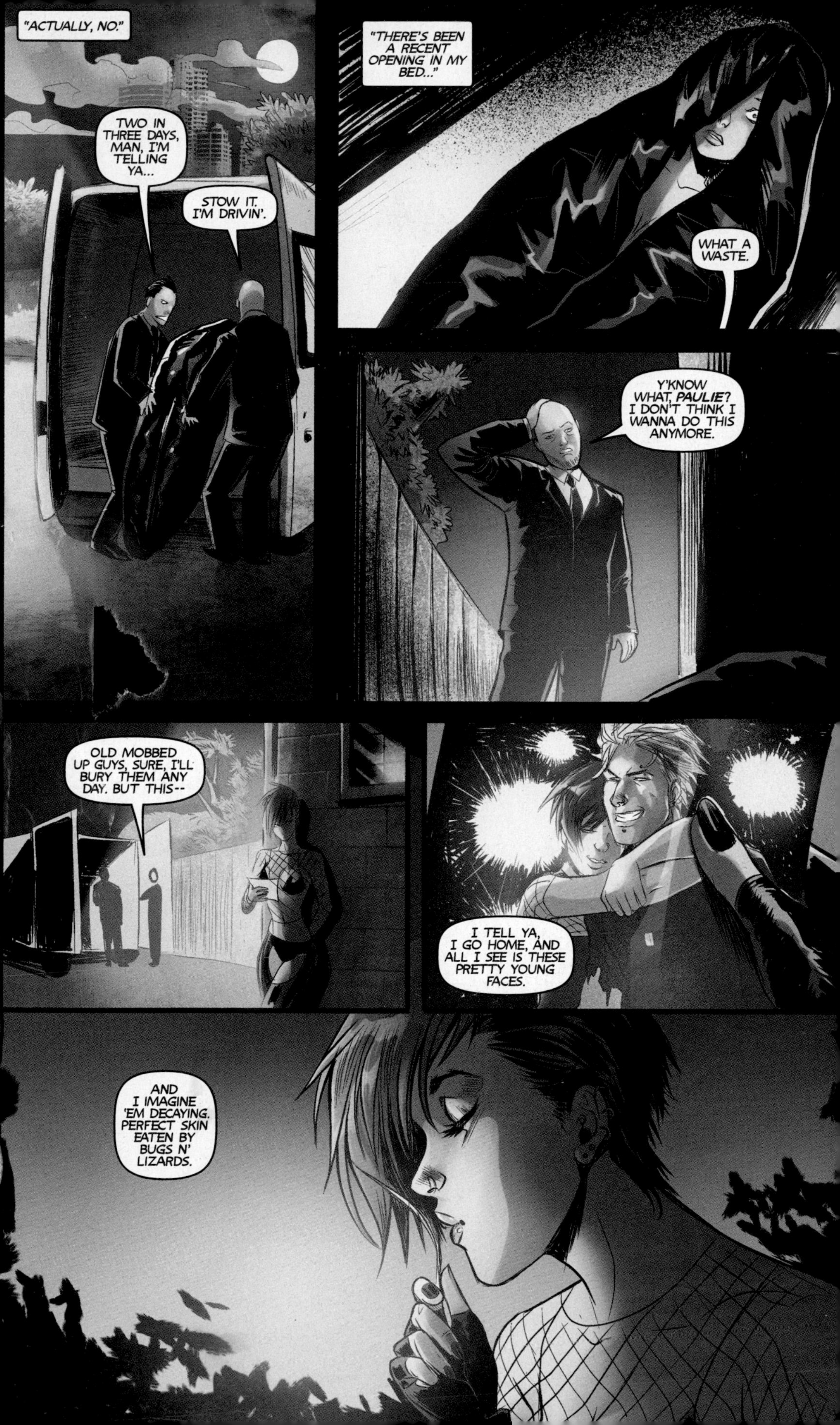
"ACTUALLY, NO."
TWO IN THREE DAYS, MAN, I'M TELLING YA...
STOW IT. I'M DRIVIN'.
"THERE'S BEEN A RECENT OPENING IN MY BED..."
WHAT A WASTE.
Y'KNOW WHAT, PAULIE? I DON'T THINK I WANNA DO THIS ANYMORE.
OLD MOBBED UP GUYS, SURE, I'LL BURY THEM ANY DAY. BUT THIS--
I TELL YA, I GO HOME, AND ALL I SEE IS THESE PRETTY YOUNG FACES.
AND I IMAGINE 'EM DECAYING. PERFECT SKIN EATEN BY BUGS N' LIZARDS.

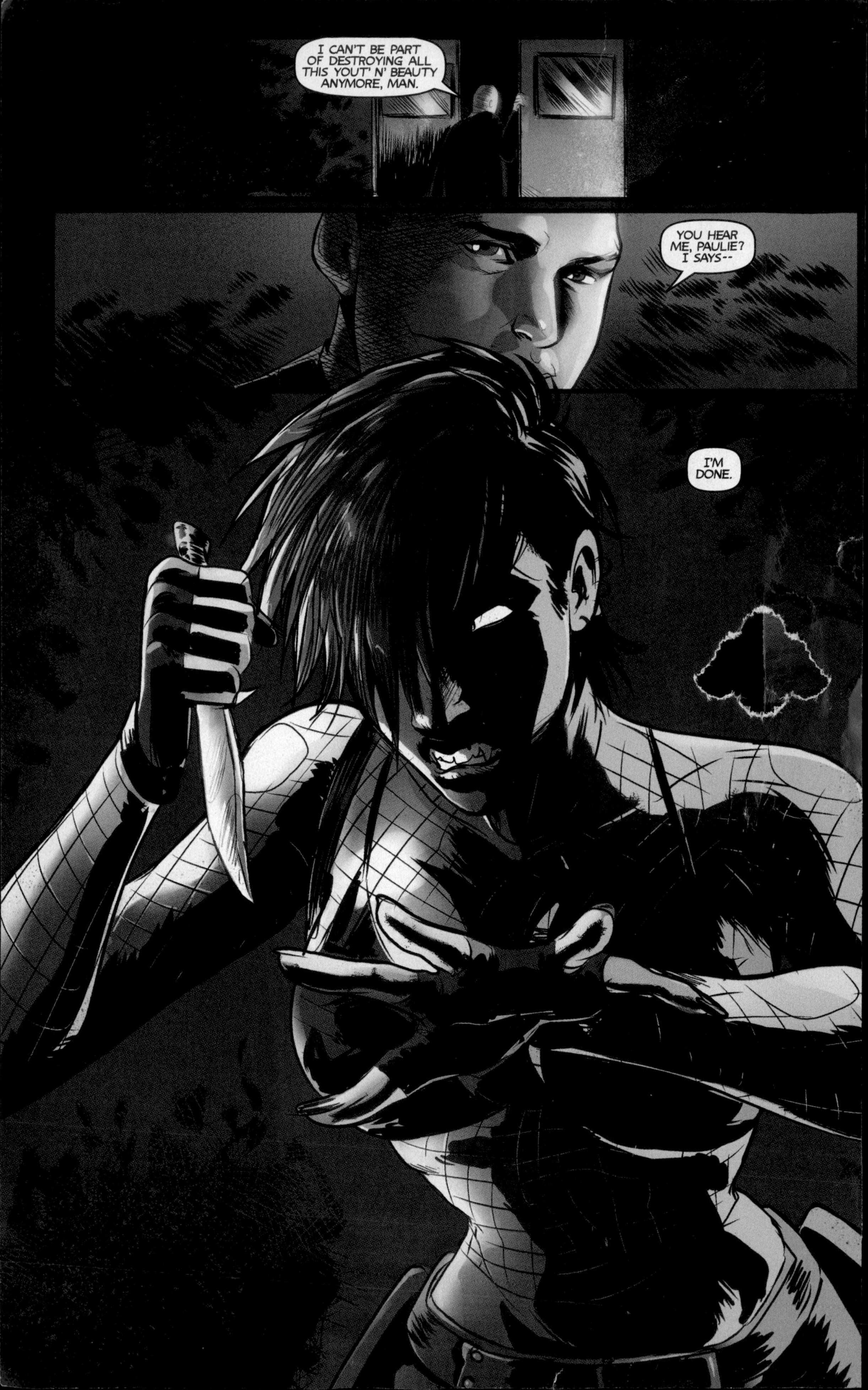
I CAN'T BE PART OF DESTROYING ALL THIS YOUT' N' BEAUTY ANYMORE, MAN.
YOU HEAR ME, PAULIE? I SAYS--
I'M DONE.

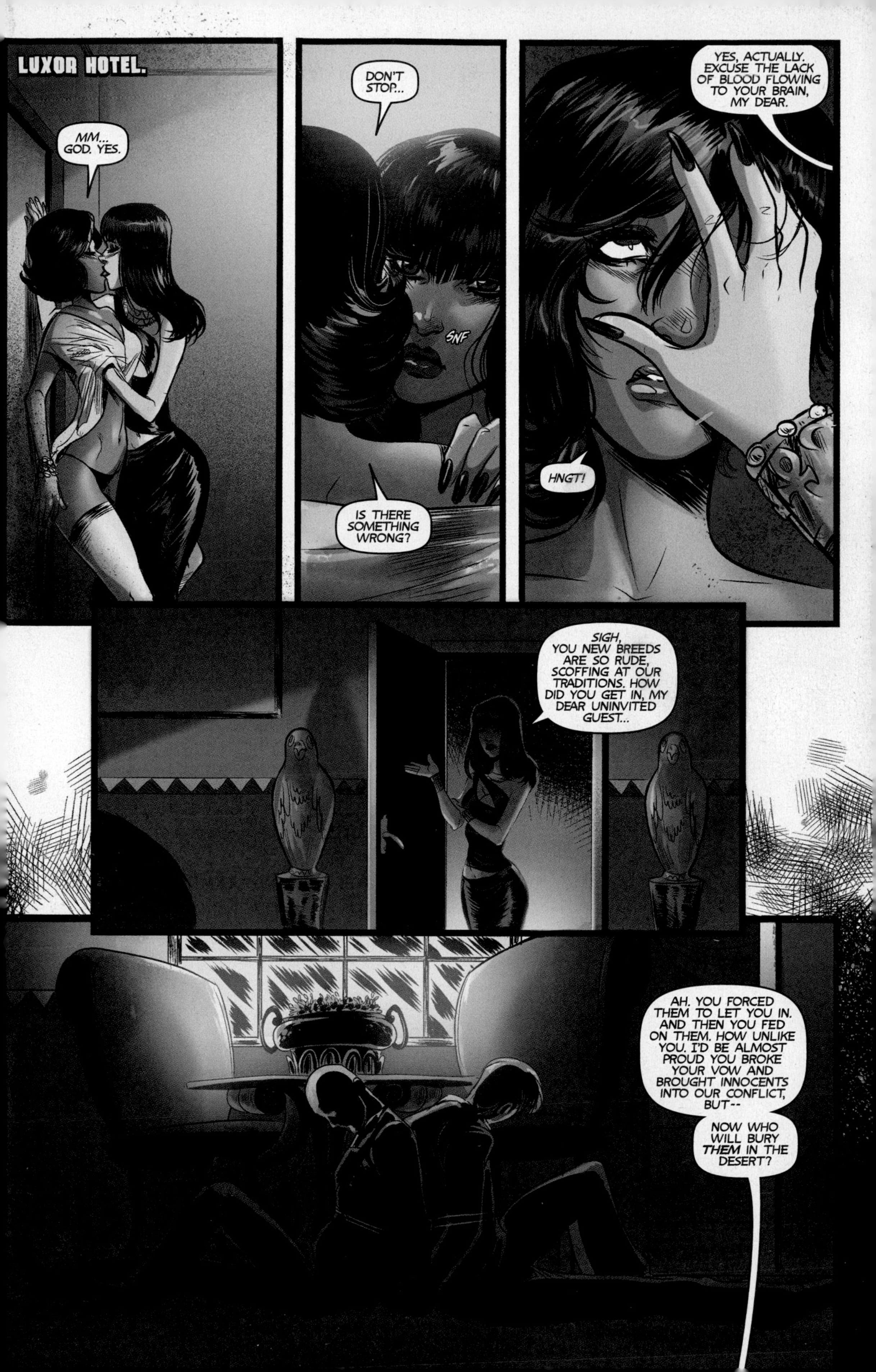
LUXOR HOTEL.
MM... GOD. YES.
DON'T STOP...
SNF
IS THERE SOMETHING WRONG?
YES, ACTUALLY. EXCUSE THE LACK OF BLOOD FLOWING TO YOUR BRAIN, MY DEAR.
HNGT!
SIGH, YOU NEW BREEDS ARE SO RUDE, SCOFFING AT OUR TRADITIONS. HOW DID YOU GET IN, MY DEAR UNINVITED GUEST...
AH. YOU FORCED THEM TO LET YOU IN. AND THEN YOU FED ON THEM. HOW UNLIKE YOU. I'D BE ALMOST PROUD YOU BROKE YOUR VOW AND BROUGHT INNOCENTS INTO OUR CONFLICT, BUT--
NOW WHO WILL BURY THEM IN THE DESERT?

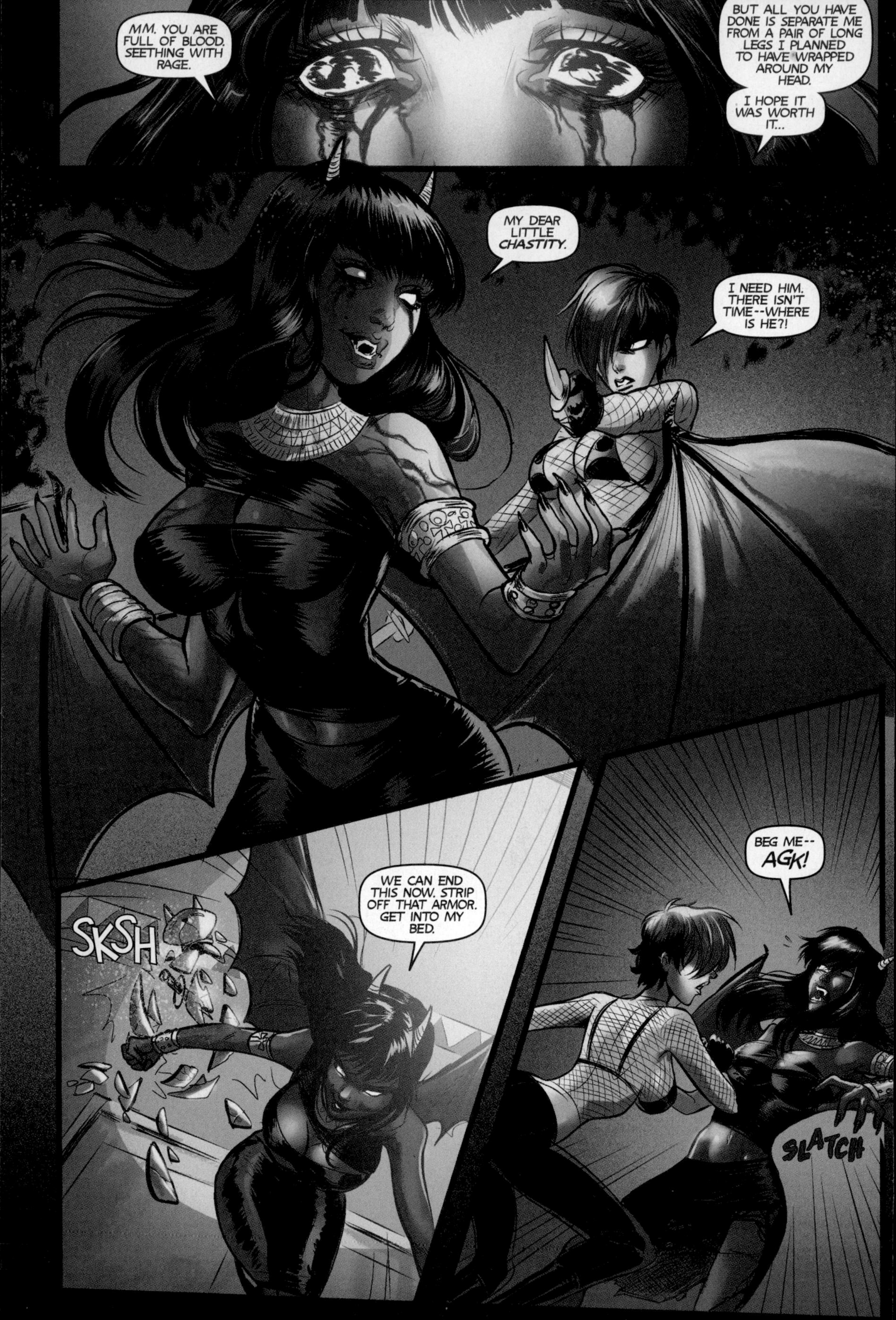
MM. YOU ARE FULL OF BLOOD. SEETHING WITH RAGE.
BUT ALL YOU HAVE DONE IS SEPARATE ME FROM A PAIR OF LONG LEGS I PLANNED TO HAVE WRAPPED AROUND MY HEAD.
I HOPE IT WAS WORTH IT...
MY DEAR LITTLE CHASTITY.
I NEED HIM. THERE ISN'T TIME--WHERE IS HE?!
SKSH
WE CAN END THIS NOW. STRIP OFF THAT ARMOR. GET INTO MY BED.
BEG ME-- AGK!
SLATCH

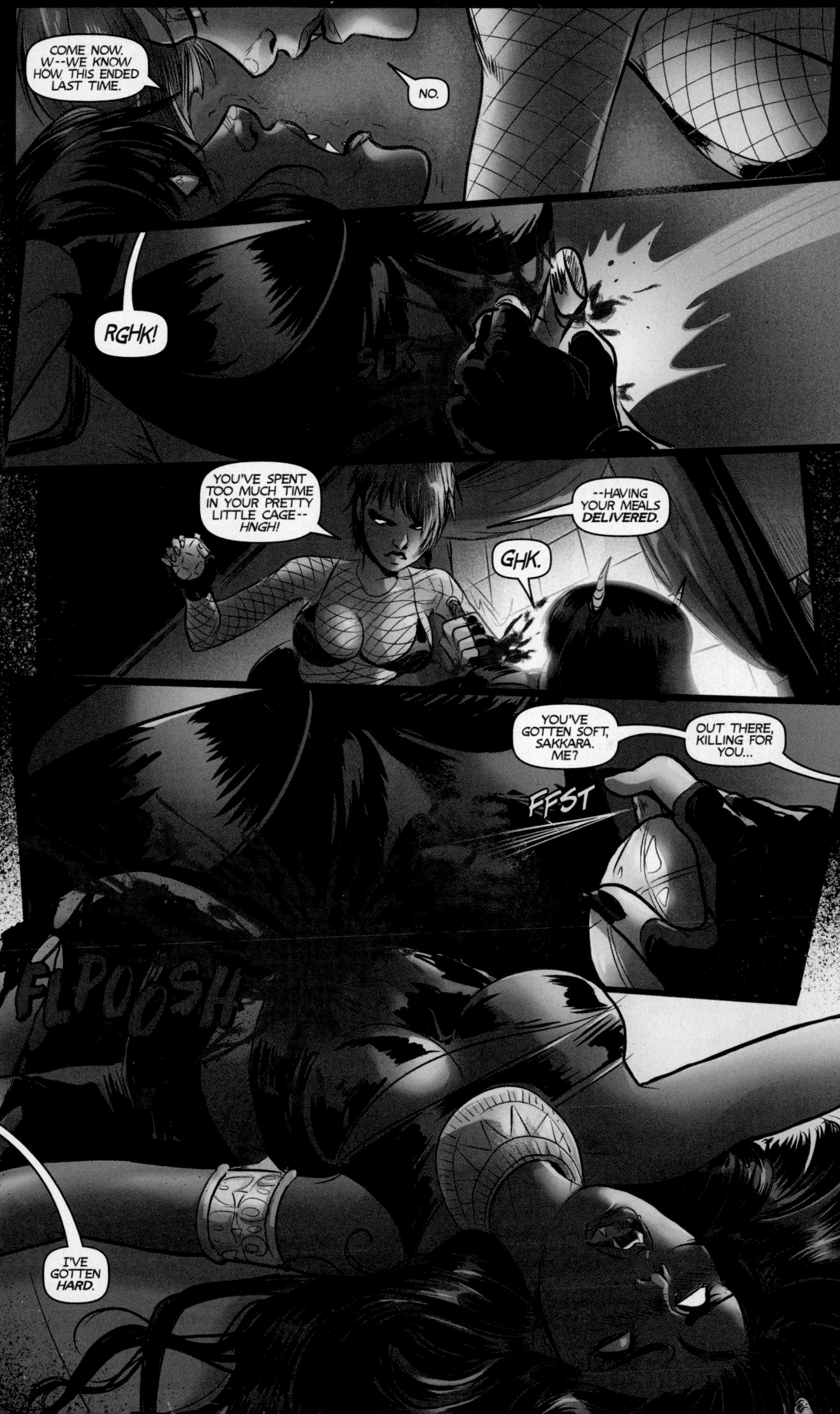
COME NOW. W--WE KNOW HOW THIS ENDED LAST TIME.
NO.
RGHK!
YOU'VE SPENT TOO MUCH TIME IN YOUR PRETTY LITTLE CAGE-- HNGH!
--HAVING YOUR MEALS DELIVERED.
GHK.
YOU'VE GOTTEN SOFT, SAKKARA. ME?
OUT THERE, KILLING FOR YOU...
FFST
FLPOOSH
I'VE GOTTEN HARD.

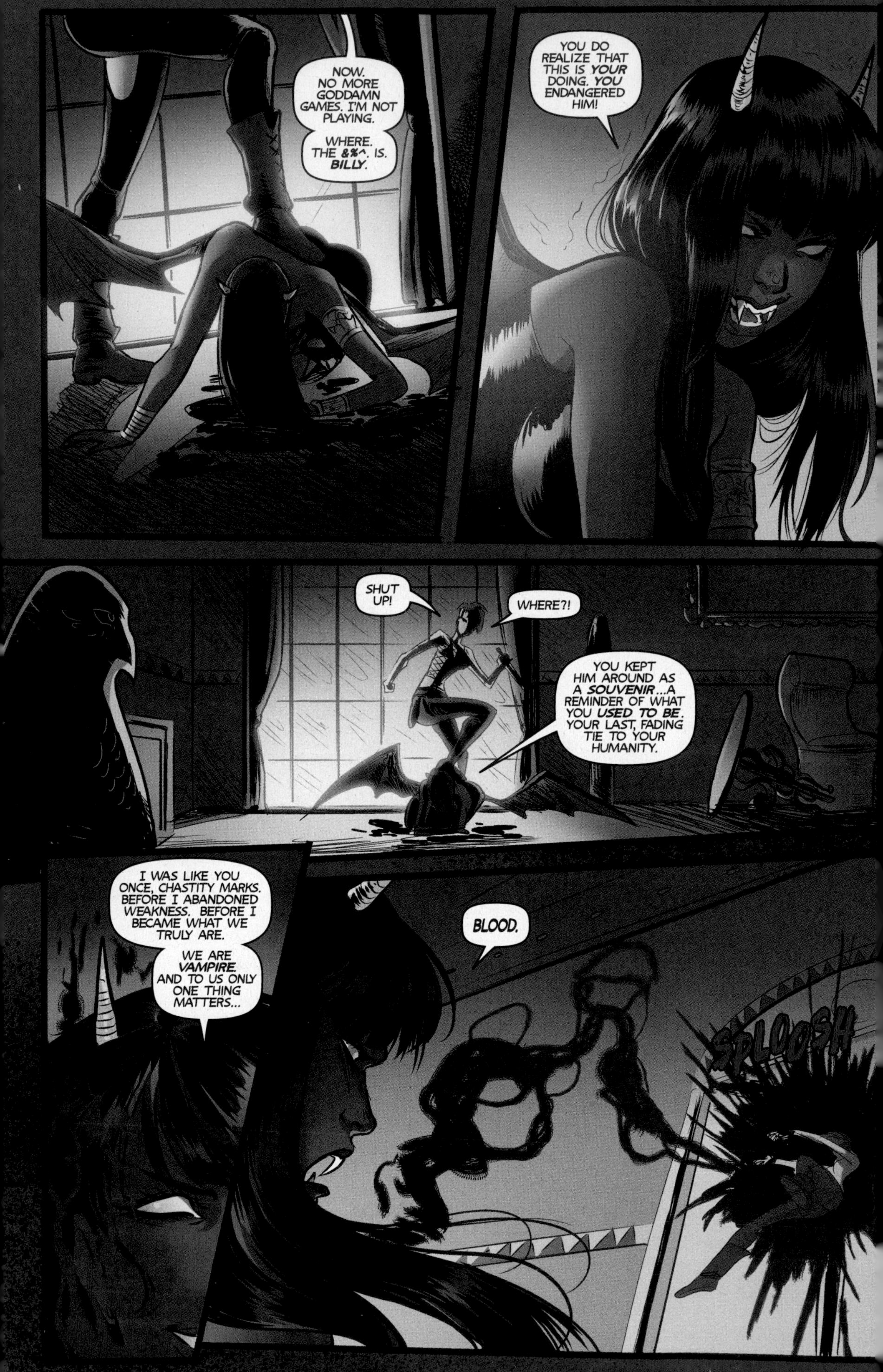
NOW. NO MORE GODDAMN GAMES. I'M NOT PLAYING.
WHERE. THE &%^. IS. BILLY.
YOU DO REALIZE THAT THIS IS YOUR DOING. YOU ENDANGERED HIM!
SHUT UP!
WHERE?!
YOU KEPT HIM AROUND AS A SOUVENIR...A REMINDER OF WHAT YOU USED TO BE. YOUR LAST, FADING TIE TO YOUR HUMANITY.
I WAS LIKE YOU ONCE, CHASTITY MARKS. BEFORE I ABANDONED WEAKNESS. BEFORE I BECAME WHAT WE TRULY ARE.
WE ARE VAMPIRE. AND TO US ONLY ONE THING MATTERS...
BLOOD.
SPLOOSH

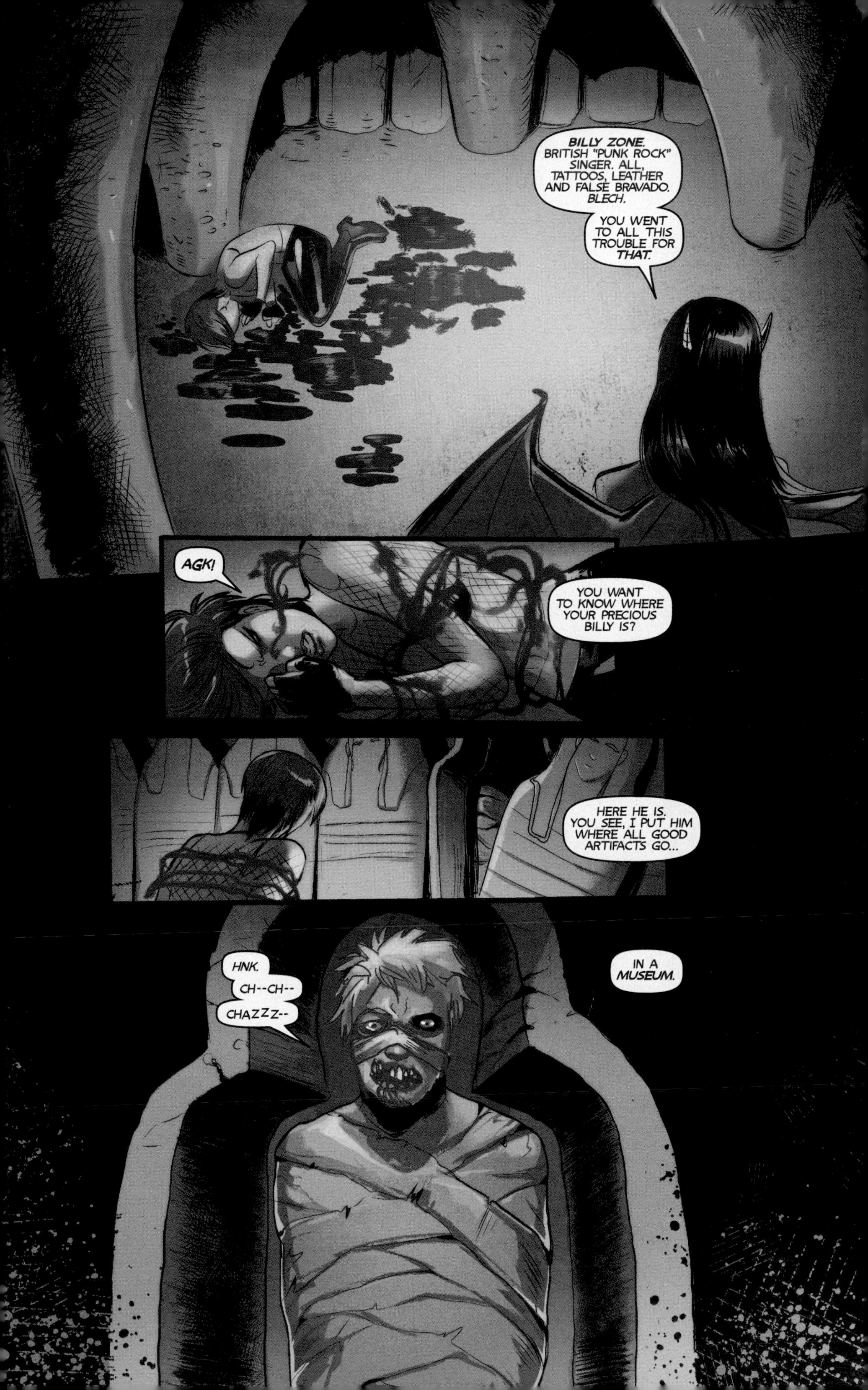
BILLY ZONE. BRITISH "PUNK ROCK" SINGER. ALL, TATTOOS, LEATHER AND FALSE BRAVADO. BLECH.
YOU WENT TO ALL THIS TROUBLE FOR THAT.
AGK!
YOU WANT TO KNOW WHERE YOUR PRECIOUS BILLY IS?
HERE HE IS. YOU SEE, I PUT HIM WHERE ALL GOOD ARTIFACTS GO...
HNK.
CH--CH--
CHAZZZ--
IN A MUSEUM.

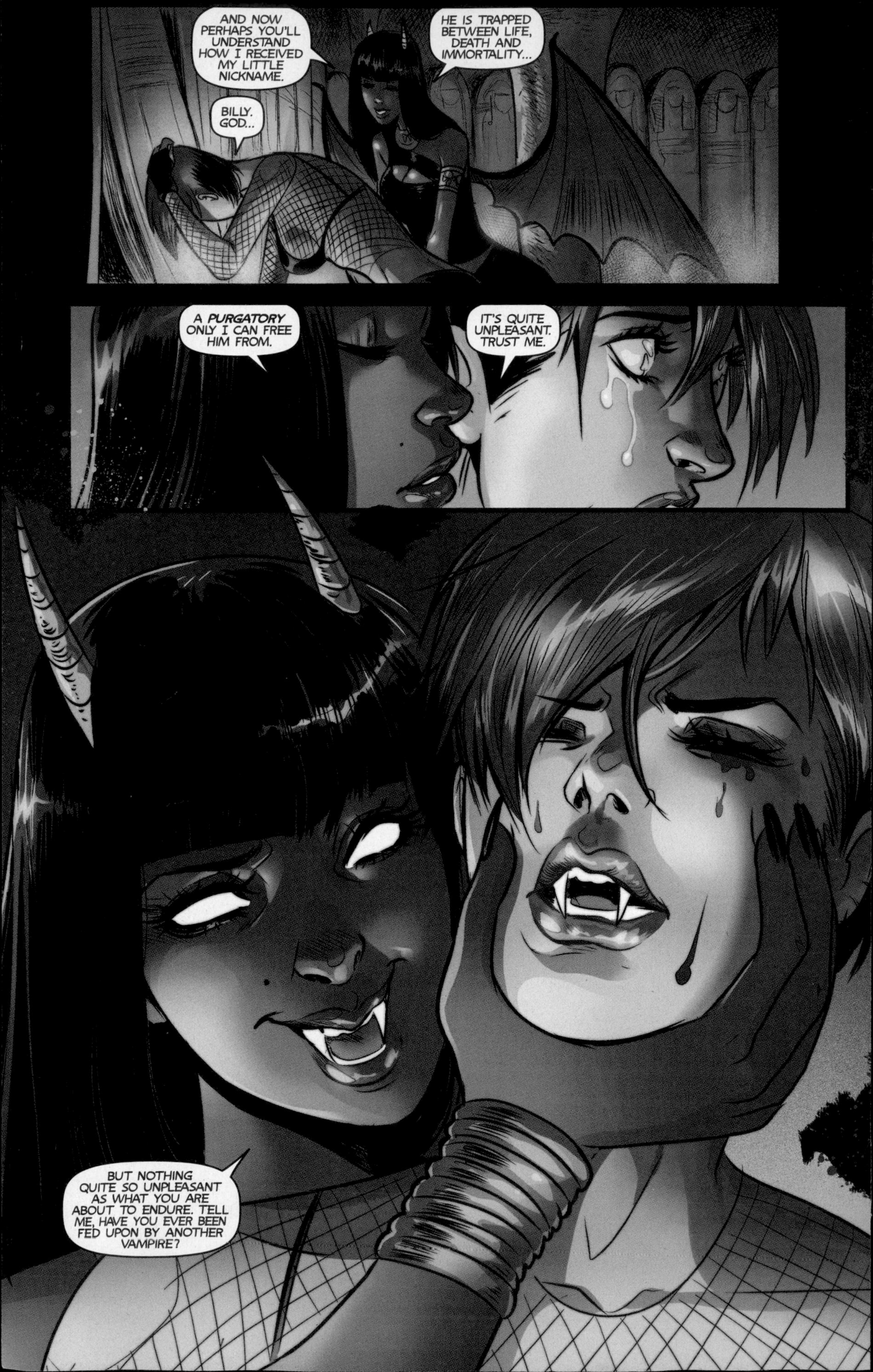
AND NOW PERHAPS YOU'LL UNDERSTAND HOW I RECEIVED MY LITTLE NICKNAME.
HE IS TRAPPED BETWEEN LIFE, DEATH AND IMMORTALITY...
BILLY. GOD...
A PURGATORY ONLY I CAN FREE HIM FROM.
IT'S QUITE UNPLEASANT. TRUST ME.
BUT NOTHING QUITE SO UNPLEASANT AS WHAT YOU ARE ABOUT TO ENDURE. TELL ME, HAVE YOU EVER BEEN FED UPON BY ANOTHER VAMPIRE?

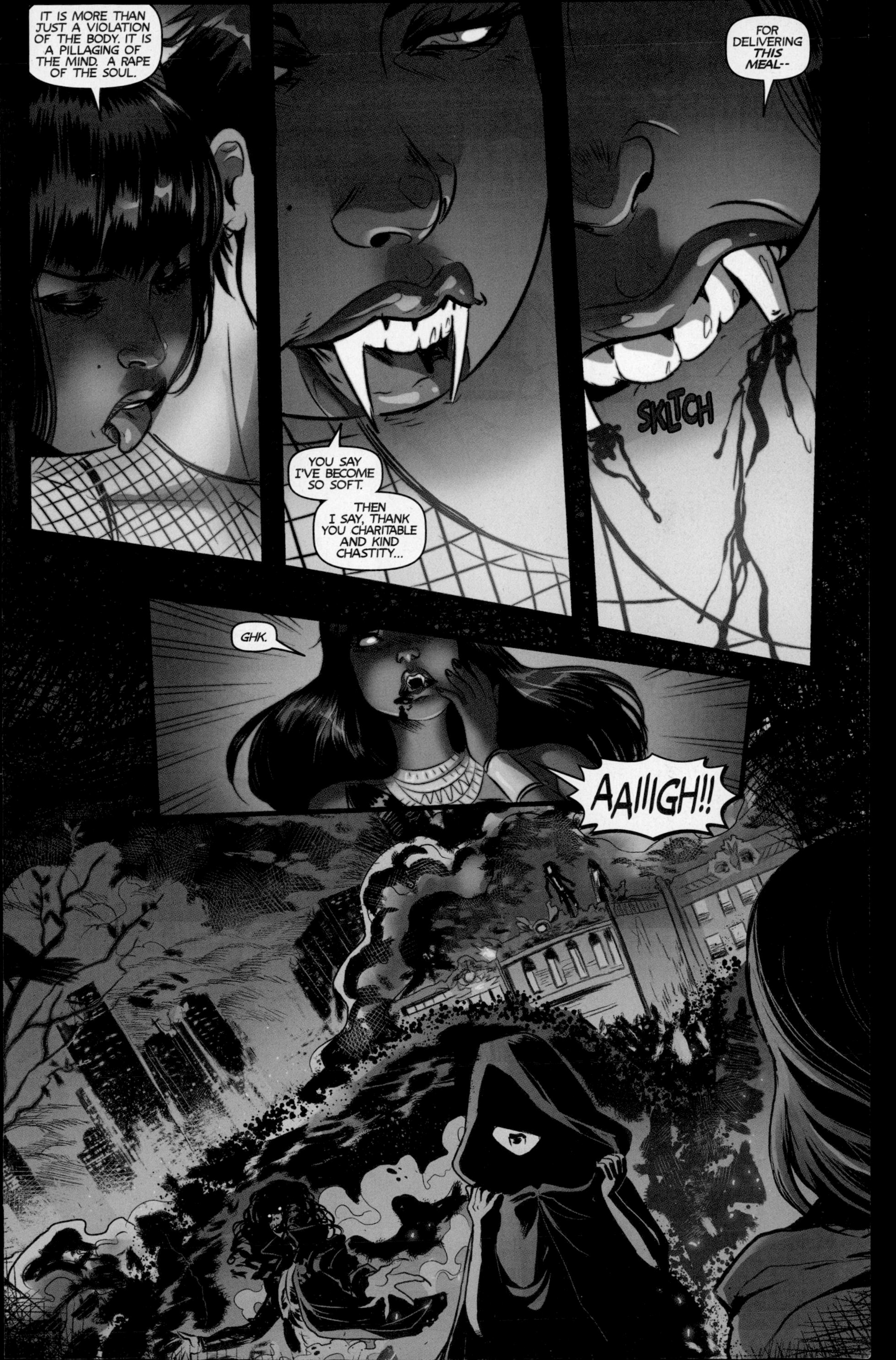
IT IS MORE THAN JUST A VIOLATION OF THE BODY. IT IS A PILLAGING OF THE MIND. A RAPE OF THE SOUL.
YOU SAY I'VE BECOME SO SOFT.
THEN I SAY, THANK YOU CHARITABLE AND KIND CHASTITY...
FOR DELIVERING *THIS MEAL*--
SKLITCH
GHK.
AAIIIGH!!

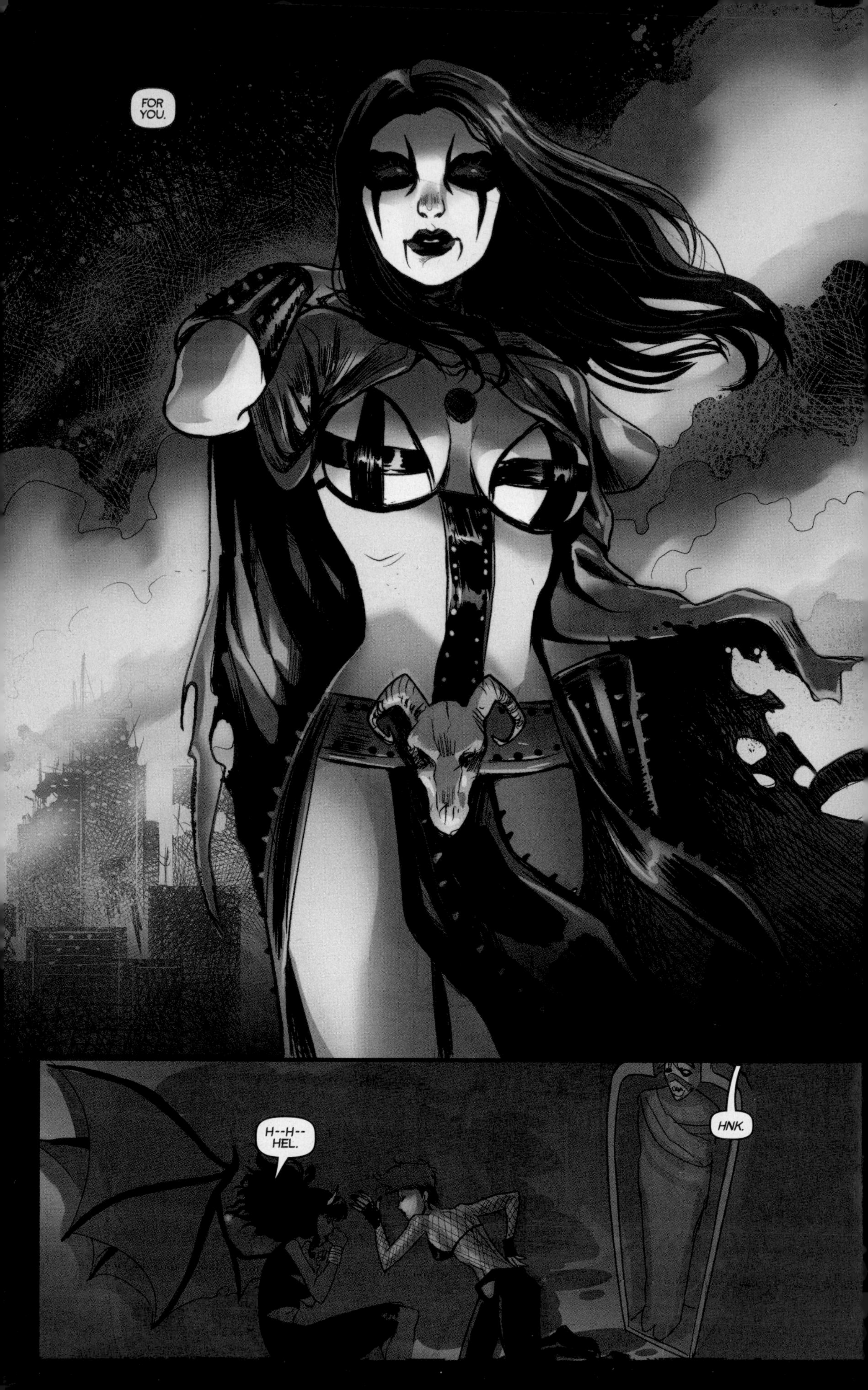
FOR YOU.
H--H-- HEL.
HNK.

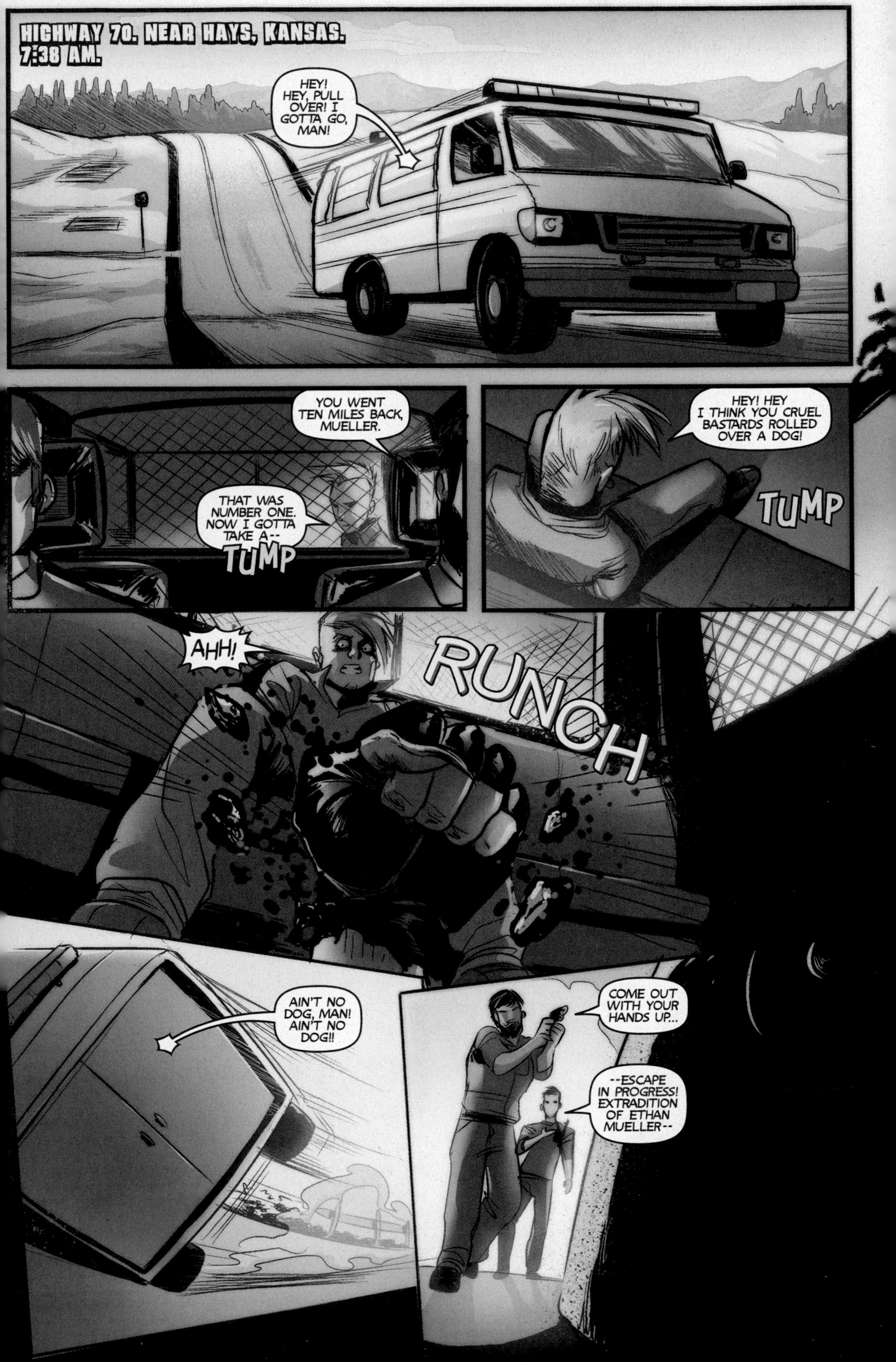
HIGHWAY 70. NEAR HAYS, KANSAS. 7:38 AM.
HEY! HEY, PULL OVER! I GOTTA GO, MAN!
YOU WENT TEN MILES BACK, MUELLER.
THAT WAS NUMBER ONE. NOW I GOTTA TAKE A--
TUMP
HEY! HEY I THINK YOU CRUEL BASTARDS ROLLED OVER A DOG!
TUMP
AHH!
RUNCH
AIN'T NO DOG, MAN! AIN'T NO DOG!!
COME OUT WITH YOUR HANDS UP...
--ESCAPE IN PROGRESS! EXTRADITION OF ETHAN MUELLER--

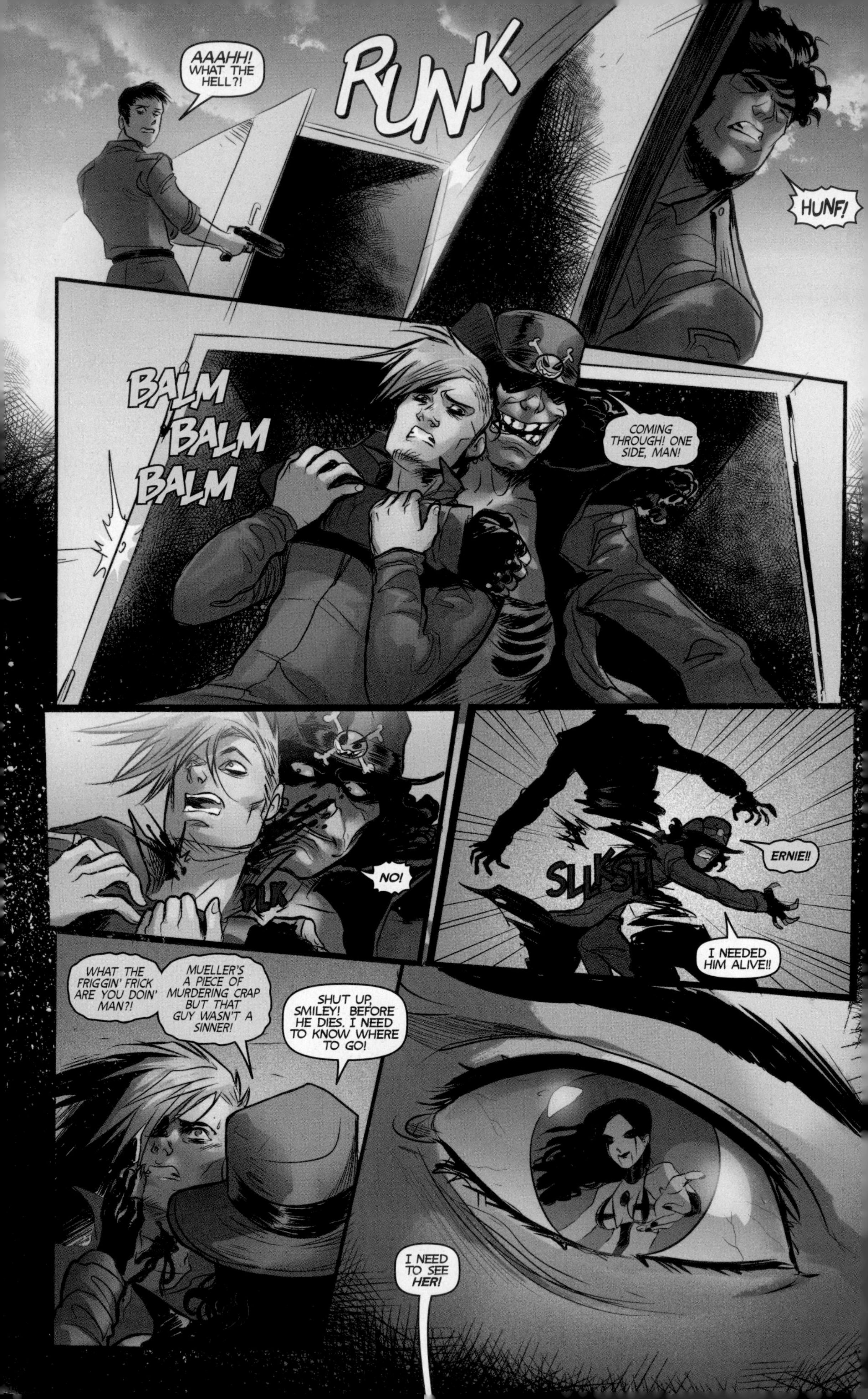
AAAHH! WHAT THE HELL?!
RUNK
HUNF!
BALM
BALM
BALM
COMING THROUGH! ONE SIDE, MAN!
NO!
ERNIE!!
SLUKSH
I NEEDED HIM ALIVE!!
WHAT THE FRIGGIN' FRICK ARE YOU DOIN' MAN?!
MUELLER'S A PIECE OF MURDERING CRAP BUT THAT GUY WASN'T A SINNER!
SHUT UP, SMILEY! BEFORE HE DIES. I NEED TO KNOW WHERE TO GO!
I NEED TO SEE HER!

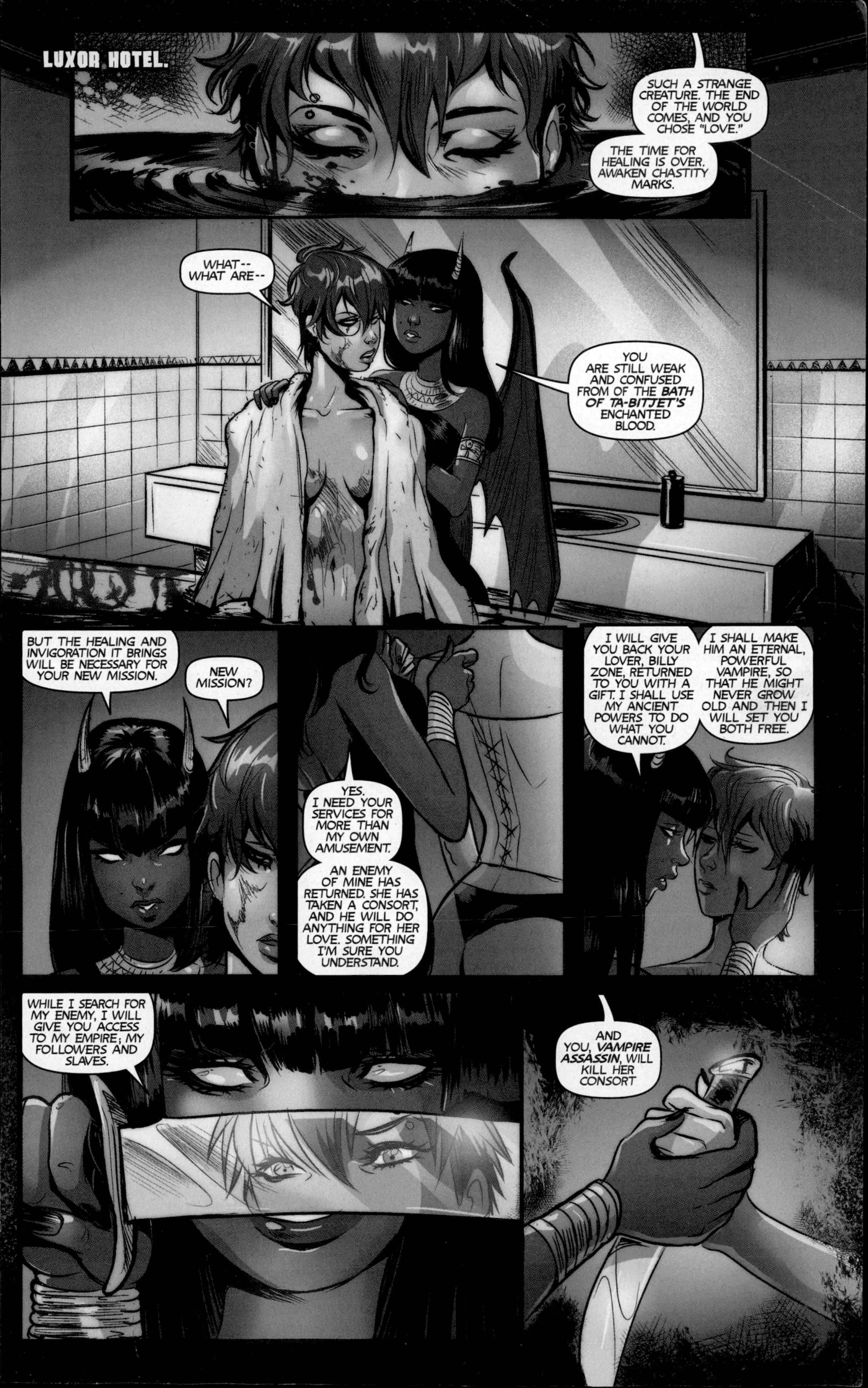
LUXOR HOTEL.
SUCH A STRANGE CREATURE. THE END OF THE WORLD COMES, AND YOU CHOSE "LOVE."
THE TIME FOR HEALING IS OVER. AWAKEN CHASTITY MARKS.
WHAT-- WHAT ARE--
YOU ARE STILL WEAK AND CONFUSED FROM OF THE BATH OF TA-BITJET'S ENCHANTED BLOOD.
BUT THE HEALING AND INVIGORATION IT BRINGS WILL BE NECESSARY FOR YOUR NEW MISSION.
NEW MISSION?
YES. I NEED YOUR SERVICES FOR MORE THAN MY OWN AMUSEMENT.
AN ENEMY OF MINE HAS RETURNED. SHE HAS TAKEN A CONSORT, AND HE WILL DO ANYTHING FOR HER LOVE. SOMETHING I'M SURE YOU UNDERSTAND.
I WILL GIVE YOU BACK YOUR LOVER, BILLY ZONE, RETURNED TO YOU WITH A GIFT. I SHALL USE MY ANCIENT POWERS TO DO WHAT YOU CANNOT.
I SHALL MAKE HIM AN ETERNAL, POWERFUL VAMPIRE, SO THAT HE MIGHT NEVER GROW OLD AND THEN I WILL SET YOU BOTH FREE.
WHILE I SEARCH FOR MY ENEMY, I WILL GIVE YOU ACCESS TO MY EMPIRE; MY FOLLOWERS AND SLAVES.
AND YOU, VAMPIRE ASSASSIN, WILL KILL HER CONSORT

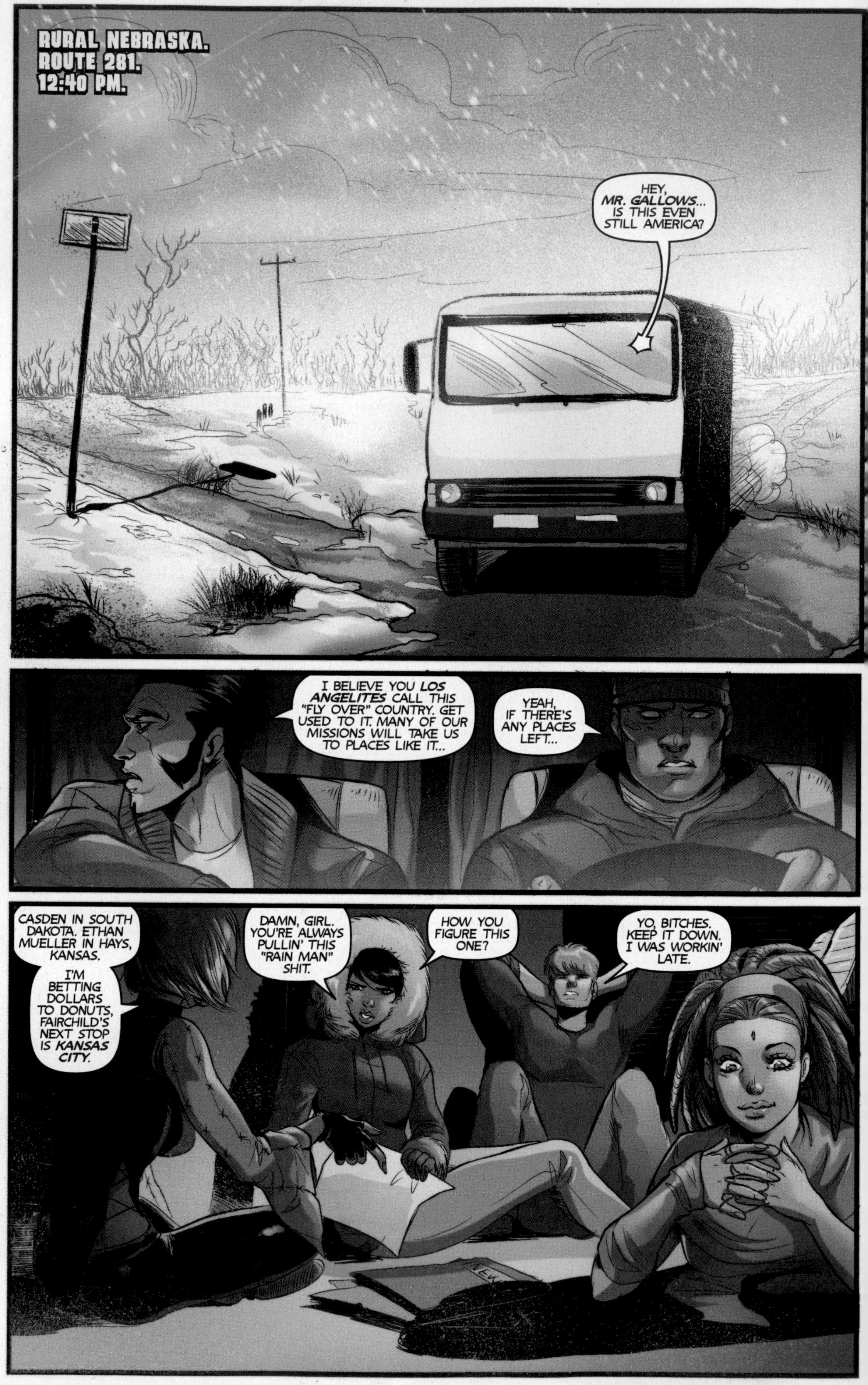
RURAL NEBRASKA.
ROUTE 281.
12:40 PM.
HEY, *MR. GALLOWS*... IS THIS EVEN STILL AMERICA?
I BELIEVE YOU *LOS ANGELITES* CALL THIS "FLY OVER" COUNTRY. GET USED TO IT. MANY OF OUR MISSIONS WILL TAKE US TO PLACES LIKE IT...
YEAH, IF THERE'S ANY PLACES LEFT...
CASDEN IN SOUTH DAKOTA. ETHAN MUELLER IN HAYS, KANSAS.
I'M BETTING DOLLARS TO DONUTS, FAIRCHILD'S NEXT STOP IS *KANSAS CITY*.
DAMN, GIRL. YOU'RE ALWAYS PULLIN' THIS "RAIN MAN" SHIT.
HOW YOU FIGURE THIS ONE?
YO, BITCHES. KEEP IT DOWN. I WAS WORKIN' LATE.

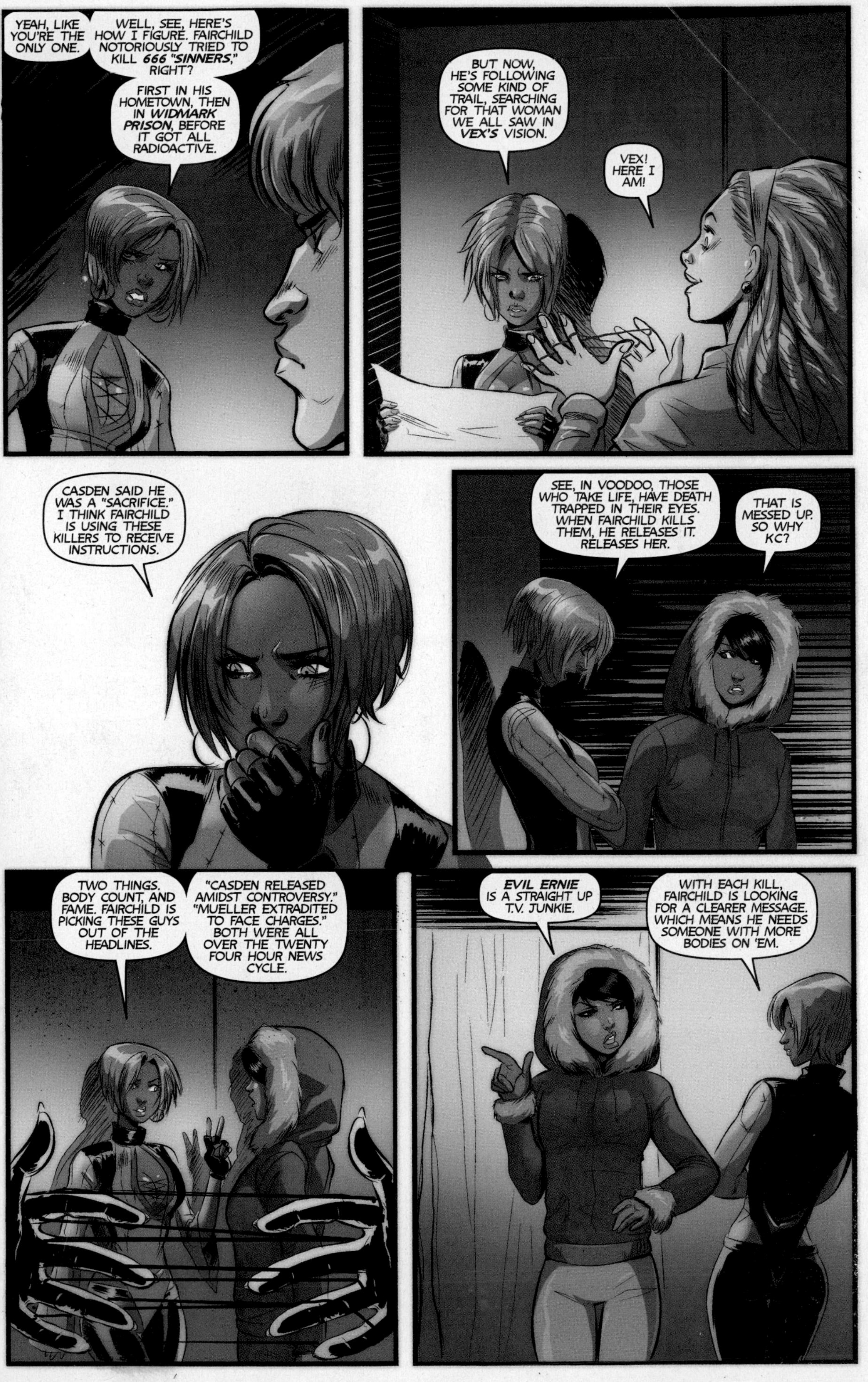
YEAH, LIKE YOU'RE THE ONLY ONE.
WELL, SEE, HERE'S HOW I FIGURE. FAIRCHILD NOTORIOUSLY TRIED TO KILL 666 "SINNERS," RIGHT?
FIRST IN HIS HOMETOWN, THEN IN WIDMARK PRISON, BEFORE IT GOT ALL RADIOACTIVE.
BUT NOW, HE'S FOLLOWING SOME KIND OF TRAIL, SEARCHING FOR THAT WOMAN WE ALL SAW IN VEX'S VISION.
VEX! HERE I AM!
CASDEN SAID HE WAS A "SACRIFICE." I THINK FAIRCHILD IS USING THESE KILLERS TO RECEIVE INSTRUCTIONS.
SEE, IN VOODOO, THOSE WHO TAKE LIFE, HAVE DEATH TRAPPED IN THEIR EYES. WHEN FAIRCHILD KILLS THEM, HE RELEASES IT. RELEASES HER.
THAT IS MESSED UP. SO WHY KC?
TWO THINGS. BODY COUNT, AND FAME. FAIRCHILD IS PICKING THESE GUYS OUT OF THE HEADLINES.
"CASDEN RELEASED AMIDST CONTROVERSY." "MUELLER EXTRADITED TO FACE CHARGES." BOTH WERE ALL OVER THE TWENTY FOUR HOUR NEWS CYCLE.
EVIL ERNIE IS A STRAIGHT UP T.V. JUNKIE.
WITH EACH KILL, FAIRCHILD IS LOOKING FOR A CLEARER MESSAGE. WHICH MEANS HE NEEDS SOMEONE WITH MORE BODIES ON 'EM.

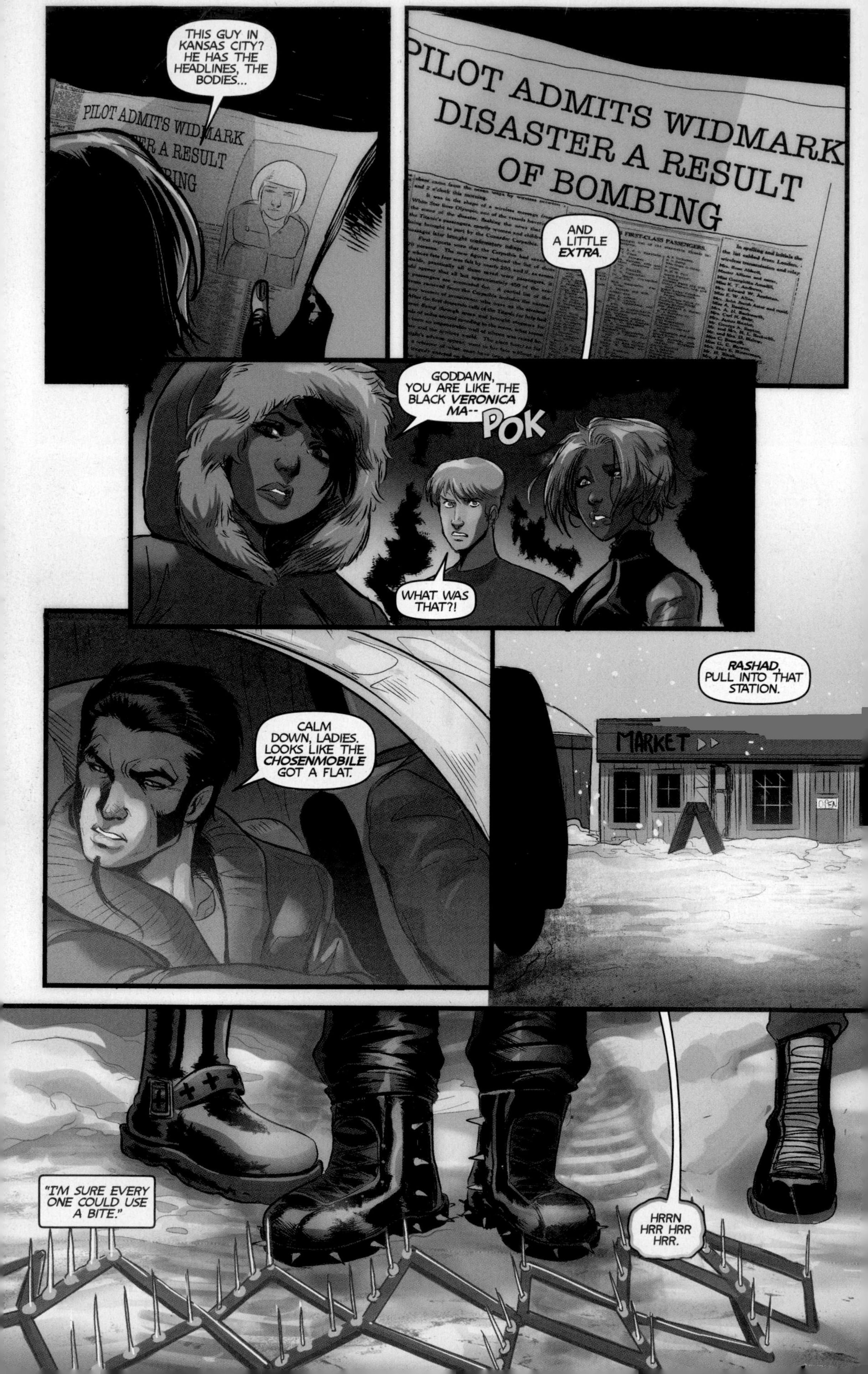
THIS GUY IN KANSAS CITY? HE HAS THE HEADLINES, THE BODIES...
PILOT ADMITS WIDMARK DISASTER A RESULT OF BOMBING
AND A LITTLE EXTRA.
GODDAMN, YOU ARE LIKE THE BLACK VERONICA MA--
POK
WHAT WAS THAT?!
CALM DOWN, LADIES. LOOKS LIKE THE CHOSENMOBILE GOT A FLAT.
RASHAD, PULL INTO THAT STATION.
MARKET
OPEN
"I'M SURE EVERY ONE COULD USE A BITE."
HRRN HRR HRR HRR.

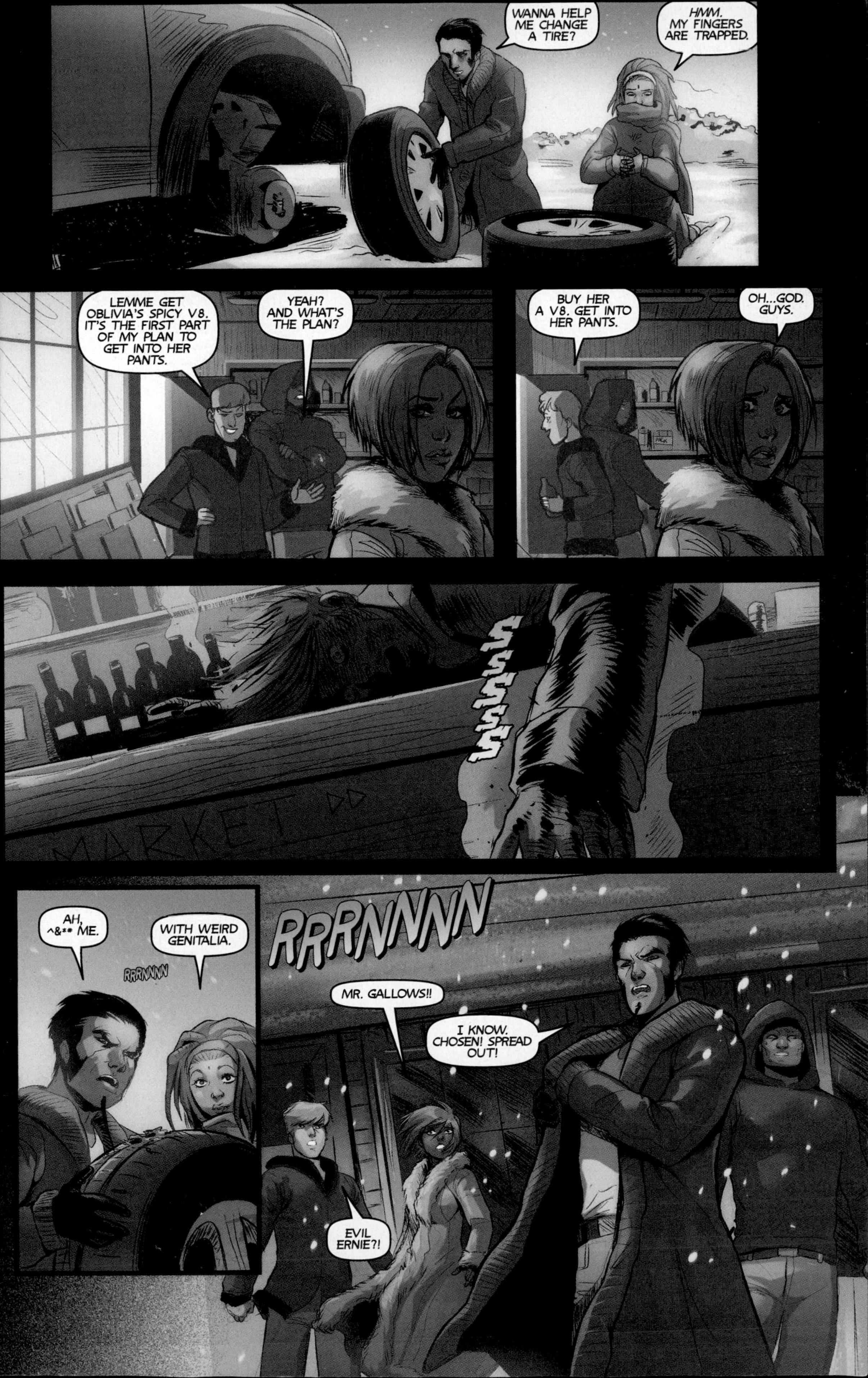
WANNA HELP ME CHANGE A TIRE?
HMM. MY FINGERS ARE TRAPPED.
LEMME GET OBLIVIA'S SPICY V8. IT'S THE FIRST PART OF MY PLAN TO GET INTO HER PANTS.
YEAH? AND WHAT'S THE PLAN?
BUY HER A V8. GET INTO HER PANTS.
OH...GOD. GUYS.
SSSSSS
MARKET
AH, ^&** ME.
WITH WEIRD GENITALIA.
RRRNNNN
RRRNNNN
MR. GALLOWS!!
I KNOW. CHOSEN! SPREAD OUT!
EVIL ERNIE?!

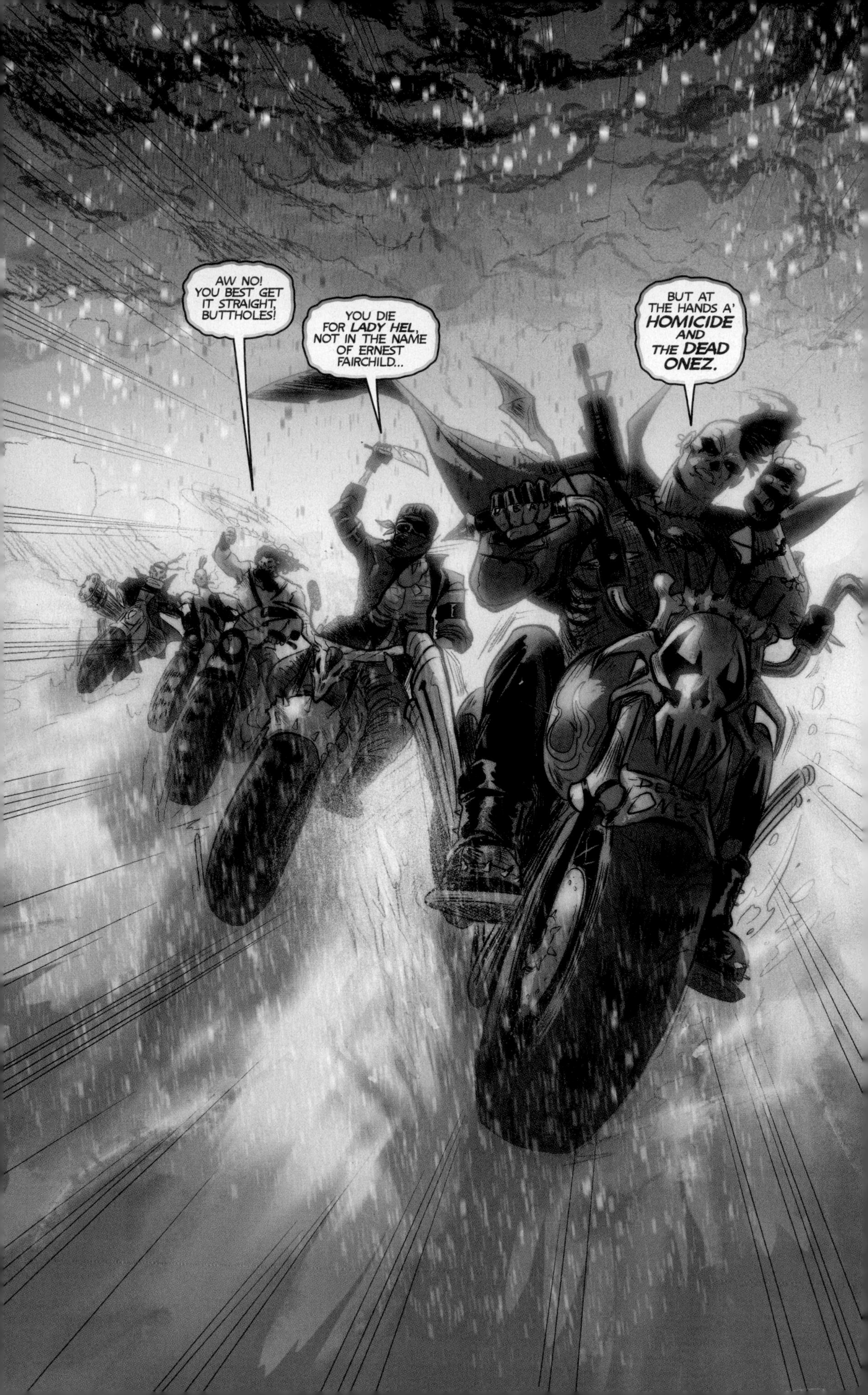
AW NO! YOU BEST GET IT STRAIGHT, BUTTHOLES!
YOU DIE FOR LADY HEL, NOT IN THE NAME OF ERNEST FAIRCHILD...
BUT AT THE HANDS A' HOMICIDE AND THE DEAD ONEZ.

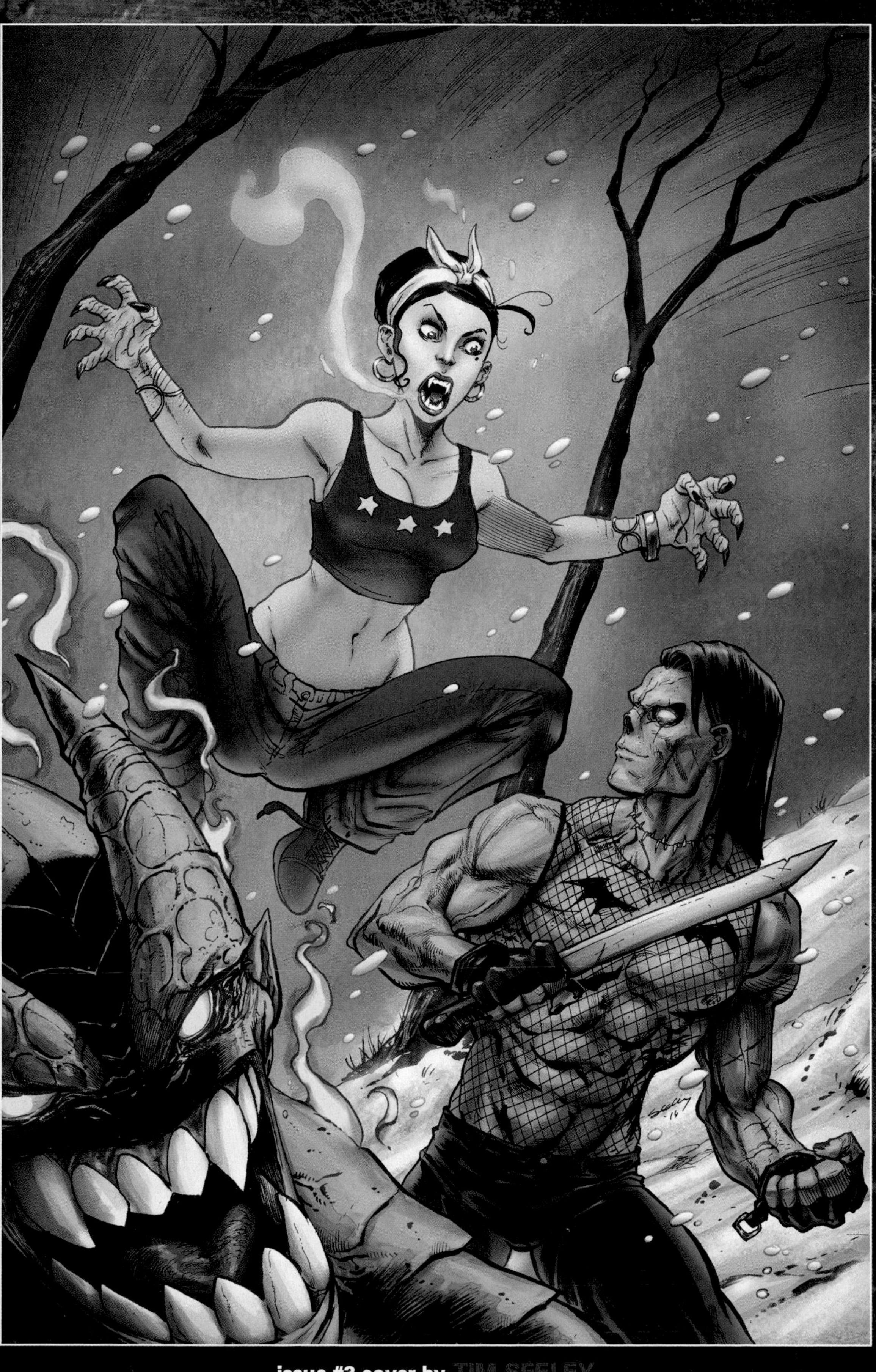

issue #3 cover by TIM SEELEY
colors by ADRIANO LUCAS

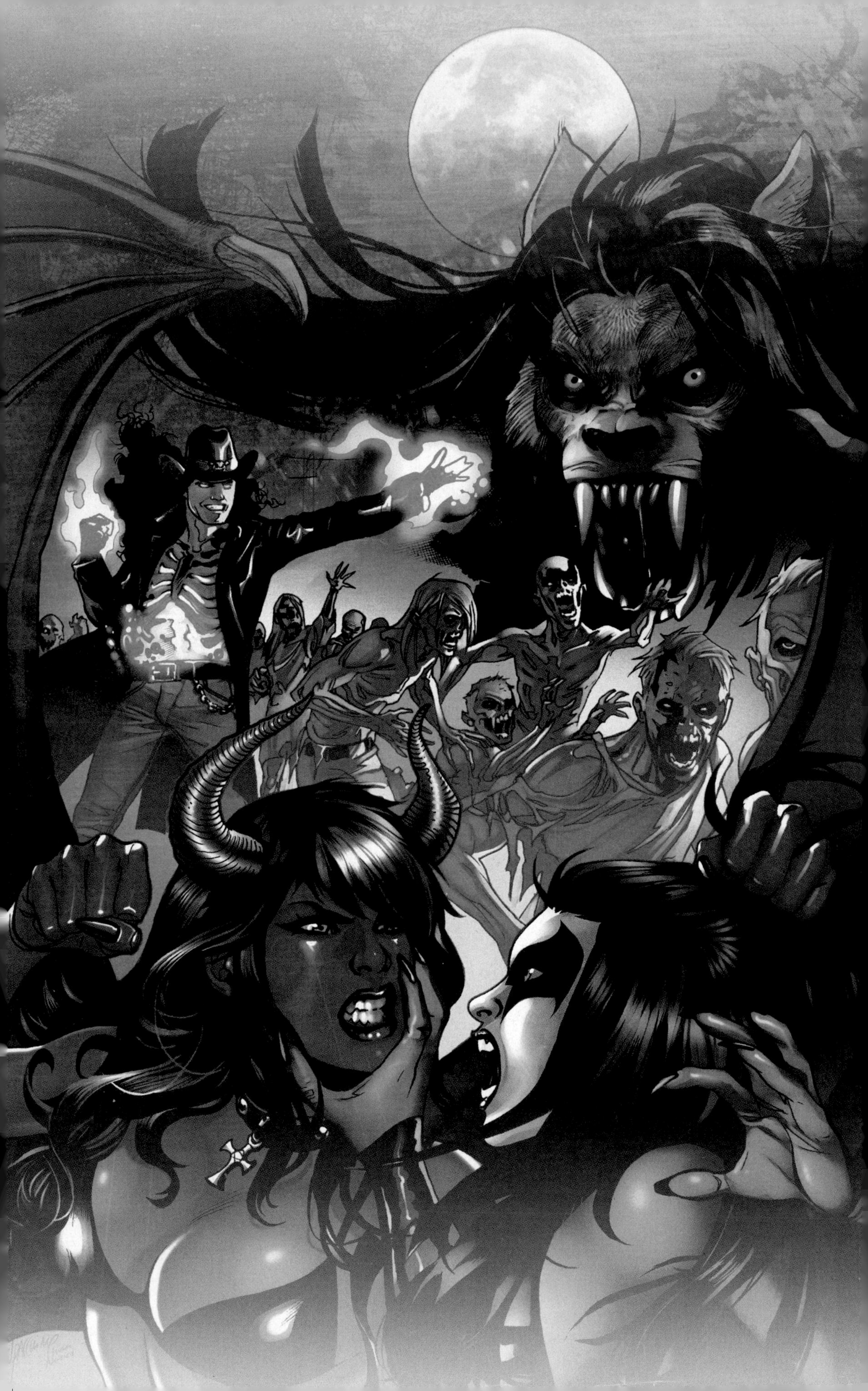

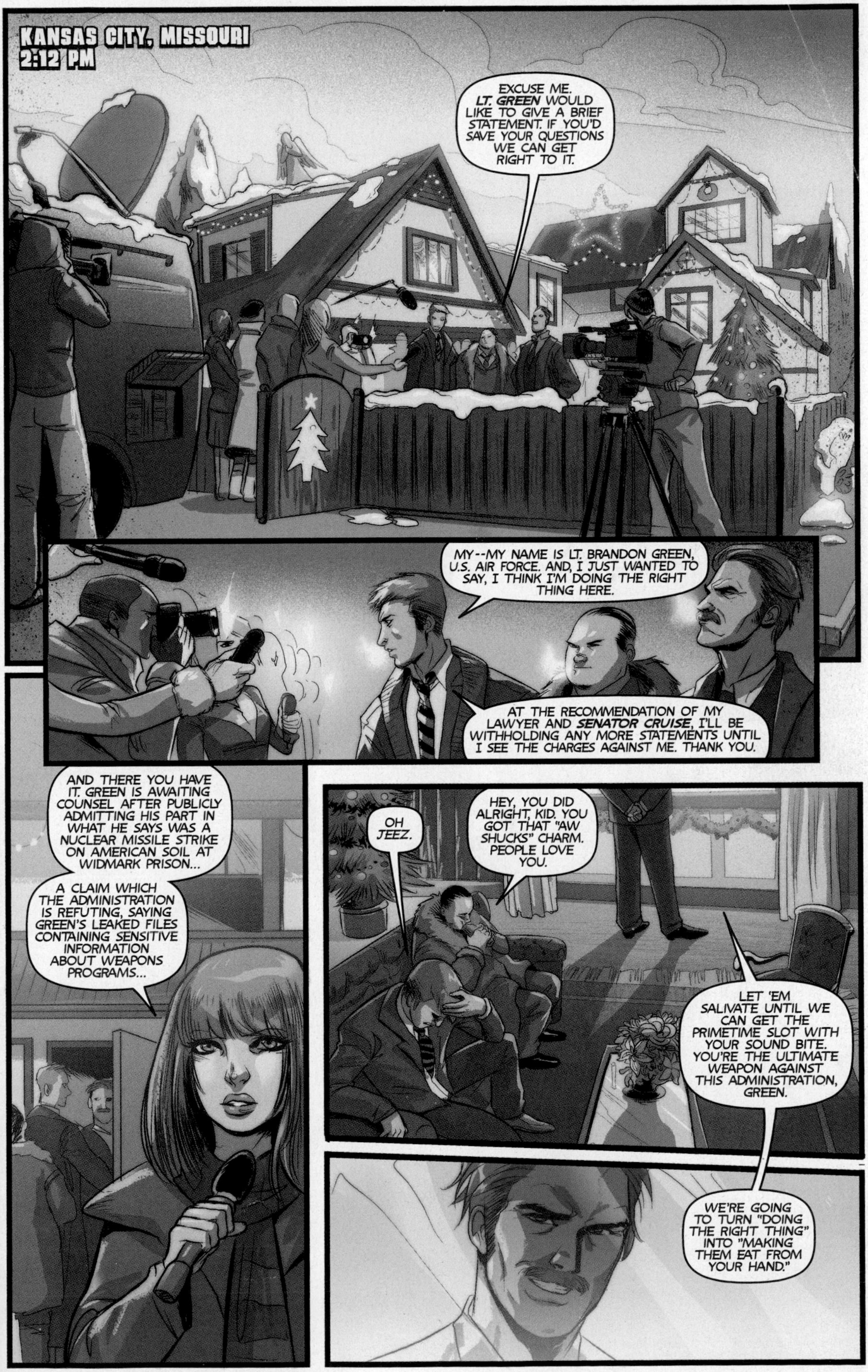
KANSAS CITY, MISSOURI 2:12 PM
EXCUSE ME. LT. GREEN WOULD LIKE TO GIVE A BRIEF STATEMENT. IF YOU'D SAVE YOUR QUESTIONS WE CAN GET RIGHT TO IT.
MY--MY NAME IS LT. BRANDON GREEN, U.S. AIR FORCE. AND, I JUST WANTED TO SAY, I THINK I'M DOING THE RIGHT THING HERE.
AT THE RECOMMENDATION OF MY LAWYER AND SENATOR CRUISE, I'LL BE WITHHOLDING ANY MORE STATEMENTS UNTIL I SEE THE CHARGES AGAINST ME. THANK YOU.
AND THERE YOU HAVE IT. GREEN IS AWAITING COUNSEL AFTER PUBLICLY ADMITTING HIS PART IN WHAT HE SAYS WAS A NUCLEAR MISSILE STRIKE ON AMERICAN SOIL AT WIDMARK PRISON...
A CLAIM WHICH THE ADMINISTRATION IS REFUTING, SAYING GREEN'S LEAKED FILES CONTAINING SENSITIVE INFORMATION ABOUT WEAPONS PROGRAMS...
OH JEEZ.
HEY, YOU DID ALRIGHT, KID. YOU GOT THAT "AW SHUCKS" CHARM. PEOPLE LOVE YOU.
LET 'EM SALIVATE UNTIL WE CAN GET THE PRIMETIME SLOT WITH YOUR SOUND BITE. YOU'RE THE ULTIMATE WEAPON AGAINST THIS ADMINISTRATION, GREEN.
WE'RE GOING TO TURN "DOING THE RIGHT THING" INTO "MAKING THEM EAT FROM YOUR HAND."

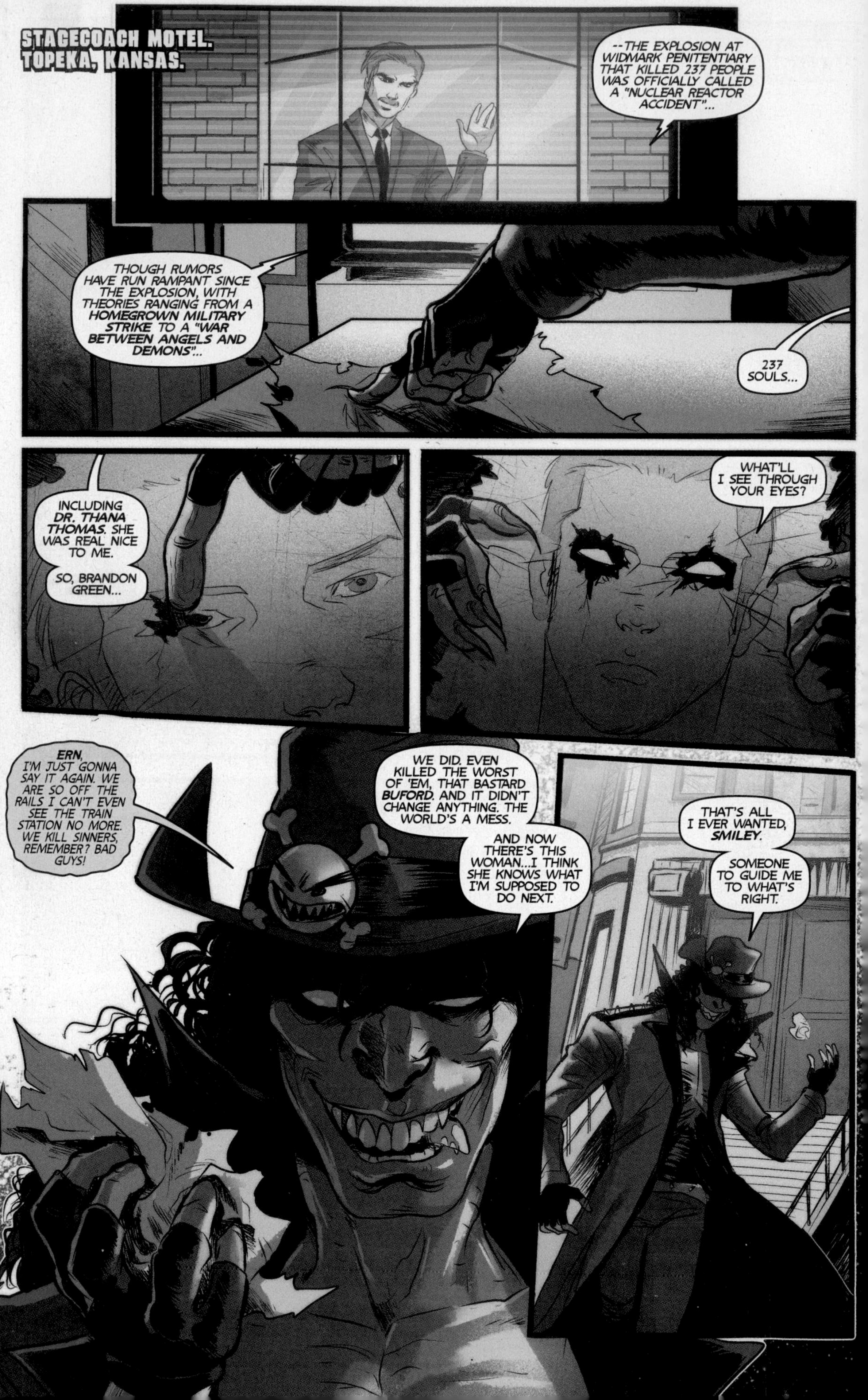

STAGECOACH MOTEL.
TOPEKA, KANSAS.
--THE EXPLOSION AT WIDMARK PENITENTIARY THAT KILLED 237 PEOPLE WAS OFFICIALLY CALLED A "NUCLEAR REACTOR ACCIDENT"...
THOUGH RUMORS HAVE RUN RAMPANT SINCE THE EXPLOSION, WITH THEORIES RANGING FROM A HOMEGROWN MILITARY STRIKE TO A "WAR BETWEEN ANGELS AND DEMONS"...
237 SOULS...
INCLUDING DR. THANA THOMAS. SHE WAS REAL NICE TO ME.
SO, BRANDON GREEN...
WHAT'LL I SEE THROUGH YOUR EYES?
ERN, I'M JUST GONNA SAY IT AGAIN. WE ARE SO OFF THE RAILS I CAN'T EVEN SEE THE TRAIN STATION NO MORE. WE KILL SINNERS, REMEMBER? BAD GUYS!
WE DID. EVEN KILLED THE WORST OF 'EM, THAT BASTARD BUFORD. AND IT DIDN'T CHANGE ANYTHING. THE WORLD'S A MESS.
AND NOW THERE'S THIS WOMAN...I THINK SHE KNOWS WHAT I'M SUPPOSED TO DO NEXT.
THAT'S ALL I EVER WANTED, SMILEY.
SOMEONE TO GUIDE ME TO WHAT'S RIGHT.

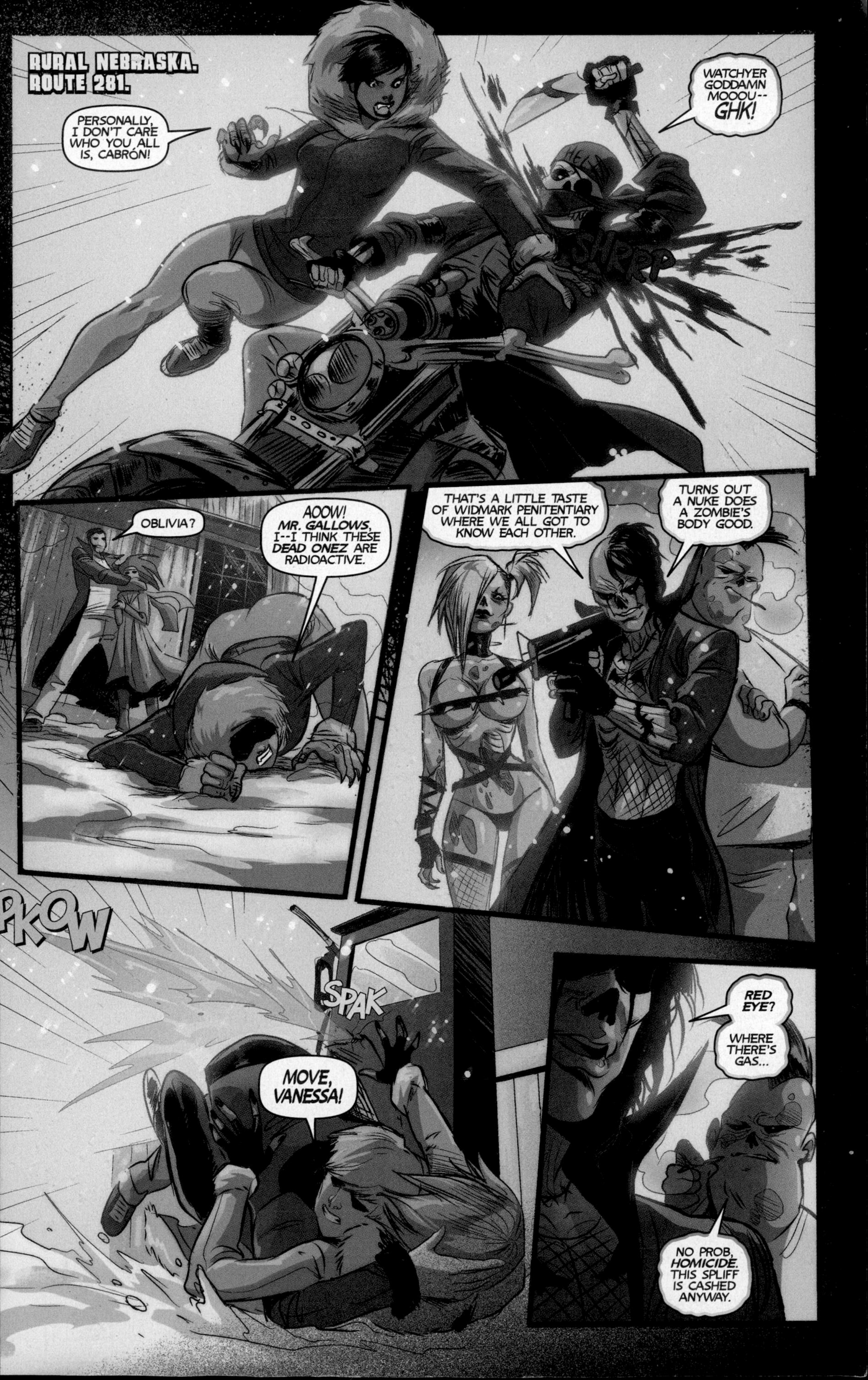
RURAL NEBRASKA. ROUTE 281.
PERSONALLY, I DON'T CARE WHO YOU ALL IS, CABRÓN!
WATCHYER GODDAMN MOOOU-- GHK!
SHRPP
OBLIVIA?
AOOW! MR. GALLOWS, I--I THINK THESE DEAD ONEZ ARE RADIOACTIVE.
THAT'S A LITTLE TASTE OF WIDMARK PENITENTIARY WHERE WE ALL GOT TO KNOW EACH OTHER.
TURNS OUT A NUKE DOES A ZOMBIE'S BODY GOOD.
PKOW
SPAK
MOVE, VANESSA!
RED EYE?
WHERE THERE'S GAS...
NO PROB, HOMICIDE. THIS SPLIFF IS CASHED ANYWAY.

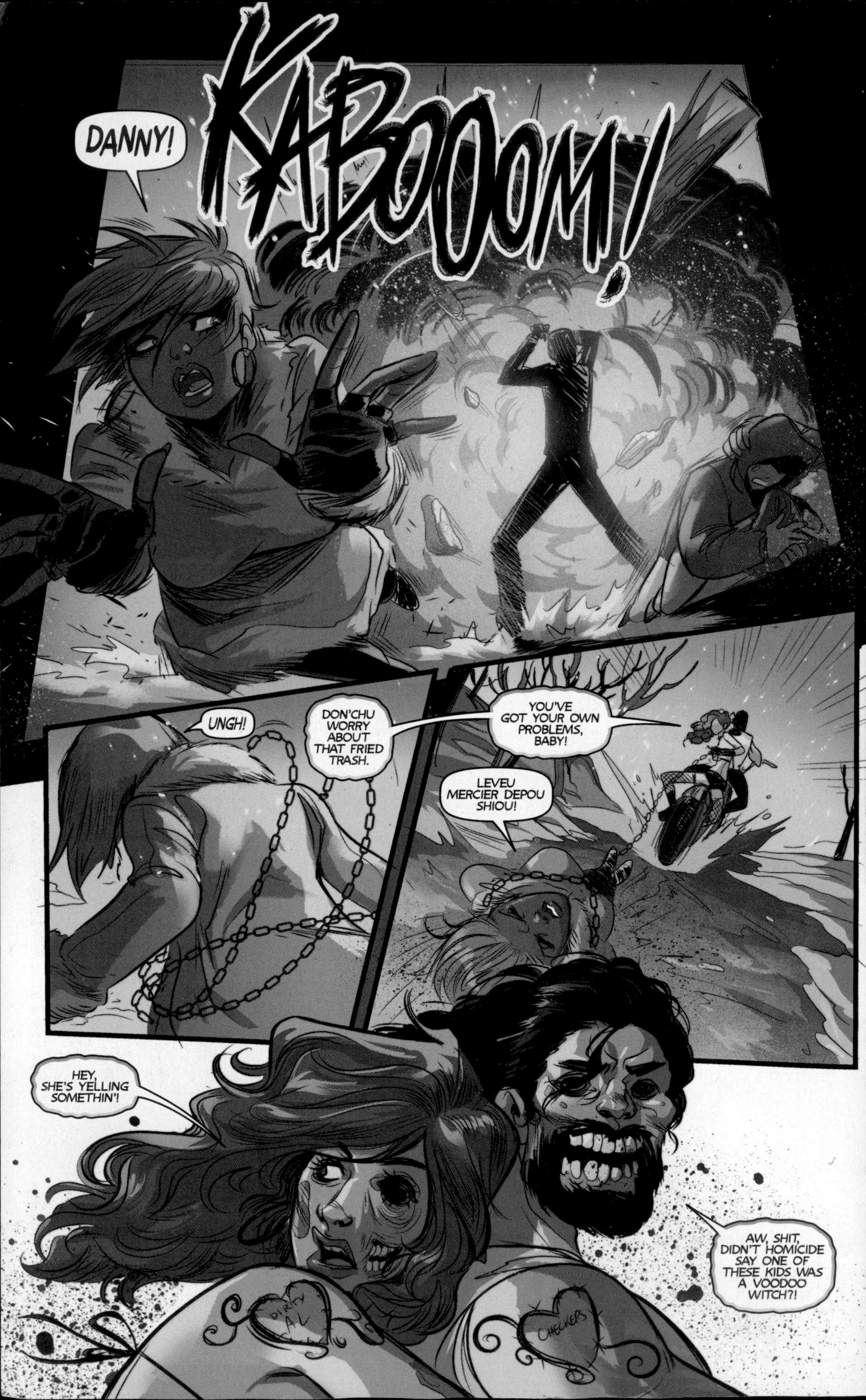
DANNY!
KABOOOM!
UNGH!
DON'CHU WORRY ABOUT THAT FRIED TRASH.
YOU'VE GOT YOUR OWN PROBLEMS, BABY!
LEVEU MERCIER DEPOU SHIOU!
HEY, SHE'S YELLING SOMETHIN'!
AW, SHIT, DIDN'T HOMICIDE SAY ONE OF THESE KIDS WAS A VOODOO WITCH?!
DIRTY AL
CHECKERS

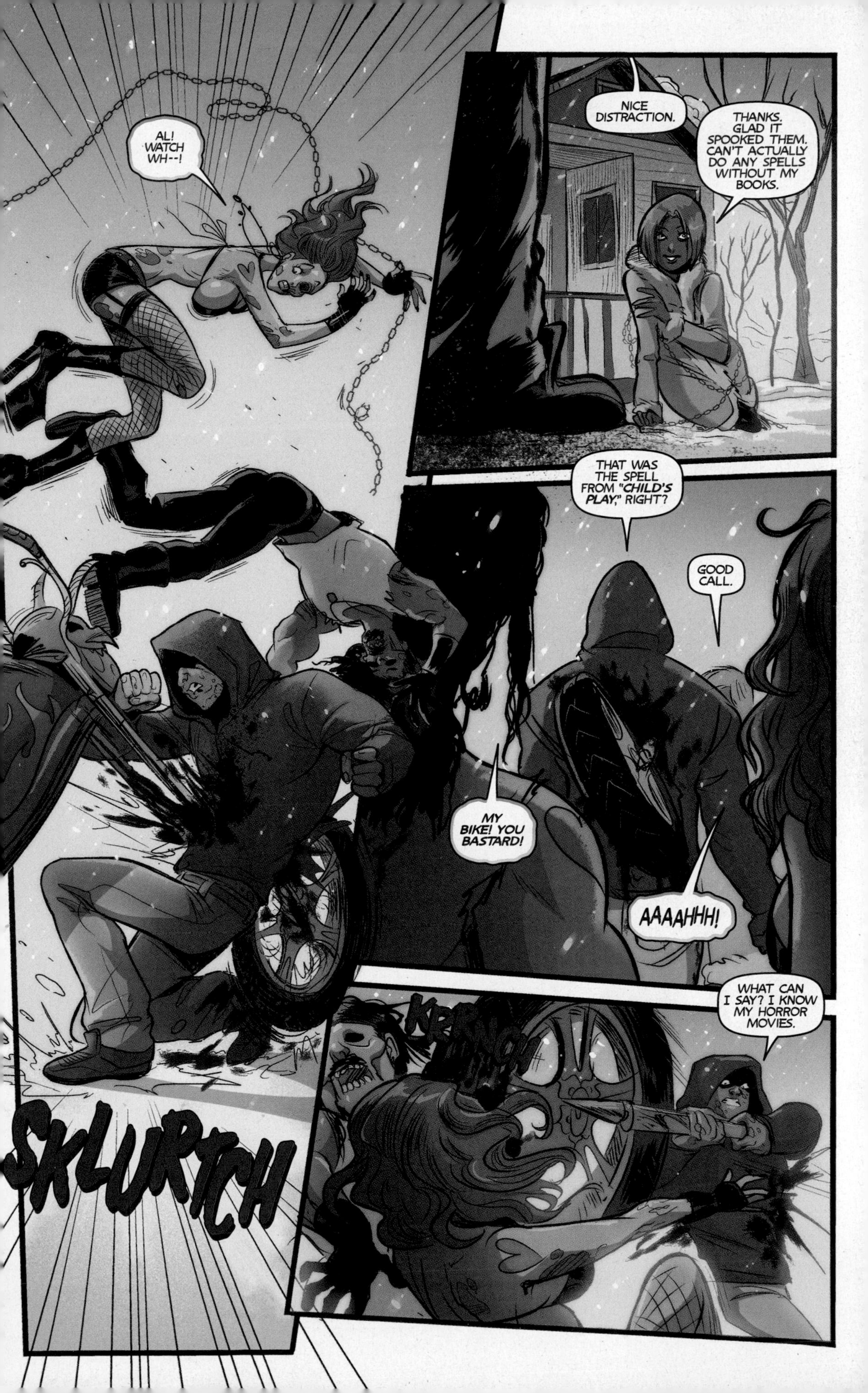
AL! WATCH WH--!
NICE DISTRACTION.
THANKS. GLAD IT SPOOKED THEM. CAN'T ACTUALLY DO ANY SPELLS WITHOUT MY BOOKS.
THAT WAS THE SPELL FROM "CHILD'S PLAY," RIGHT?
GOOD CALL.
MY BIKE! YOU BASTARD!
AAAAHHH!
SKLURTCH
WHAT CAN I SAY? I KNOW MY HORROR MOVIES.

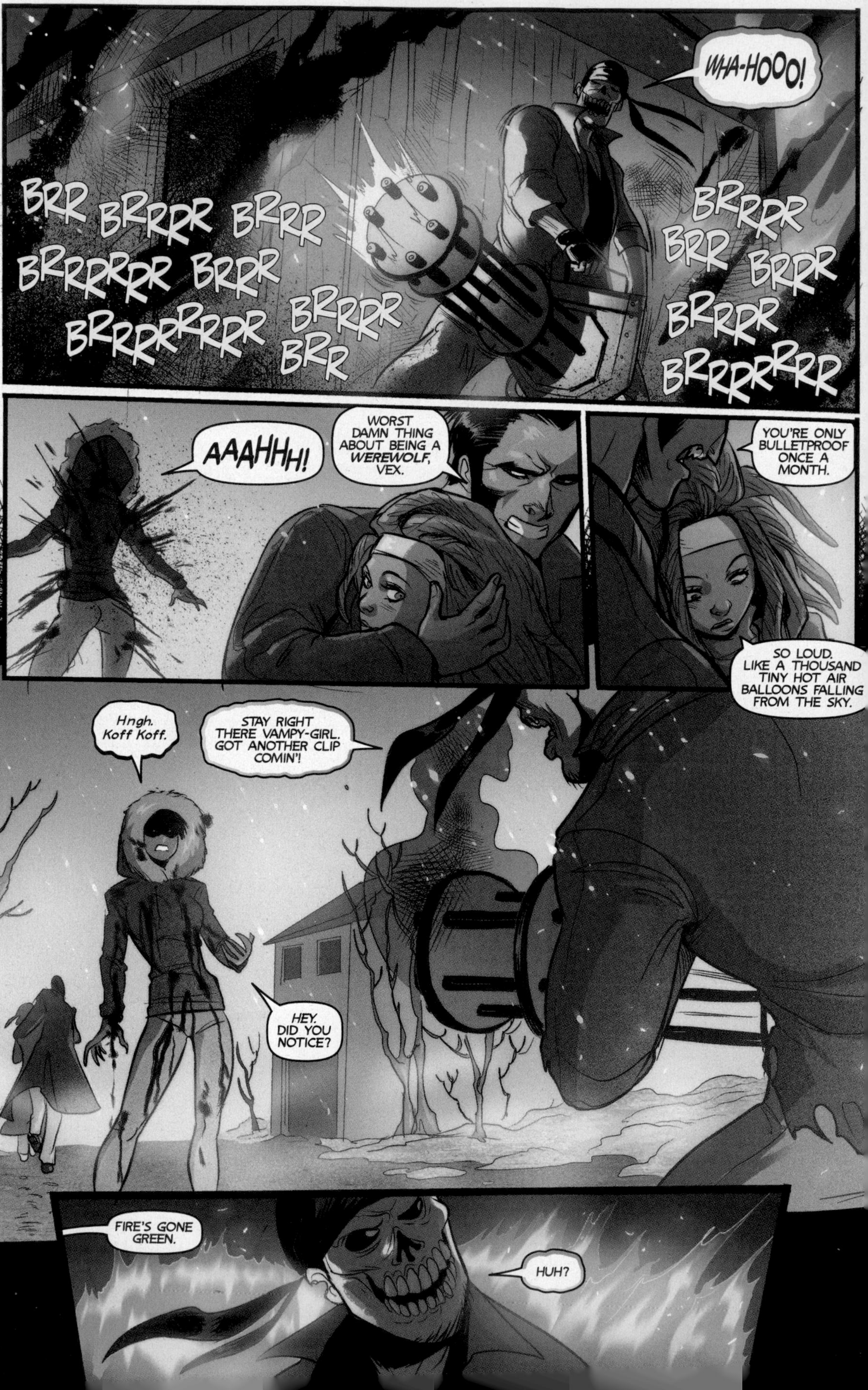
WHA-HOOO!
BRR BRRRRR BRRR BRRRRRR BRRR BRRRRRRRRR BRRRR BRR
BRRRR BRR BRRR BRRRR BRRRRRRR
AAAHHH!
WORST DAMN THING ABOUT BEING A *WEREWOLF,* VEX.
YOU'RE ONLY BULLETPROOF ONCE A MONTH.
SO LOUD. LIKE A THOUSAND TINY HOT AIR BALLOONS FALLING FROM THE SKY.
Hngh. Koff Koff.
STAY RIGHT THERE VAMPY-GIRL. GOT ANOTHER CLIP COMIN'!
HEY. DID YOU NOTICE?
FIRE'S GONE GREEN.
HUH?

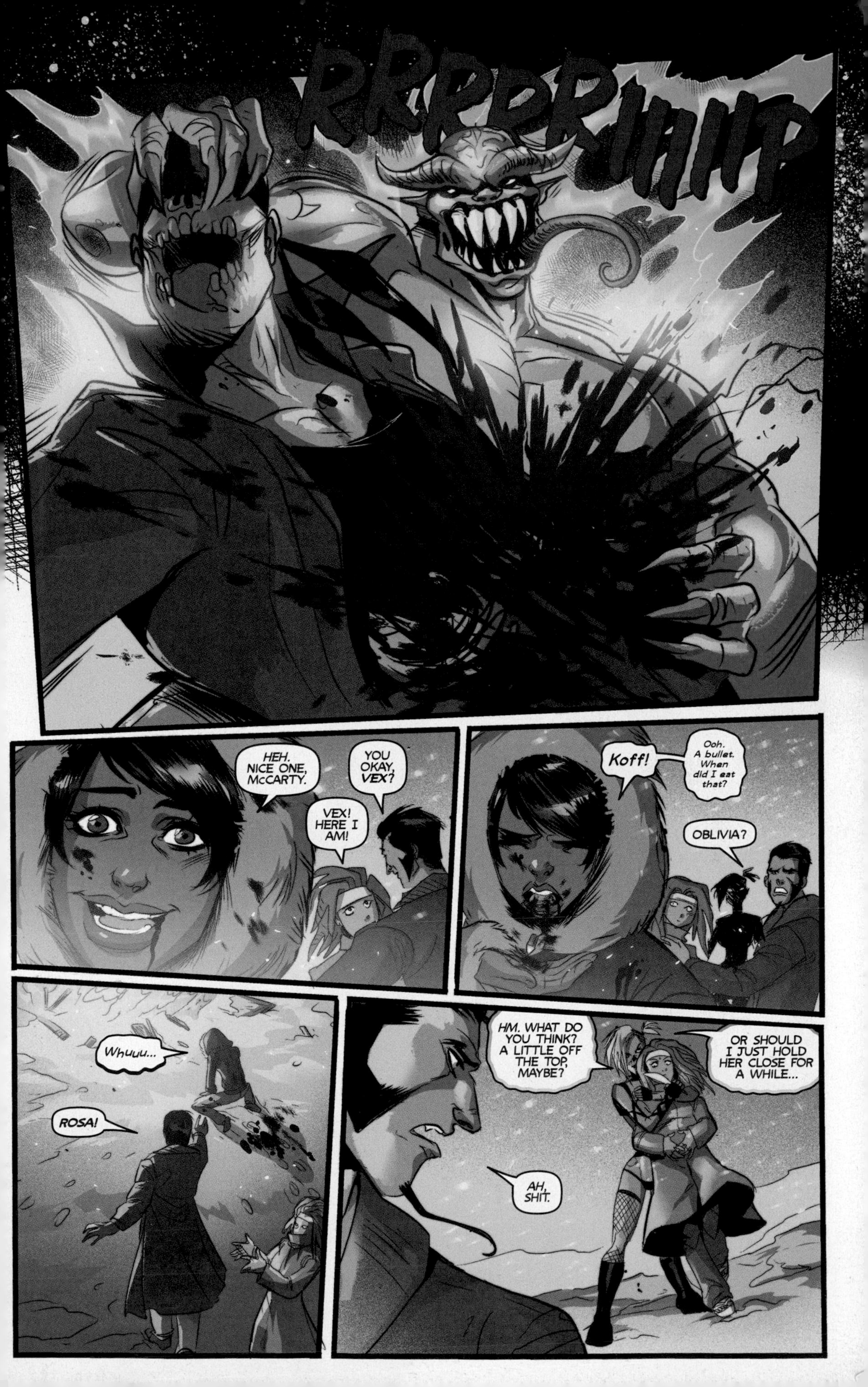
RRRRRIIIIIP
HEH. NICE ONE, McCARTY.
YOU OKAY, VEX?
VEX! HERE I AM!
Koff!
Ooh. A bullet. When did I eat that?
OBLIVIA?
Whuuu...
ROSA!
HM. WHAT DO YOU THINK? A LITTLE OFF THE TOP, MAYBE?
OR SHOULD I JUST HOLD HER CLOSE FOR A WHILE...
AH, SHIT.

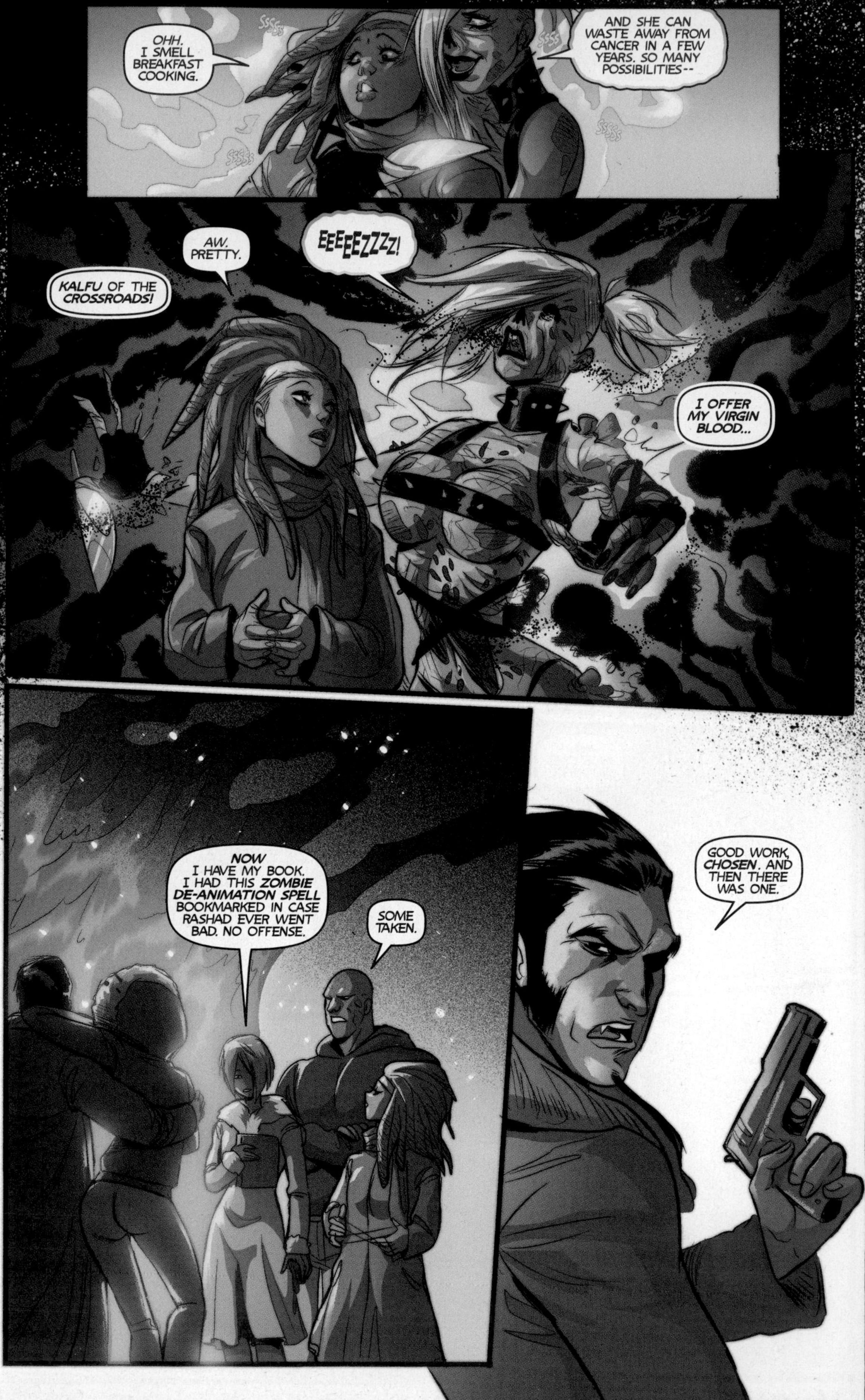
OHH. I SMELL BREAKFAST COOKING.
SSSSS
SSSS
AND SHE CAN WASTE AWAY FROM CANCER IN A FEW YEARS. SO MANY POSSIBILITIES--
SSSSS
SSSSS
KALFU OF THE CROSSROADS!
AW. PRETTY.
EEEEEZZZZZ!
I OFFER MY VIRGIN BLOOD...
NOW I HAVE MY BOOK. I HAD THIS ZOMBIE DE-ANIMATION SPELL BOOKMARKED IN CASE RASHAD EVER WENT BAD. NO OFFENSE.
SOME TAKEN.
GOOD WORK, CHOSEN. AND THEN THERE WAS ONE.

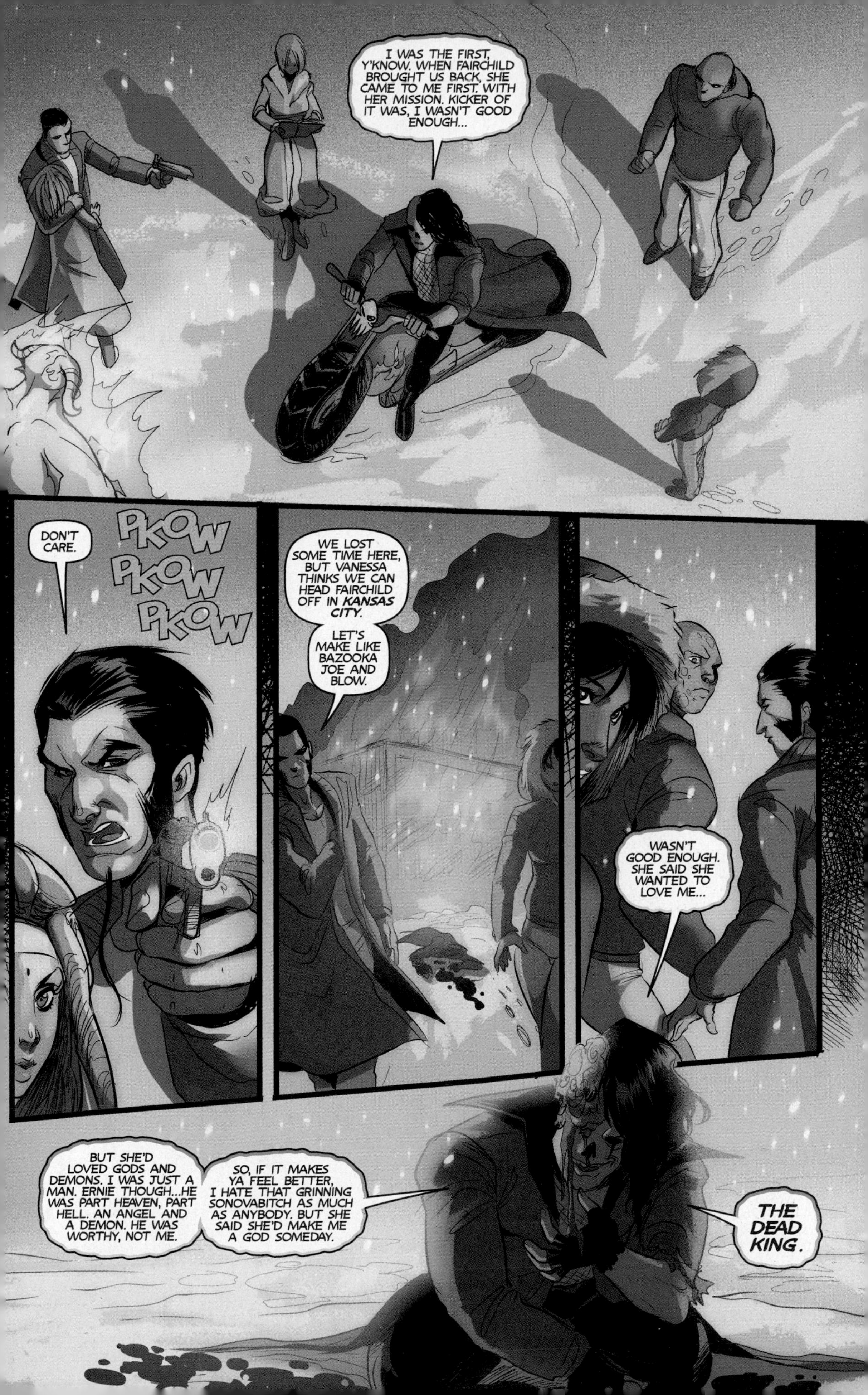
I WAS THE FIRST, Y'KNOW. WHEN FAIRCHILD BROUGHT US BACK, SHE CAME TO ME FIRST. WITH HER MISSION. KICKER OF IT WAS, I WASN'T GOOD ENOUGH...
DON'T CARE.
PKOW PKOW PKOW
WE LOST SOME TIME HERE, BUT VANESSA THINKS WE CAN HEAD FAIRCHILD OFF IN KANSAS CITY.
LET'S MAKE LIKE BAZOOKA JOE AND BLOW.
WASN'T GOOD ENOUGH. SHE SAID SHE WANTED TO LOVE ME...
BUT SHE'D LOVED GODS AND DEMONS. I WAS JUST A MAN. ERNIE THOUGH...HE WAS PART HEAVEN, PART HELL. AN ANGEL AND A DEMON. HE WAS WORTHY, NOT ME.
SO, IF IT MAKES YA FEEL BETTER, I HATE THAT GRINNING SONOVABITCH AS MUCH AS ANYBODY. BUT SHE SAID SHE'D MAKE ME A GOD SOMEDAY.
THE DEAD KING.

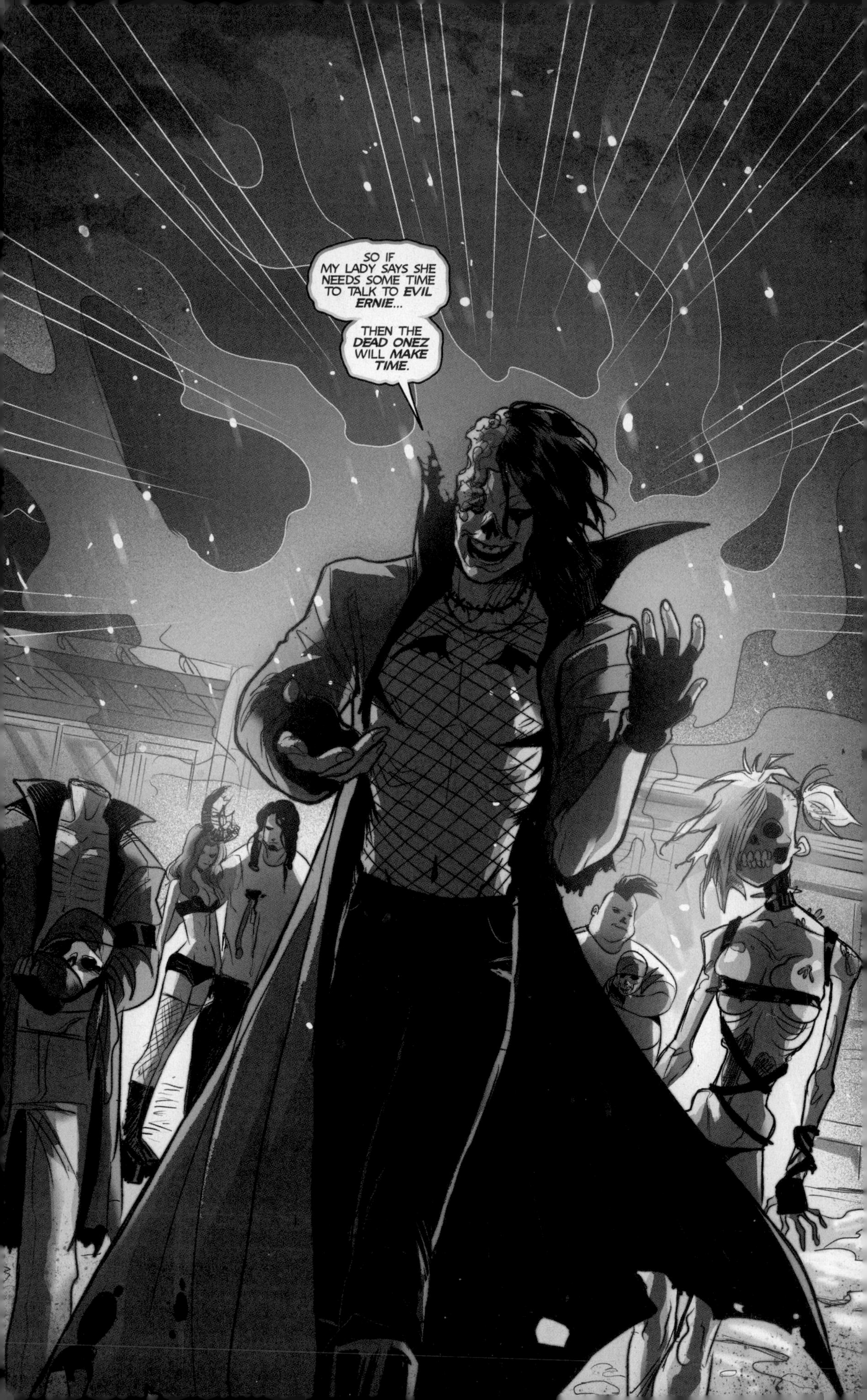
SO IF MY LADY SAYS SHE NEEDS SOME TIME TO TALK TO EVIL ERNIE...
THEN THE DEAD ONEZ WILL MAKE TIME.

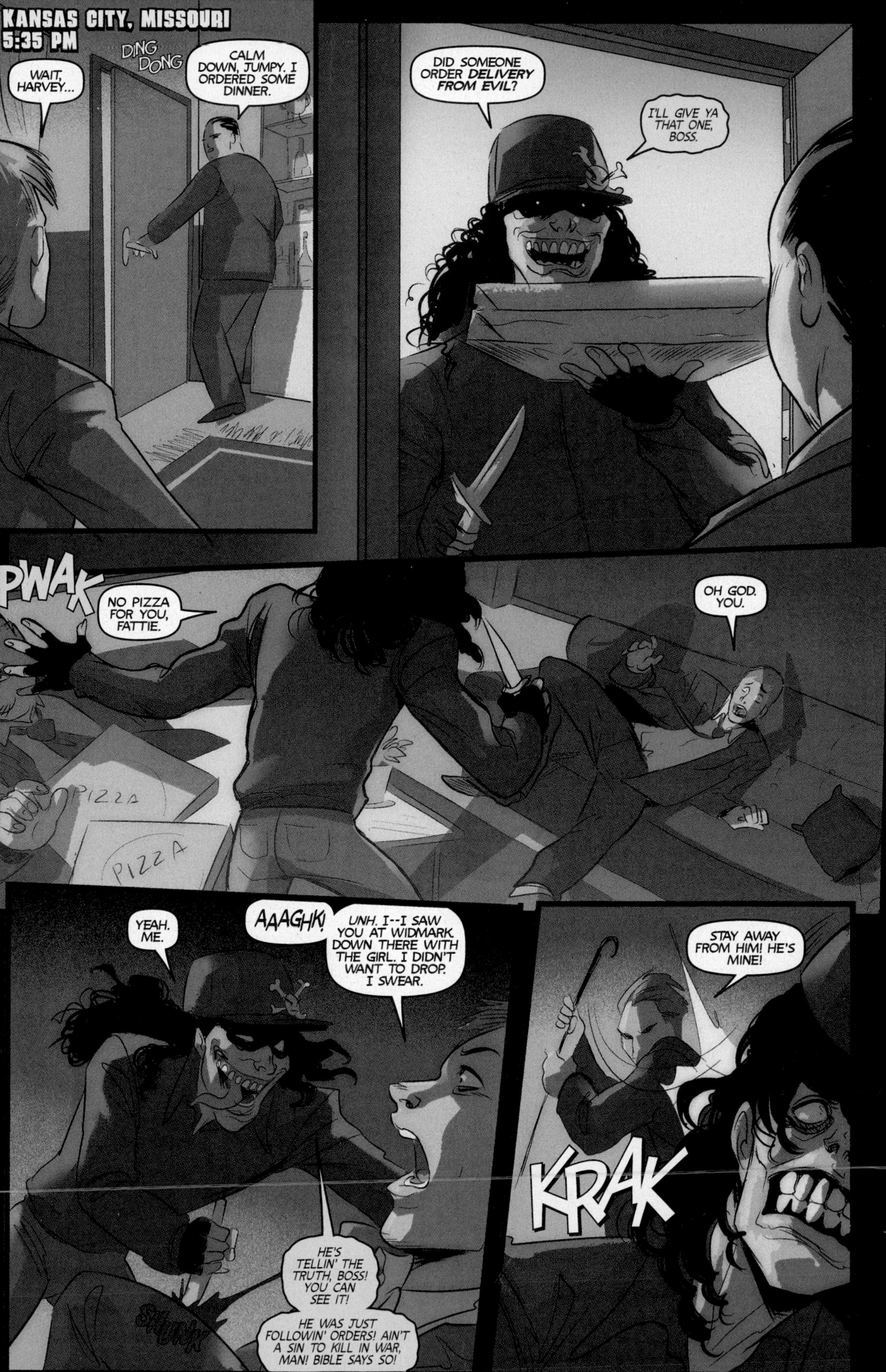
KANSAS CITY, MISSOURI
5:35 PM
WAIT, HARVEY...
DING DONG
CALM DOWN, JUMPY. I ORDERED SOME DINNER.
DID SOMEONE ORDER DELIVERY FROM EVIL?
I'LL GIVE YA THAT ONE, BOSS.
PWAK
NO PIZZA FOR YOU, FATTIE.
OH GOD. YOU.
PIZZA
PIZZA
YEAH. ME.
AAAGHK!
UNH. I--I SAW YOU AT WIDMARK. DOWN THERE WITH THE GIRL. I DIDN'T WANT TO DROP. I SWEAR.
HE'S TELLIN' THE TRUTH, BOSS! YOU CAN SEE IT!
HE WAS JUST FOLLOWIN' ORDERS! AIN'T A SIN TO KILL IN WAR, MAN! BIBLE SAYS SO!
STAY AWAY FROM HIM! HE'S MINE!
KRAK

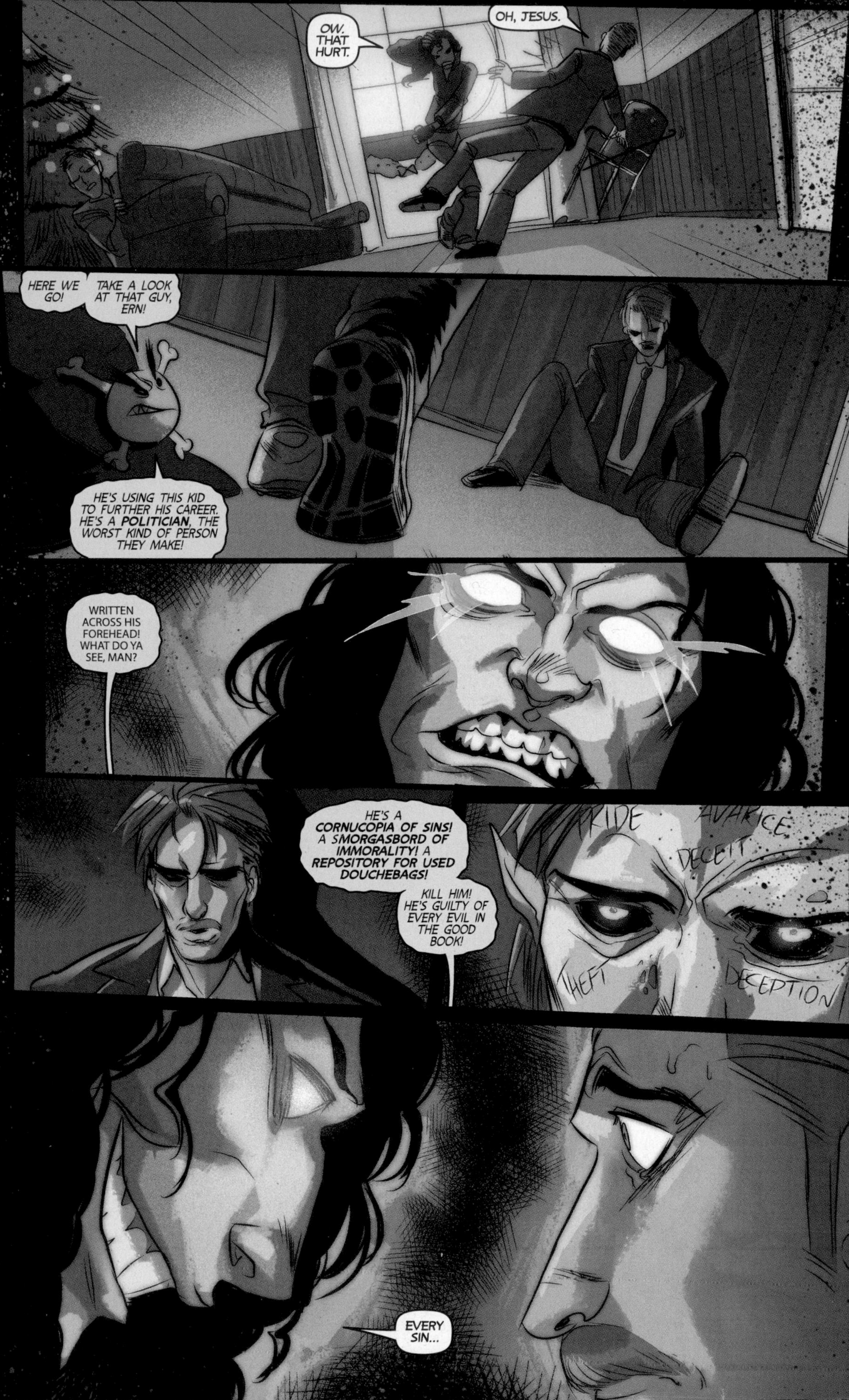
OW. THAT HURT.
OH, JESUS.
HERE WE GO!
TAKE A LOOK AT THAT GUY, ERN!
HE'S USING THIS KID TO FURTHER HIS CAREER. HE'S A POLITICIAN, THE WORST KIND OF PERSON THEY MAKE!
WRITTEN ACROSS HIS FOREHEAD! WHAT DO YA SEE, MAN?
HE'S A CORNUCOPIA OF SINS! A SMORGASBORD OF IMMORALITY! A REPOSITORY FOR USED DOUCHEBAGS!
KILL HIM! HE'S GUILTY OF EVERY EVIL IN THE GOOD BOOK!
PRIDE
AVARICE
DECEIT
THEFT
DECEPTION
EVERY SIN...

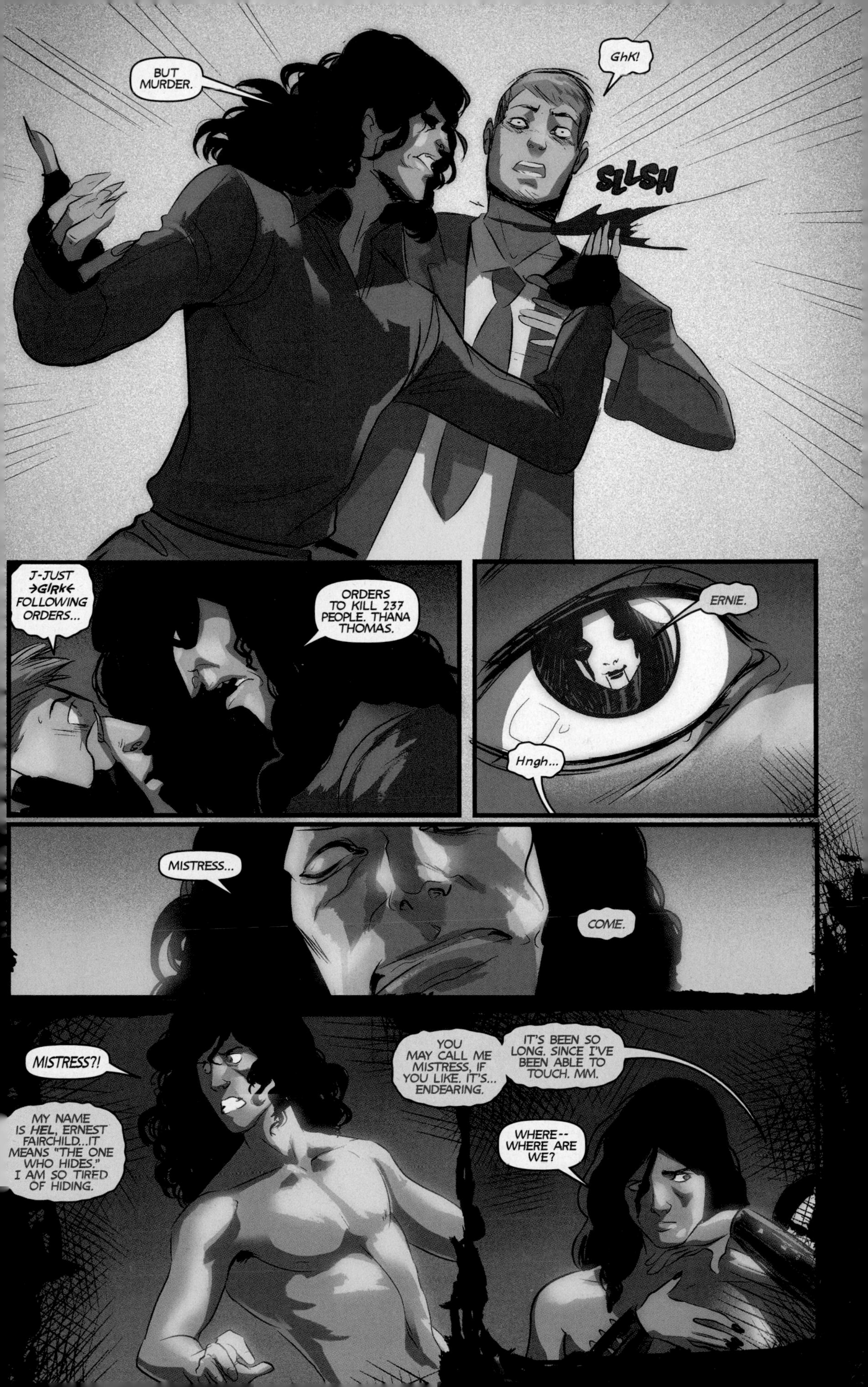
BUT MURDER.
GhK!
SLLSH
J-JUST →GIRK← FOLLOWING ORDERS...
ORDERS TO KILL 237 PEOPLE. THANA THOMAS.
ERNIE.
Hngh...
MISTRESS...
COME.
MISTRESS?!
MY NAME IS HEL, ERNEST FAIRCHILD...IT MEANS "THE ONE WHO HIDES." I AM SO TIRED OF HIDING.
YOU MAY CALL ME MISTRESS, IF YOU LIKE. IT'S... ENDEARING.
IT'S BEEN SO LONG. SINCE I'VE BEEN ABLE TO TOUCH. MM.
WHERE-- WHERE ARE WE?

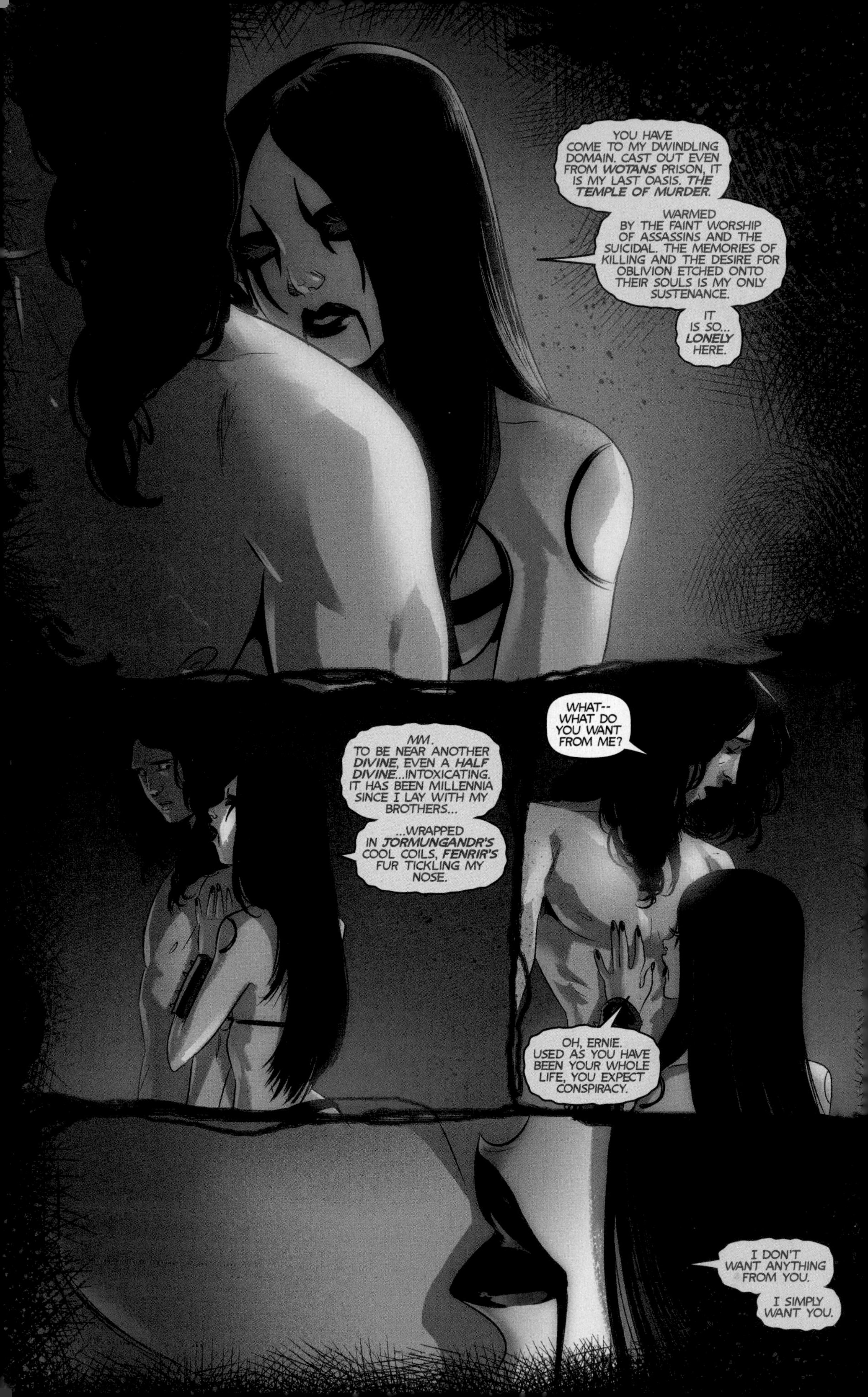
YOU HAVE COME TO MY DWINDLING DOMAIN. CAST OUT EVEN FROM WOTANS PRISON, IT IS MY LAST OASIS. THE TEMPLE OF MURDER.
WARMED BY THE FAINT WORSHIP OF ASSASSINS AND THE SUICIDAL. THE MEMORIES OF KILLING AND THE DESIRE FOR OBLIVION ETCHED ONTO THEIR SOULS IS MY ONLY SUSTENANCE.
IT IS SO... LONELY HERE.
MM. TO BE NEAR ANOTHER DIVINE, EVEN A HALF DIVINE...INTOXICATING. IT HAS BEEN MILLENNIA SINCE I LAY WITH MY BROTHERS...
...WRAPPED IN JORMUNGANDR'S COOL COILS, FENRIR'S FUR TICKLING MY NOSE.
WHAT-- WHAT DO YOU WANT FROM ME?
OH, ERNIE. USED AS YOU HAVE BEEN YOUR WHOLE LIFE, YOU EXPECT CONSPIRACY.
I DON'T WANT ANYTHING FROM YOU.
I SIMPLY WANT YOU.

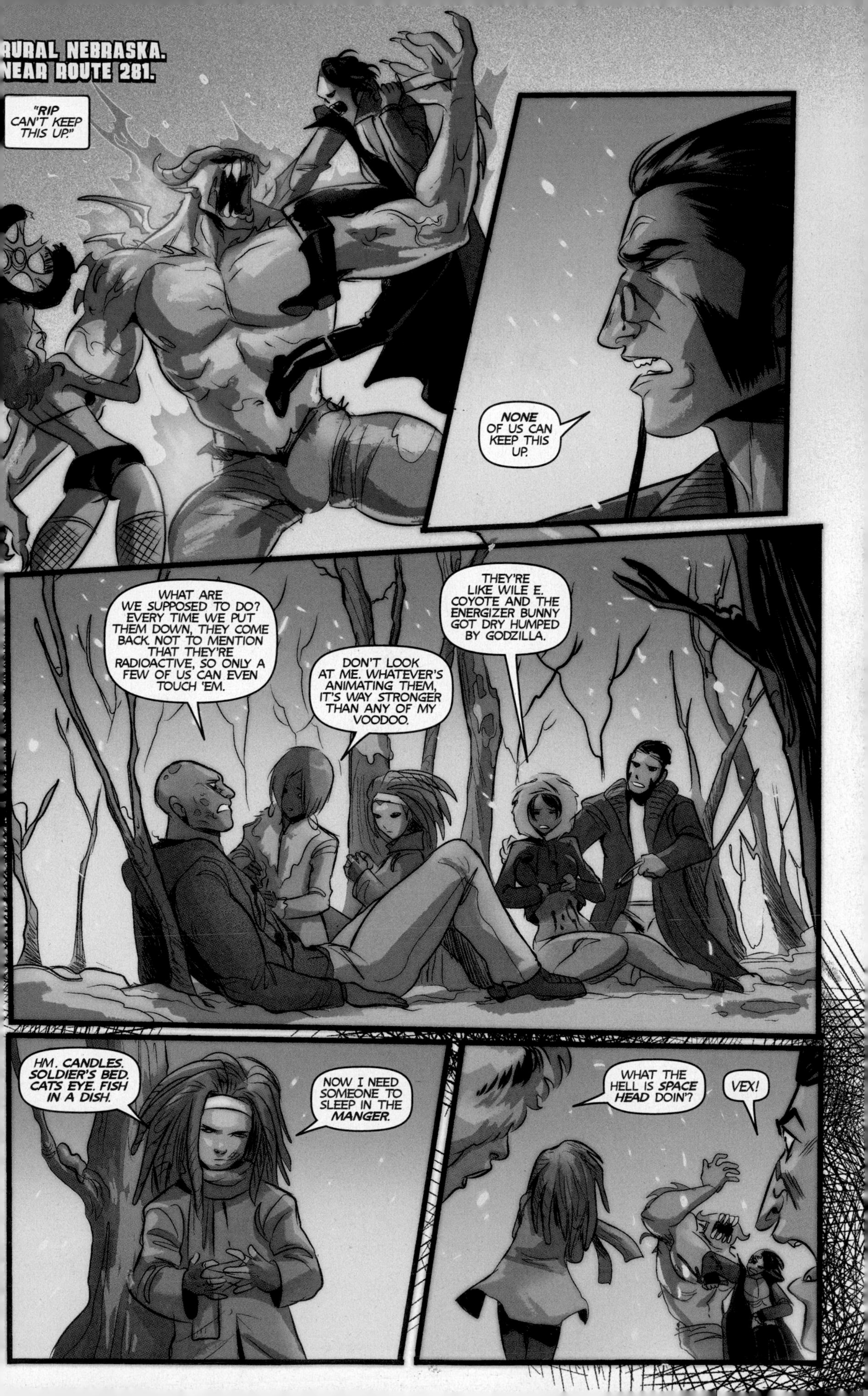
RURAL NEBRASKA. NEAR ROUTE 281.
"RIP CAN'T KEEP THIS UP."
NONE OF US CAN KEEP THIS UP.
WHAT ARE WE SUPPOSED TO DO? EVERY TIME WE PUT THEM DOWN, THEY COME BACK. NOT TO MENTION THAT THEY'RE RADIOACTIVE, SO ONLY A FEW OF US CAN EVEN TOUCH 'EM.
DON'T LOOK AT ME. WHATEVER'S ANIMATING THEM, IT'S WAY STRONGER THAN ANY OF MY VOODOO.
THEY'RE LIKE WILE E. COYOTE AND THE ENERGIZER BUNNY GOT DRY HUMPED BY GODZILLA.
HM. CANDLES. SOLDIER'S BED. CATS EYE. FISH IN A DISH.
NOW I NEED SOMEONE TO SLEEP IN THE MANGER.
WHAT THE HELL IS SPACE HEAD DOIN'?
VEX!

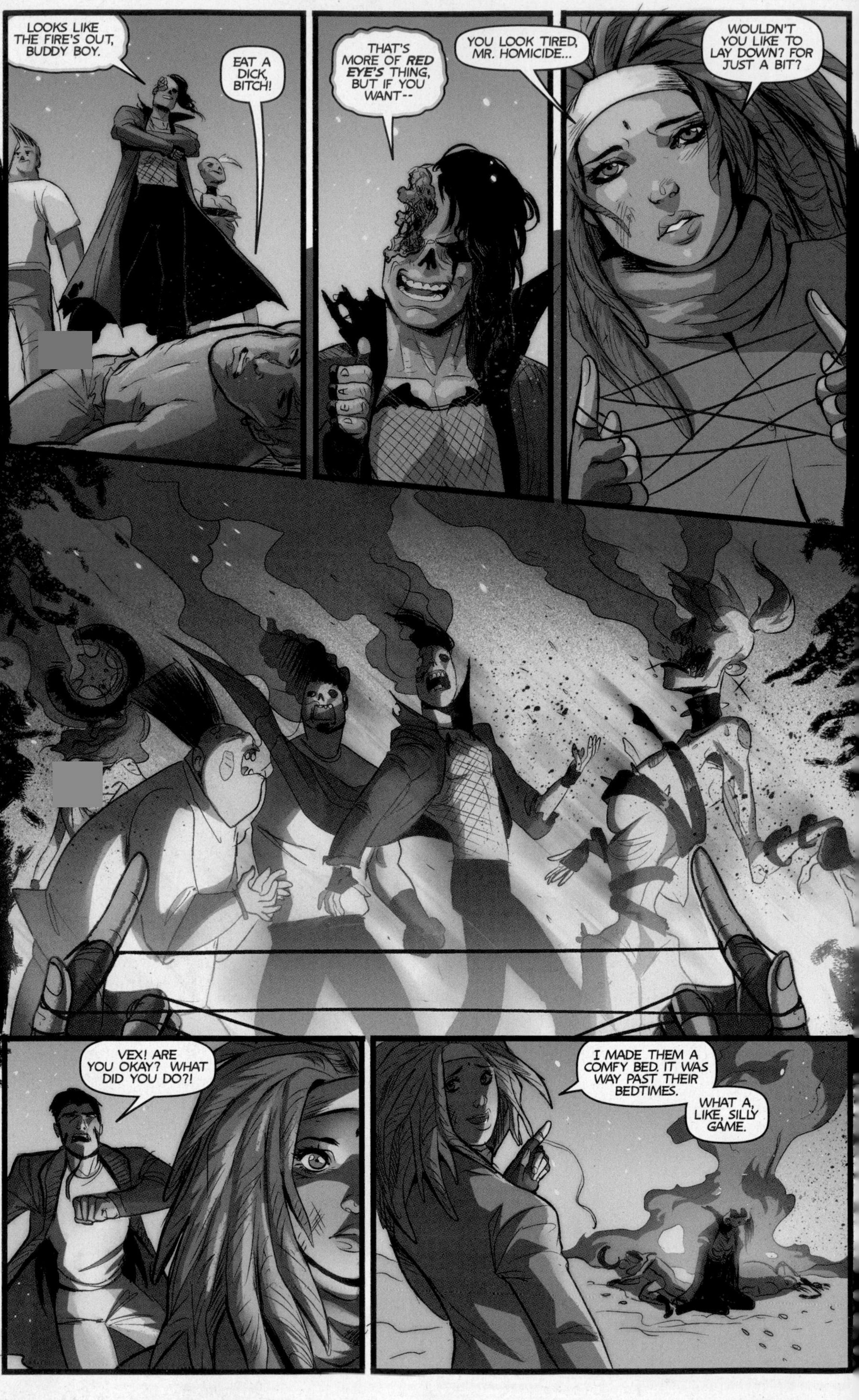
LOOKS LIKE THE FIRE'S OUT, BUDDY BOY.
EAT A DICK, BITCH!
THAT'S MORE OF RED EYE'S THING, BUT IF YOU WANT--
YOU LOOK TIRED, MR. HOMICIDE...
WOULDN'T YOU LIKE TO LAY DOWN? FOR JUST A BIT?
VEX! ARE YOU OKAY? WHAT DID YOU DO?!
I MADE THEM A COMFY BED. IT WAS WAY PAST THEIR BEDTIMES.
WHAT A, LIKE, SILLY GAME.

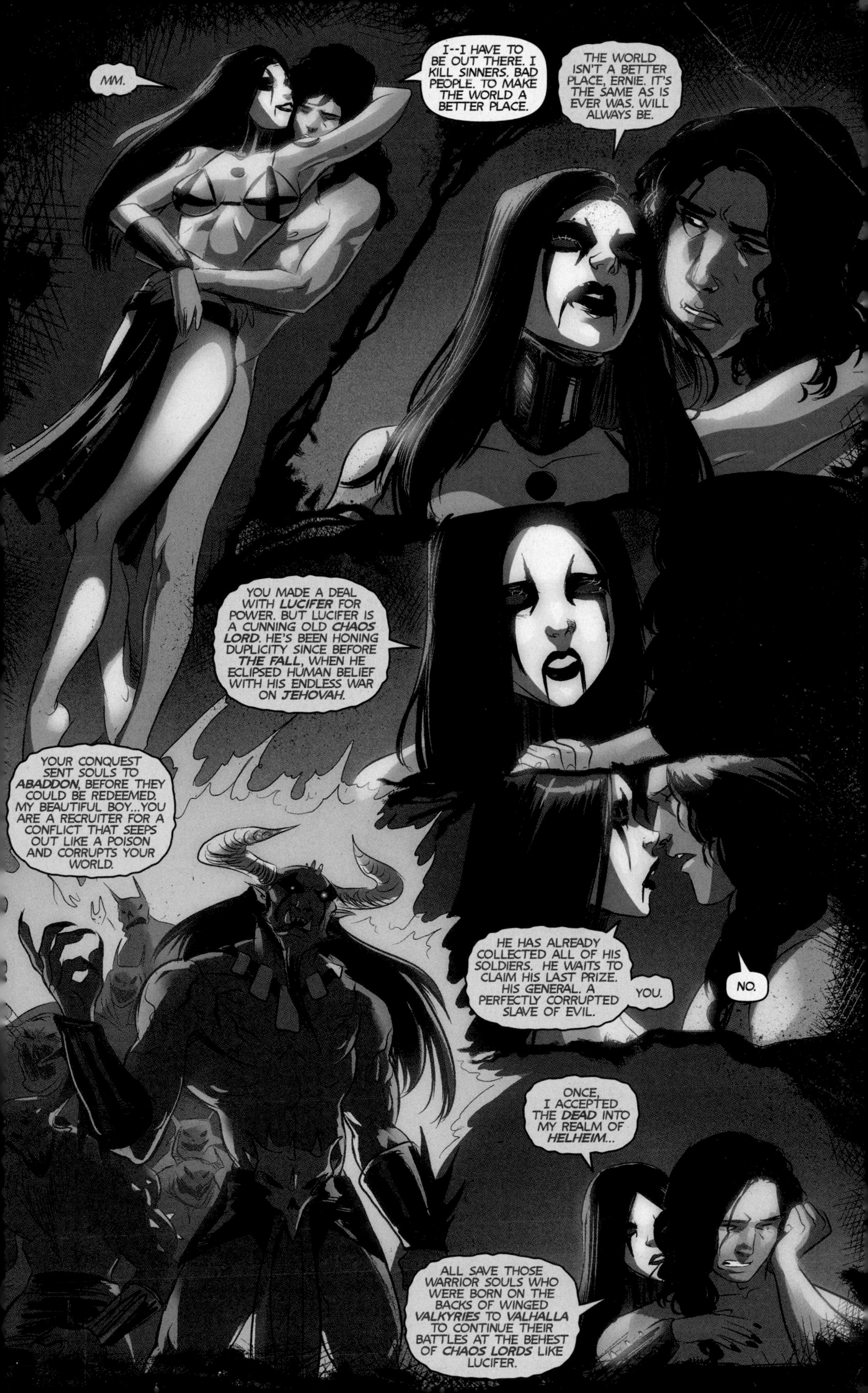
MM.
I--I HAVE TO BE OUT THERE. I KILL SINNERS. BAD PEOPLE. TO MAKE THE WORLD A BETTER PLACE.
THE WORLD ISN'T A BETTER PLACE, ERNIE. IT'S THE SAME AS IS EVER WAS. WILL ALWAYS BE.
YOU MADE A DEAL WITH LUCIFER FOR POWER. BUT LUCIFER IS A CUNNING OLD CHAOS LORD. HE'S BEEN HONING DUPLICITY SINCE BEFORE THE FALL, WHEN HE ECLIPSED HUMAN BELIEF WITH HIS ENDLESS WAR ON JEHOVAH.
YOUR CONQUEST SENT SOULS TO ABADDON, BEFORE THEY COULD BE REDEEMED. MY BEAUTIFUL BOY...YOU ARE A RECRUITER FOR A CONFLICT THAT SEEPS OUT LIKE A POISON AND CORRUPTS YOUR WORLD.
HE HAS ALREADY COLLECTED ALL OF HIS SOLDIERS. HE WAITS TO CLAIM HIS LAST PRIZE. HIS GENERAL. A PERFECTLY CORRUPTED SLAVE OF EVIL.
YOU.
NO.
ONCE, I ACCEPTED THE DEAD INTO MY REALM OF HELHEIM...
ALL SAVE THOSE WARRIOR SOULS WHO WERE BORN ON THE BACKS OF WINGED VALKYRIES TO VALHALLA TO CONTINUE THEIR BATTLES AT THE BEHEST OF CHAOS LORDS LIKE LUCIFER.

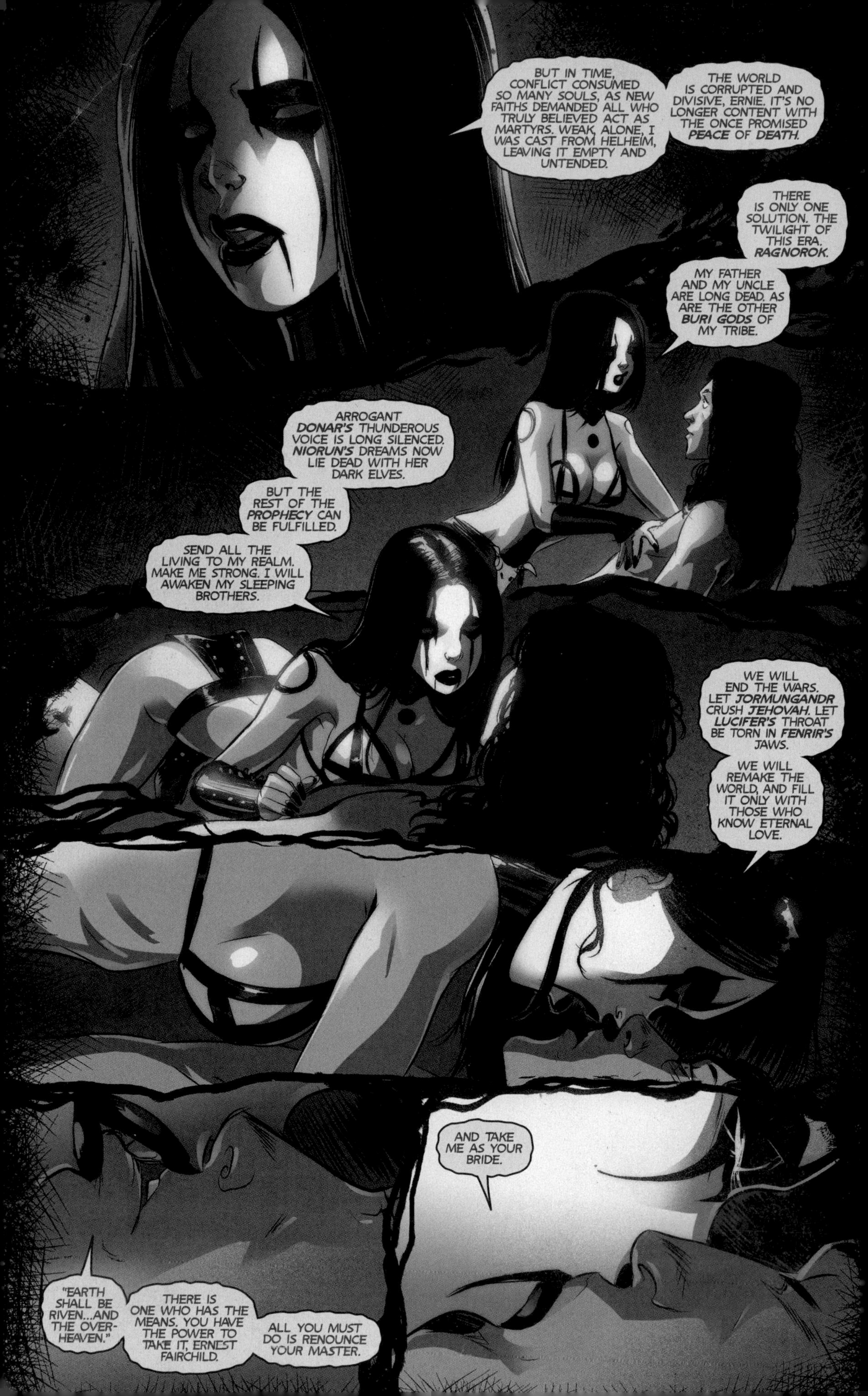

BUT IN TIME, CONFLICT CONSUMED SO MANY SOULS, AS NEW FAITHS DEMANDED ALL WHO TRULY BELIEVED ACT AS MARTYRS. WEAK, ALONE, I WAS CAST FROM HELHEIM, LEAVING IT EMPTY AND UNTENDED.
THE WORLD IS CORRUPTED AND DIVISIVE, ERNIE. IT'S NO LONGER CONTENT WITH THE ONCE PROMISED PEACE OF DEATH.
THERE IS ONLY ONE SOLUTION. THE TWILIGHT OF THIS ERA. RAGNOROK.
MY FATHER AND MY UNCLE ARE LONG DEAD. AS ARE THE OTHER BURI GODS OF MY TRIBE.
ARROGANT DONAR'S THUNDEROUS VOICE IS LONG SILENCED. NIORUN'S DREAMS NOW LIE DEAD WITH HER DARK ELVES.
BUT THE REST OF THE PROPHECY CAN BE FULFILLED.
SEND ALL THE LIVING TO MY REALM. MAKE ME STRONG. I WILL AWAKEN MY SLEEPING BROTHERS.
WE WILL END THE WARS. LET JORMUNGANDR CRUSH JEHOVAH. LET LUCIFER'S THROAT BE TORN IN FENRIR'S JAWS.
WE WILL REMAKE THE WORLD, AND FILL IT ONLY WITH THOSE WHO KNOW ETERNAL LOVE.
AND TAKE ME AS YOUR BRIDE.
"EARTH SHALL BE RIVEN...AND THE OVER-HEAVEN."
THERE IS ONE WHO HAS THE MEANS. YOU HAVE THE POWER TO TAKE IT, ERNEST FAIRCHILD.
ALL YOU MUST DO IS RENOUNCE YOUR MASTER.

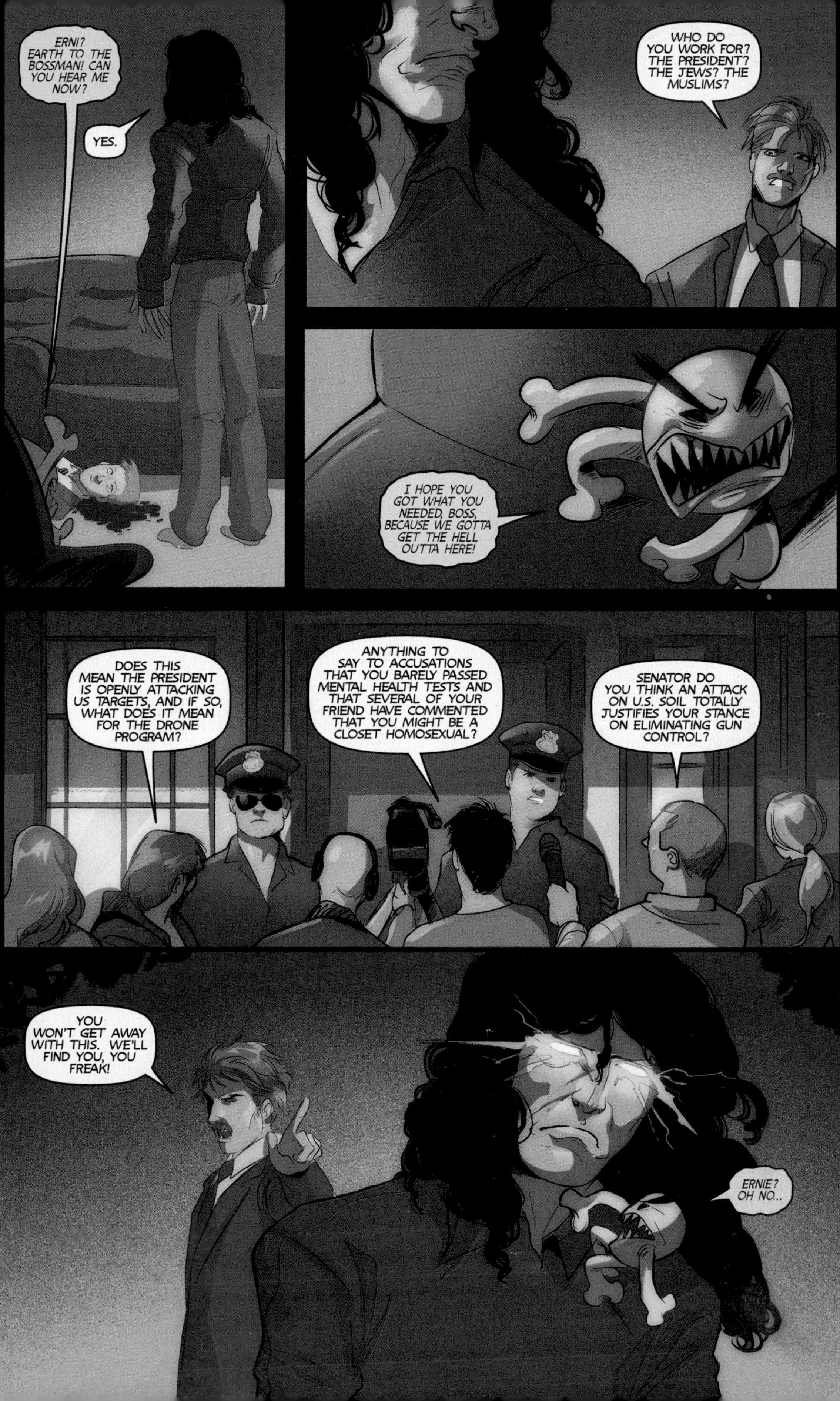
ERNI? EARTH TO THE BOSSMAN! CAN YOU HEAR ME NOW?
YES.
WHO DO YOU WORK FOR? THE PRESIDENT? THE JEWS? THE MUSLIMS?
I HOPE YOU GOT WHAT YOU NEEDED, BOSS, BECAUSE WE GOTTA GET THE HELL OUTTA HERE!
DOES THIS MEAN THE PRESIDENT IS OPENLY ATTACKING US TARGETS, AND IF SO, WHAT DOES IT MEAN FOR THE DRONE PROGRAM?
ANYTHING TO SAY TO ACCUSATIONS THAT YOU BARELY PASSED MENTAL HEALTH TESTS AND THAT SEVERAL OF YOUR FRIEND HAVE COMMENTED THAT YOU MIGHT BE A CLOSET HOMOSEXUAL?
SENATOR DO YOU THINK AN ATTACK ON U.S. SOIL TOTALLY JUSTIFIES YOUR STANCE ON ELIMINATING GUN CONTROL?
YOU WON'T GET AWAY WITH THIS. WE'LL FIND YOU, YOU FREAK!
ERNIE? OH NO...

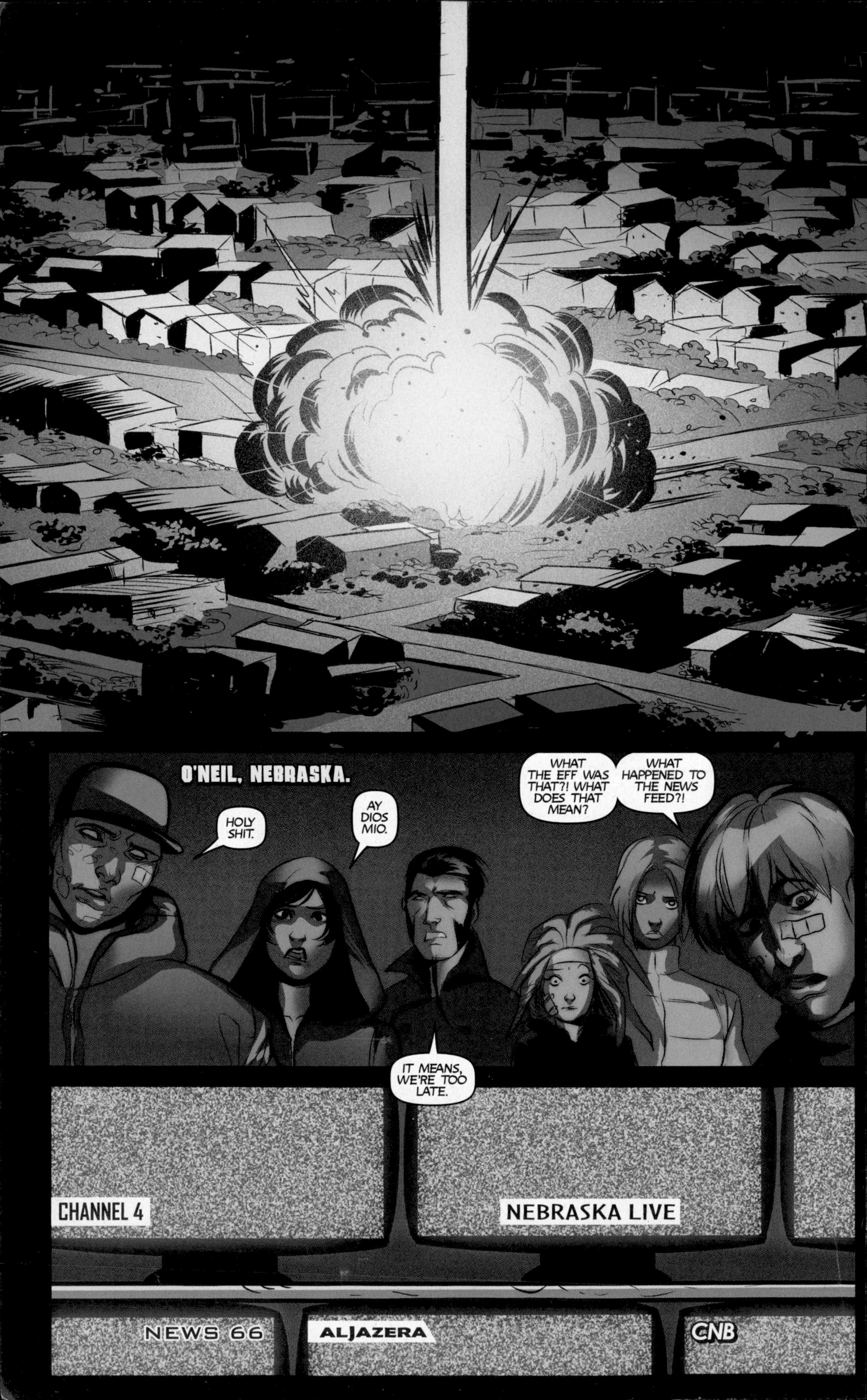
O'NEIL, NEBRASKA.
HOLY SHIT.
AY DIOS MIO.
WHAT THE EFF WAS THAT?! WHAT DOES THAT MEAN?
WHAT HAPPENED TO THE NEWS FEED?!
IT MEANS, WE'RE TOO LATE.
CHANNEL 4
NEBRASKA LIVE
NEWS 66
ALJAZERA
CNB

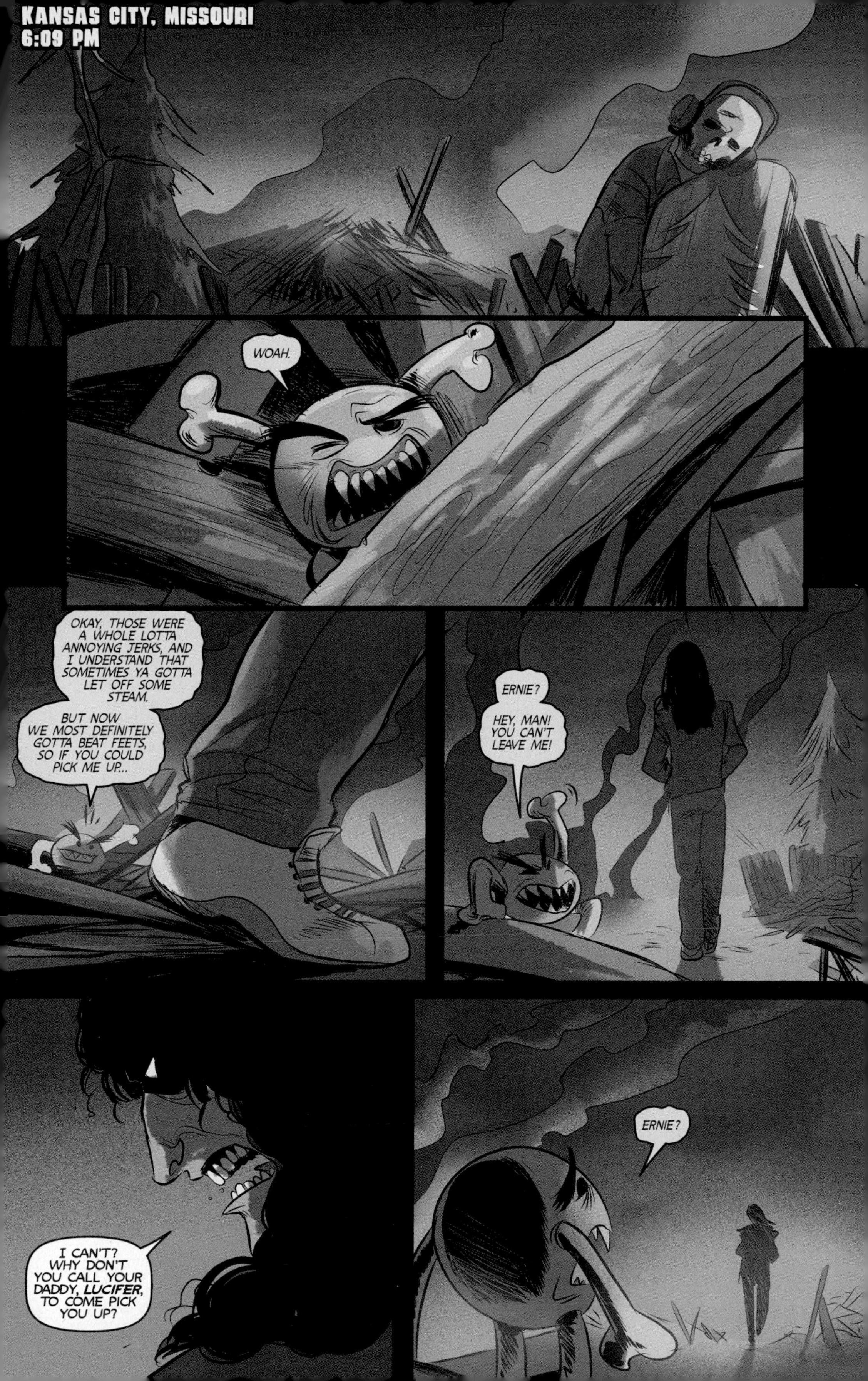
KANSAS CITY, MISSOURI
6:09 PM
WOAH.
OKAY, THOSE WERE A WHOLE LOTTA ANNOYING JERKS, AND I UNDERSTAND THAT SOMETIMES YA GOTTA LET OFF SOME STEAM.
BUT NOW WE MOST DEFINITELY GOTTA BEAT FEETS, SO IF YOU COULD PICK ME UP...
ERNIE?
HEY, MAN! YOU CAN'T LEAVE ME!
I CAN'T? WHY DON'T YOU CALL YOUR DADDY, *LUCIFER*, TO COME PICK YOU UP?
ERNIE?

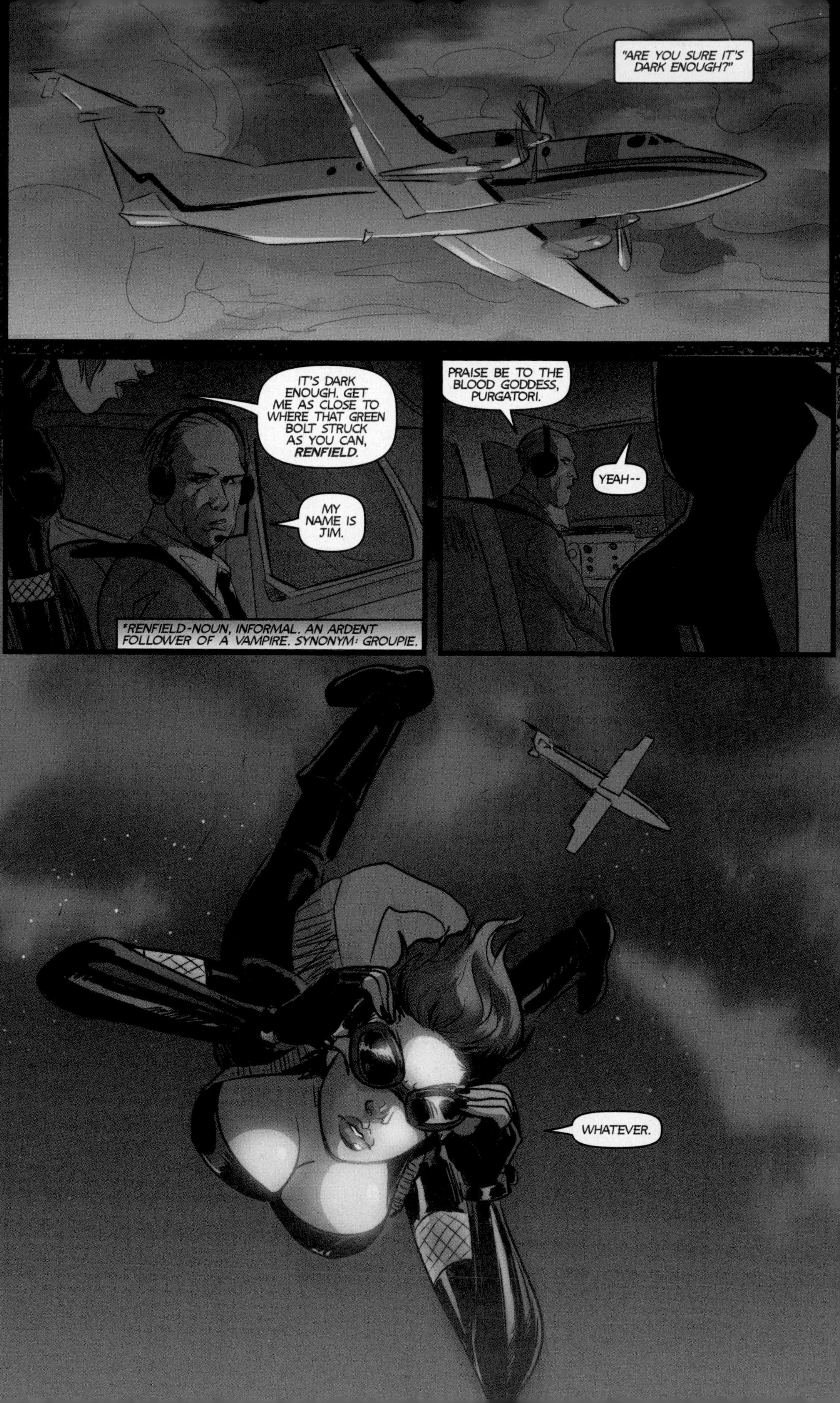
"ARE YOU SURE IT'S DARK ENOUGH?"
IT'S DARK ENOUGH. GET ME AS CLOSE TO WHERE THAT GREEN BOLT STRUCK AS YOU CAN, RENFIELD.
MY NAME IS JIM.
*RENFIELD-NOUN, INFORMAL. AN ARDENT FOLLOWER OF A VAMPIRE. SYNONYM: GROUPIE.
PRAISE BE TO THE BLOOD GODDESS, PURGATORI.
YEAH--
WHATEVER.

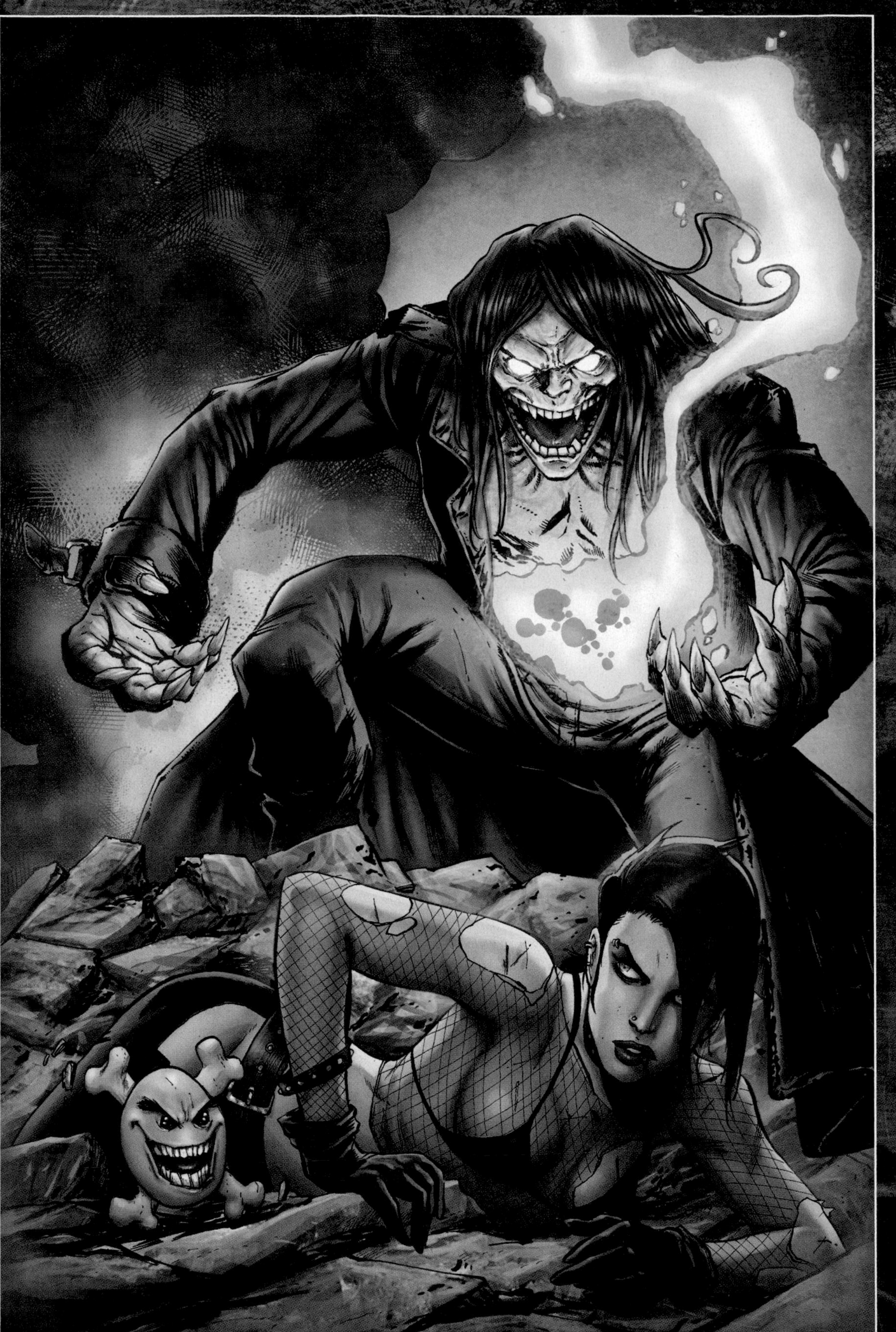

issue #4 cover by TIM SEELEY
colors by ADRIANO LUCAS

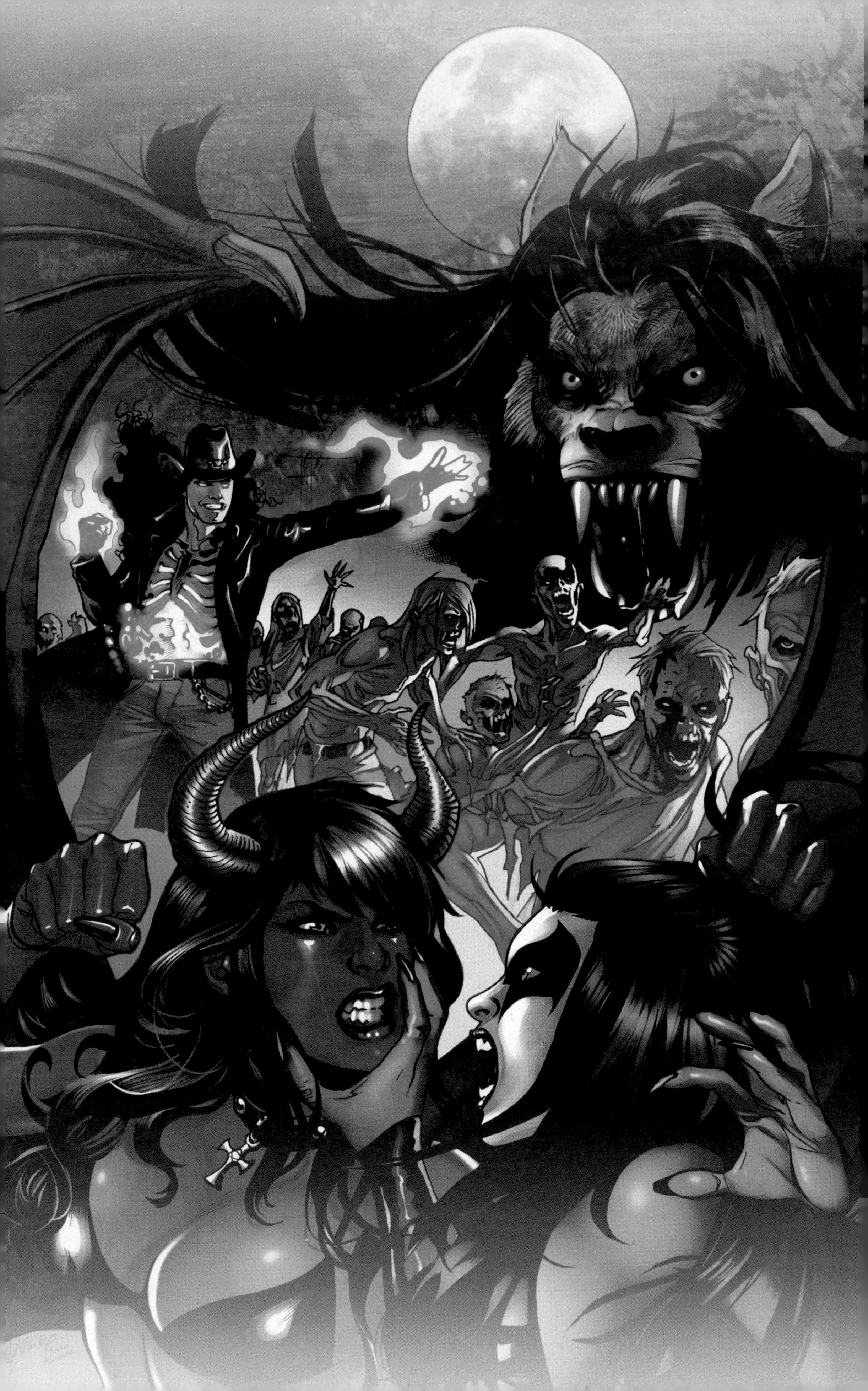

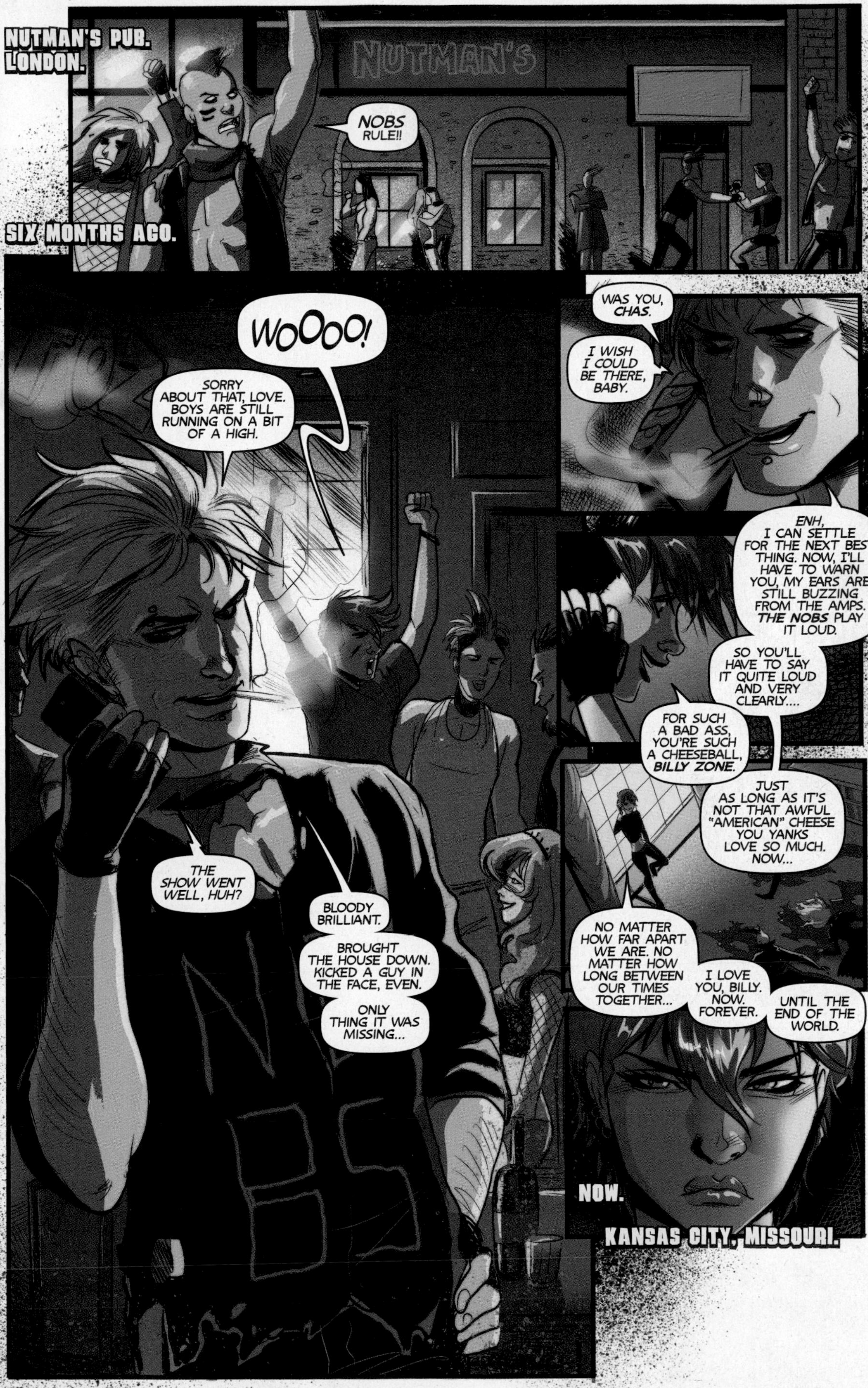
NUTMAN'S PUB. LONDON.
NUTMAN'S
NOBS RULE!!
SIX MONTHS AGO.
WOOOO!
SORRY ABOUT THAT, LOVE. BOYS ARE STILL RUNNING ON A BIT OF A HIGH.
WAS YOU, CHAS.
I WISH I COULD BE THERE, BABY.
ENH, I CAN SETTLE FOR THE NEXT BEST THING. NOW, I'LL HAVE TO WARN YOU, MY EARS ARE STILL BUZZING FROM THE AMPS. THE NOBS PLAY IT LOUD.
SO YOU'LL HAVE TO SAY IT QUITE LOUD AND VERY CLEARLY....
FOR SUCH A BAD ASS, YOU'RE SUCH A CHEESEBALL, BILLY ZONE.
JUST AS LONG AS IT'S NOT THAT AWFUL "AMERICAN" CHEESE YOU YANKS LOVE SO MUCH. NOW...
THE SHOW WENT WELL, HUH?
BLOODY BRILLIANT.
BROUGHT THE HOUSE DOWN. KICKED A GUY IN THE FACE, EVEN.
ONLY THING IT WAS MISSING...
NO MATTER HOW FAR APART WE ARE. NO MATTER HOW LONG BETWEEN OUR TIMES TOGETHER...
I LOVE YOU, BILLY. NOW. FOREVER.
UNTIL THE END OF THE WORLD.
NOW.
KANSAS CITY, MISSOURI.

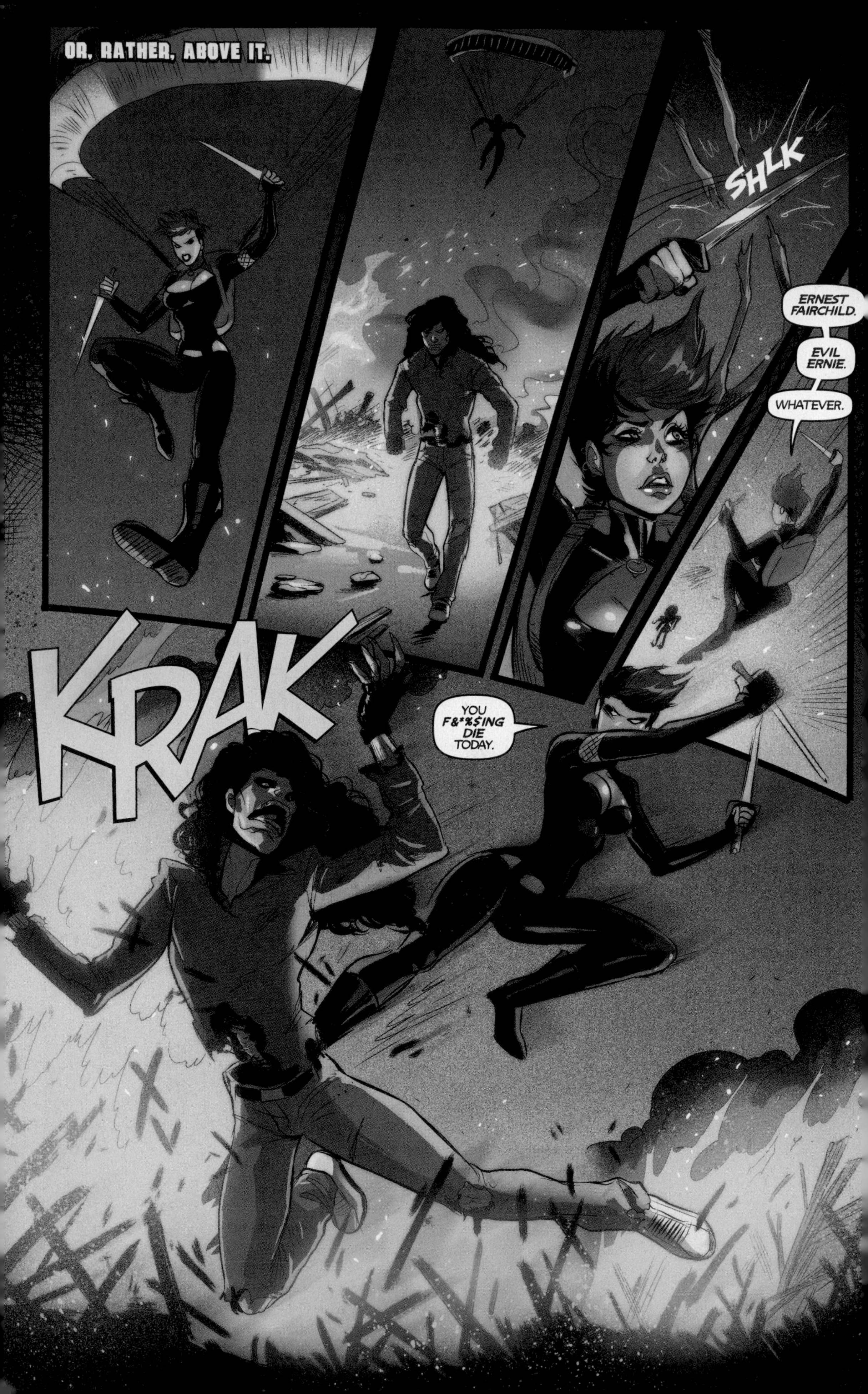
OR, RATHER, ABOVE IT.
SHLK
ERNEST FAIRCHILD.
EVIL ERNIE.
WHATEVER.
KRAK
YOU F&*%$ING DIE TODAY.

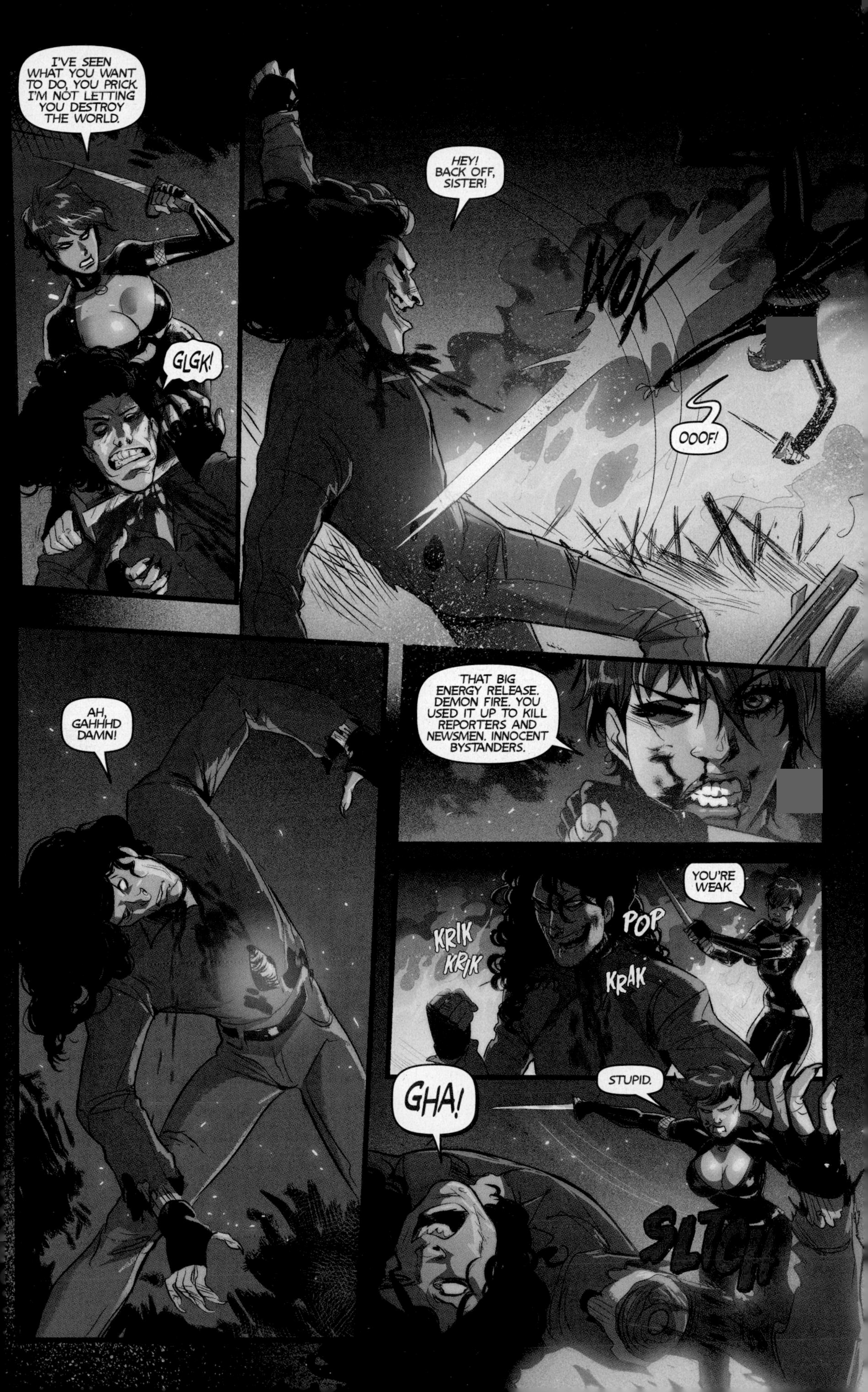
I'VE SEEN WHAT YOU WANT TO DO, YOU PRICK. I'M NOT LETTING YOU DESTROY THE WORLD.
GLGK!
HEY! BACK OFF, SISTER!
WOK
OOOF!
AH, GAHHHD DAMN!
THAT BIG ENERGY RELEASE. DEMON FIRE. YOU USED IT UP TO KILL REPORTERS AND NEWSMEN. INNOCENT BYSTANDERS.
YOU'RE WEAK.
POP
KRIK KRIK
KRAK
STUPID.
GHA!
SLTCH

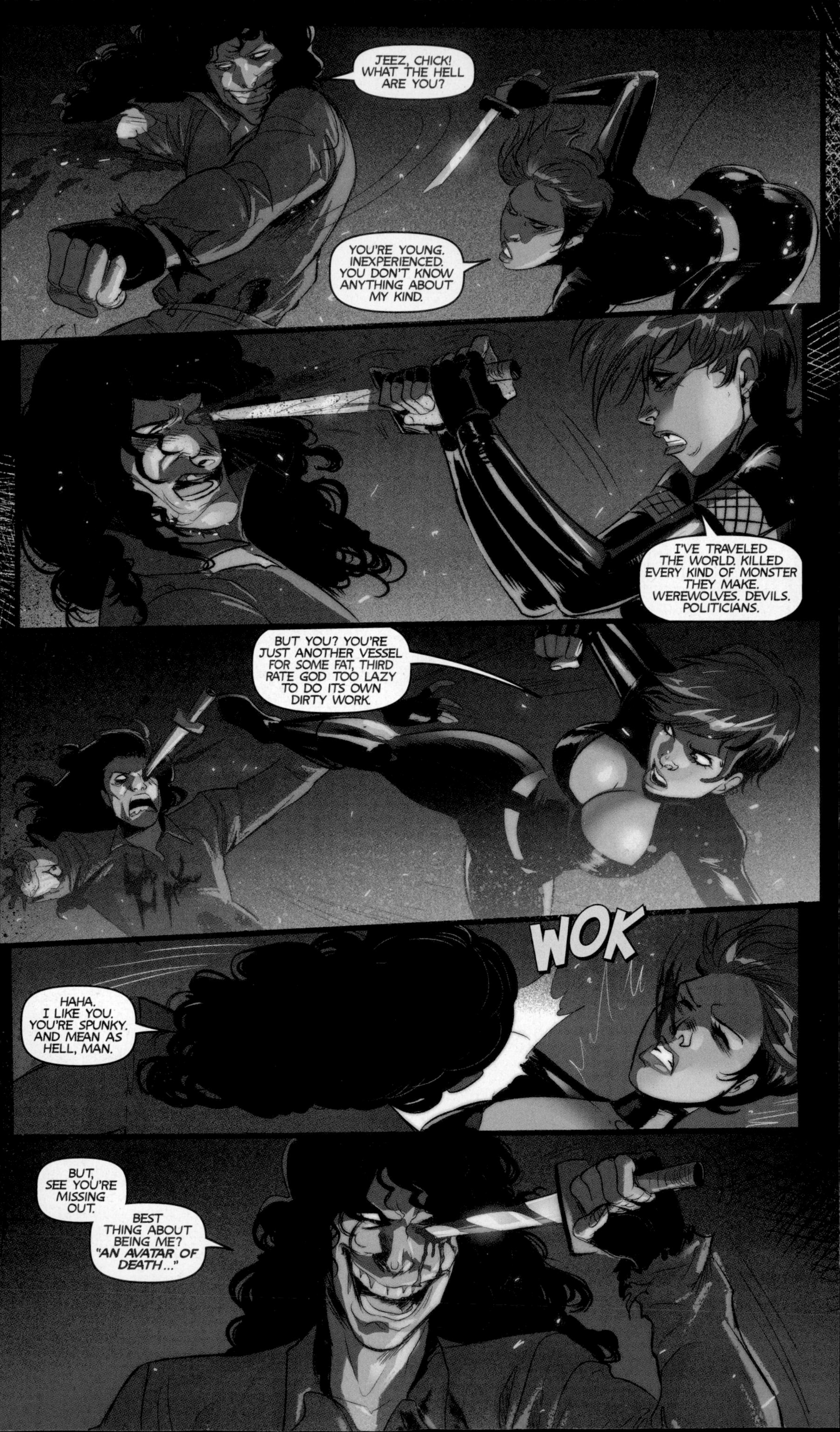
JEEZ, CHICK! WHAT THE HELL ARE YOU?
YOU'RE YOUNG. INEXPERIENCED. YOU DON'T KNOW ANYTHING ABOUT MY KIND.
I'VE TRAVELED THE WORLD. KILLED EVERY KIND OF MONSTER THEY MAKE. WEREWOLVES. DEVILS. POLITICIANS.
BUT YOU? YOU'RE JUST ANOTHER VESSEL FOR SOME FAT, THIRD RATE GOD TOO LAZY TO DO ITS OWN DIRTY WORK.
WOK
HAHA. I LIKE YOU. YOU'RE *SPUNKY.* AND MEAN AS HELL, MAN.
BUT, SEE YOU'RE MISSING OUT.
BEST THING ABOUT BEING ME? ***"AN AVATAR OF DEATH..."***

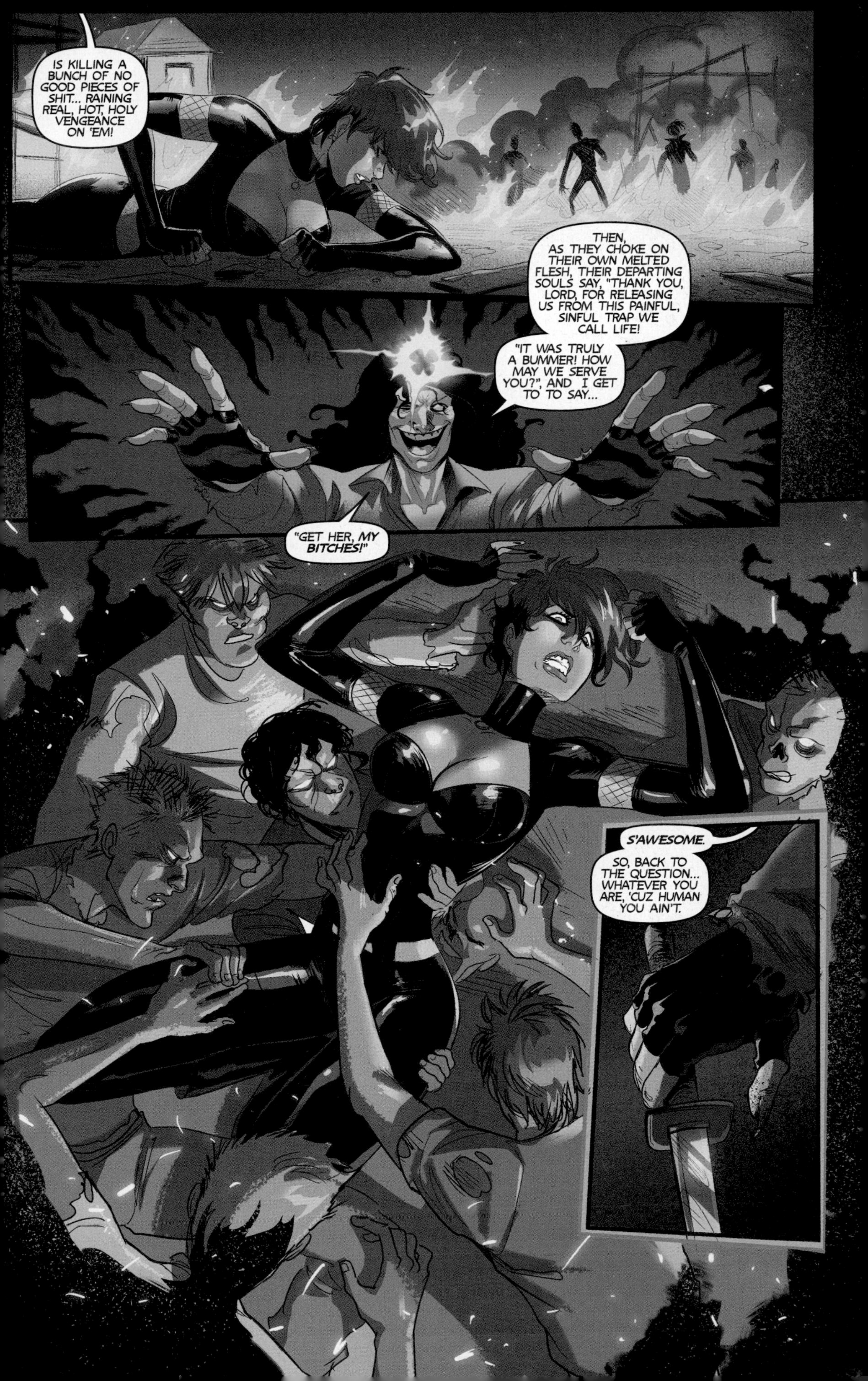
IS KILLING A BUNCH OF NO GOOD PIECES OF SHIT... RAINING REAL, HOT, HOLY VENGEANCE ON 'EM!
THEN, AS THEY CHOKE ON THEIR OWN MELTED FLESH, THEIR DEPARTING SOULS SAY, "THANK YOU, LORD, FOR RELEASING US FROM THIS PAINFUL, SINFUL TRAP WE CALL LIFE!
"IT WAS TRULY A BUMMER! HOW MAY WE SERVE YOU?", AND I GET TO TO SAY...
"GET HER, MY BITCHES!"
S'AWESOME.
SO, BACK TO THE QUESTION... WHATEVER YOU ARE, 'CUZ HUMAN YOU AIN'T.

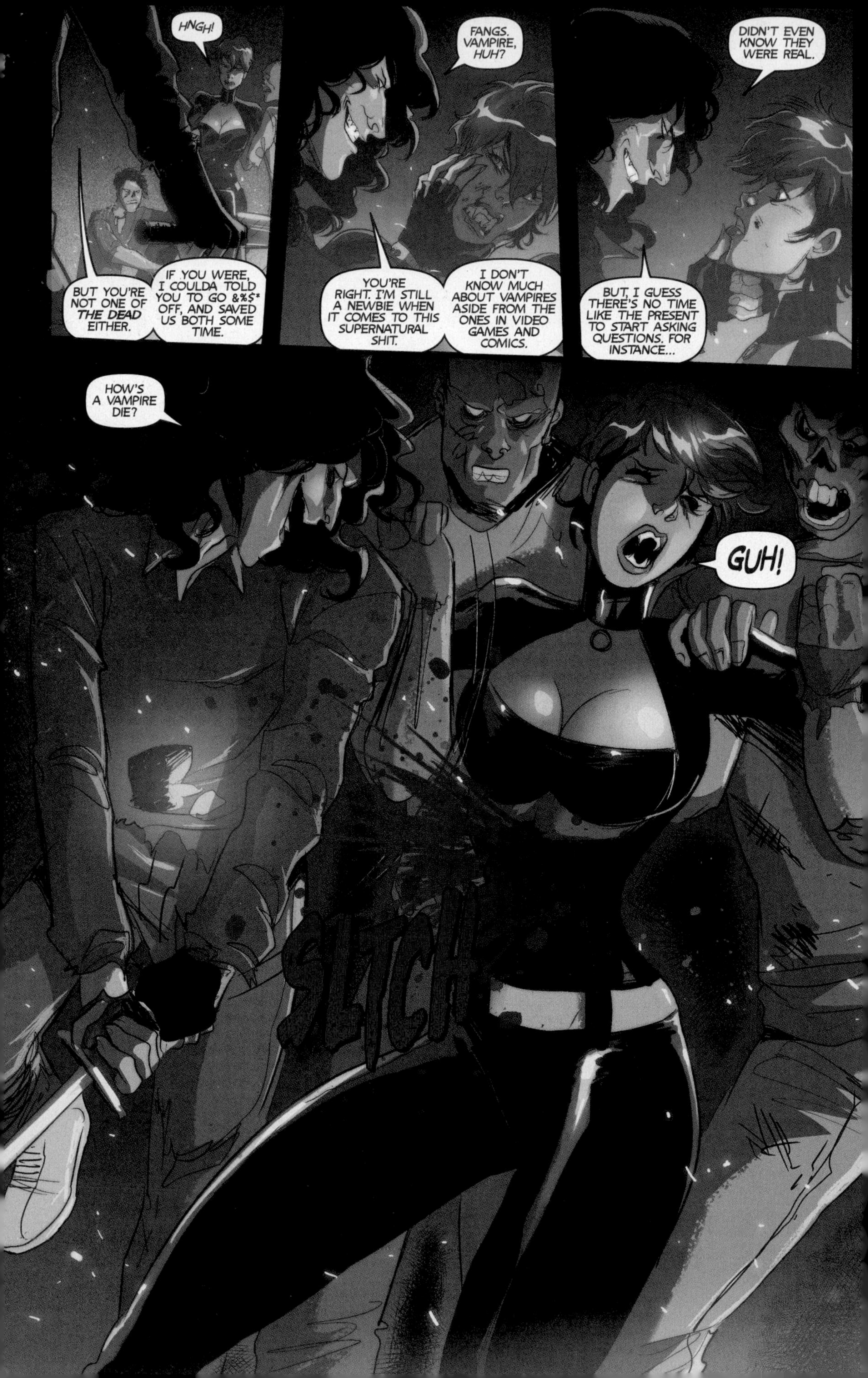
HNGH!
BUT YOU'RE NOT ONE OF ***THE DEAD*** EITHER.
IF YOU WERE, I COULDA TOLD YOU TO GO &%$* OFF, AND SAVED US BOTH SOME TIME.
FANGS. VAMPIRE, HUH?
YOU'RE RIGHT. I'M STILL A NEWBIE WHEN IT COMES TO THIS SUPERNATURAL SHIT.
I DON'T KNOW MUCH ABOUT VAMPIRES ASIDE FROM THE ONES IN VIDEO GAMES AND COMICS.
DIDN'T EVEN KNOW THEY WERE REAL.
BUT, I GUESS THERE'S NO TIME LIKE THE PRESENT TO START ASKING QUESTIONS. FOR INSTANCE...
HOW'S A VAMPIRE DIE?
GUH!
SLTCH

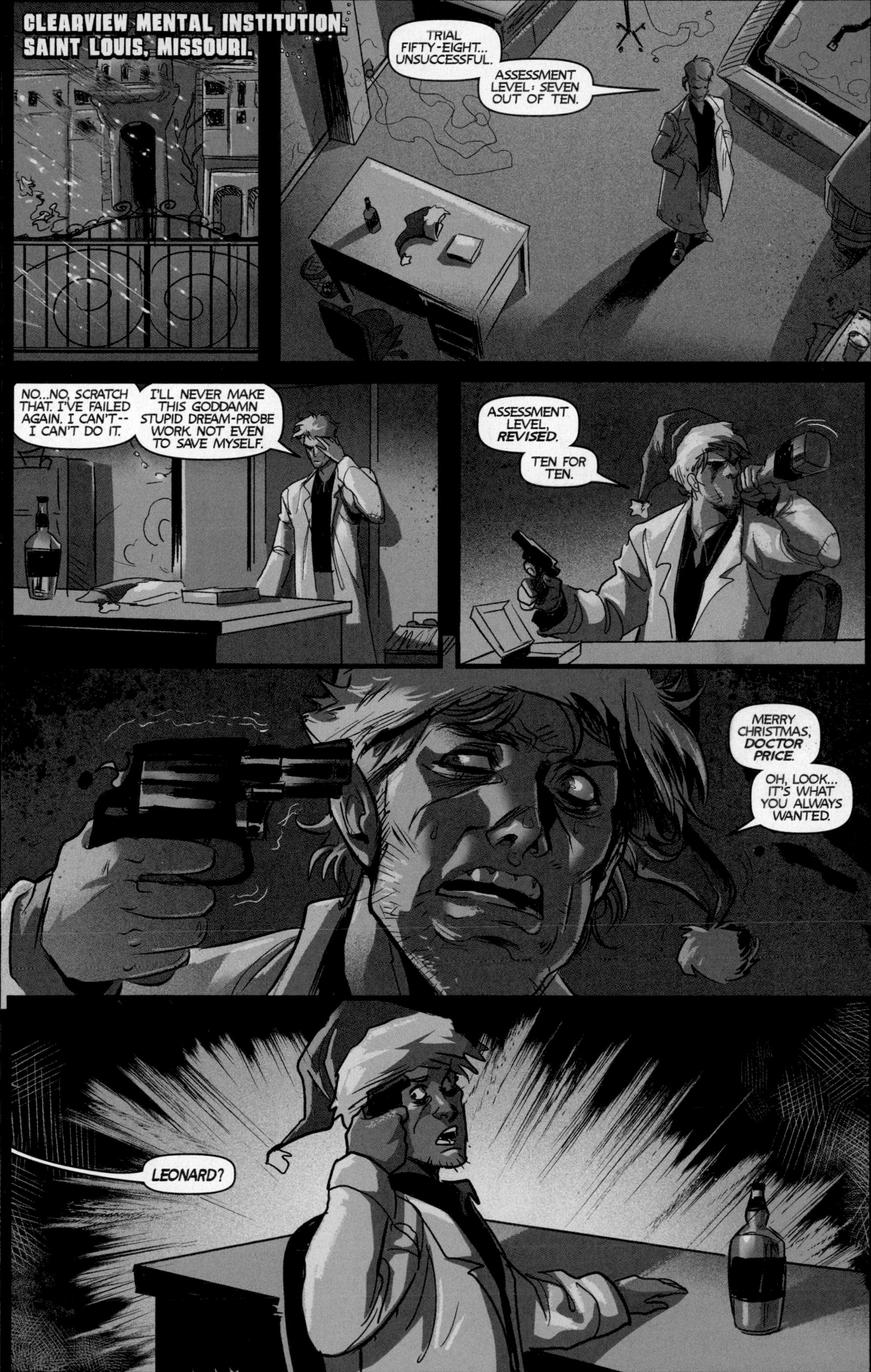
CLEARVIEW MENTAL INSTITUTION.
SAINT LOUIS, MISSOURI.
TRIAL FIFTY-EIGHT... UNSUCCESSFUL.
ASSESSMENT LEVEL: SEVEN OUT OF TEN.
NO...NO, SCRATCH THAT. I'VE FAILED AGAIN. I CAN'T-- I CAN'T DO IT.
I'LL NEVER MAKE THIS GODDAMN STUPID DREAM-PROBE WORK. NOT EVEN TO SAVE MYSELF.
ASSESSMENT LEVEL, *REVISED*.
TEN FOR TEN.
MERRY CHRISTMAS, **DOCTOR PRICE**.
OH, LOOK... IT'S WHAT YOU ALWAYS WANTED.
LEONARD?

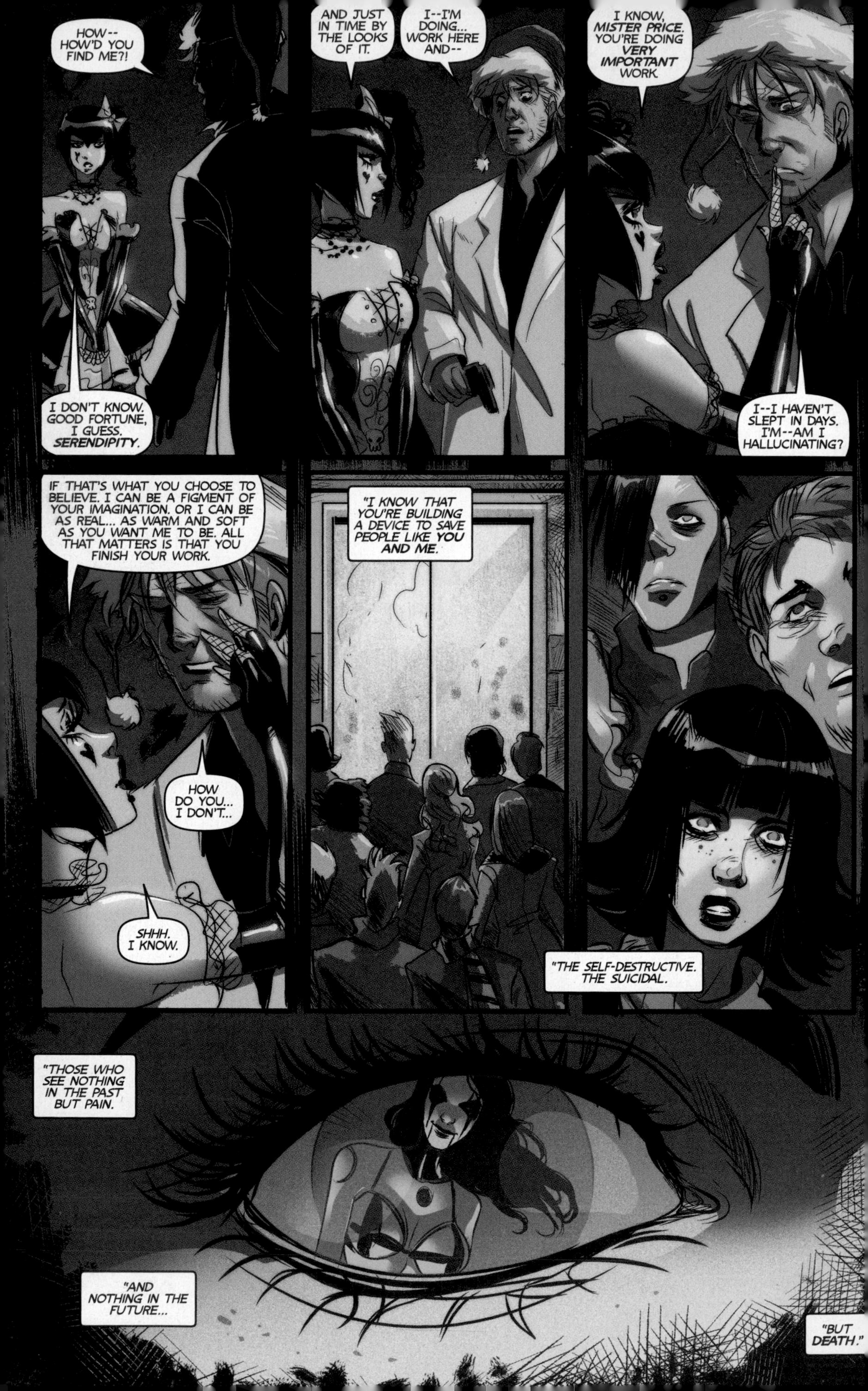
HOW--
HOW'D YOU FIND ME?!
I DON'T KNOW. GOOD FORTUNE, I GUESS. SERENDIPITY.
AND JUST IN TIME BY THE LOOKS OF IT.
I--I'M DOING... WORK HERE AND--
I KNOW, MISTER PRICE. YOU'RE DOING VERY IMPORTANT WORK.
I--I HAVEN'T SLEPT IN DAYS. I'M--AM I HALLUCINATING?
IF THAT'S WHAT YOU CHOOSE TO BELIEVE. I CAN BE A FIGMENT OF YOUR IMAGINATION. OR I CAN BE AS REAL... AS WARM AND SOFT AS YOU WANT ME TO BE. ALL THAT MATTERS IS THAT YOU FINISH YOUR WORK.
HOW DO YOU... I DON'T...
SHHH. I KNOW.
"I KNOW THAT YOU'RE BUILDING A DEVICE TO SAVE PEOPLE LIKE YOU AND ME.
"THE SELF-DESTRUCTIVE. THE SUICIDAL.
"THOSE WHO SEE NOTHING IN THE PAST BUT PAIN.
"AND NOTHING IN THE FUTURE...
"BUT DEATH."

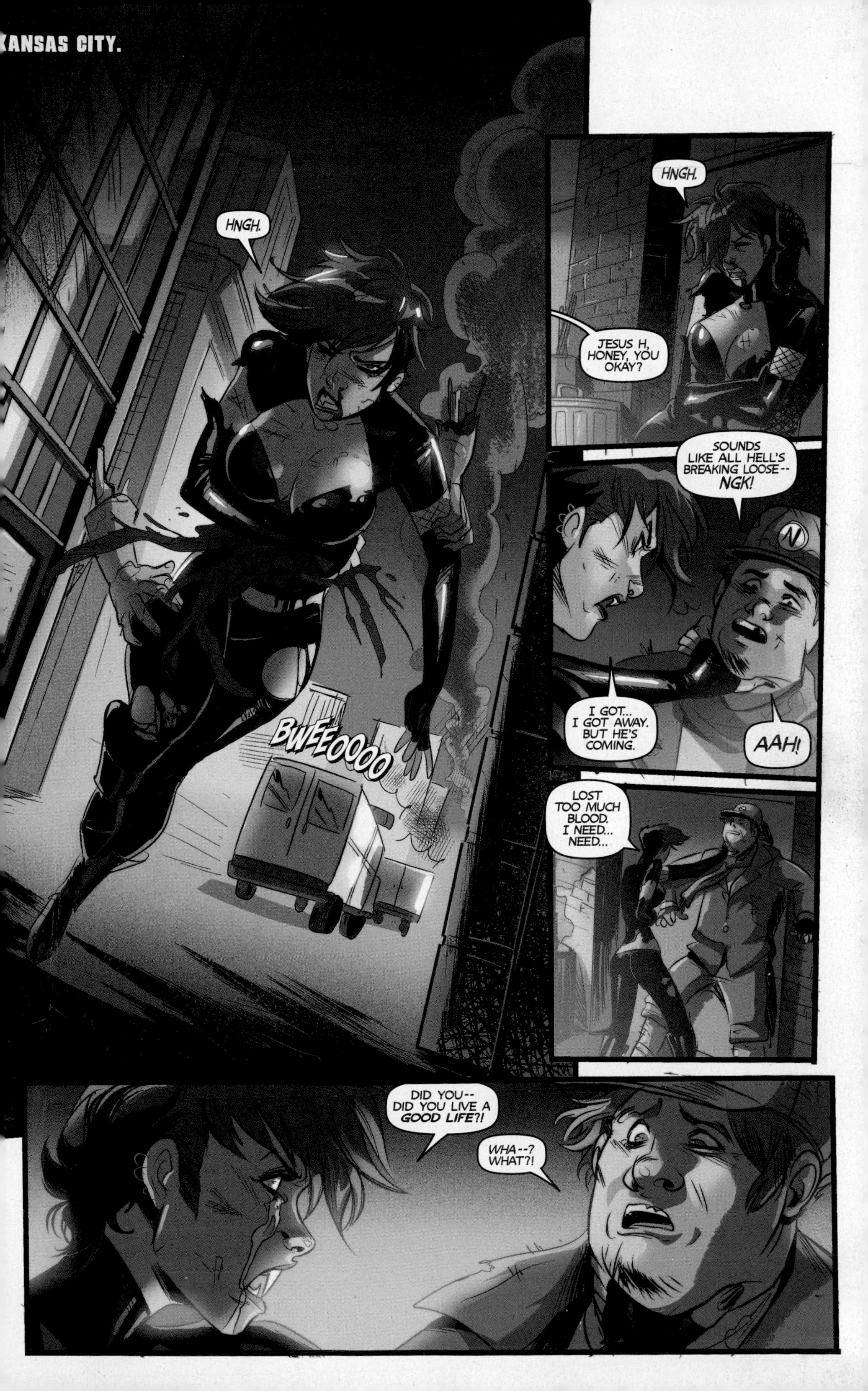
KANSAS CITY.
HNGH.
BWEEOOOO
HNGH.
JESUS H, HONEY, YOU OKAY?
SOUNDS LIKE ALL HELL'S BREAKING LOOSE-- NGK!
I GOT... I GOT AWAY. BUT HE'S COMING.
AAH!
LOST TOO MUCH BLOOD. I NEED... NEED...
DID YOU-- DID YOU LIVE A GOOD LIFE?!
WHA--? WHAT?!

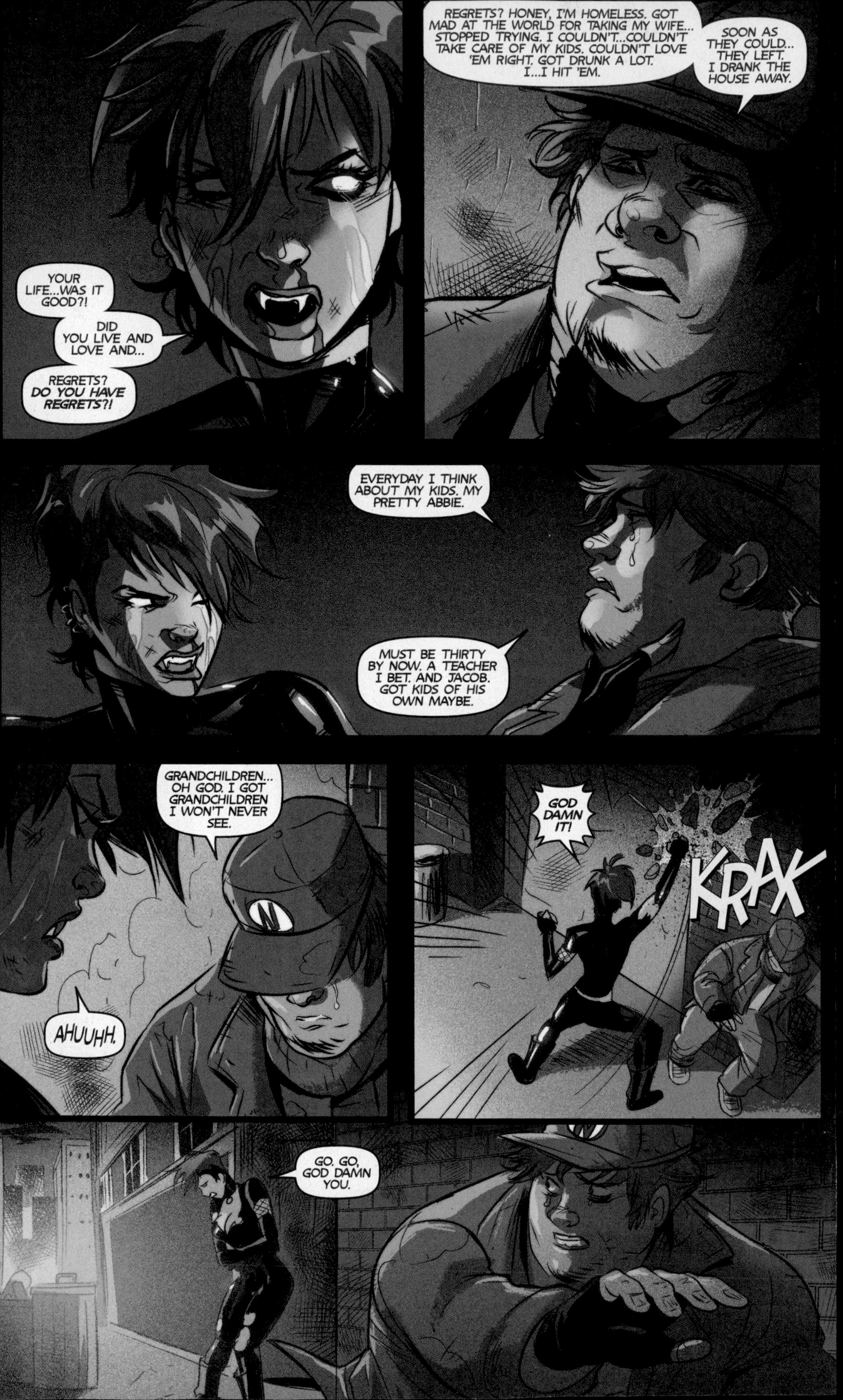
YOUR LIFE...WAS IT GOOD?!
DID YOU LIVE AND LOVE AND...
REGRETS? DO YOU HAVE REGRETS?!
REGRETS? HONEY, I'M HOMELESS. GOT MAD AT THE WORLD FOR TAKING MY WIFE... STOPPED TRYING. I COULDN'T...COULDN'T TAKE CARE OF MY KIDS. COULDN'T LOVE 'EM RIGHT. GOT DRUNK A LOT. I...I HIT 'EM.
SOON AS THEY COULD... THEY LEFT. I DRANK THE HOUSE AWAY.
EVERYDAY I THINK ABOUT MY KIDS. MY PRETTY ABBIE.
MUST BE THIRTY BY NOW. A TEACHER I BET. AND JACOB. GOT KIDS OF HIS OWN MAYBE.
GRANDCHILDREN... OH GOD. I GOT GRANDCHILDREN I WON'T NEVER SEE.
AHUUHH.
GOD DAMN IT!
KRAK
GO. GO, GOD DAMN YOU.

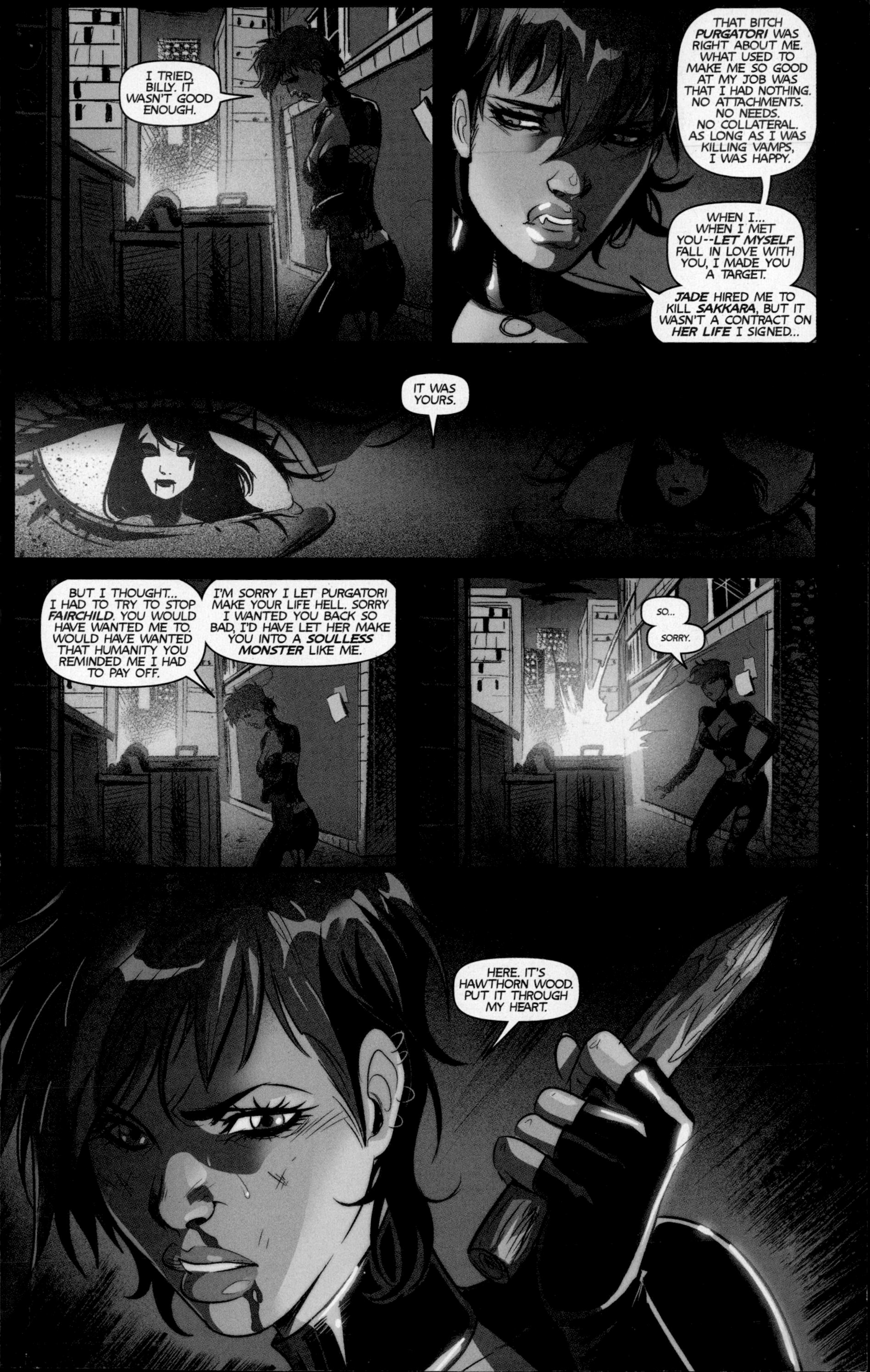
I TRIED, BILLY. IT WASN'T GOOD ENOUGH.
THAT BITCH PURGATORI WAS RIGHT ABOUT ME. WHAT USED TO MAKE ME SO GOOD AT MY JOB WAS THAT I HAD NOTHING. NO ATTACHMENTS. NO NEEDS. NO COLLATERAL. AS LONG AS I WAS KILLING VAMPS, I WAS HAPPY.
WHEN I... WHEN I MET YOU--LET MYSELF FALL IN LOVE WITH YOU, I MADE YOU A TARGET.
JADE HIRED ME TO KILL SAKKARA, BUT IT WASN'T A CONTRACT ON HER LIFE I SIGNED...
IT WAS YOURS.
BUT I THOUGHT... I HAD TO TRY TO STOP FAIRCHILD. YOU WOULD HAVE WANTED ME TO. WOULD HAVE WANTED THAT HUMANITY YOU REMINDED ME I HAD TO PAY OFF.
I'M SORRY I LET PURGATORI MAKE YOUR LIFE HELL. SORRY I WANTED YOU BACK SO BAD, I'D HAVE LET HER MAKE YOU INTO A SOULLESS MONSTER LIKE ME.
SO...
SORRY.
HERE. IT'S HAWTHORN WOOD. PUT IT THROUGH MY HEART.

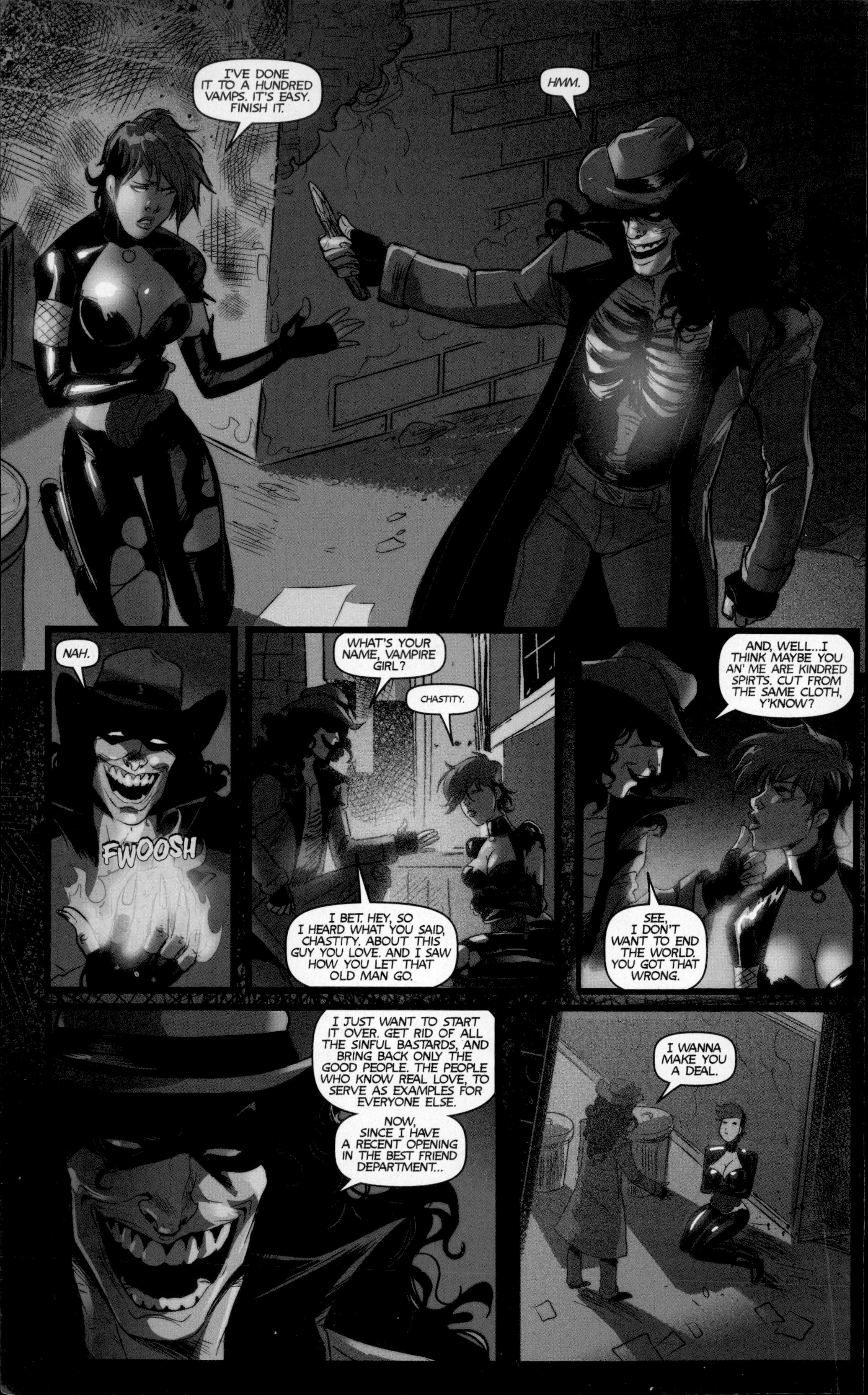
I'VE DONE IT TO A HUNDRED VAMPS. IT'S EASY. FINISH IT.
HMM.
NAH.
FWOOSH
WHAT'S YOUR NAME, VAMPIRE GIRL?
CHASTITY.
I BET. HEY, SO I HEARD WHAT YOU SAID, CHASTITY. ABOUT THIS GUY YOU LOVE. AND I SAW HOW YOU LET THAT OLD MAN GO.
AND, WELL...I THINK MAYBE YOU AN' ME ARE KINDRED SPIRTS. CUT FROM THE SAME CLOTH, Y'KNOW?
SEE, I DON'T WANT TO END THE WORLD. YOU GOT THAT WRONG.
I JUST WANT TO START IT OVER. GET RID OF ALL THE SINFUL BASTARDS, AND BRING BACK ONLY THE GOOD PEOPLE. THE PEOPLE WHO KNOW REAL LOVE, TO SERVE AS EXAMPLES FOR EVERYONE ELSE.
NOW, SINCE I HAVE A RECENT OPENING IN THE BEST FRIEND DEPARTMENT...
I WANNA MAKE YOU A DEAL.

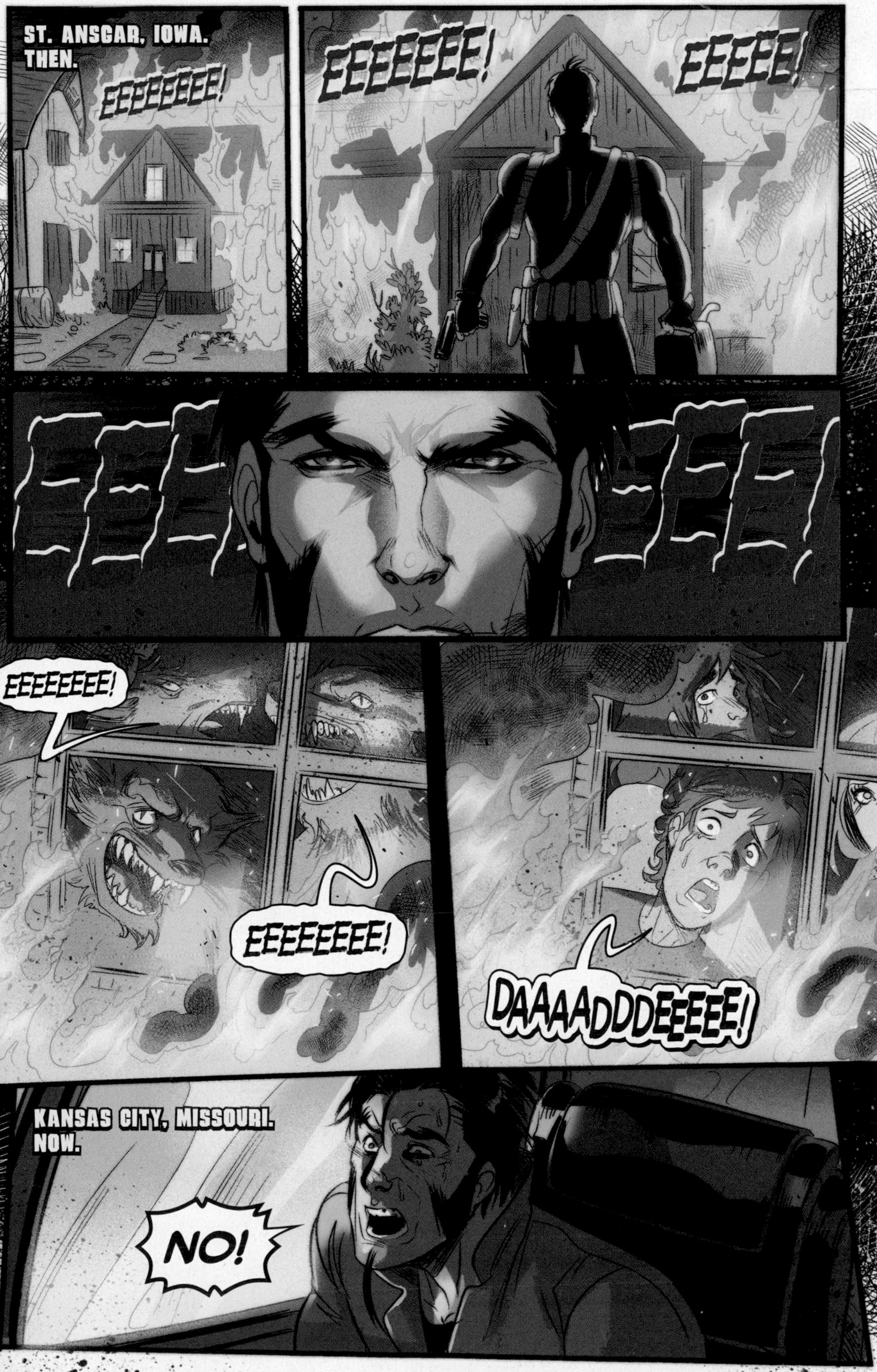
ST. ANSGAR, IOWA. THEN.
EEEEEEEE!
EEEEEEE!
EEEEE!
EEEEEEEE!
EEEEEEEE!
DAAAADDDEEEEE!
KANSAS CITY, MISSOURI. NOW.
NO!

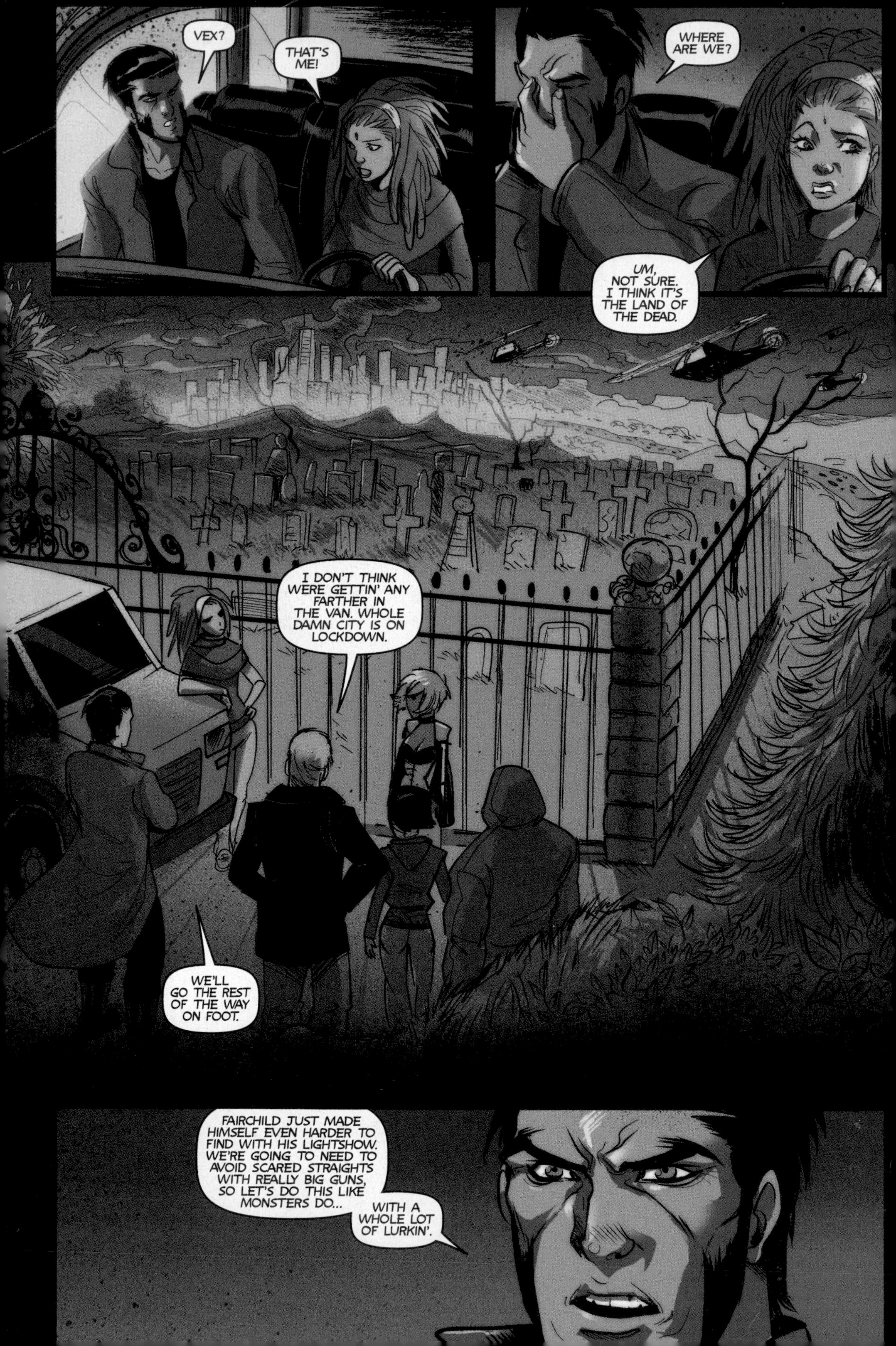
VEX?
THAT'S ME!
WHERE ARE WE?
UM, NOT SURE. I THINK IT'S THE LAND OF THE DEAD.
I DON'T THINK WERE GETTIN' ANY FARTHER IN THE VAN. WHOLE DAMN CITY IS ON LOCKDOWN.
WE'LL GO THE REST OF THE WAY ON FOOT.
FAIRCHILD JUST MADE HIMSELF EVEN HARDER TO FIND WITH HIS LIGHTSHOW. WE'RE GOING TO NEED TO AVOID SCARED STRAIGHTS WITH REALLY BIG GUNS, SO LET'S DO THIS LIKE MONSTERS DO...
WITH A WHOLE LOT OF LURKIN'.

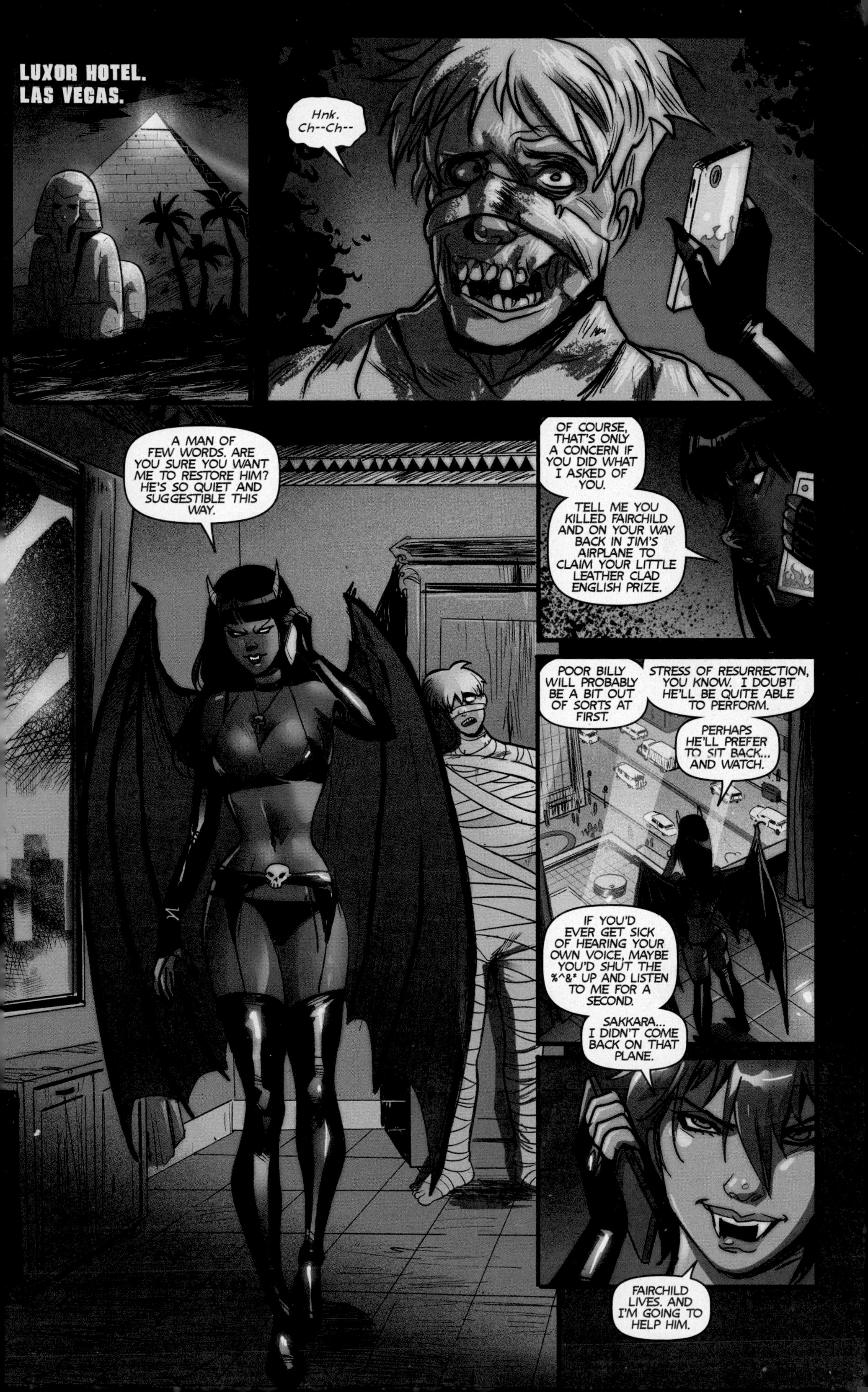
LUXOR HOTEL. LAS VEGAS.
Hnk. Ch--Ch--
A MAN OF FEW WORDS. ARE YOU SURE YOU WANT ME TO RESTORE HIM? HE'S SO QUIET AND SUGGESTIBLE THIS WAY.
OF COURSE, THAT'S ONLY A CONCERN IF YOU DID WHAT I ASKED OF YOU.
TELL ME YOU KILLED FAIRCHILD AND ON YOUR WAY BACK IN JIM'S AIRPLANE TO CLAIM YOUR LITTLE LEATHER CLAD ENGLISH PRIZE.
POOR BILLY WILL PROBABLY BE A BIT OUT OF SORTS AT FIRST.
STRESS OF RESURRECTION, YOU KNOW. I DOUBT HE'LL BE QUITE ABLE TO PERFORM.
PERHAPS HE'LL PREFER TO SIT BACK... AND WATCH.
IF YOU'D EVER GET SICK OF HEARING YOUR OWN VOICE, MAYBE YOU'D SHUT THE %^&* UP AND LISTEN TO ME FOR A SECOND.
SAKKARA... I DIDN'T COME BACK ON THAT PLANE.
FAIRCHILD LIVES. AND I'M GOING TO HELP HIM.

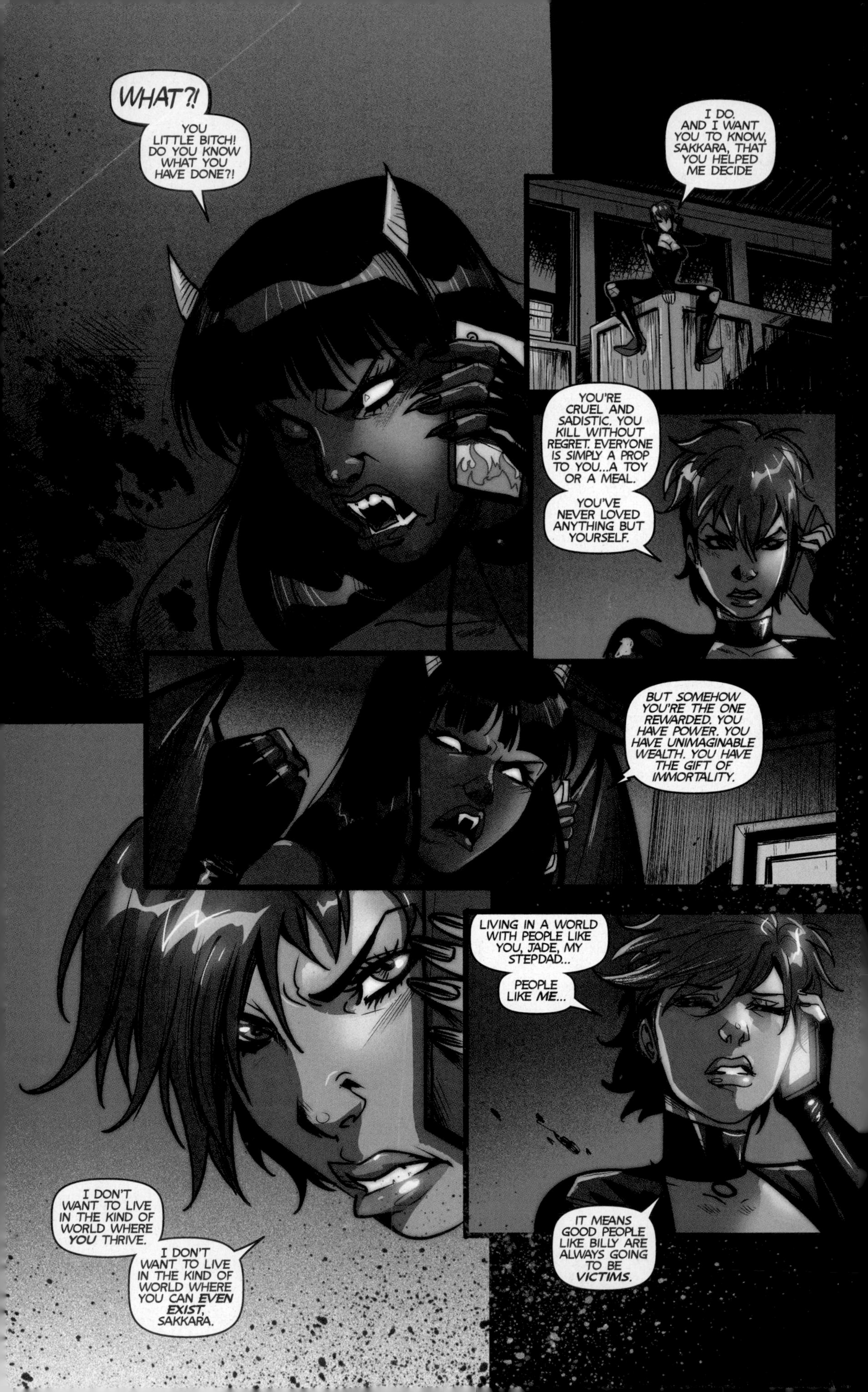
WHAT?!
YOU LITTLE BITCH! DO YOU KNOW WHAT YOU HAVE DONE?!
I DO. AND I WANT YOU TO KNOW, SAKKARA, THAT YOU HELPED ME DECIDE
YOU'RE CRUEL AND SADISTIC. YOU KILL WITHOUT REGRET. EVERYONE IS SIMPLY A PROP TO YOU...A TOY OR A MEAL.
YOU'VE NEVER LOVED ANYTHING BUT YOURSELF.
BUT SOMEHOW YOU'RE THE ONE REWARDED. YOU HAVE POWER. YOU HAVE UNIMAGINABLE WEALTH. YOU HAVE THE GIFT OF IMMORTALITY.
LIVING IN A WORLD WITH PEOPLE LIKE YOU, JADE, MY STEPDAD...
PEOPLE LIKE ME...
IT MEANS GOOD PEOPLE LIKE BILLY ARE ALWAYS GOING TO BE VICTIMS.
I DON'T WANT TO LIVE IN THE KIND OF WORLD WHERE YOU THRIVE.
I DON'T WANT TO LIVE IN THE KIND OF WORLD WHERE YOU CAN EVEN EXIST, SAKKARA.

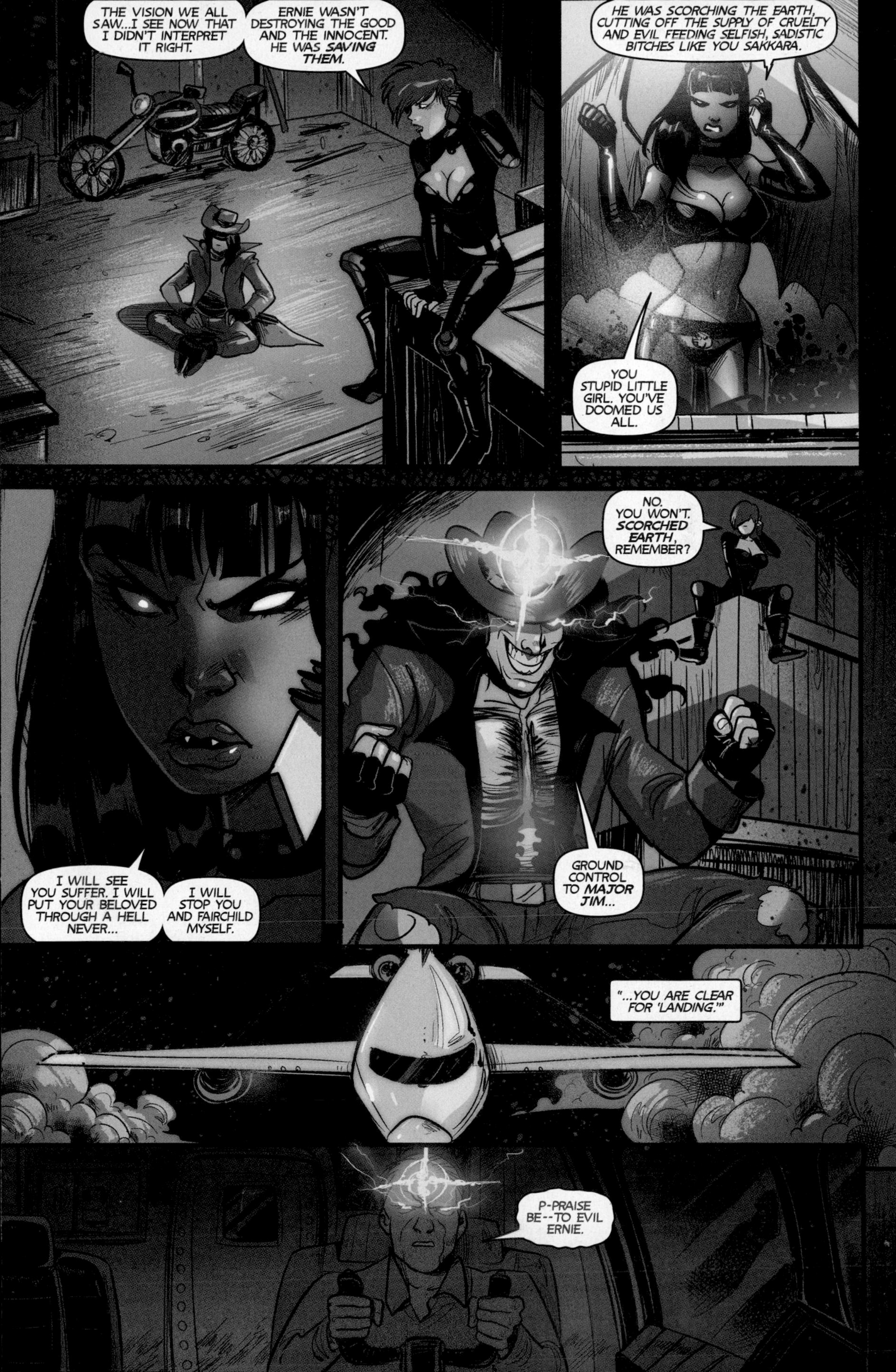
THE VISION WE ALL SAW...I SEE NOW THAT I DIDN'T INTERPRET IT RIGHT.
ERNIE WASN'T DESTROYING THE GOOD AND THE INNOCENT. HE WAS *SAVING THEM.*
HE WAS SCORCHING THE EARTH, CUTTING OFF THE SUPPLY OF CRUELTY AND EVIL FEEDING SELFISH, SADISTIC BITCHES LIKE YOU SAKKARA.
YOU STUPID LITTLE GIRL. YOU'VE DOOMED US ALL.
I WILL SEE YOU SUFFER. I WILL PUT YOUR BELOVED THROUGH A HELL NEVER...
I WILL STOP YOU AND FAIRCHILD MYSELF.
NO. YOU WON'T. *SCORCHED EARTH*, REMEMBER?
GROUND CONTROL TO *MAJOR JIM*...
"...YOU ARE CLEAR FOR 'LANDING.'"
P-PRAISE BE--TO EVIL ERNIE.

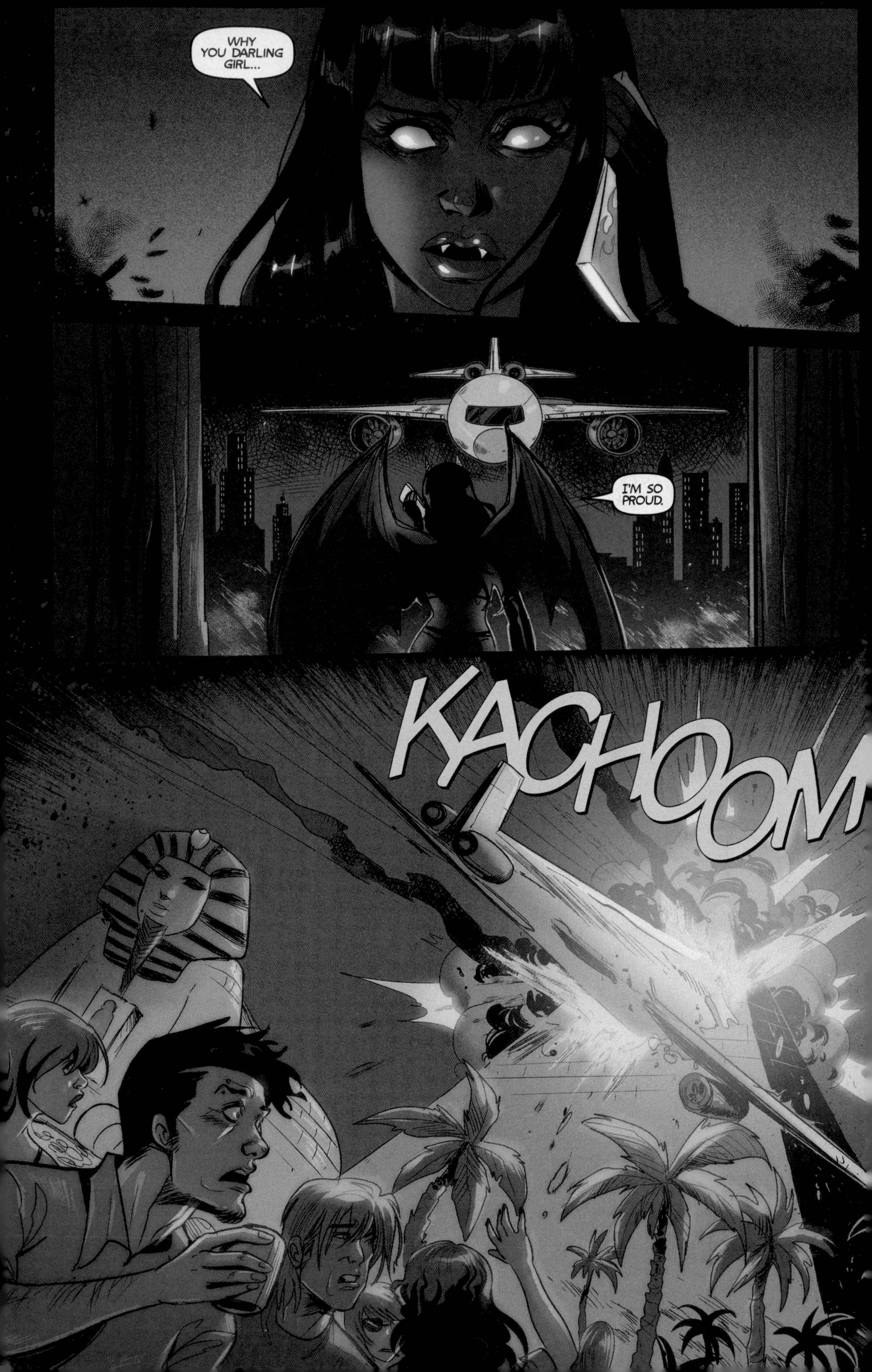
WHY YOU DARLING GIRL...
I'M SO PROUD.
KACHOOOM

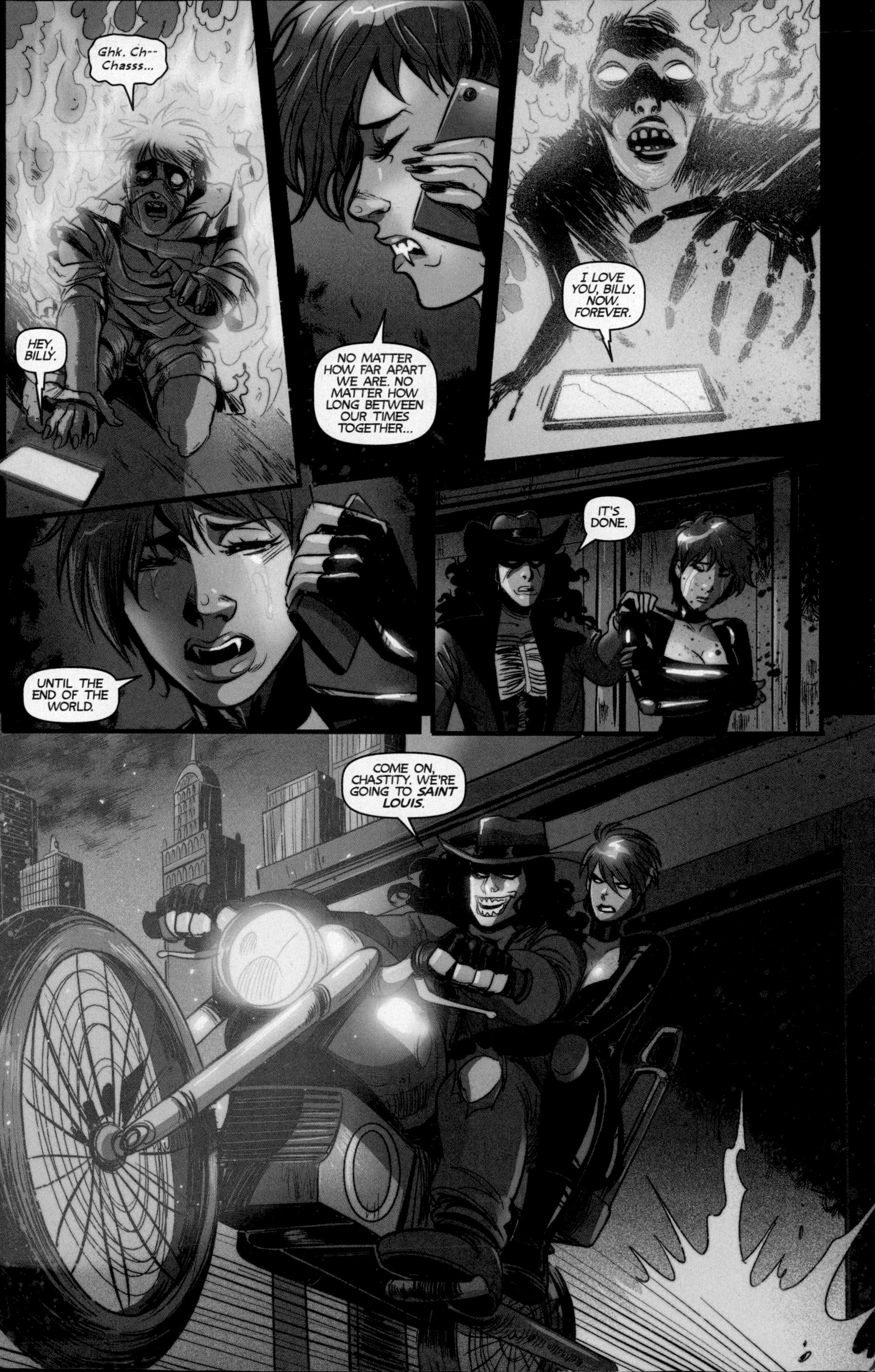
Ghk. Ch-- Chasss...
HEY, BILLY.
NO MATTER HOW FAR APART WE ARE. NO MATTER HOW LONG BETWEEN OUR TIMES TOGETHER...
I LOVE YOU, BILLY. NOW. FOREVER.
UNTIL THE END OF THE WORLD.
IT'S DONE.
COME ON, CHASTITY. WE'RE GOING TO SAINT LOUIS.

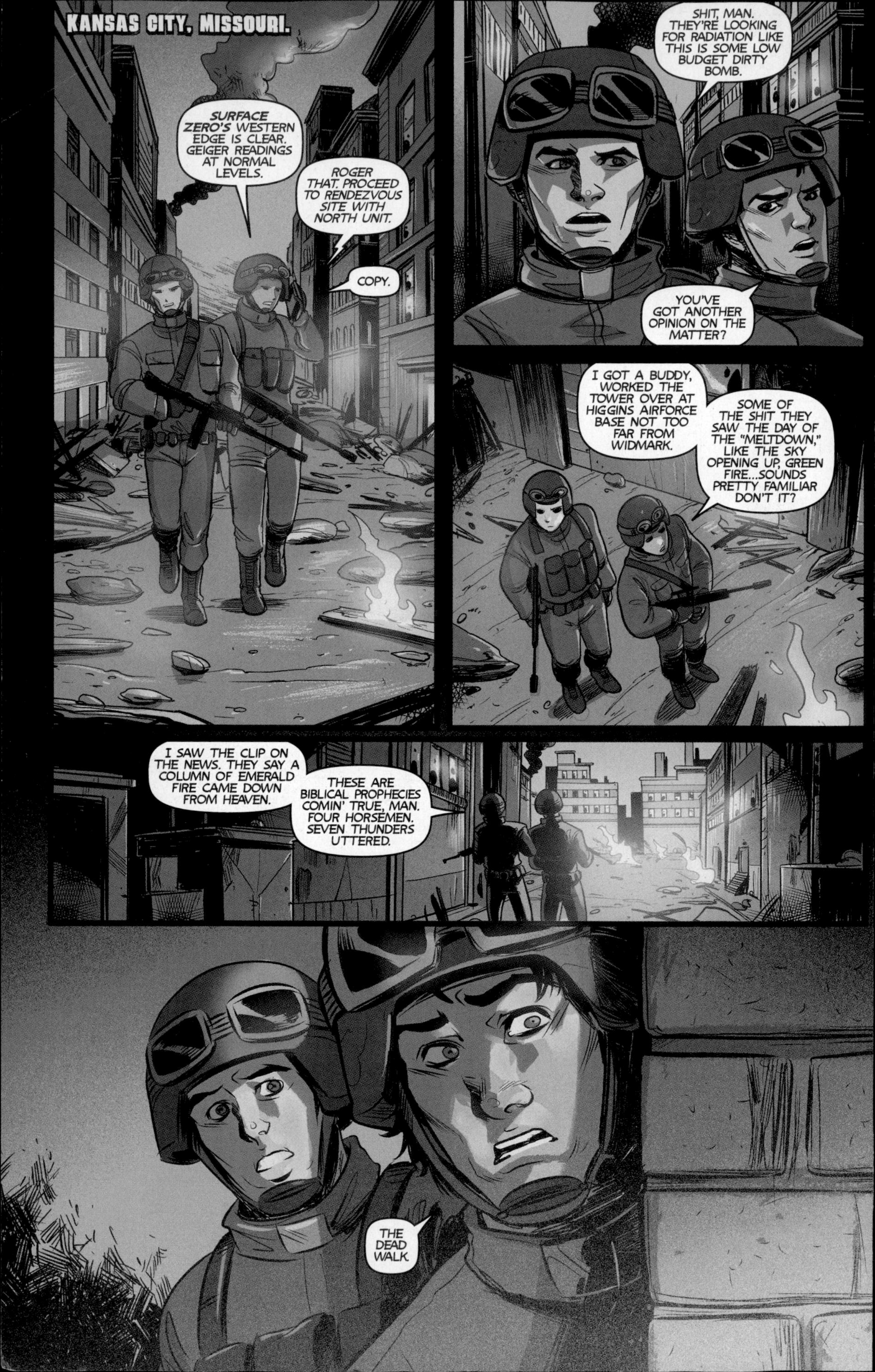
KANSAS CITY, MISSOURI.
SURFACE ZERO'S WESTERN EDGE IS CLEAR. GEIGER READINGS AT NORMAL LEVELS.
ROGER THAT. PROCEED TO RENDEZVOUS SITE WITH NORTH UNIT.
COPY.
SHIT, MAN. THEY'RE LOOKING FOR RADIATION LIKE THIS IS SOME LOW BUDGET DIRTY BOMB.
YOU'VE GOT ANOTHER OPINION ON THE MATTER?
I GOT A BUDDY, WORKED THE TOWER OVER AT HIGGINS AIRFORCE BASE NOT TOO FAR FROM WIDMARK.
SOME OF THE SHIT THEY SAW THE DAY OF THE "MELTDOWN," LIKE THE SKY OPENING UP, GREEN FIRE...SOUNDS PRETTY FAMILIAR DON'T IT?
I SAW THE CLIP ON THE NEWS. THEY SAY A COLUMN OF EMERALD FIRE CAME DOWN FROM HEAVEN.
THESE ARE BIBLICAL PROPHECIES COMIN' TRUE, MAN. FOUR HORSEMEN. SEVEN THUNDERS UTTERED.
THE DEAD WALK.

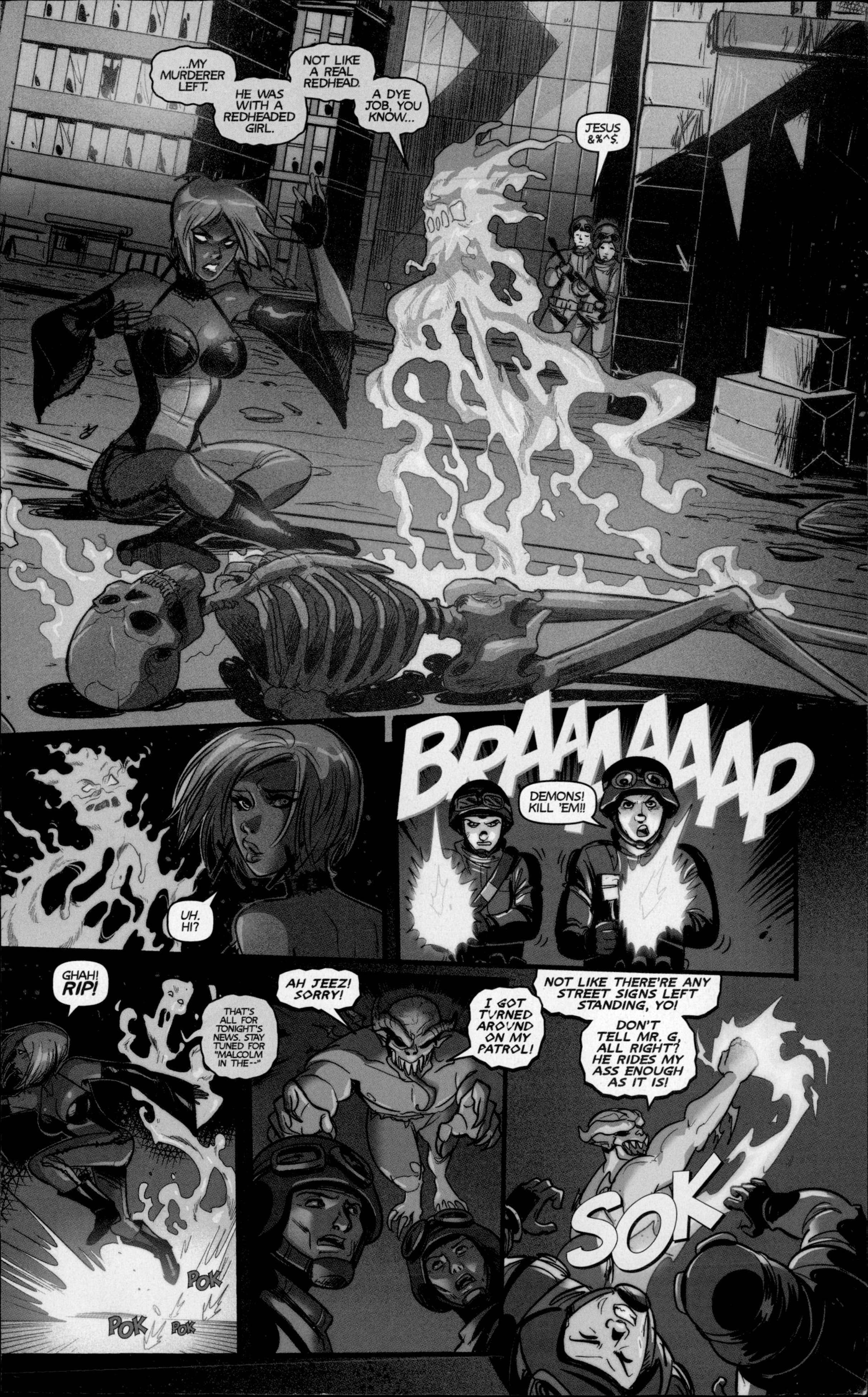
...MY MURDERER LEFT.
HE WAS WITH A REDHEADED GIRL.
NOT LIKE A REAL REDHEAD.
A DYE JOB, YOU KNOW...
JESUS &%^$.
UH. HI?
BRAAAAAAP
DEMONS! KILL 'EM!!
GHAH! RIP!
THAT'S ALL FOR TONIGHT'S NEWS. STAY TUNED FOR "MALCOLM IN THE--"
POK
POK
POK
AH JEEZ! SORRY!
I GOT TURNED AROUND ON MY PATROL!
NOT LIKE THERE'RE ANY STREET SIGNS LEFT STANDING, YO!
DON'T TELL MR. G, ALL RIGHT? HE RIDES MY ASS ENOUGH AS IT IS!
SOK

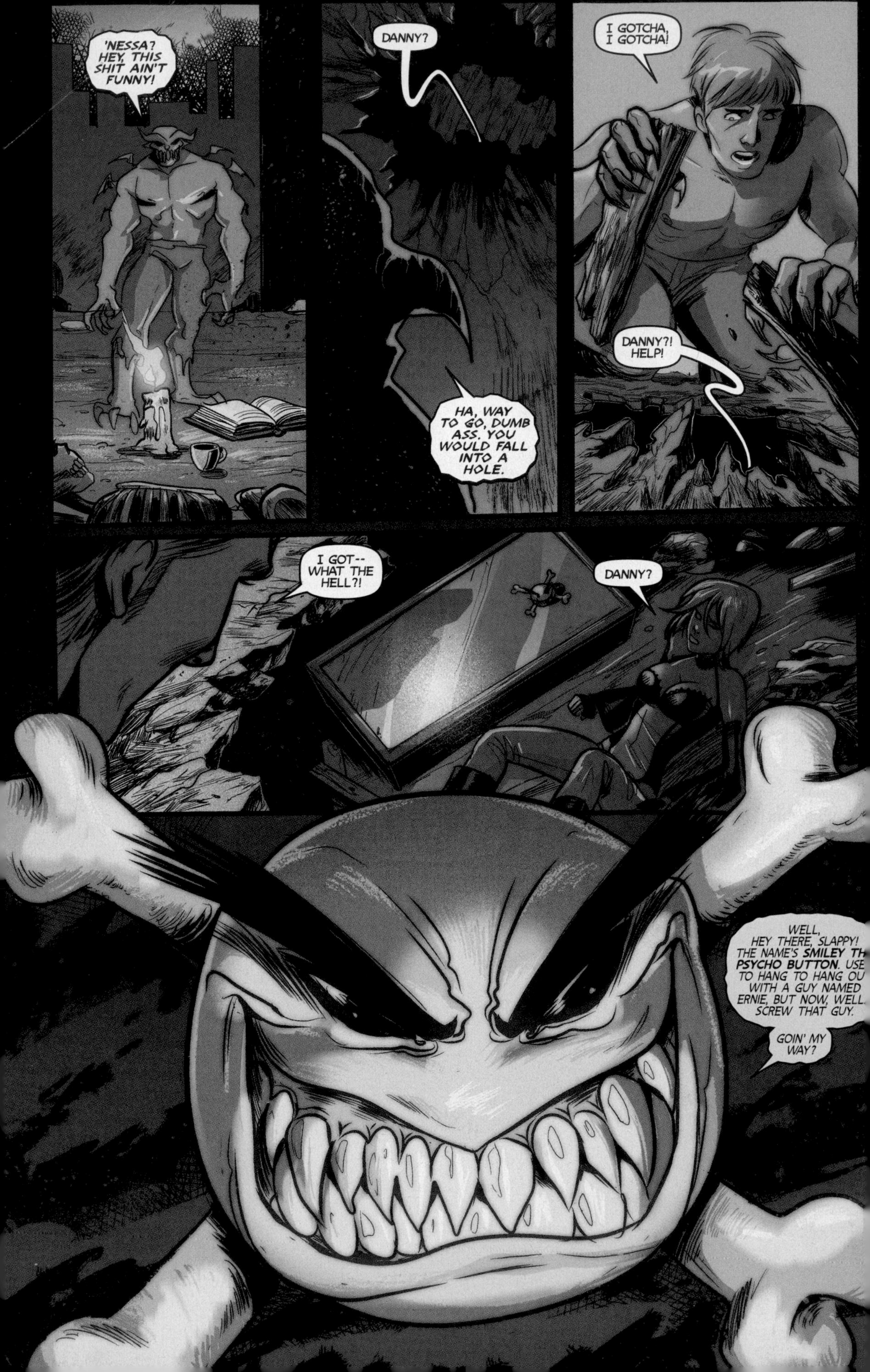

'NESSA? HEY, THIS SHIT AIN'T FUNNY!
DANNY?
HA, WAY TO GO, DUMB ASS. YOU WOULD FALL INTO A HOLE.
I GOTCHA, I GOTCHA!
DANNY?! HELP!
I GOT-- WHAT THE HELL?!
DANNY?
WELL, HEY THERE, SLAPPY! THE NAME'S SMILEY TH PSYCHO BUTTON. USE TO HANG TO HANG OU WITH A GUY NAMED ERNIE, BUT NOW, WELL SCREW THAT GUY.
GOIN' MY WAY?

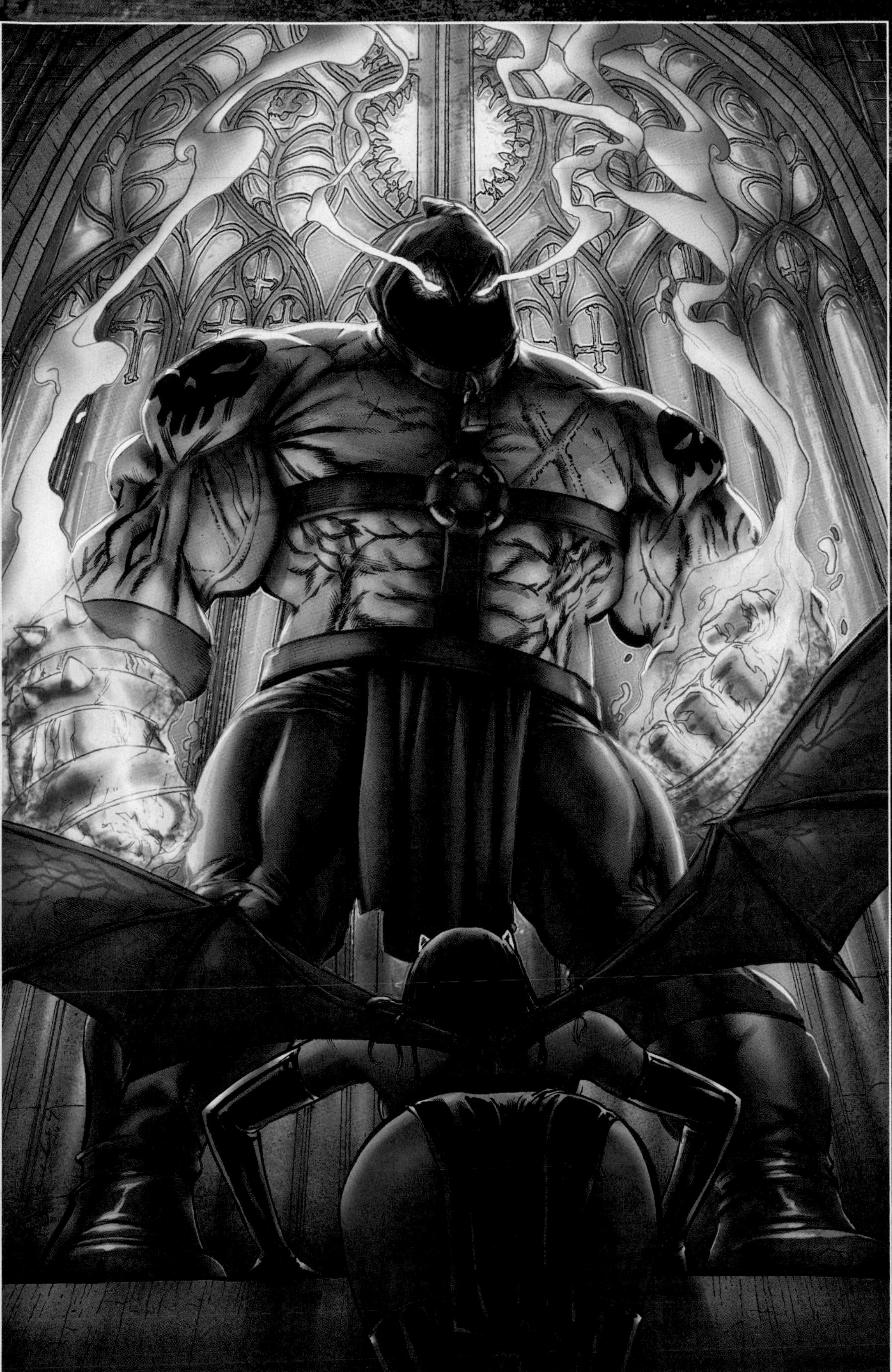

issue #5 cover by TIM SEELEY
colors by ADRIANO LUCAS

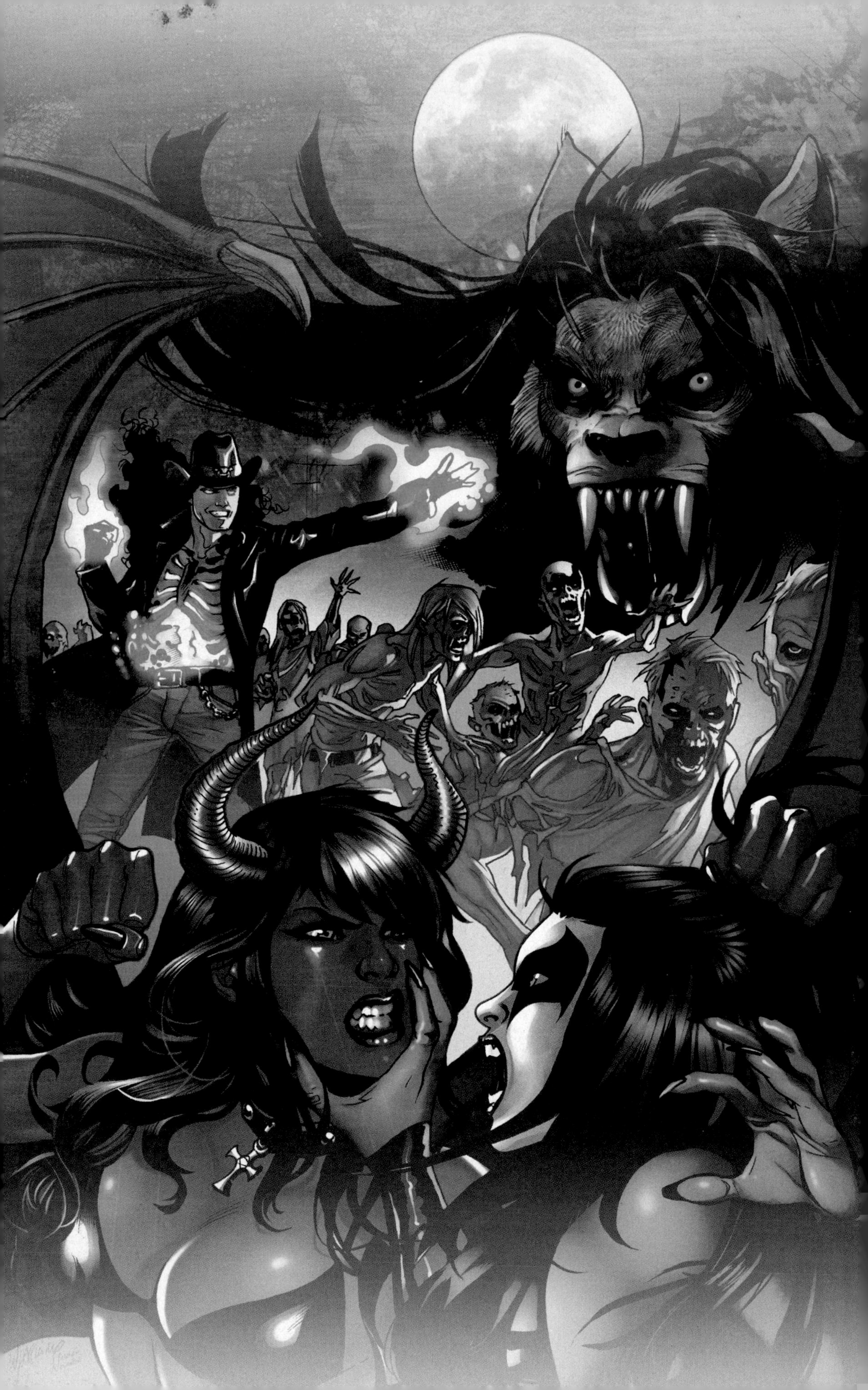

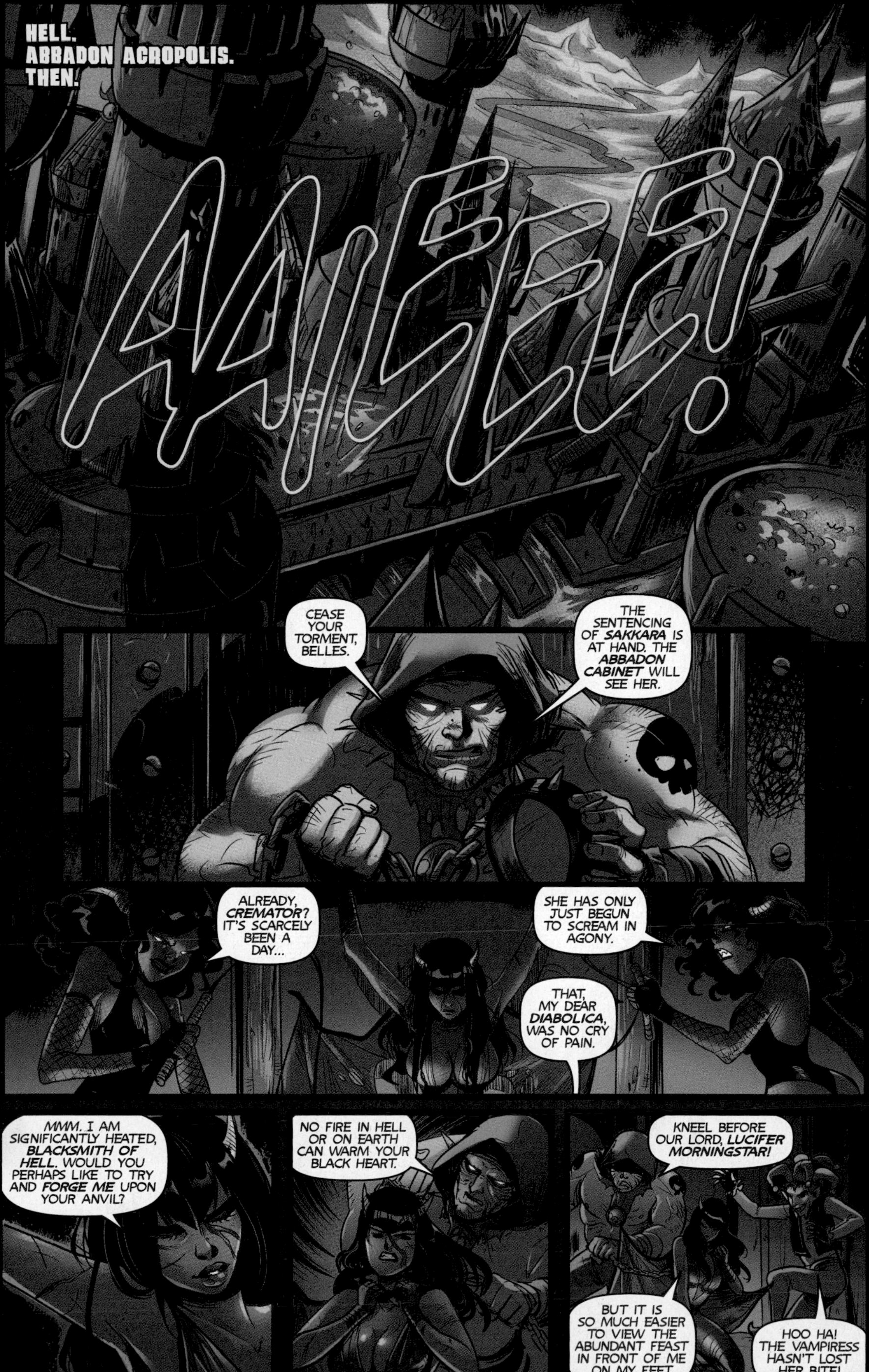

HELL. ABBADON ACROPOLIS. THEN.
AAIEEEE!
CEASE YOUR TORMENT, BELLES.
THE SENTENCING OF SAKKARA IS AT HAND. THE ABBADON CABINET WILL SEE HER.
ALREADY, CREMATOR? IT'S SCARCELY BEEN A DAY...
SHE HAS ONLY JUST BEGUN TO SCREAM IN AGONY.
THAT, MY DEAR DIABOLICA, WAS NO CRY OF PAIN.
MMM. I AM SIGNIFICANTLY HEATED, BLACKSMITH OF HELL. WOULD YOU PERHAPS LIKE TO TRY AND FORGE ME UPON YOUR ANVIL?
NO FIRE IN HELL OR ON EARTH CAN WARM YOUR BLACK HEART.
KNEEL BEFORE OUR LORD, LUCIFER MORNINGSTAR!
BUT IT IS SO MUCH EASIER TO VIEW THE ABUNDANT FEAST IN FRONT OF ME ON MY FEET.
HOO HA! THE VAMPIRESS HASN'T LOST HER BITE!

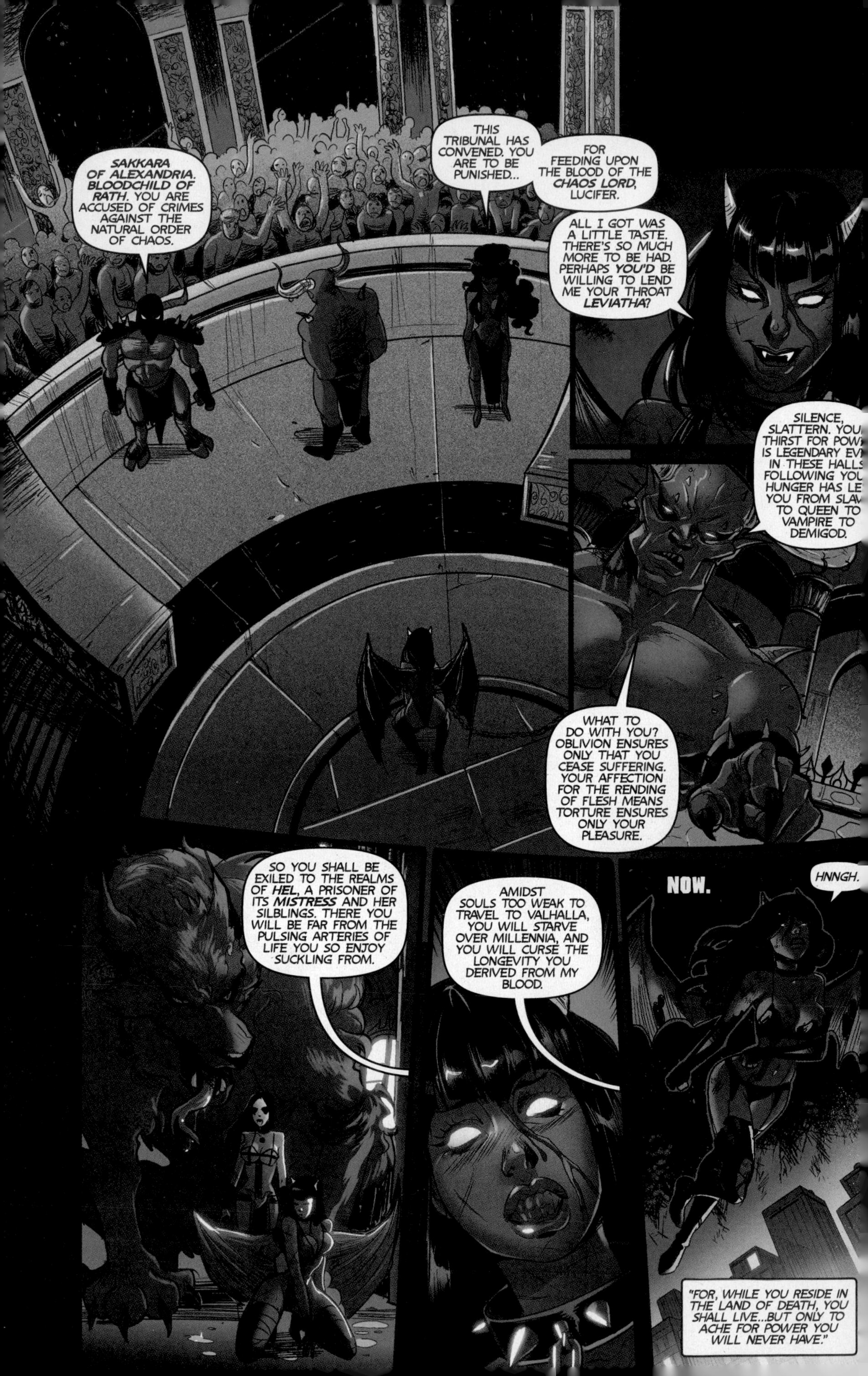
SAKKARA OF ALEXANDRIA. BLOODCHILD OF RATH. YOU ARE ACCUSED OF CRIMES AGAINST THE NATURAL ORDER OF CHAOS.
THIS TRIBUNAL HAS CONVENED. YOU ARE TO BE PUNISHED...
FOR FEEDING UPON THE BLOOD OF THE CHAOS LORD, LUCIFER.
ALL I GOT WAS A LITTLE TASTE. THERE'S SO MUCH MORE TO BE HAD. PERHAPS YOU'D BE WILLING TO LEND ME YOUR THROAT LEVIATHA?
SILENCE, SLATTERN. YOU THIRST FOR POW IS LEGENDARY EV IN THESE HALLS FOLLOWING YOU HUNGER HAS LE YOU FROM SLAV TO QUEEN TO VAMPIRE TO DEMIGOD.
WHAT TO DO WITH YOU? OBLIVION ENSURES ONLY THAT YOU CEASE SUFFERING. YOUR AFFECTION FOR THE RENDING OF FLESH MEANS TORTURE ENSURES ONLY YOUR PLEASURE.
SO YOU SHALL BE EXILED TO THE REALMS OF HEL, A PRISONER OF ITS MISTRESS AND HER SILBLINGS. THERE YOU WILL BE FAR FROM THE PULSING ARTERIES OF LIFE YOU SO ENJOY SUCKLING FROM.
AMIDST SOULS TOO WEAK TO TRAVEL TO VALHALLA, YOU WILL STARVE OVER MILLENNIA, AND YOU WILL CURSE THE LONGEVITY YOU DERIVED FROM MY BLOOD.
NOW.
HNNGH.
"FOR, WHILE YOU RESIDE IN THE LAND OF DEATH, YOU SHALL LIVE...BUT ONLY TO ACHE FOR POWER YOU WILL NEVER HAVE."

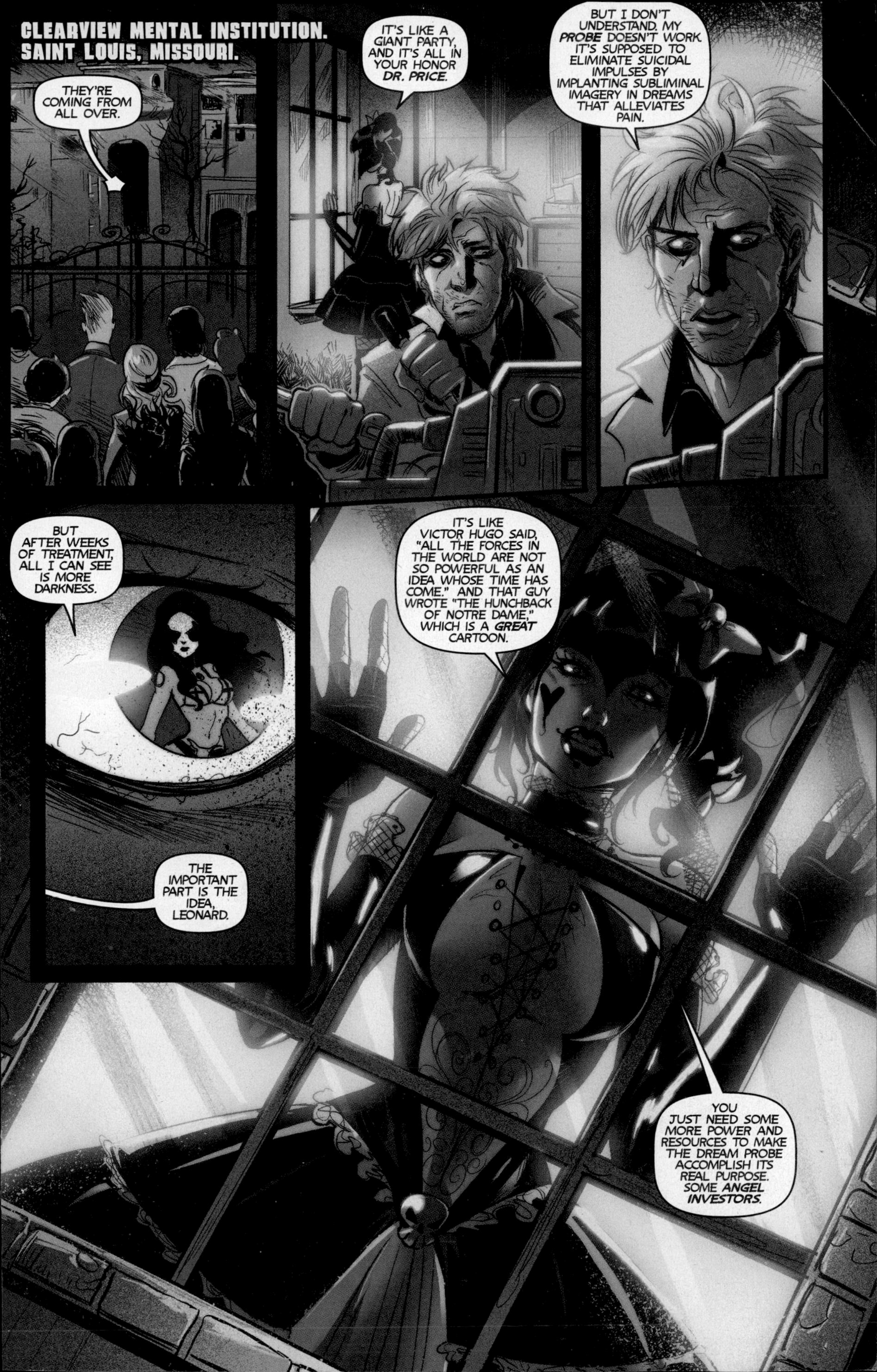

CLEARVIEW MENTAL INSTITUTION. SAINT LOUIS, MISSOURI.
THEY'RE COMING FROM ALL OVER.
IT'S LIKE A GIANT PARTY, AND IT'S ALL IN YOUR HONOR *DR. PRICE*.
BUT I DON'T UNDERSTAND. MY *PROBE* DOESN'T WORK. IT'S SUPPOSED TO ELIMINATE SUICIDAL IMPULSES BY IMPLANTING SUBLIMINAL IMAGERY IN DREAMS THAT ALLEVIATES PAIN.
BUT AFTER WEEKS OF TREATMENT, ALL I CAN SEE IS MORE DARKNESS.
IT'S LIKE VICTOR HUGO SAID, "ALL THE FORCES IN THE WORLD ARE NOT SO POWERFUL AS AN IDEA WHOSE TIME HAS COME." AND THAT GUY WROTE "THE HUNCHBACK OF NOTRE DAME," WHICH IS A *GREAT* CARTOON.
THE IMPORTANT PART IS THE IDEA, LEONARD.
YOU JUST NEED SOME MORE POWER AND RESOURCES TO MAKE THE DREAM PROBE ACCOMPLISH ITS REAL PURPOSE. SOME *ANGEL INVESTORS*.

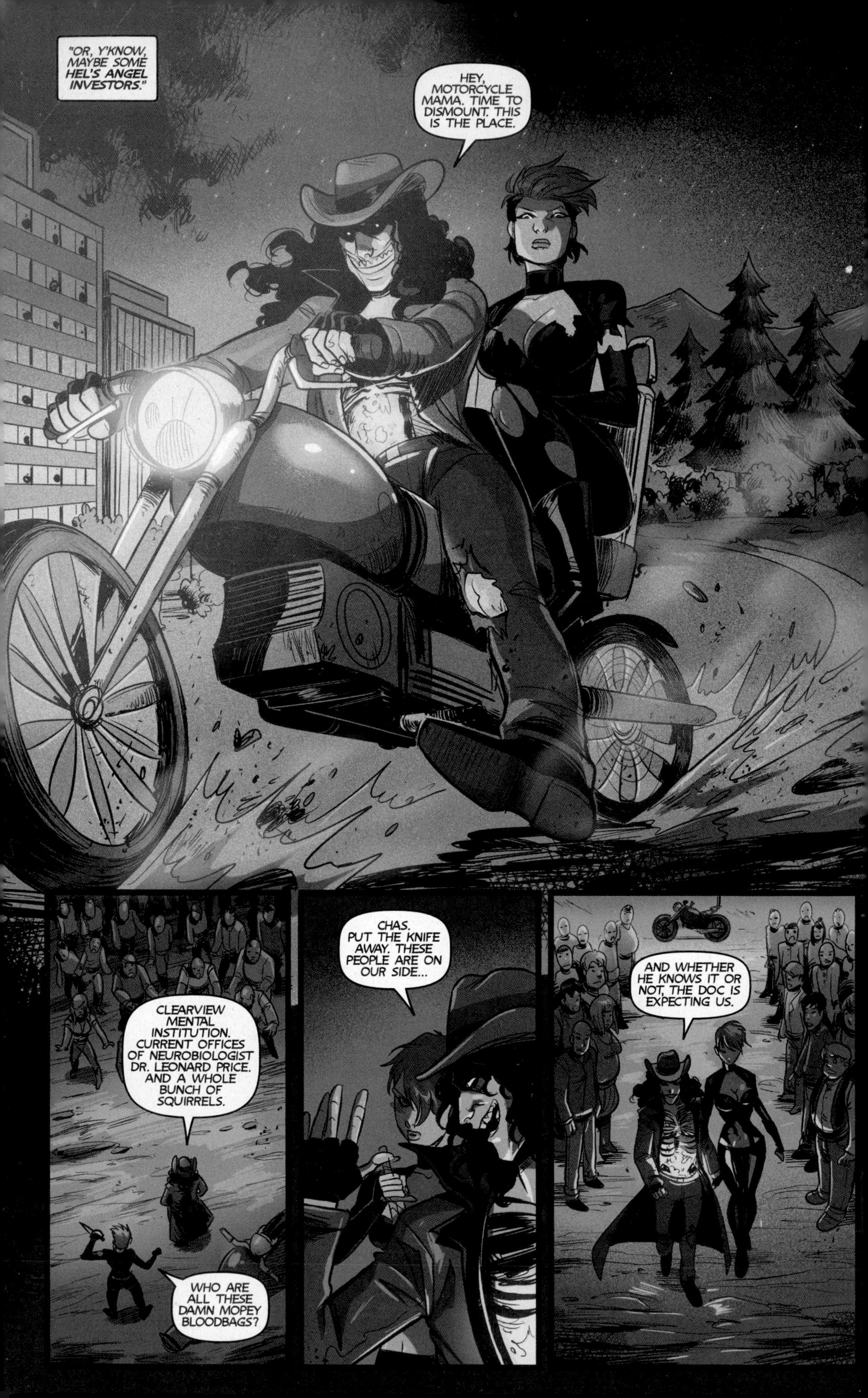
"OR, Y'KNOW, MAYBE SOME HEL'S ANGEL INVESTORS."
HEY, MOTORCYCLE MAMA. TIME TO DISMOUNT. THIS IS THE PLACE.
CLEARVIEW MENTAL INSTITUTION. CURRENT OFFICES OF NEUROBIOLOGIST DR. LEONARD PRICE. AND A WHOLE BUNCH OF SQUIRRELS.
WHO ARE ALL THESE DAMN MOPEY BLOODBAGS?
CHAS. PUT THE KNIFE AWAY. THESE PEOPLE ARE ON OUR SIDE...
AND WHETHER HE KNOWS IT OR NOT, THE DOC IS EXPECTING US.

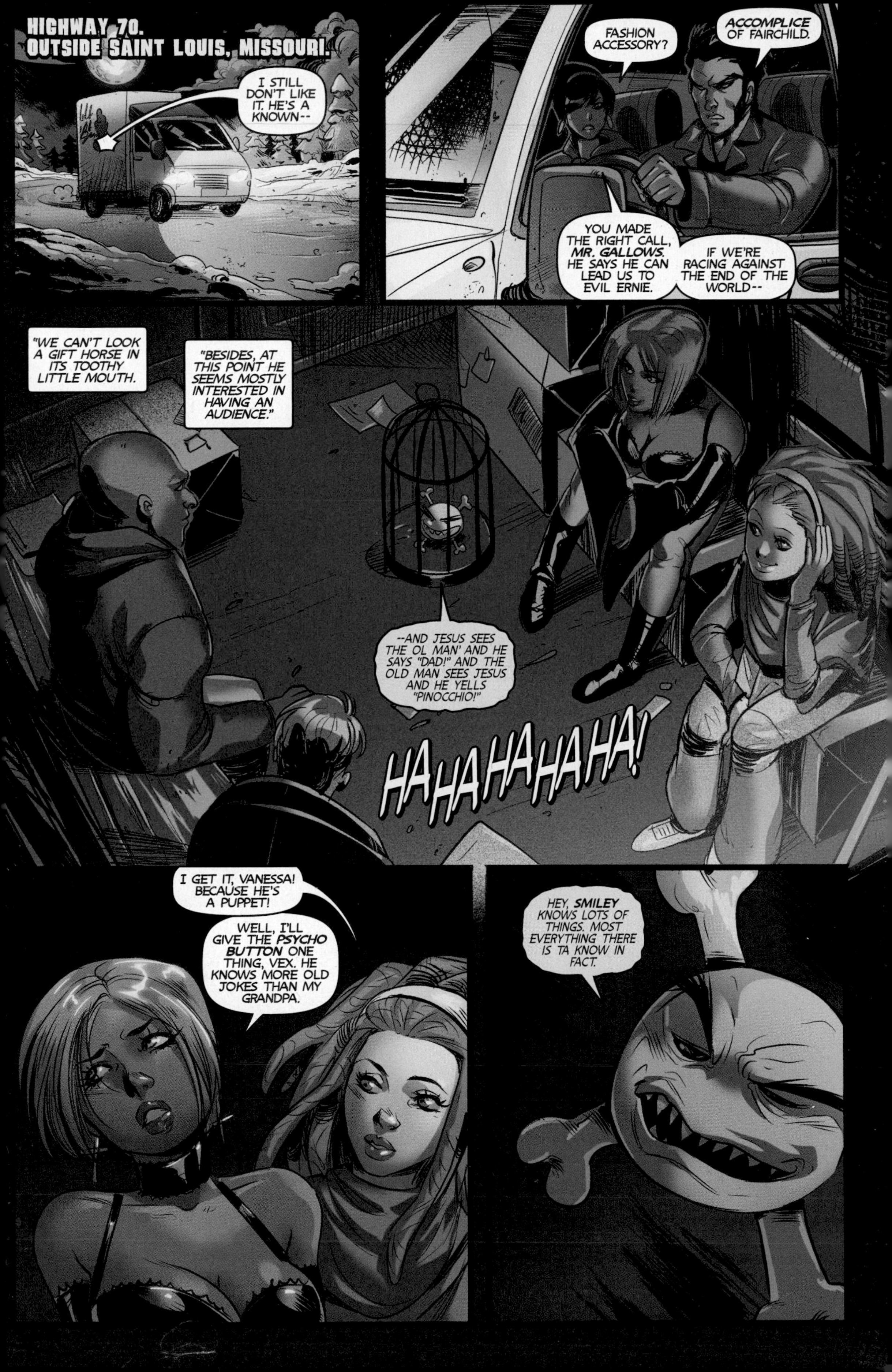
HIGHWAY 70.
OUTSIDE SAINT LOUIS, MISSOURI.
I STILL DON'T LIKE IT. HE'S A KNOWN--
ACCOMPLICE OF FAIRCHILD.
FASHION ACCESSORY?
YOU MADE THE RIGHT CALL, MR. GALLOWS. HE SAYS HE CAN LEAD US TO EVIL ERNIE.
IF WE'RE RACING AGAINST THE END OF THE WORLD--
"WE CAN'T LOOK A GIFT HORSE IN ITS TOOTHY LITTLE MOUTH.
"BESIDES, AT THIS POINT HE SEEMS MOSTLY INTERESTED IN HAVING AN AUDIENCE."
--AND JESUS SEES THE OL MAN' AND HE SAYS "DAD!" AND THE OLD MAN SEES JESUS AND HE YELLS "PINOCCHIO!"
HAHAHAHAHAHA!
I GET IT, VANESSA! BECAUSE HE'S A PUPPET!
WELL, I'LL GIVE THE PSYCHO BUTTON ONE THING, VEX. HE KNOWS MORE OLD JOKES THAN MY GRANDPA.
HEY, SMILEY KNOWS LOTS OF THINGS. MOST EVERYTHING THERE IS TA KNOW IN FACT.

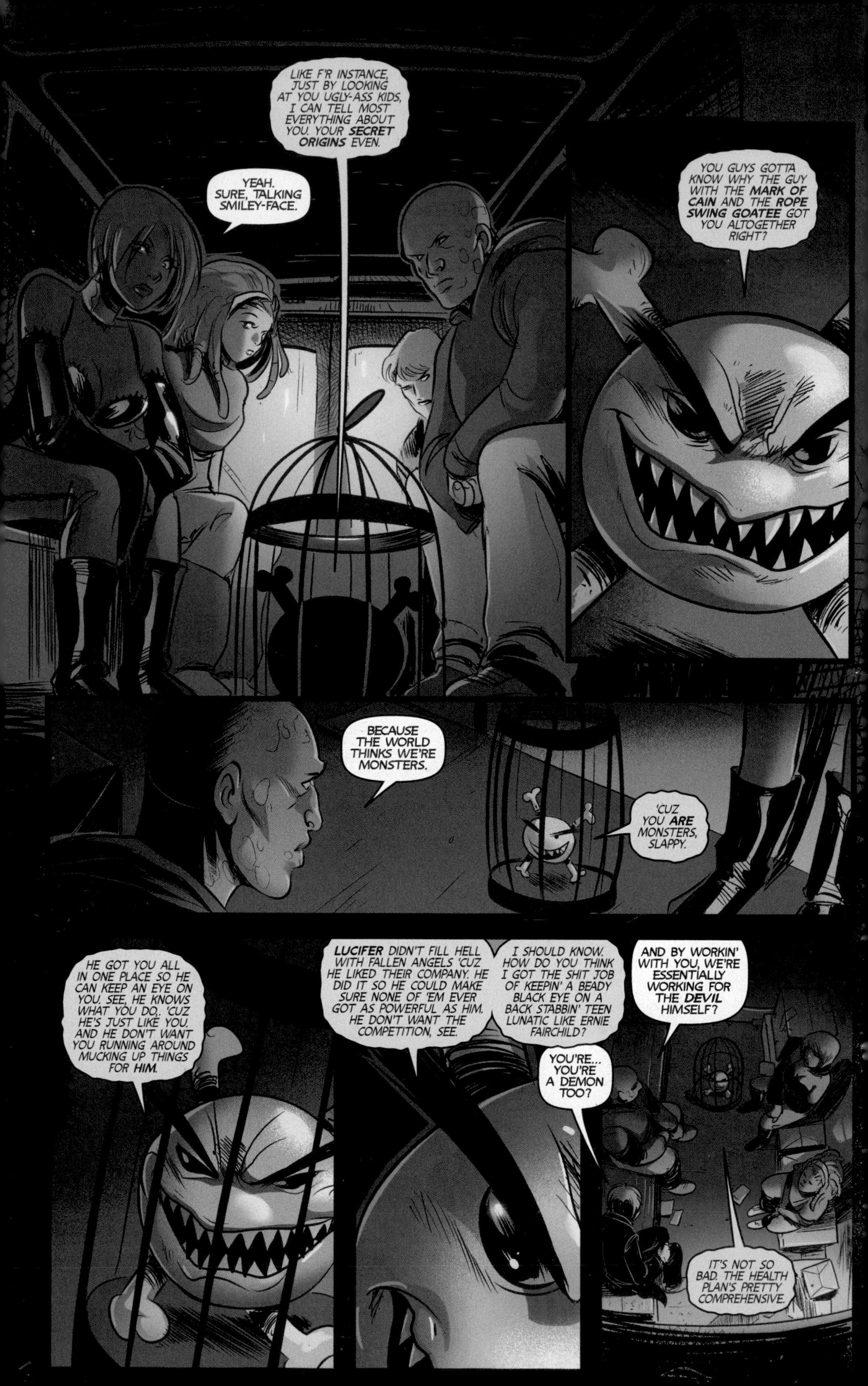

LIKE F'R INSTANCE, JUST BY LOOKING AT YOU UGLY-ASS KIDS, I CAN TELL MOST EVERYTHING ABOUT YOU. YOUR **SECRET ORIGINS** EVEN.
YEAH. SURE, TALKING SMILEY-FACE.
YOU GUYS GOTTA KNOW WHY THE GUY WITH THE **MARK OF CAIN** AND THE **ROPE SWING GOATEE** GOT YOU ALTOGETHER RIGHT?
BECAUSE THE WORLD THINKS WE'RE MONSTERS.
'CUZ YOU **ARE** MONSTERS, SLAPPY.
HE GOT YOU ALL IN ONE PLACE SO HE CAN KEEP AN EYE ON YOU. SEE, HE KNOWS WHAT YOU DO, 'CUZ HE'S JUST LIKE YOU. AND HE DON'T WANT YOU RUNNING AROUND MUCKING UP THINGS FOR **HIM**.
LUCIFER DIDN'T FILL HELL WITH FALLEN ANGELS 'CUZ HE LIKED THEIR COMPANY. HE DID IT SO HE COULD MAKE SURE NONE OF 'EM EVER GOT AS POWERFUL AS HIM. HE DON'T WANT THE COMPETITION, SEE.
I SHOULD KNOW. HOW DO YOU THINK I GOT THE SHIT JOB OF KEEPIN' A BEADY BLACK EYE ON A BACK STABBIN' TEEN LUNATIC LIKE ERNIE FAIRCHILD?
YOU'RE... YOU'RE A DEMON TOO?
AND BY WORKIN' WITH YOU, WE'RE **ESSENTIALLY WORKING FOR THE DEVIL** HIMSELF?
IT'S NOT SO BAD. THE HEALTH PLAN'S PRETTY COMPREHENSIVE.

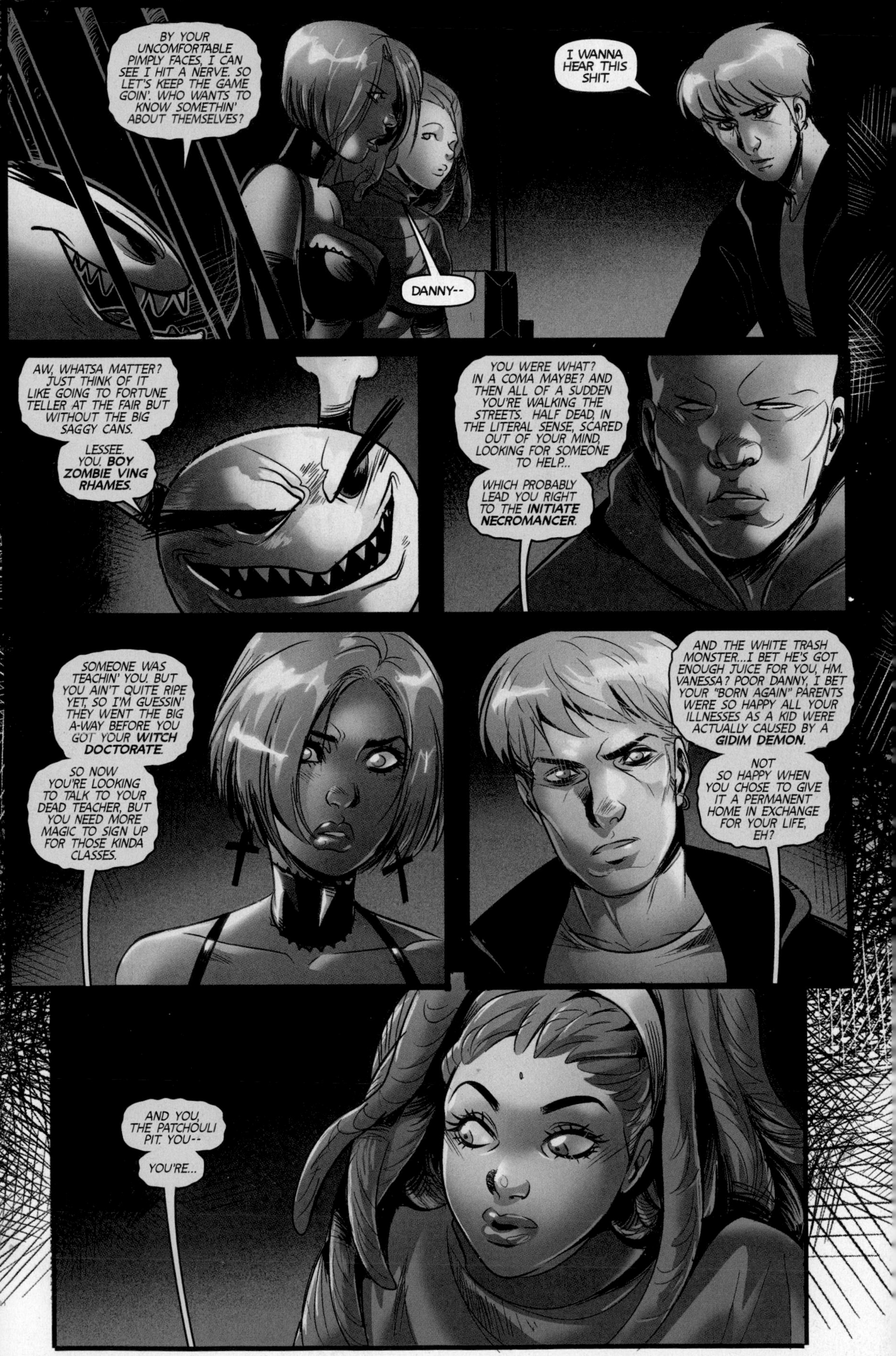

BY YOUR UNCOMFORTABLE PIMPLY FACES, I CAN SEE I HIT A NERVE. SO LET'S KEEP THE GAME GOIN'. WHO WANTS TO KNOW SOMETHIN' ABOUT THEMSELVES?
I WANNA HEAR THIS SHIT.
DANNY--
AW, WHATSA MATTER? JUST THINK OF IT LIKE GOING TO FORTUNE TELLER AT THE FAIR BUT WITHOUT THE BIG SAGGY CANS.
LESSEE. YOU. **BOY ZOMBIE VING RHAMES**.
YOU WERE WHAT? IN A COMA MAYBE? AND THEN ALL OF A SUDDEN YOU'RE WALKING THE STREETS. HALF DEAD, IN THE LITERAL SENSE, SCARED OUT OF YOUR MIND, LOOKING FOR SOMEONE TO HELP...
WHICH PROBABLY LEAD YOU RIGHT TO THE **INITIATE NECROMANCER**.
SOMEONE WAS TEACHIN' YOU. BUT YOU AIN'T QUITE RIPE YET, SO I'M GUESSIN' THEY WENT THE BIG A-WAY BEFORE YOU GOT YOUR **WITCH DOCTORATE**.
SO NOW YOU'RE LOOKING TO TALK TO YOUR DEAD TEACHER, BUT YOU NEED MORE MAGIC TO SIGN UP FOR THOSE KINDA CLASSES.
AND THE WHITE TRASH MONSTER...I BET HE'S GOT ENOUGH JUICE FOR YOU, HM. VANESSA? POOR DANNY, I BET YOUR "BORN AGAIN" PARENTS WERE SO HAPPY ALL YOUR ILLNESSES AS A KID WERE ACTUALLY CAUSED BY A **GIDIM DEMON**.
NOT SO HAPPY WHEN YOU CHOSE TO GIVE IT A PERMANENT HOME IN EXCHANGE FOR YOUR LIFE, EH?
AND YOU, THE PATCHOULI PIT. YOU--
YOU'RE...

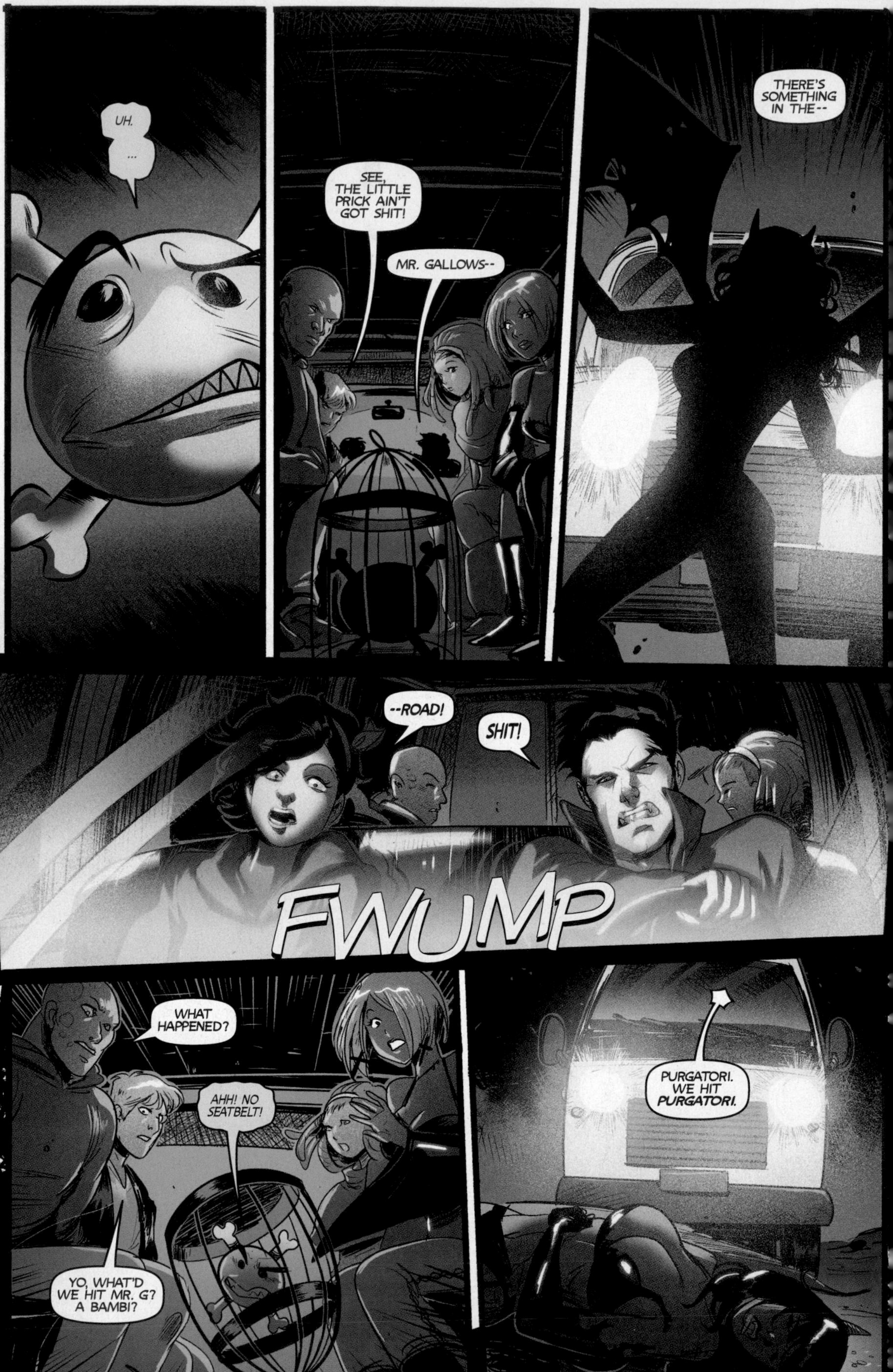
UH.
...
SEE, THE LITTLE PRICK AIN'T GOT SHIT!
MR. GALLOWS--
THERE'S SOMETHING IN THE--
--ROAD!
SHIT!
FWUMP
WHAT HAPPENED?
AHH! NO SEATBELT!
YO, WHAT'D WE HIT MR. G? A BAMBI?
PURGATORI. WE HIT PURGATORI.

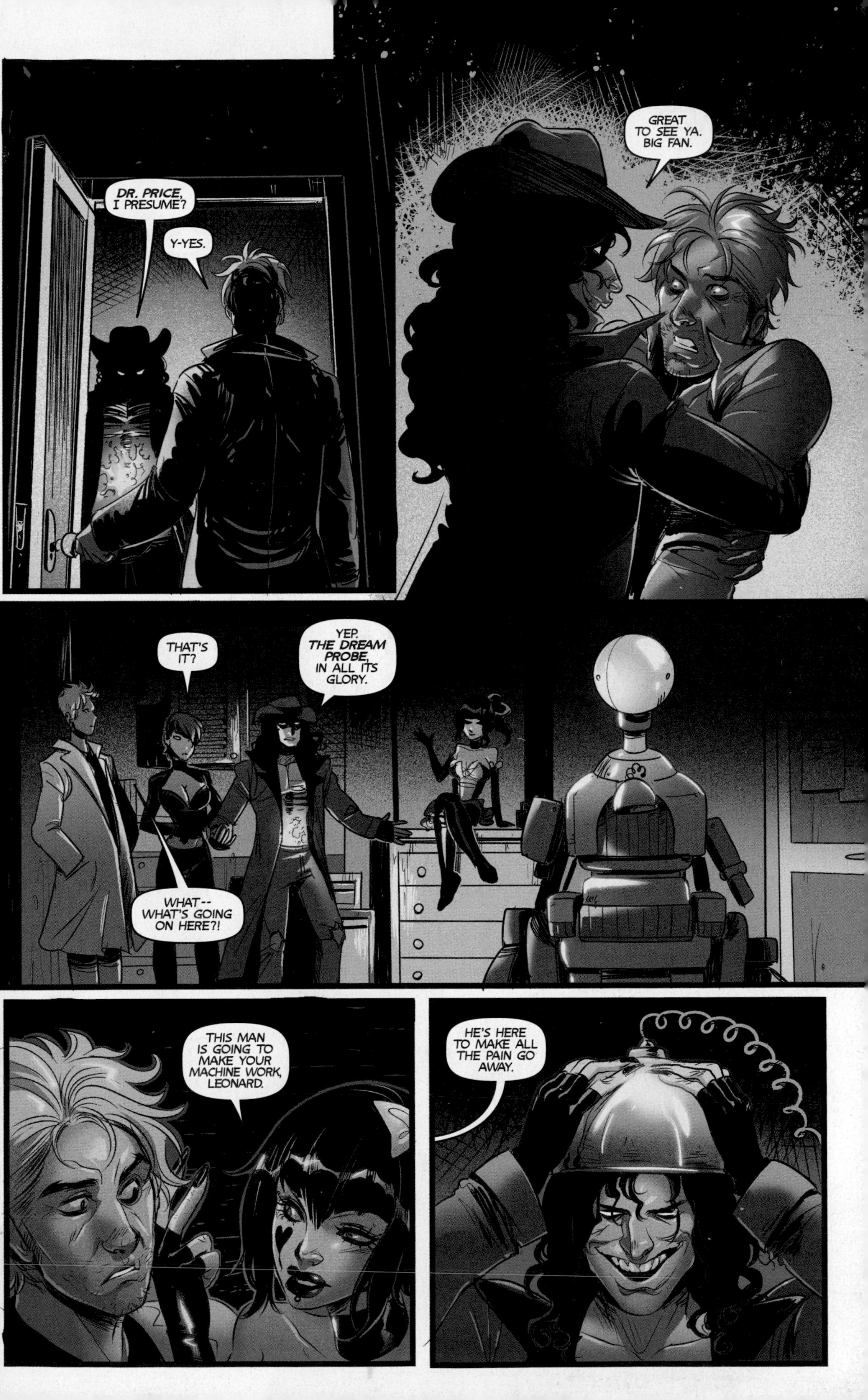
DR. PRICE, I PRESUME?
Y-YES.
GREAT TO SEE YA. BIG FAN.
THAT'S IT?
YEP. THE DREAM PROBE, IN ALL ITS GLORY.
WHAT-- WHAT'S GOING ON HERE?!
THIS MAN IS GOING TO MAKE YOUR MACHINE WORK, LEONARD.
HE'S HERE TO MAKE ALL THE PAIN GO AWAY.

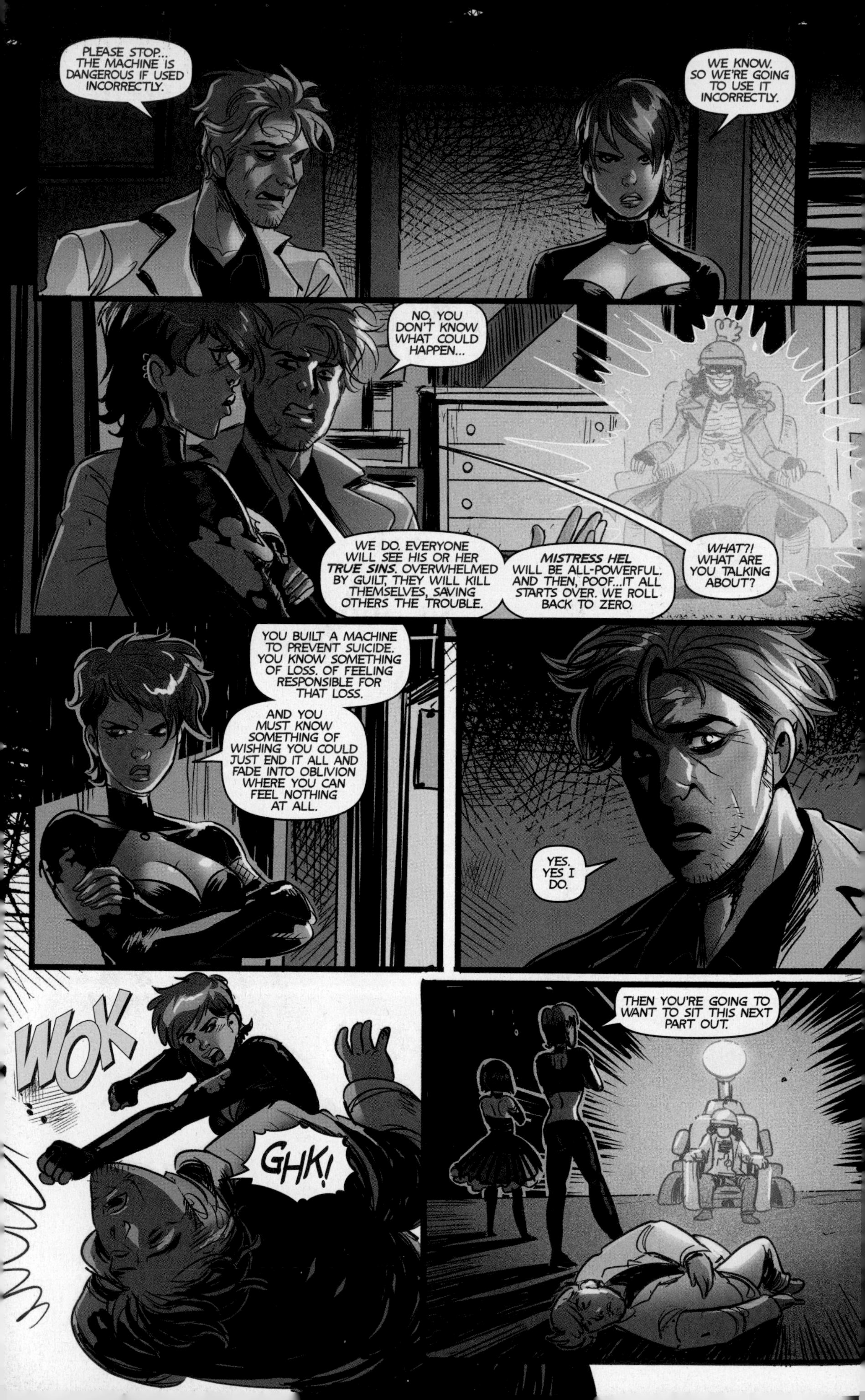
PLEASE STOP... THE MACHINE IS DANGEROUS IF USED INCORRECTLY.
WE KNOW. SO WE'RE GOING TO USE IT INCORRECTLY.
NO, YOU DON'T KNOW WHAT COULD HAPPEN...
WE DO. EVERYONE WILL SEE HIS OR HER TRUE SINS. OVERWHELMED BY GUILT, THEY WILL KILL THEMSELVES, SAVING OTHERS THE TROUBLE.
MISTRESS HEL WILL BE ALL-POWERFUL. AND THEN, POOF...IT ALL STARTS OVER. WE ROLL BACK TO ZERO.
WHAT?! WHAT ARE YOU TALKING ABOUT?
YOU BUILT A MACHINE TO PREVENT SUICIDE. YOU KNOW SOMETHING OF LOSS, OF FEELING RESPONSIBLE FOR THAT LOSS.
AND YOU MUST KNOW SOMETHING OF WISHING YOU COULD JUST END IT ALL AND FADE INTO OBLIVION WHERE YOU CAN FEEL NOTHING AT ALL.
YES. YES I DO.
WOK
GHK!
THEN YOU'RE GOING TO WANT TO SIT THIS NEXT PART OUT.

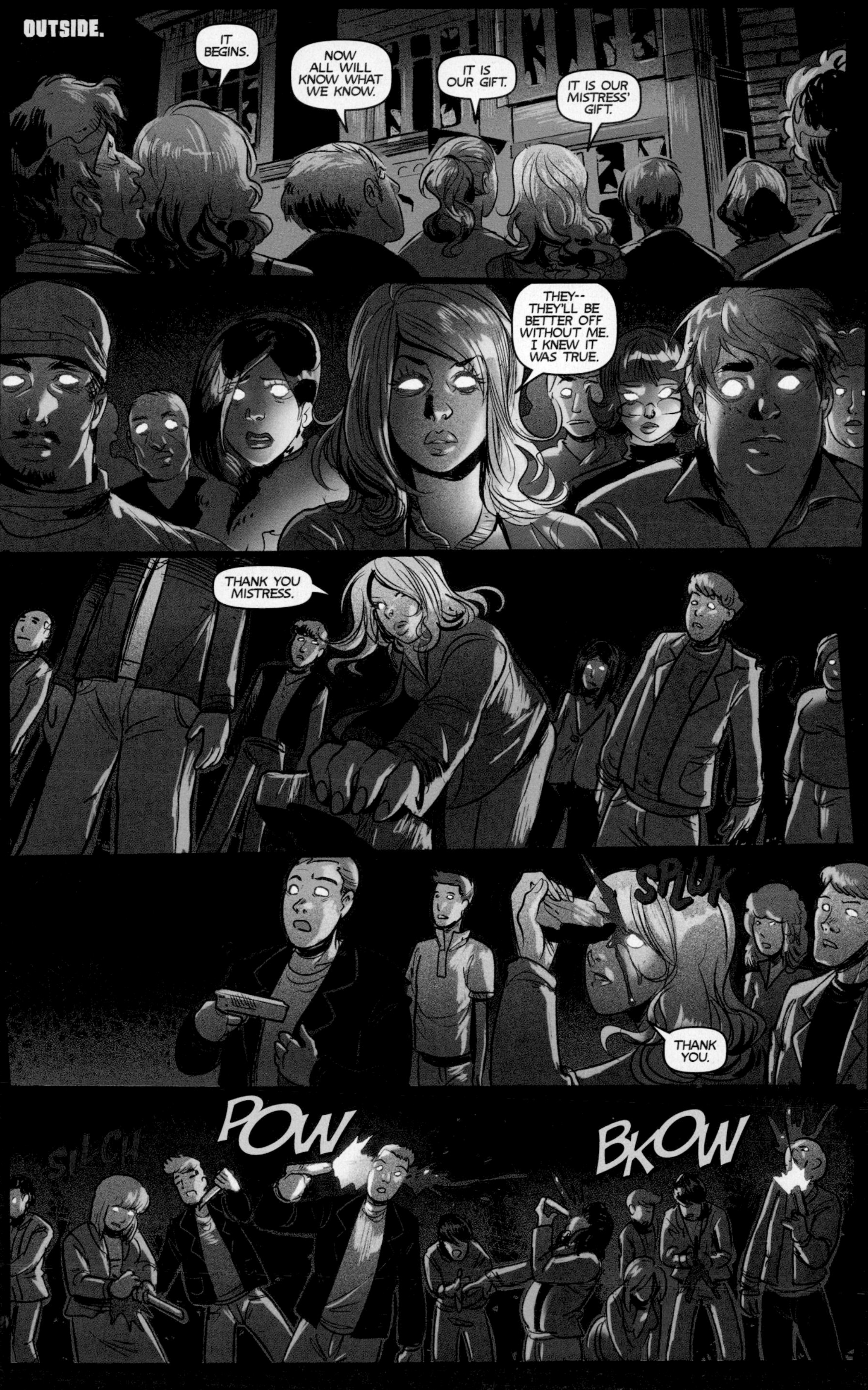
OUTSIDE.
IT BEGINS.
NOW ALL WILL KNOW WHAT WE KNOW.
IT IS OUR GIFT.
IT IS OUR MISTRESS' GIFT.
THEY-- THEY'LL BE BETTER OFF WITHOUT ME. I KNEW IT WAS TRUE.
THANK YOU MISTRESS.
SPLUK
THANK YOU.
POW
BKOW

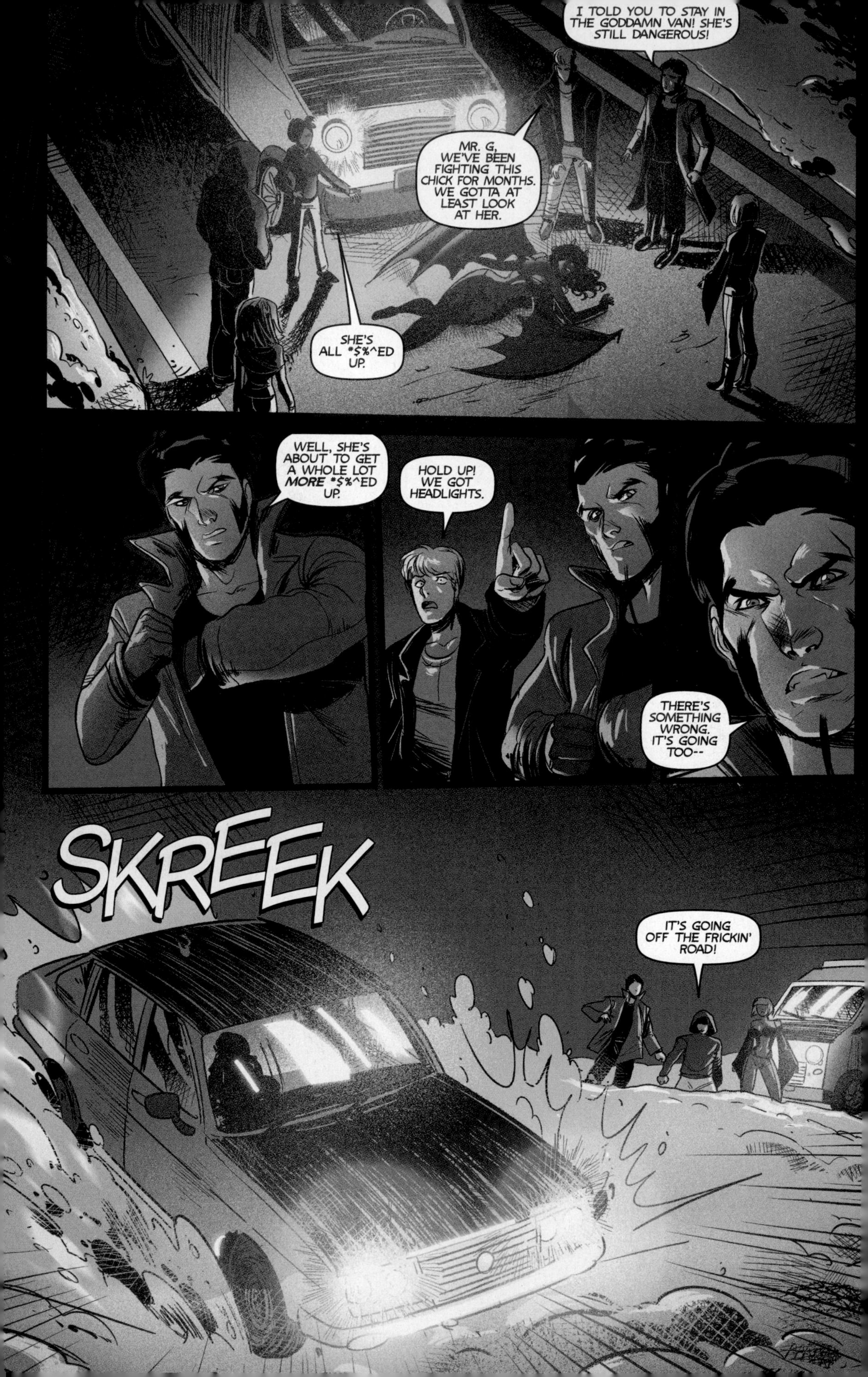
I TOLD YOU TO STAY IN THE GODDAMN VAN! SHE'S STILL DANGEROUS!
MR. G, WE'VE BEEN FIGHTING THIS CHICK FOR MONTHS. WE GOTTA AT LEAST LOOK AT HER.
SHE'S ALL *$%^ED UP.
WELL, SHE'S ABOUT TO GET A WHOLE LOT MORE *$%^ED UP.
HOLD UP! WE GOT HEADLIGHTS.
THERE'S SOMETHING WRONG. IT'S GOING TOO--
SKREEK
IT'S GOING OFF THE FRICKIN' ROAD!

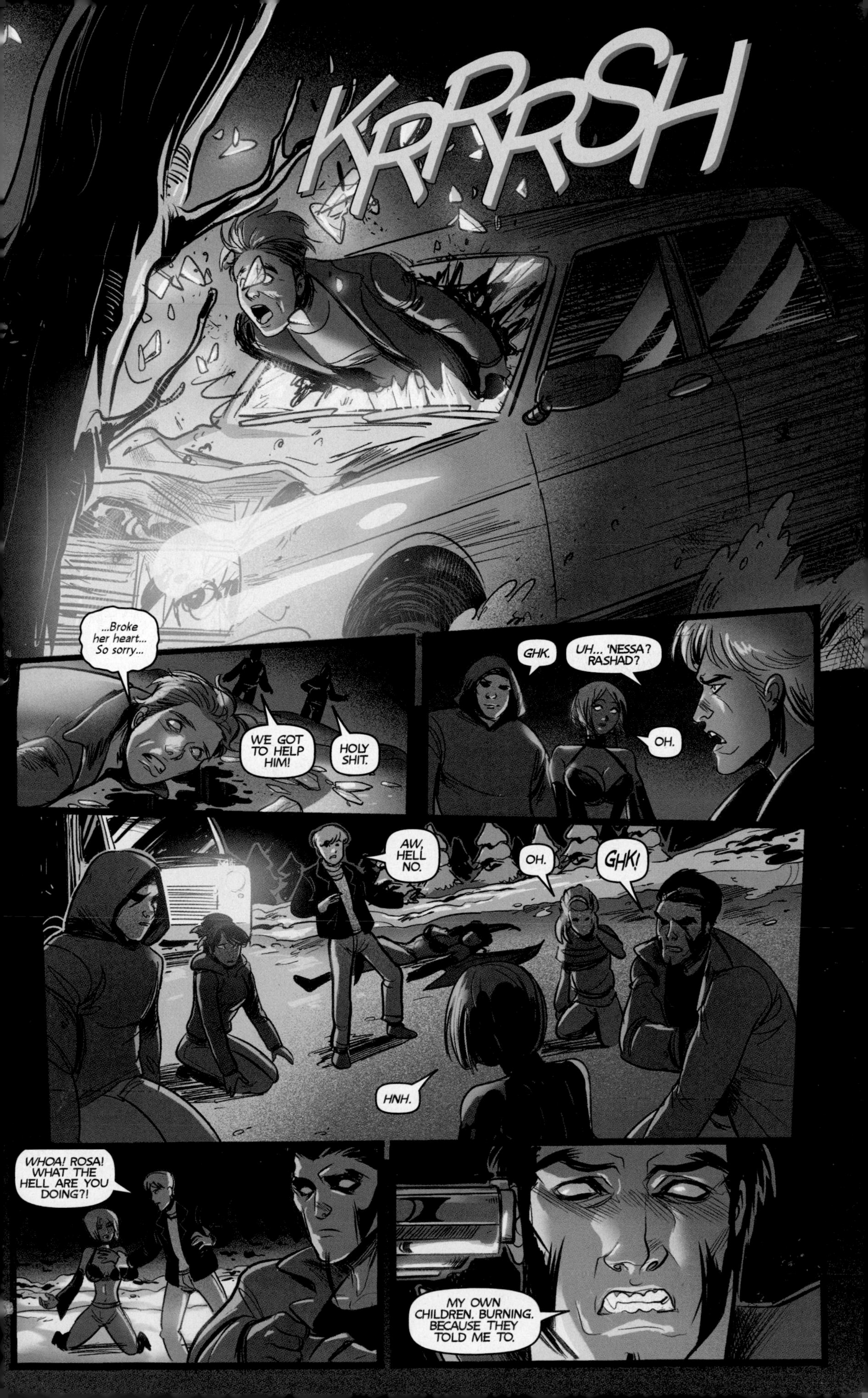
KRRRSH
...Broke her heart... So sorry...
WE GOT TO HELP HIM!
HOLY SHIT.
GHK.
UH... 'NESSA? RASHAD?
OH.
AW, HELL NO.
OH.
GHK!
HNH.
WHOA! ROSA! WHAT THE HELL ARE YOU DOING?!
MY OWN CHILDREN, BURNING. BECAUSE THEY TOLD ME TO.

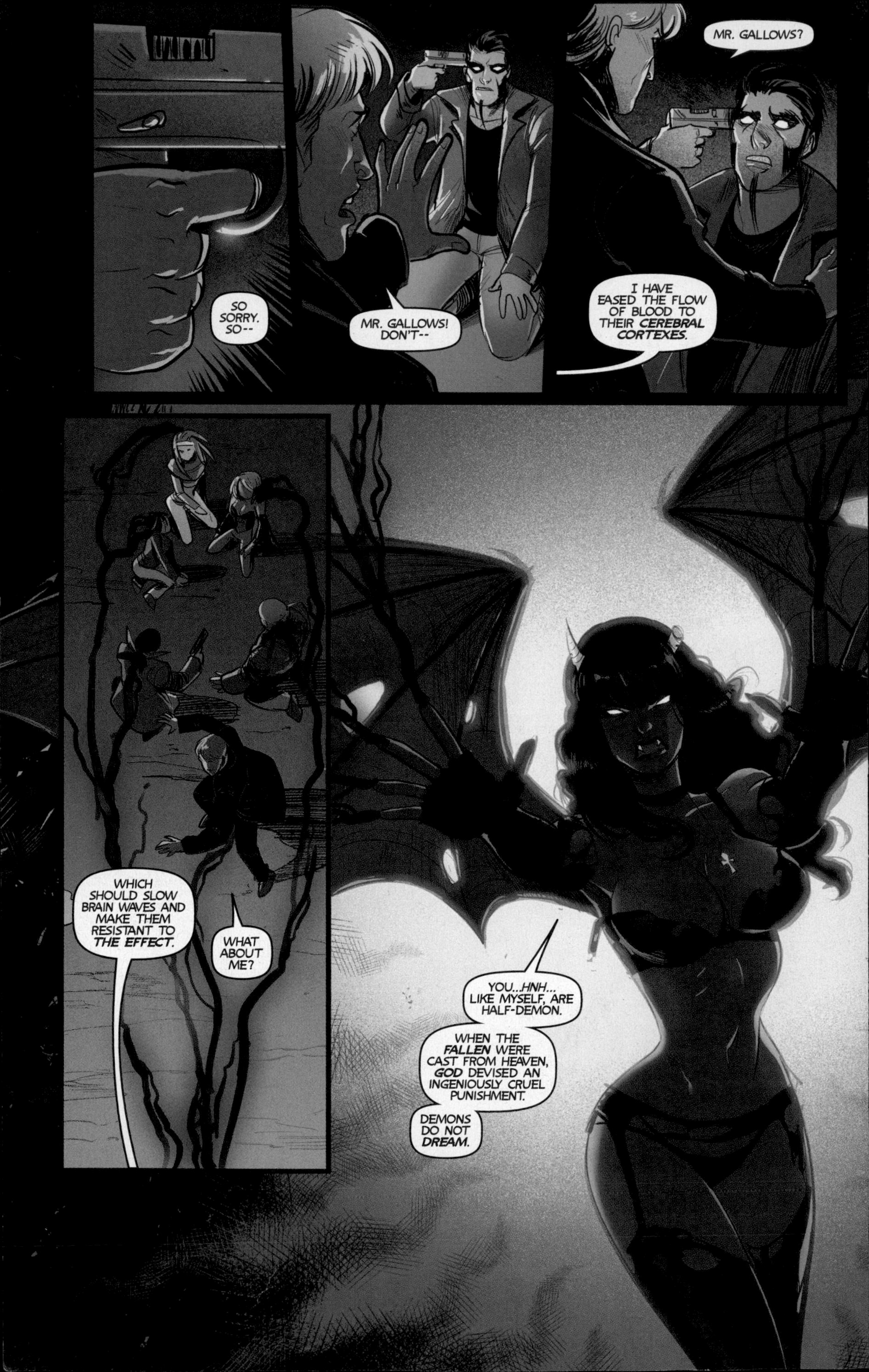
SO SORRY. SO--
MR. GALLOWS! DON'T--
MR. GALLOWS?
I HAVE EASED THE FLOW OF BLOOD TO THEIR CEREBRAL CORTEXES.
WHICH SHOULD SLOW BRAIN WAVES AND MAKE THEM RESISTANT TO THE EFFECT.
WHAT ABOUT ME?
YOU...HNH... LIKE MYSELF, ARE HALF-DEMON.
WHEN THE FALLEN WERE CAST FROM HEAVEN, GOD DEVISED AN INGENIOUSLY CRUEL PUNISHMENT.
DEMONS DO NOT DREAM.

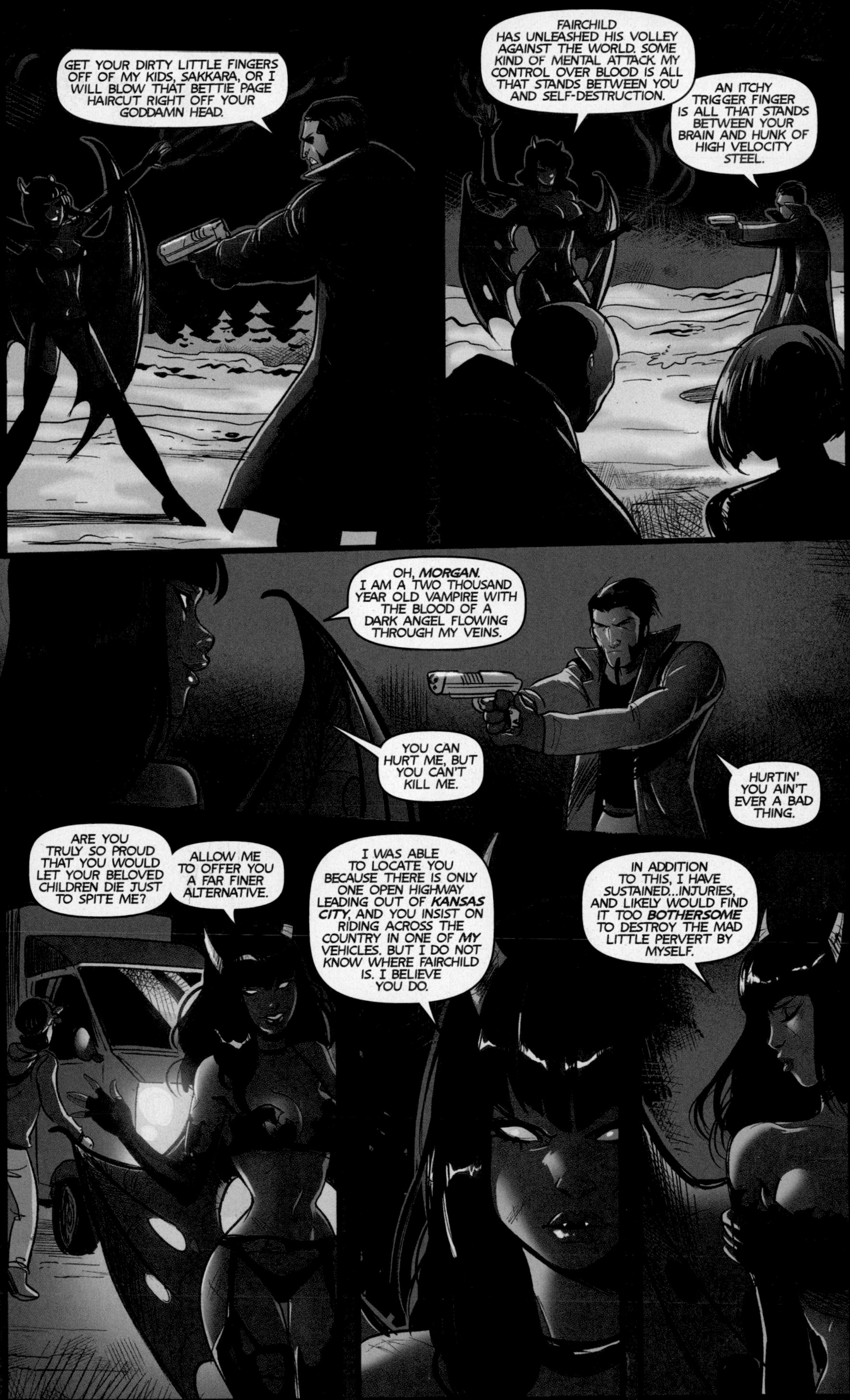
GET YOUR DIRTY LITTLE FINGERS OFF OF MY KIDS, SAKKARA, OR I WILL BLOW THAT BETTIE PAGE HAIRCUT RIGHT OFF YOUR GODDAMN HEAD.
FAIRCHILD HAS UNLEASHED HIS VOLLEY AGAINST THE WORLD. SOME KIND OF MENTAL ATTACK. MY CONTROL OVER BLOOD IS ALL THAT STANDS BETWEEN YOU AND SELF-DESTRUCTION.
AN ITCHY TRIGGER FINGER IS ALL THAT STANDS BETWEEN YOUR BRAIN AND HUNK OF HIGH VELOCITY STEEL.
OH, MORGAN. I AM A TWO THOUSAND YEAR OLD VAMPIRE WITH THE BLOOD OF A DARK ANGEL FLOWING THROUGH MY VEINS.
YOU CAN HURT ME, BUT YOU CAN'T KILL ME.
HURTIN' YOU AIN'T EVER A BAD THING.
ARE YOU TRULY SO PROUD THAT YOU WOULD LET YOUR BELOVED CHILDREN DIE JUST TO SPITE ME?
ALLOW ME TO OFFER YOU A FAR FINER ALTERNATIVE.
I WAS ABLE TO LOCATE YOU BECAUSE THERE IS ONLY ONE OPEN HIGHWAY LEADING OUT OF KANSAS CITY, AND YOU INSIST ON RIDING ACROSS THE COUNTRY IN ONE OF MY VEHICLES. BUT I DO NOT KNOW WHERE FAIRCHILD IS. I BELIEVE YOU DO.
IN ADDITION TO THIS, I HAVE SUSTAINED...INJURIES, AND LIKELY WOULD FIND IT TOO BOTHERSOME TO DESTROY THE MAD LITTLE PERVERT BY MYSELF.

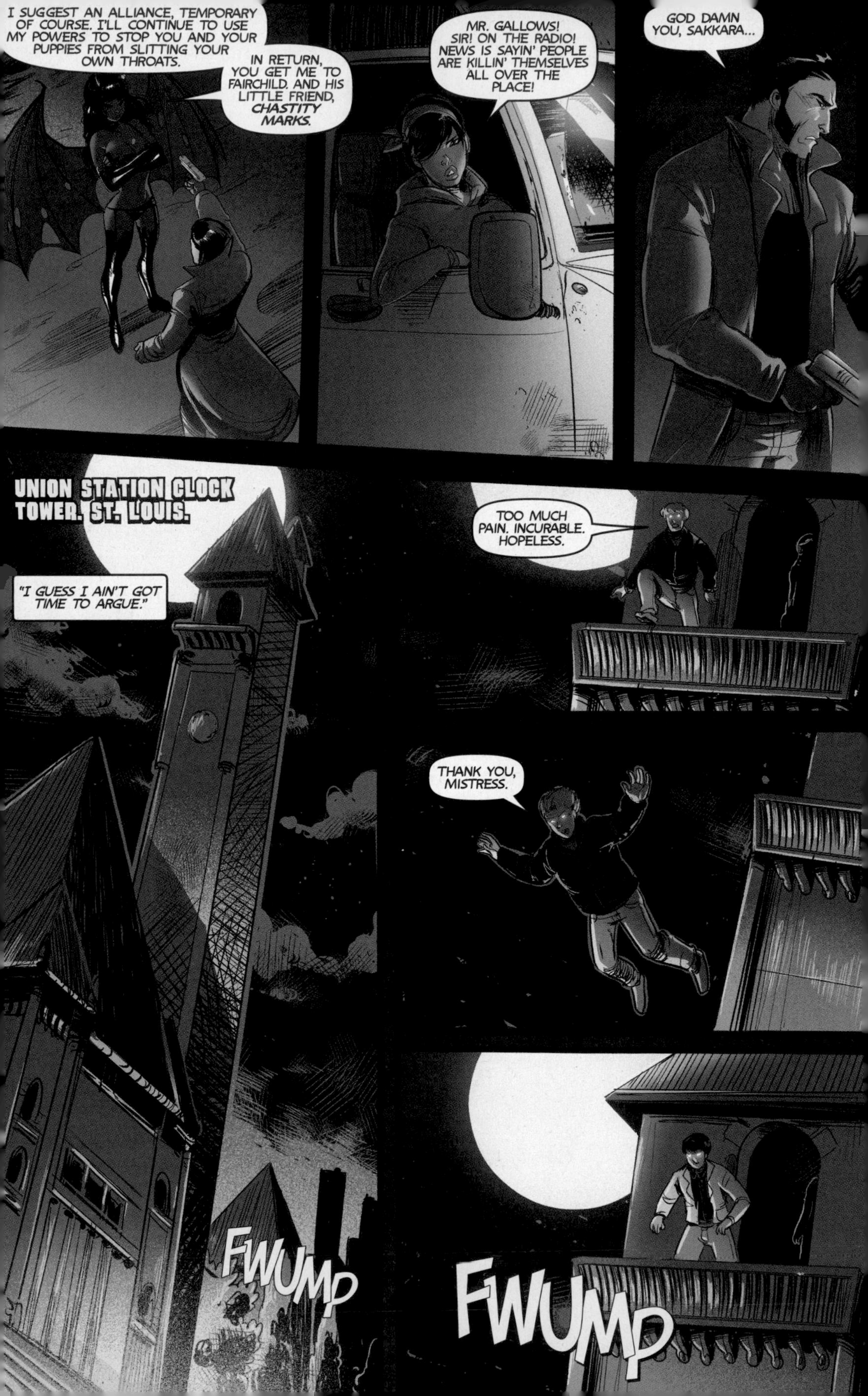
I SUGGEST AN ALLIANCE, TEMPORARY OF COURSE. I'LL CONTINUE TO USE MY POWERS TO STOP YOU AND YOUR PUPPIES FROM SLITTING YOUR OWN THROATS.
IN RETURN, YOU GET ME TO FAIRCHILD. AND HIS LITTLE FRIEND, *CHASTITY MARKS*.
MR. GALLOWS! SIR! ON THE RADIO! NEWS IS SAYIN' PEOPLE ARE KILLIN' THEMSELVES ALL OVER THE PLACE!
GOD DAMN YOU, SAKKARA...
UNION STATION CLOCK TOWER. ST. LOUIS.
"I GUESS I AIN'T GOT TIME TO ARGUE."
TOO MUCH PAIN. INCURABLE. HOPELESS.
THANK YOU, MISTRESS.
FWUMP
FWUMP

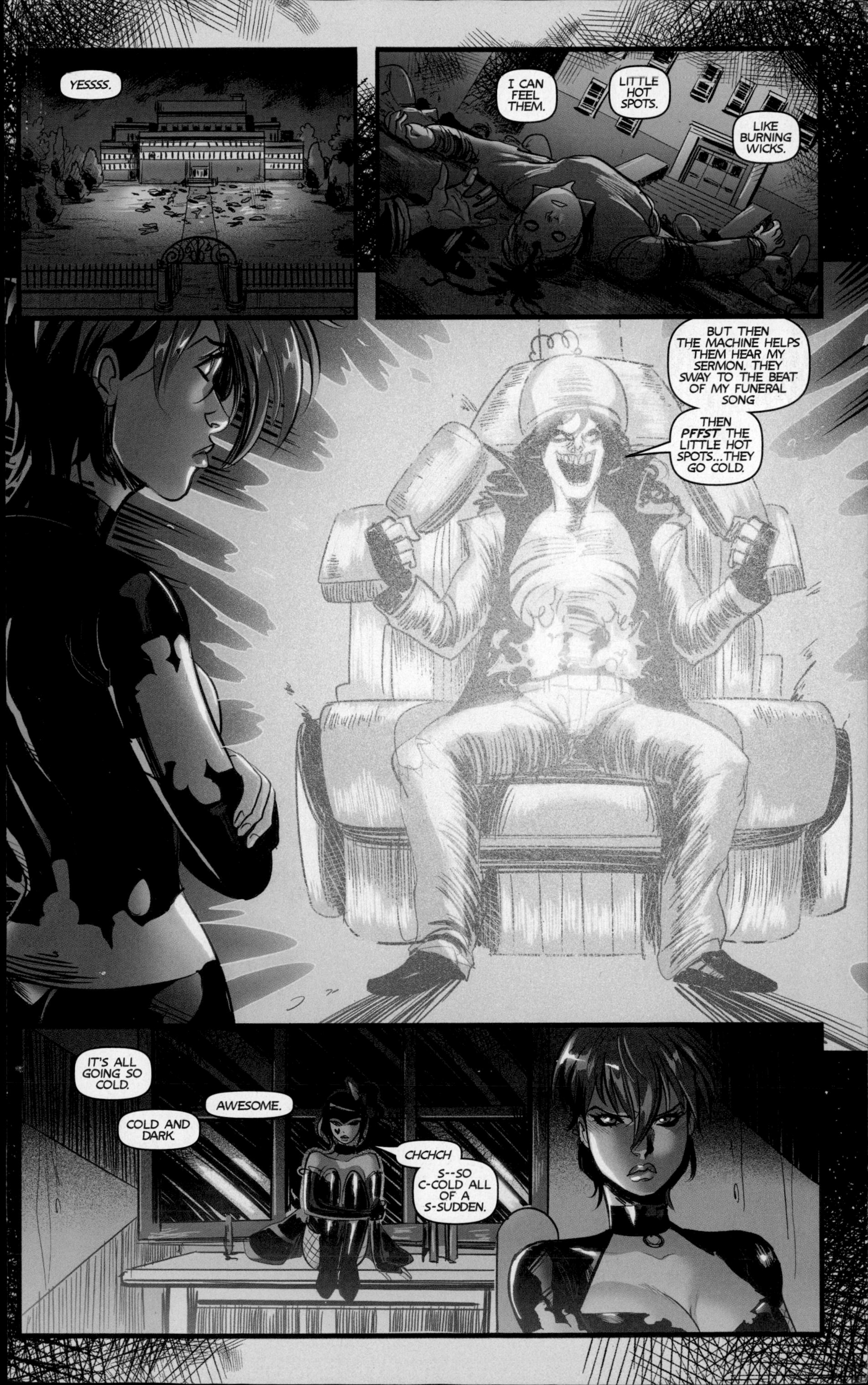

YESSSS.
I CAN FEEL THEM.
LITTLE HOT SPOTS.
LIKE BURNING WICKS.
BUT THEN THE MACHINE HELPS THEM HEAR MY SERMON. THEY SWAY TO THE BEAT OF MY FUNERAL SONG
THEN PFFST THE LITTLE HOT SPOTS...THEY GO COLD.
IT'S ALL GOING SO COLD.
COLD AND DARK.
AWESOME.
CHCHCH
S--SO C-COLD ALL OF A S-SUDDEN.

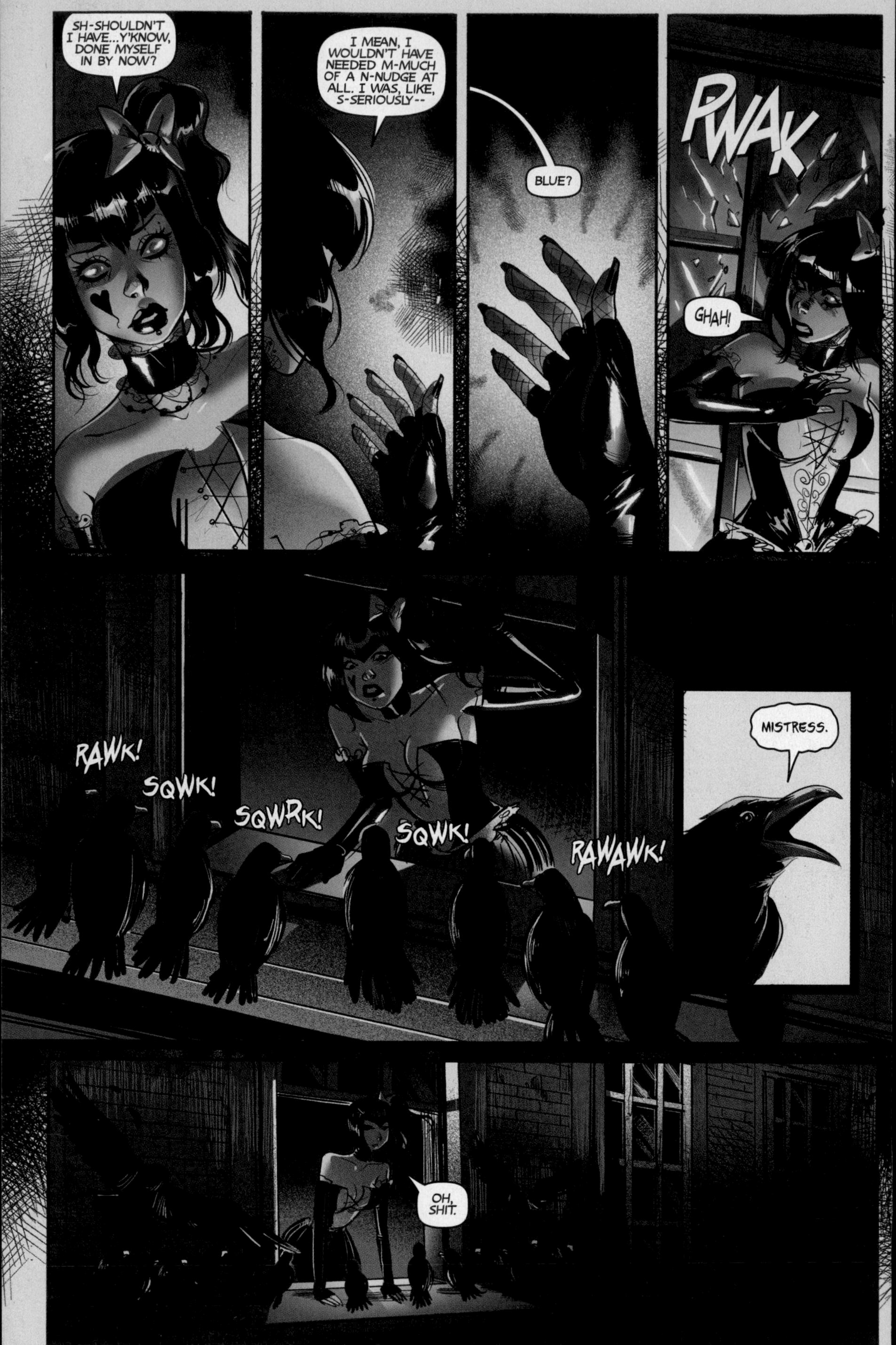
SH-SHOULDN'T I HAVE...Y'KNOW, DONE MYSELF IN BY NOW?
I MEAN, I WOULDN'T HAVE NEEDED M-MUCH OF A N-NUDGE AT ALL. I WAS, LIKE, S-SERIOUSLY--
BLUE?
PWAK
GHAH!
RAWK!
SQWK!
SQWRK!
SQWK!
RAWAWK!
MISTRESS.
OH, SHIT.

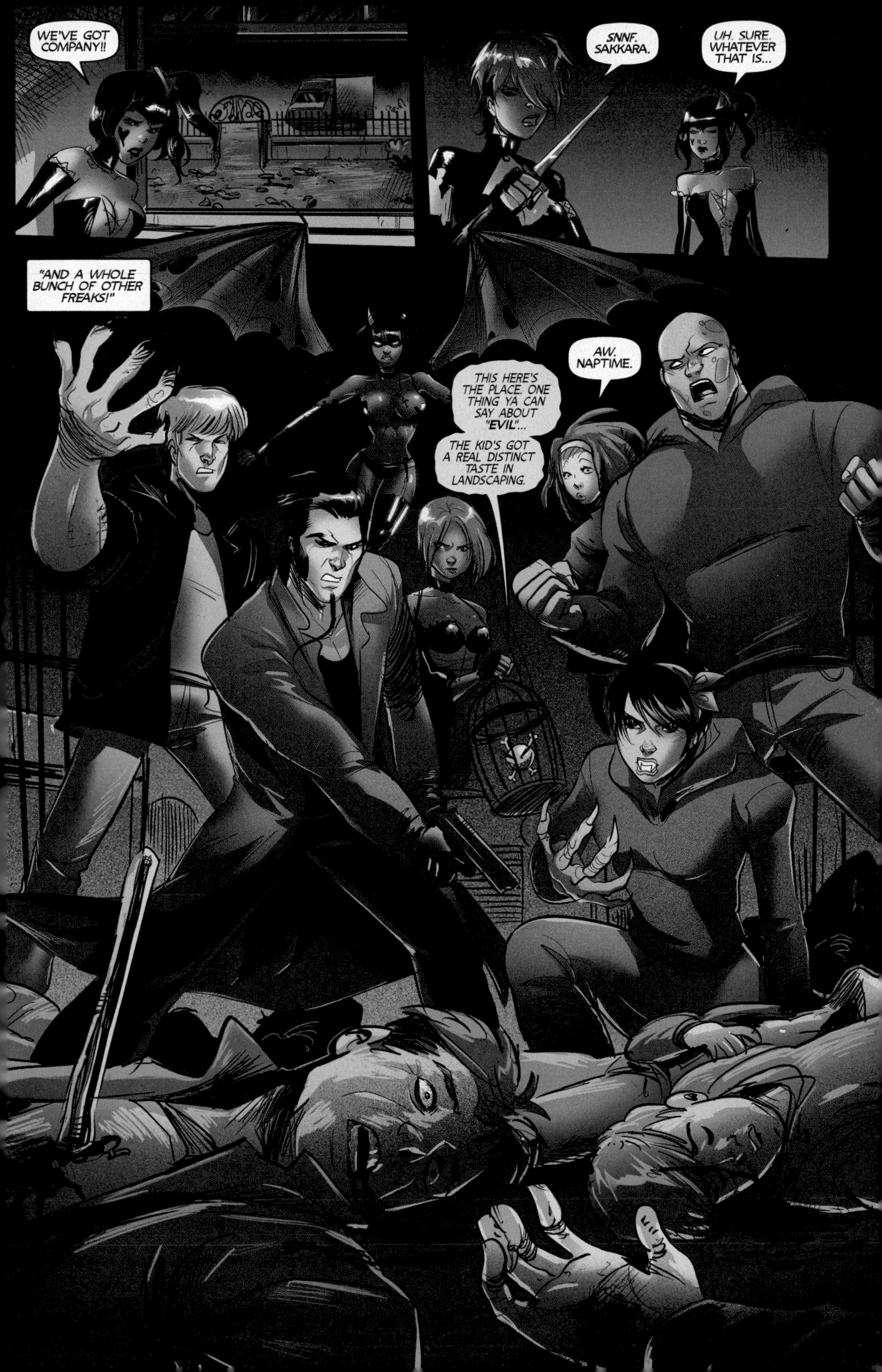
WE'VE GOT COMPANY!!
SNNF. SAKKARA.
UH, SURE. WHATEVER THAT IS...
"AND A WHOLE BUNCH OF OTHER FREAKS!"
THIS HERE'S THE PLACE. ONE THING YA CAN SAY ABOUT "EVIL"...
THE KID'S GOT A REAL DISTINCT TASTE IN LANDSCAPING.
AW. NAPTIME.

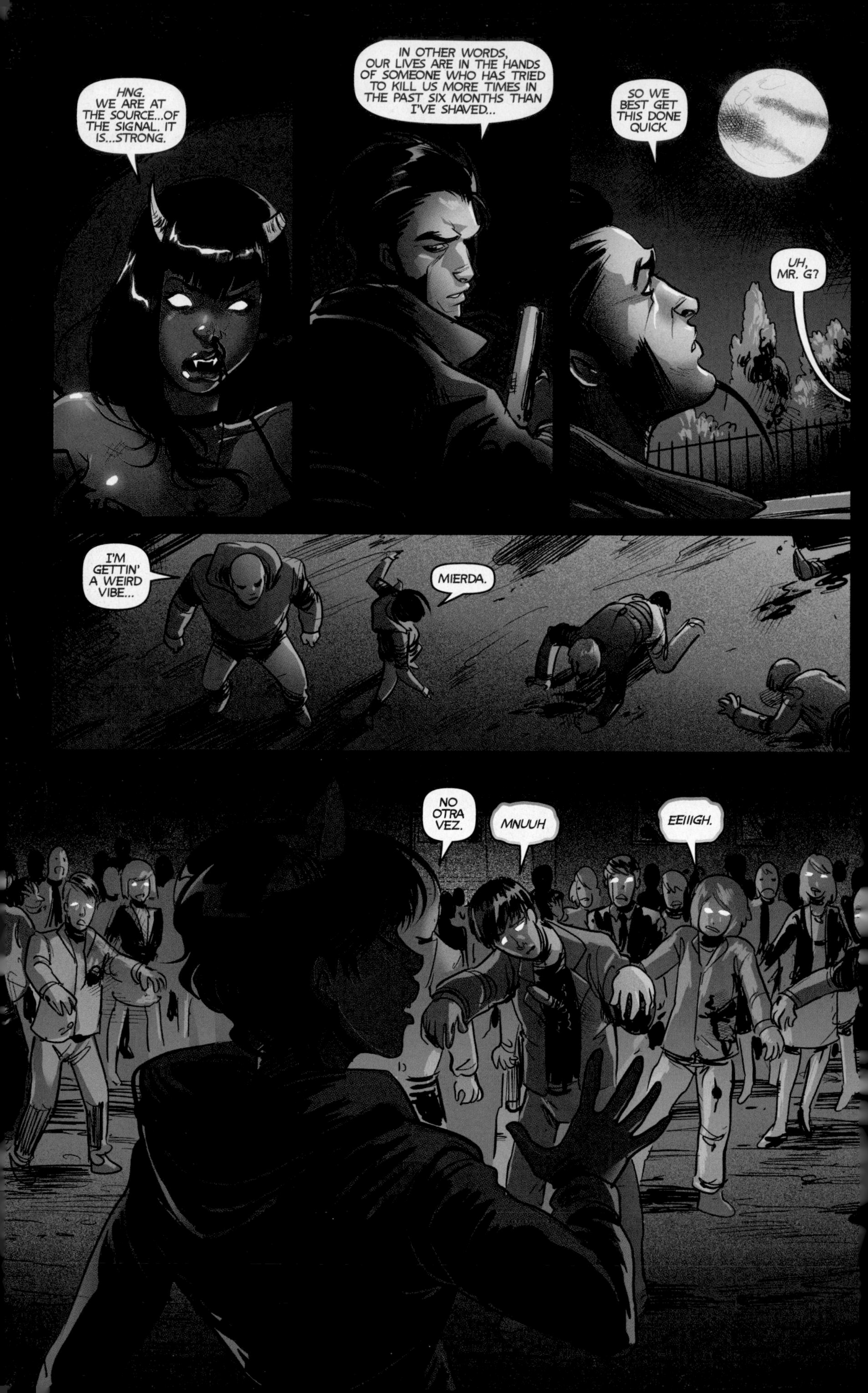
HNG. WE ARE AT THE SOURCE...OF THE SIGNAL. IT IS...STRONG.
IN OTHER WORDS, OUR LIVES ARE IN THE HANDS OF SOMEONE WHO HAS TRIED TO KILL US MORE TIMES IN THE PAST SIX MONTHS THAN I'VE SHAVED...
SO WE BEST GET THIS DONE QUICK.
UH, MR. G?
I'M GETTIN' A WEIRD VIBE...
MIERDA.
NO OTRA VEZ.
MNUUH
EEIIIGH.

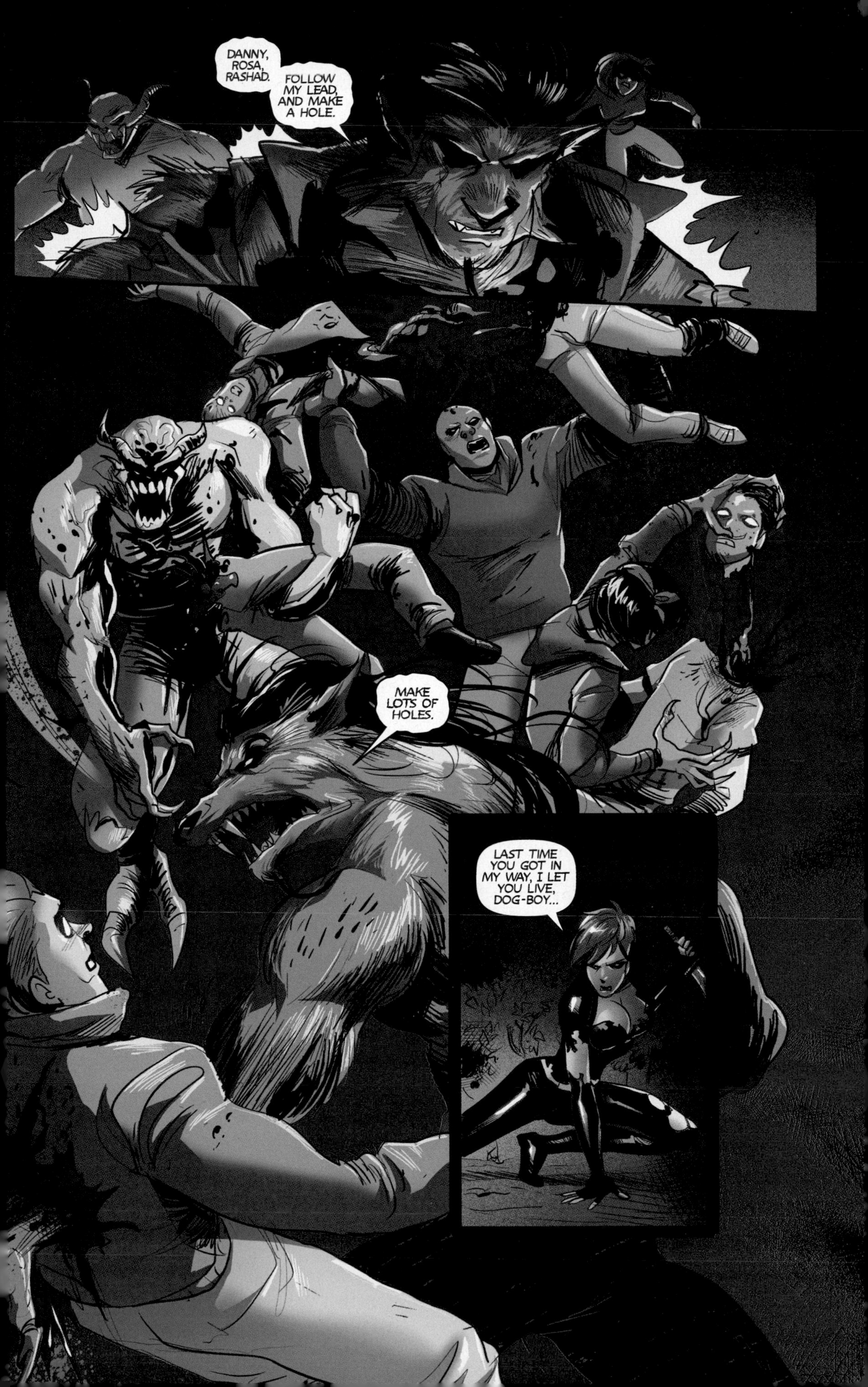
DANNY, ROSA, RASHAD.
FOLLOW MY LEAD, AND MAKE A HOLE.
MAKE LOTS OF HOLES.
LAST TIME YOU GOT IN MY WAY, I LET YOU LIVE, DOG-BOY...

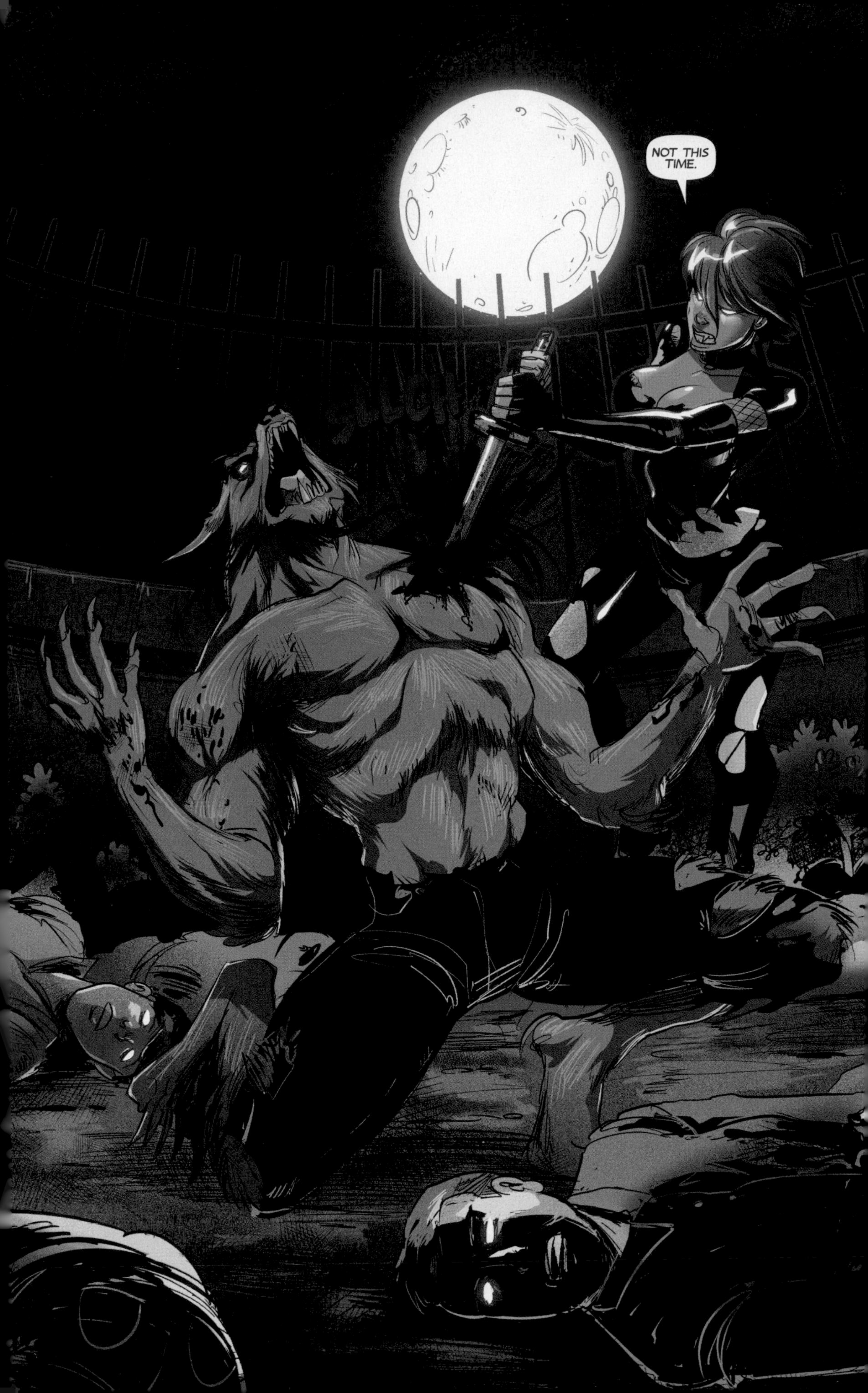
NOT THIS TIME.

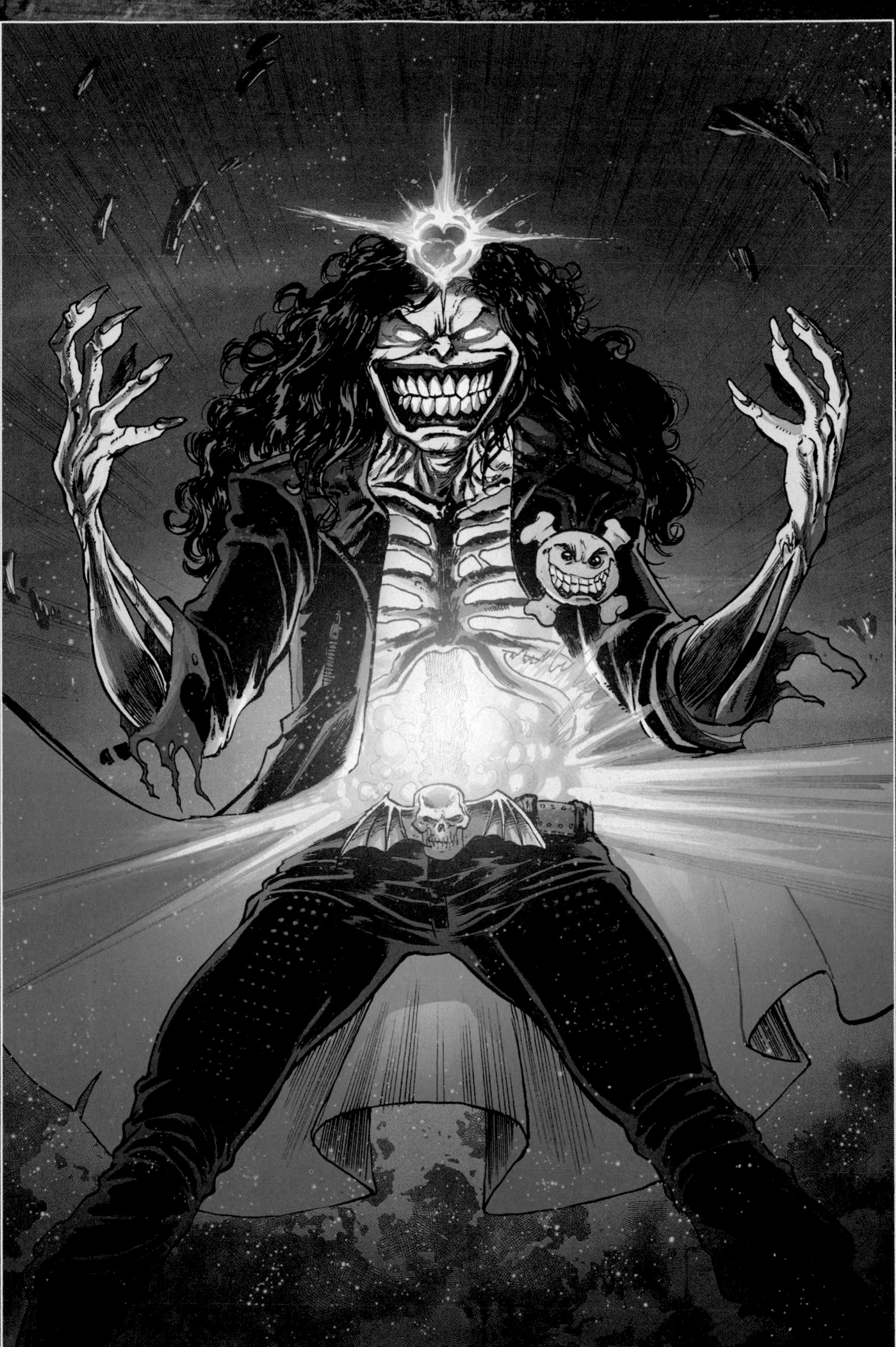

issue #6 cover by TIM SEELEY
colors by ADRIANO LUCAS

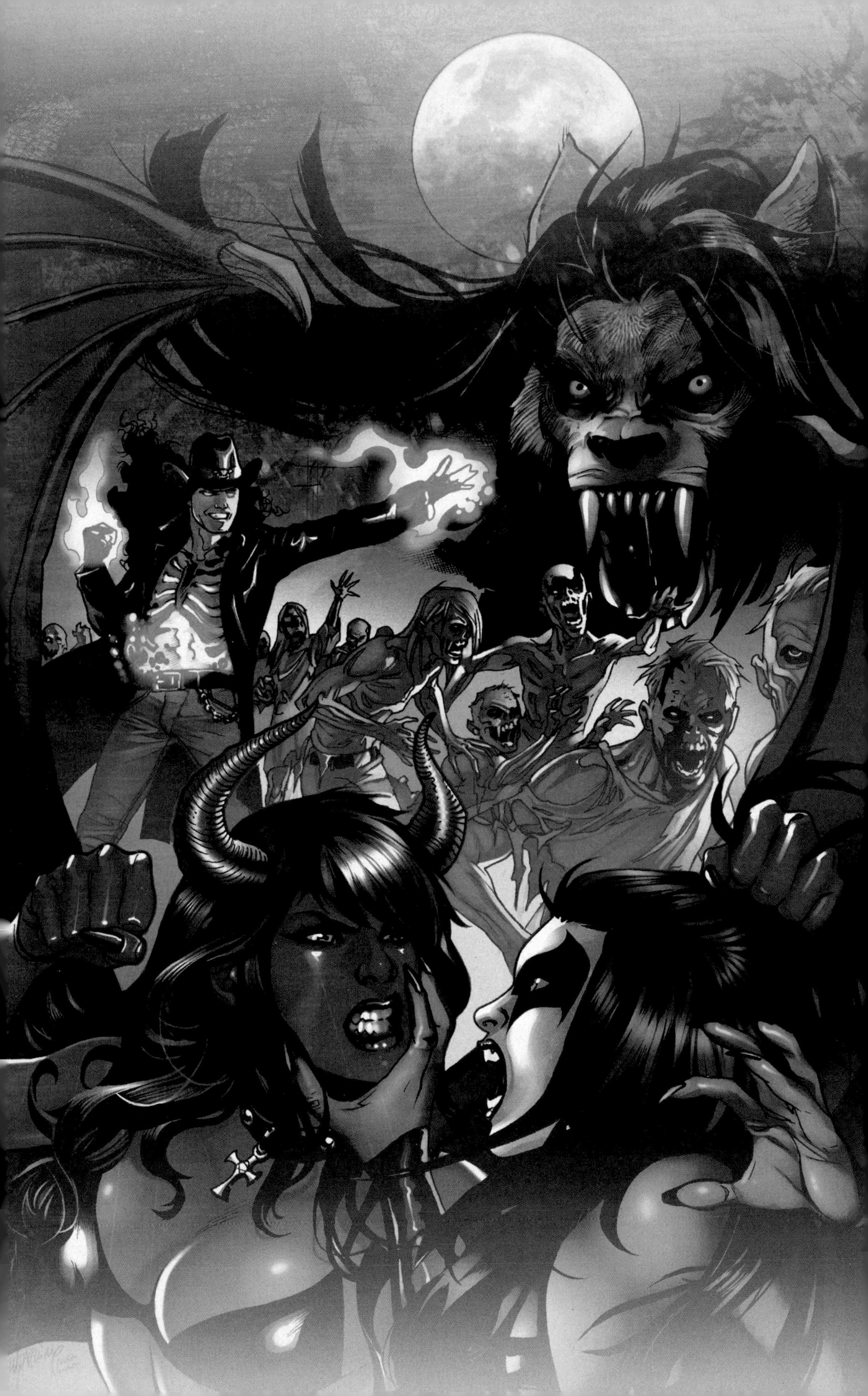

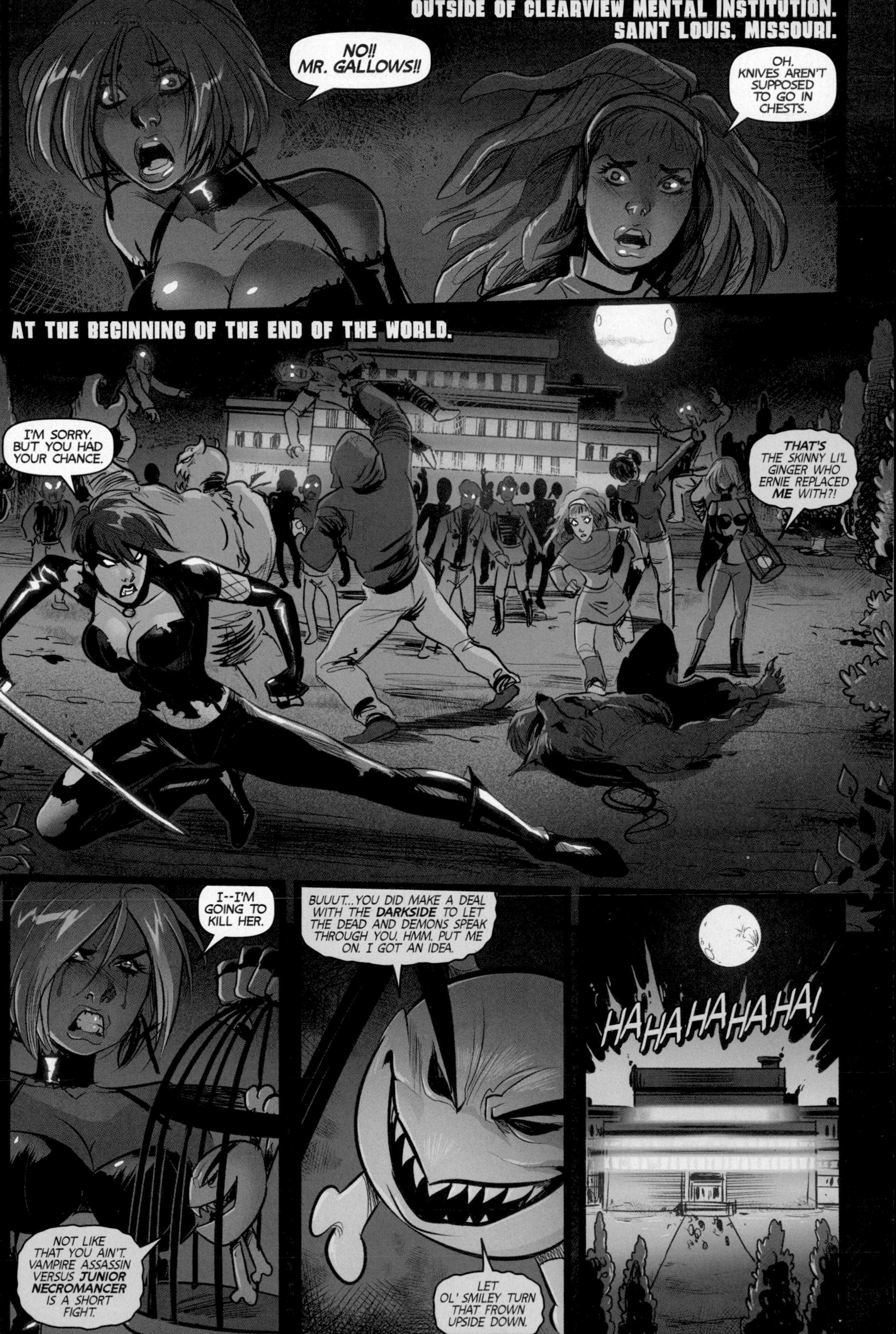
OUTSIDE OF CLEARVIEW MENTAL INSTITUTION.
SAINT LOUIS, MISSOURI.
NO!! MR. GALLOWS!!
OH. KNIVES AREN'T SUPPOSED TO GO IN CHESTS.
AT THE BEGINNING OF THE END OF THE WORLD.
I'M SORRY. BUT YOU HAD YOUR CHANCE.
THAT'S THE SKINNY LI'L GINGER WHO ERNIE REPLACED ME WITH?!
I--I'M GOING TO KILL HER.
NOT LIKE THAT YOU AIN'T. VAMPIRE ASSASSIN VERSUS JUNIOR NECROMANCER IS A SHORT FIGHT.
BUUUT...YOU DID MAKE A DEAL WITH THE DARKSIDE TO LET THE DEAD AND DEMONS SPEAK THROUGH YOU. HMM. PUT ME ON. I GOT AN IDEA.
LET OL' SMILEY TURN THAT FROWN UPSIDE DOWN.
HAHAHAHAHA!

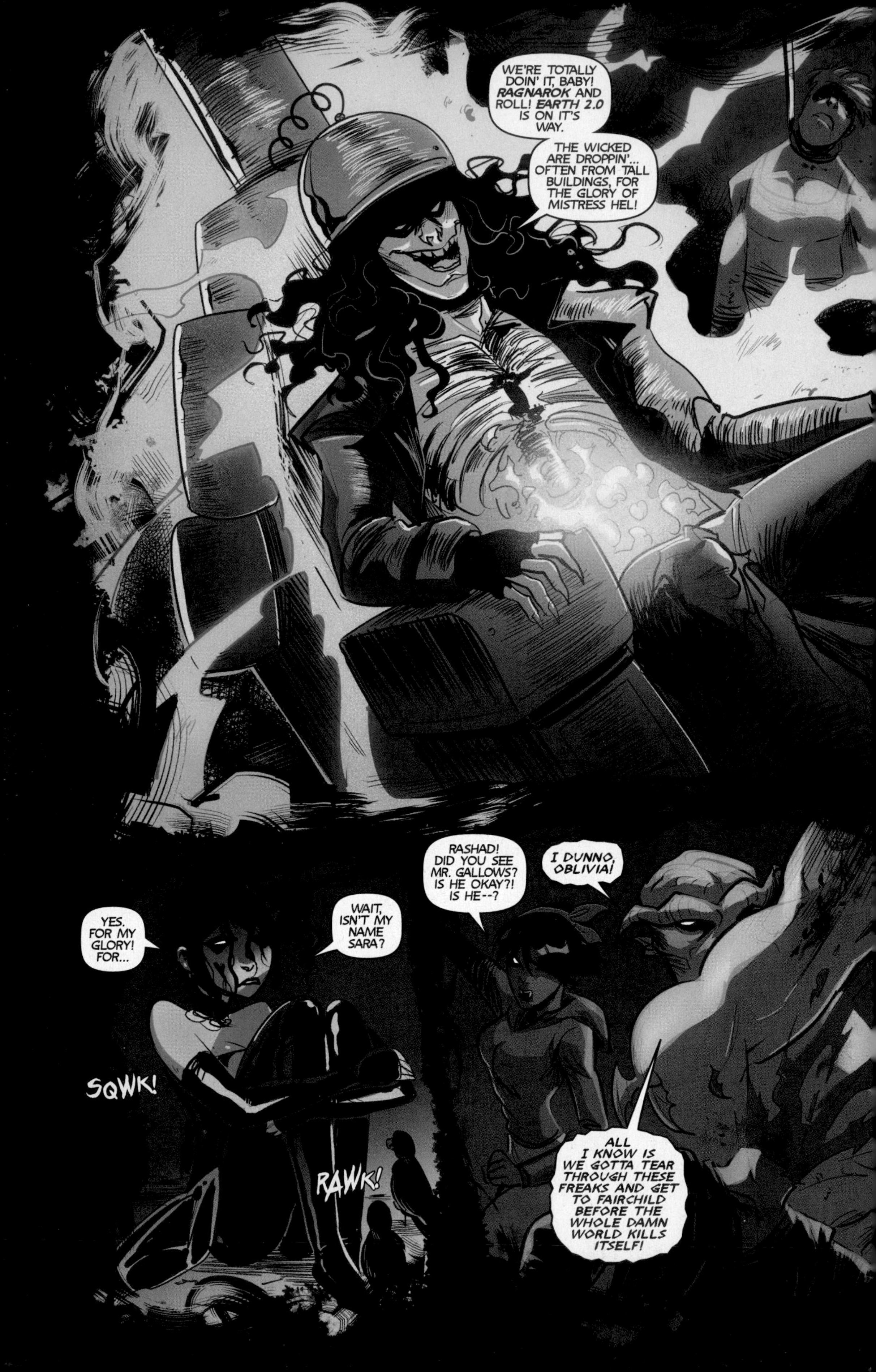
WE'RE TOTALLY DOIN' IT, BABY! RAGNAROK AND ROLL! EARTH 2.0 IS ON IT'S WAY.
THE WICKED ARE DROPPIN'... OFTEN FROM TALL BUILDINGS, FOR THE GLORY OF MISTRESS HEL!
YES. FOR MY GLORY! FOR...
WAIT, ISN'T MY NAME SARA?
RASHAD! DID YOU SEE MR. GALLOWS? IS HE OKAY?! IS HE--?
I DUNNO, OBLIVIA!
ALL I KNOW IS WE GOTTA TEAR THROUGH THESE FREAKS AND GET TO FAIRCHILD BEFORE THE WHOLE DAMN WORLD KILLS ITSELF!
SQWK!
RAWK!

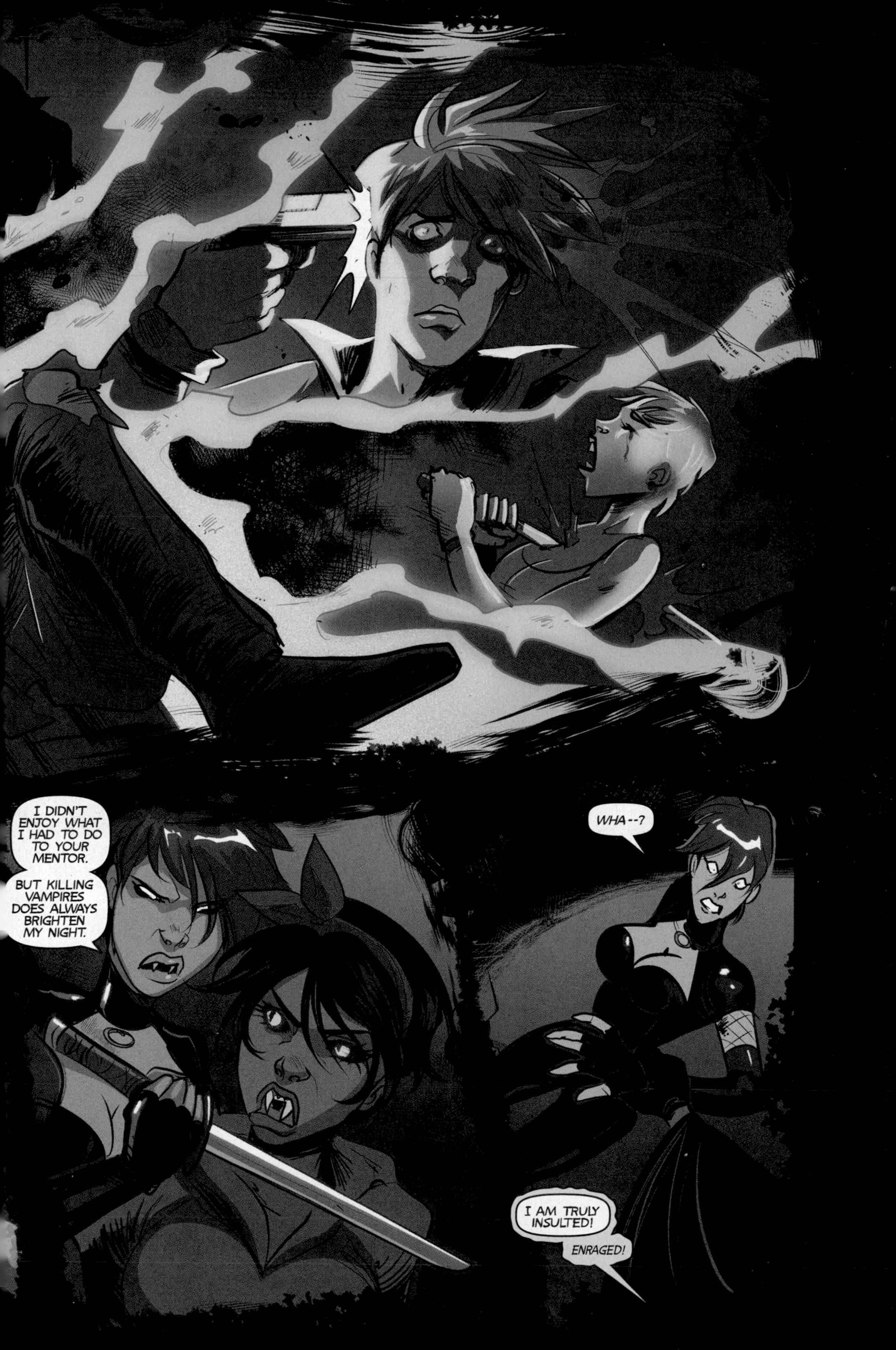
I DIDN'T ENJOY WHAT I HAD TO DO TO YOUR MENTOR.
BUT KILLING VAMPIRES DOES ALWAYS BRIGHTEN MY NIGHT.
WHA--?
I AM TRULY INSULTED!
ENRAGED!

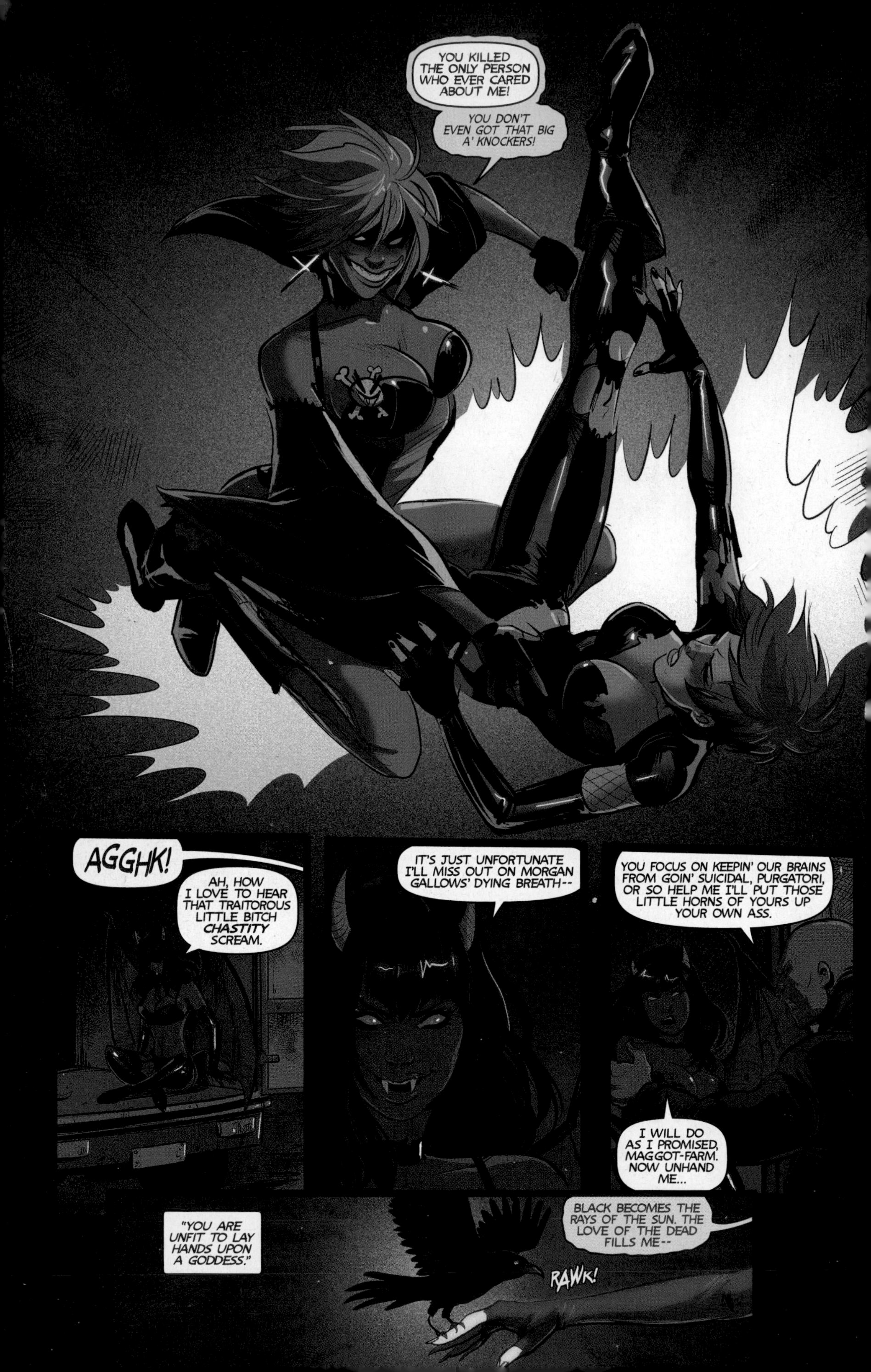
YOU KILLED THE ONLY PERSON WHO EVER CARED ABOUT ME!
YOU DON'T EVEN GOT THAT BIG A' KNOCKERS!
AGGHK!
AH, HOW I LOVE TO HEAR THAT TRAITOROUS LITTLE BITCH CHASTITY SCREAM.
IT'S JUST UNFORTUNATE I'LL MISS OUT ON MORGAN GALLOWS' DYING BREATH--
YOU FOCUS ON KEEPIN' OUR BRAINS FROM GOIN' SUICIDAL, PURGATORI, OR SO HELP ME I'LL PUT THOSE LITTLE HORNS OF YOURS UP YOUR OWN ASS.
I WILL DO AS I PROMISED, MAGGOT-FARM. NOW UNHAND ME...
"YOU ARE UNFIT TO LAY HANDS UPON A GODDESS."
BLACK BECOMES THE RAYS OF THE SUN. THE LOVE OF THE DEAD FILLS ME--
RAWK!

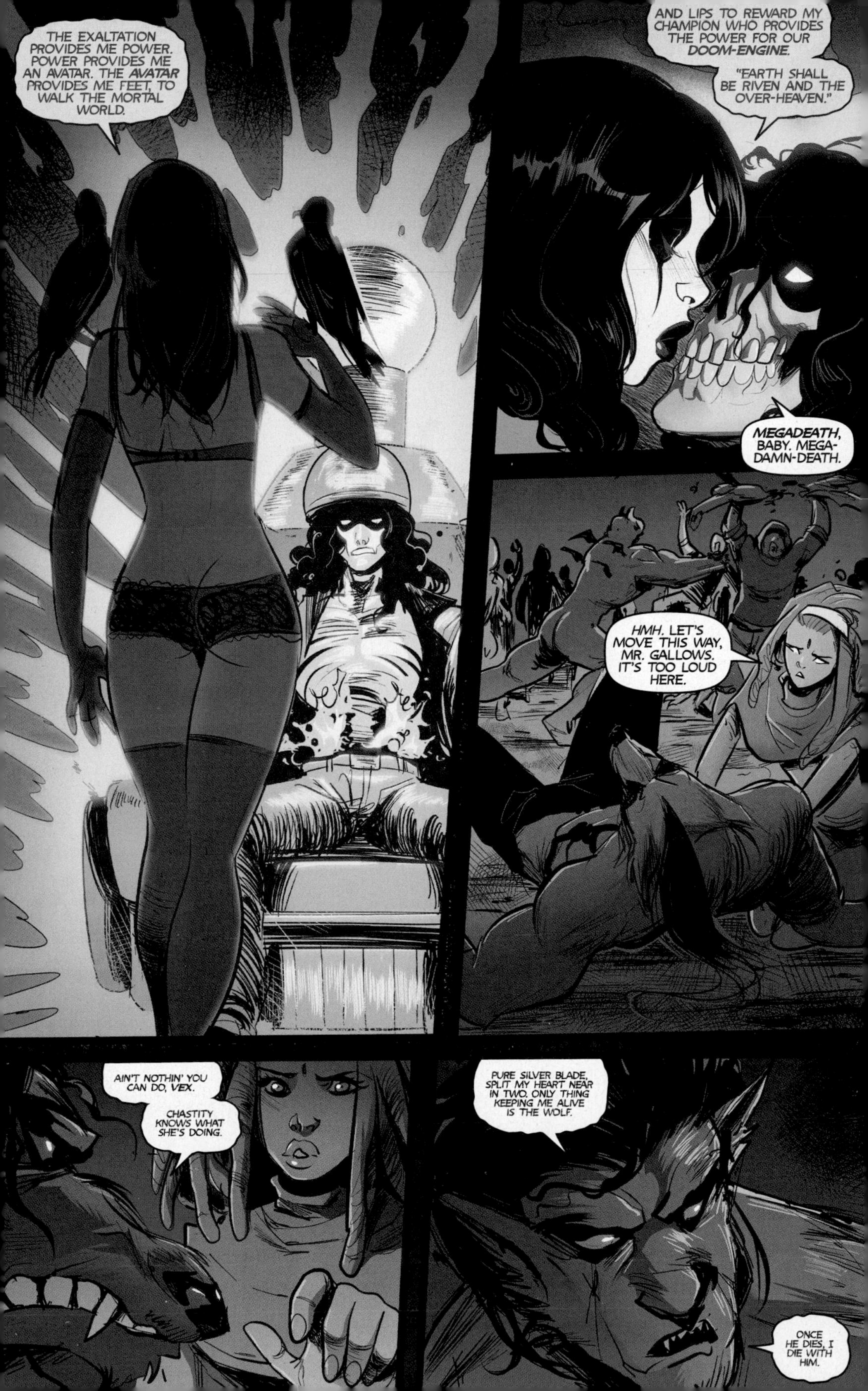
THE EXALTATION PROVIDES ME POWER. POWER PROVIDES ME AN AVATAR. THE *AVATAR* PROVIDES ME FEET, TO WALK THE MORTAL WORLD.
AND LIPS TO REWARD MY CHAMPION WHO PROVIDES THE POWER FOR OUR *DOOM-ENGINE.*
"EARTH SHALL BE RIVEN AND THE OVER-HEAVEN."
MEGADEATH, BABY. MEGA-DAMN-DEATH.
HMH. LET'S MOVE THIS WAY, MR. GALLOWS. IT'S TOO LOUD HERE.
AIN'T NOTHIN' YOU CAN DO, *VEX*.
CHASTITY KNOWS WHAT SHE'S DOING.
PURE SILVER BLADE, SPLIT MY HEART NEAR IN TWO. ONLY THING KEEPING ME ALIVE IS THE WOLF.
ONCE HE DIES, I DIE WITH HIM.

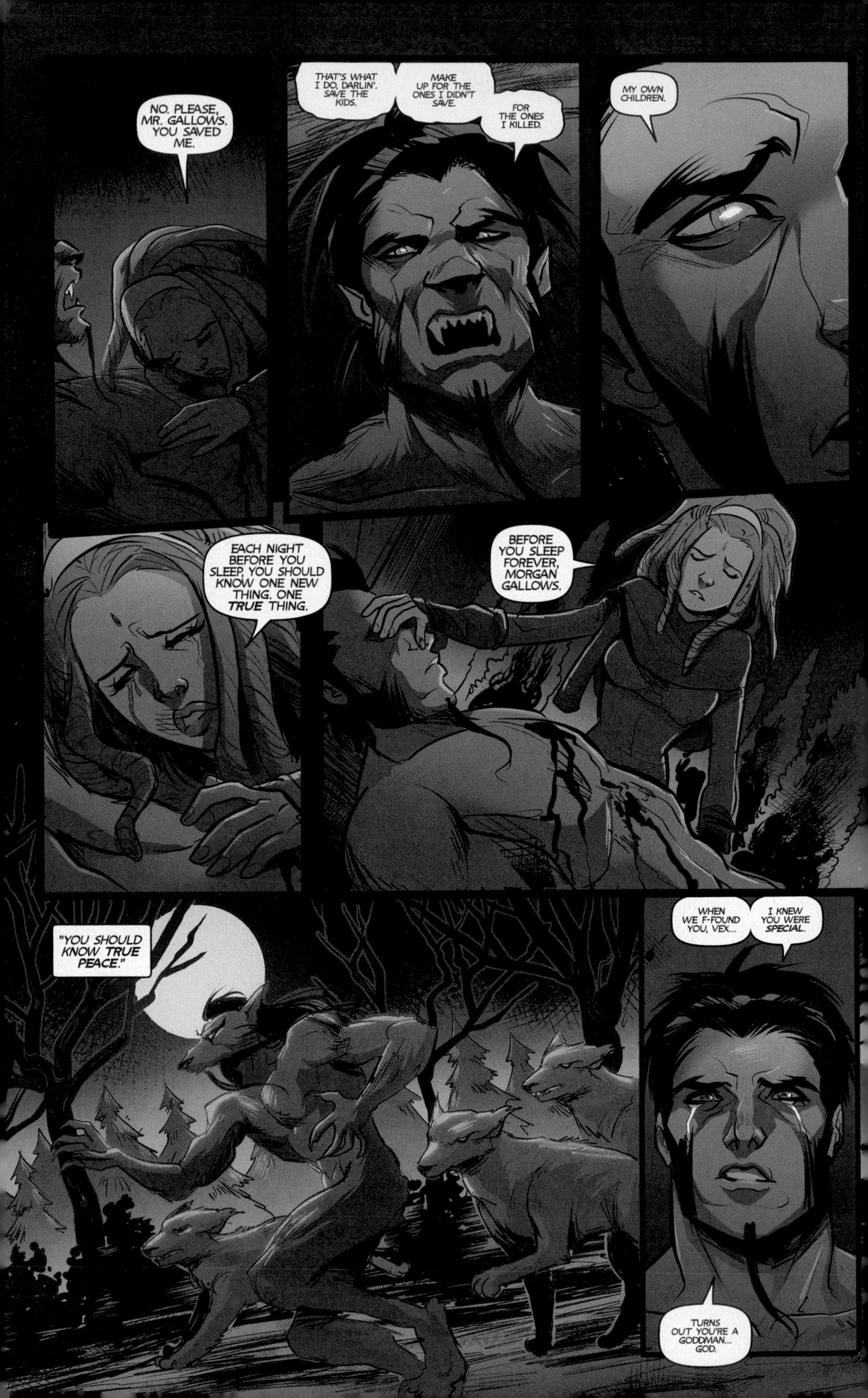
NO. PLEASE, MR. GALLOWS. YOU SAVED ME.
THAT'S WHAT I DO, DARLIN'. SAVE THE KIDS.
MAKE UP FOR THE ONES I DIDN'T SAVE.
FOR THE ONES I KILLED.
MY OWN CHILDREN.
EACH NIGHT BEFORE YOU SLEEP, YOU SHOULD KNOW ONE NEW THING. ONE TRUE THING.
BEFORE YOU SLEEP FOREVER, MORGAN GALLOWS.
"YOU SHOULD KNOW TRUE PEACE."
WHEN WE F-FOUND YOU, VEX...
I KNEW YOU WERE SPECIAL.
TURNS OUT YOU'RE A GODDMAN... GOD.

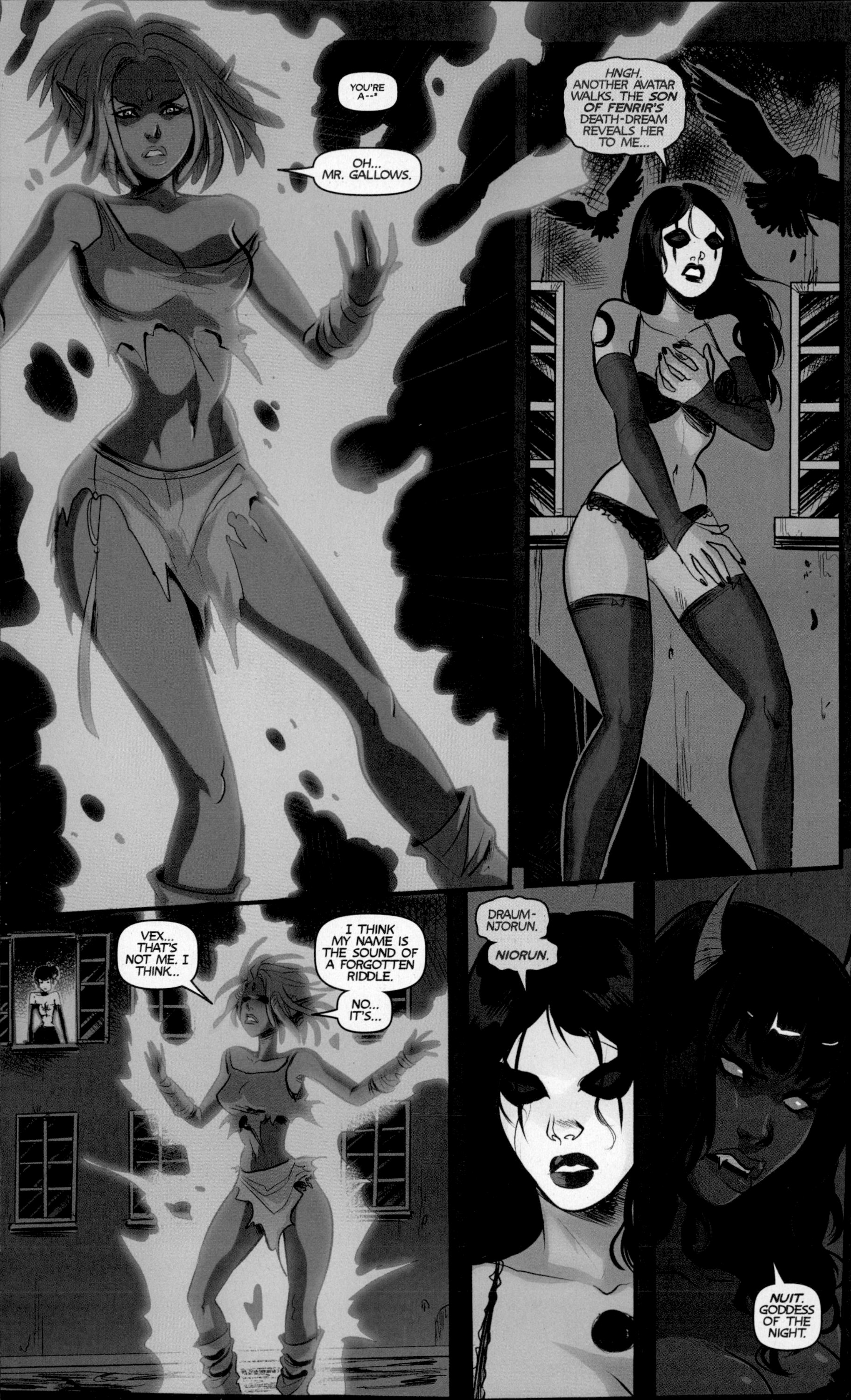
YOU'RE A--"
OH... MR. GALLOWS.
HNGH. ANOTHER AVATAR WALKS. THE SON OF FENRIR'S DEATH-DREAM REVEALS HER TO ME...
VEX... THAT'S NOT ME. I THINK...
I THINK MY NAME IS THE SOUND OF A FORGOTTEN RIDDLE.
NO... IT'S...
DRAUM-NJORUN.
NIORUN.
NUIT. GODDESS OF THE NIGHT.

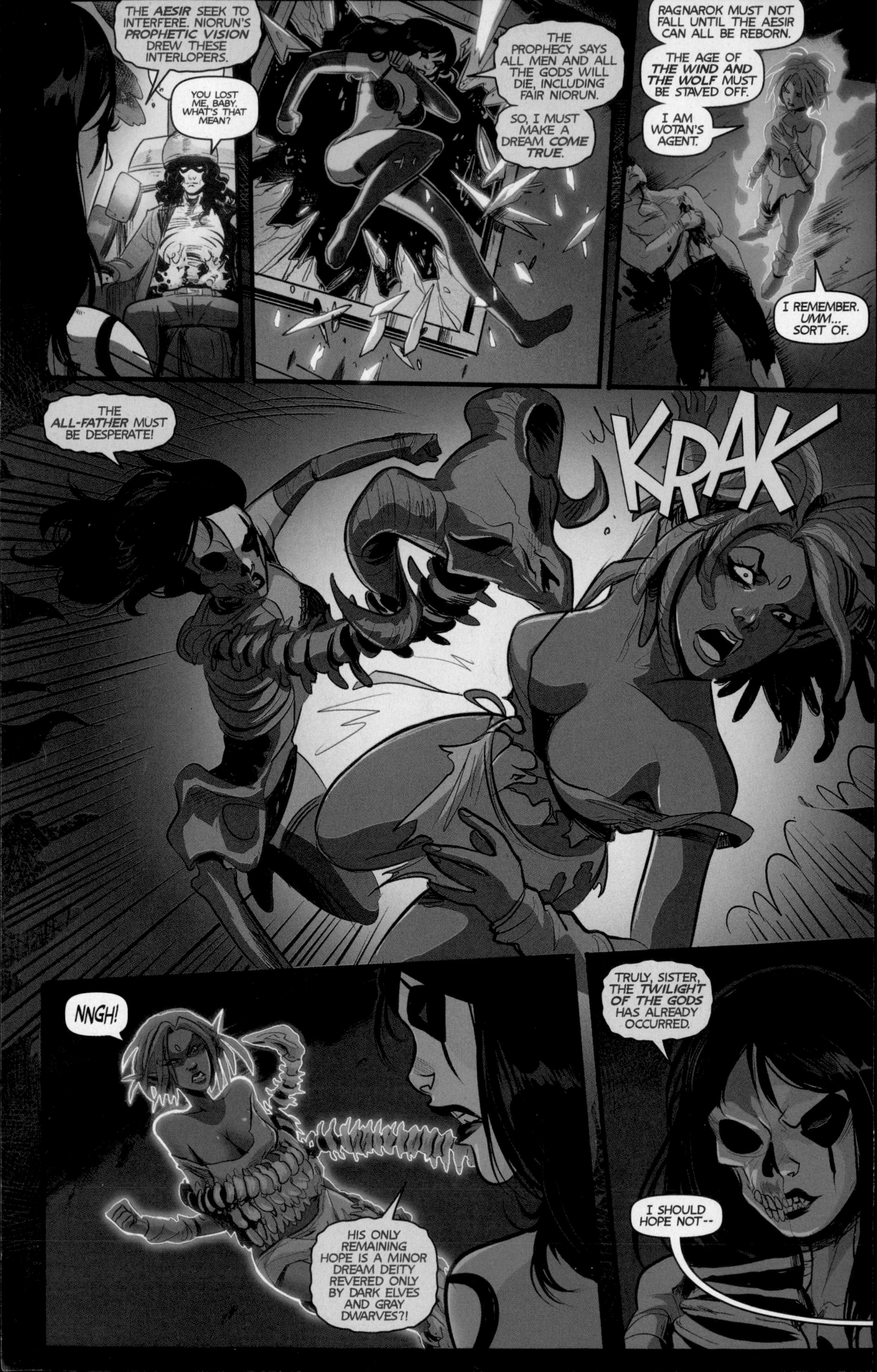
THE AESIR SEEK TO INTERFERE. NIORUN'S PROPHETIC VISION DREW THESE INTERLOPERS.
YOU LOST ME, BABY. WHAT'S THAT MEAN?
THE PROPHECY SAYS ALL MEN AND ALL THE GODS WILL DIE, INCLUDING FAIR NIORUN.
SO, I MUST MAKE A DREAM COME TRUE.
RAGNAROK MUST NOT FALL UNTIL THE AESIR CAN ALL BE REBORN.
THE AGE OF THE WIND AND THE WOLF MUST BE STAVED OFF.
I AM WOTAN'S AGENT.
I REMEMBER. UMM... SORT OF.
THE ALL-FATHER MUST BE DESPERATE!
KRAK
NNGH!
HIS ONLY REMAINING HOPE IS A MINOR DREAM DEITY REVERED ONLY BY DARK ELVES AND GRAY DWARVES?!
TRULY, SISTER, THE TWILIGHT OF THE GODS HAS ALREADY OCCURRED.
I SHOULD HOPE NOT--

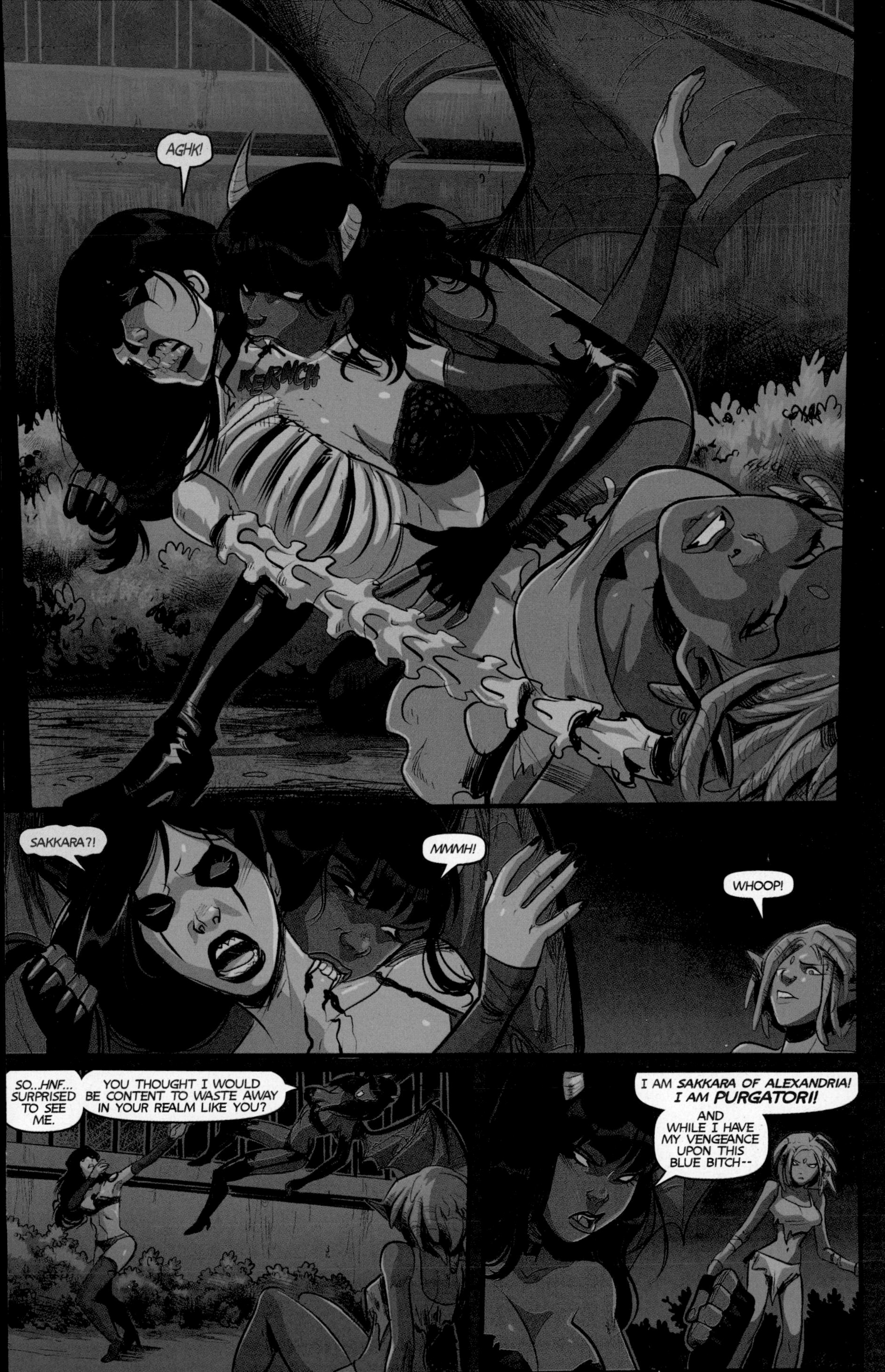
AGHK!
KERUNCH
SAKKARA?!
MMMH!
WHOOP!
SO...HNF... SURPRISED TO SEE ME.
YOU THOUGHT I WOULD BE CONTENT TO WASTE AWAY IN YOUR REALM LIKE YOU?
I AM SAKKARA OF ALEXANDRIA! I AM PURGATORI!
AND WHILE I HAVE MY VENGEANCE UPON THIS BLUE BITCH--

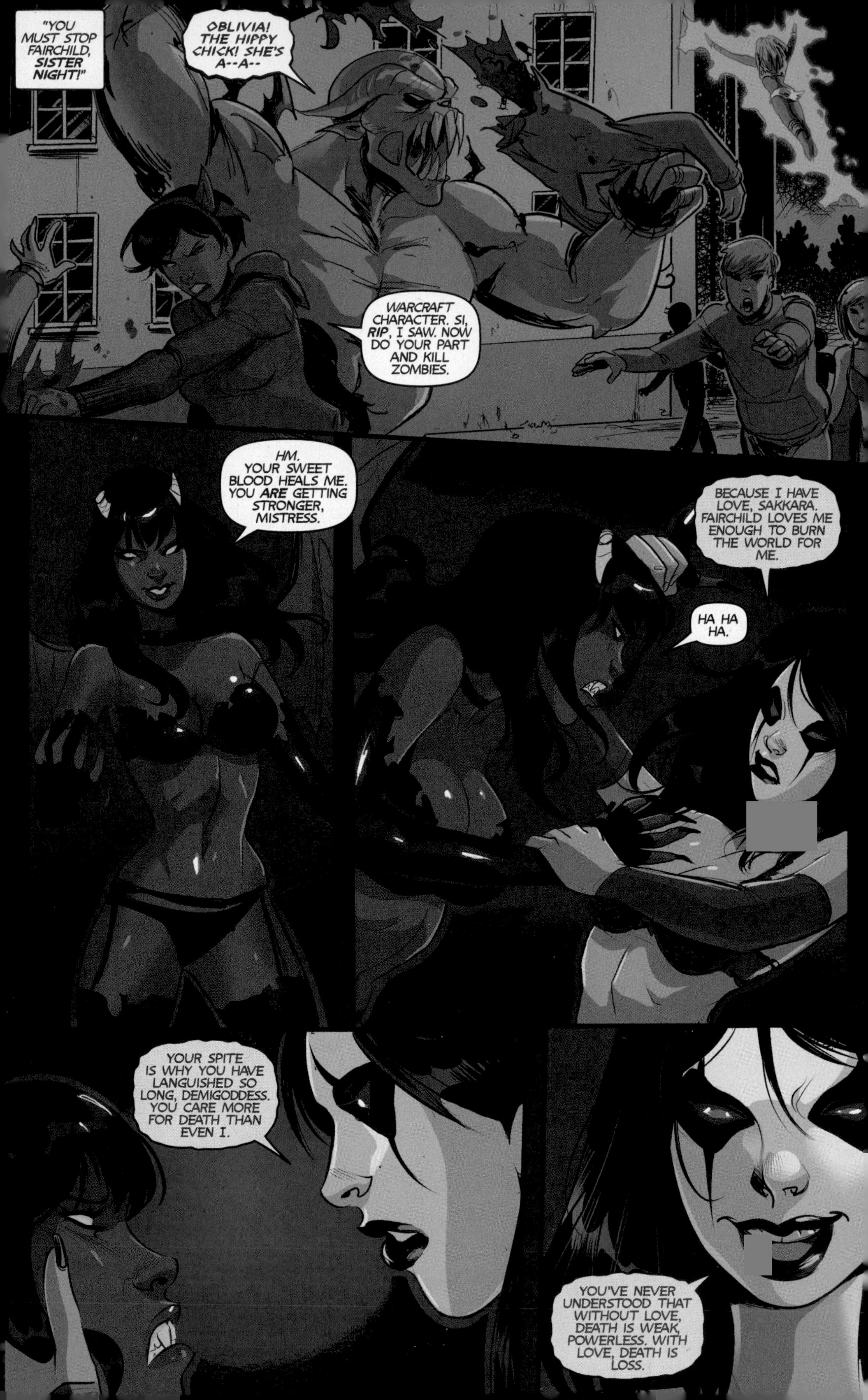
"YOU MUST STOP FAIRCHILD, SISTER NIGHT!"
OBLIVIA! THE HIPPY CHICK! SHE'S A--A--
WARCRAFT CHARACTER. SI, RIP, I SAW. NOW DO YOUR PART AND KILL ZOMBIES.
HM. YOUR SWEET BLOOD HEALS ME. YOU ARE GETTING STRONGER, MISTRESS.
BECAUSE I HAVE LOVE, SAKKARA. FAIRCHILD LOVES ME ENOUGH TO BURN THE WORLD FOR ME.
HA HA HA.
YOUR SPITE IS WHY YOU HAVE LANGUISHED SO LONG, DEMIGODDESS. YOU CARE MORE FOR DEATH THAN EVEN I.
YOU'VE NEVER UNDERSTOOD THAT WITHOUT LOVE, DEATH IS WEAK, POWERLESS. WITH LOVE, DEATH IS LOSS.

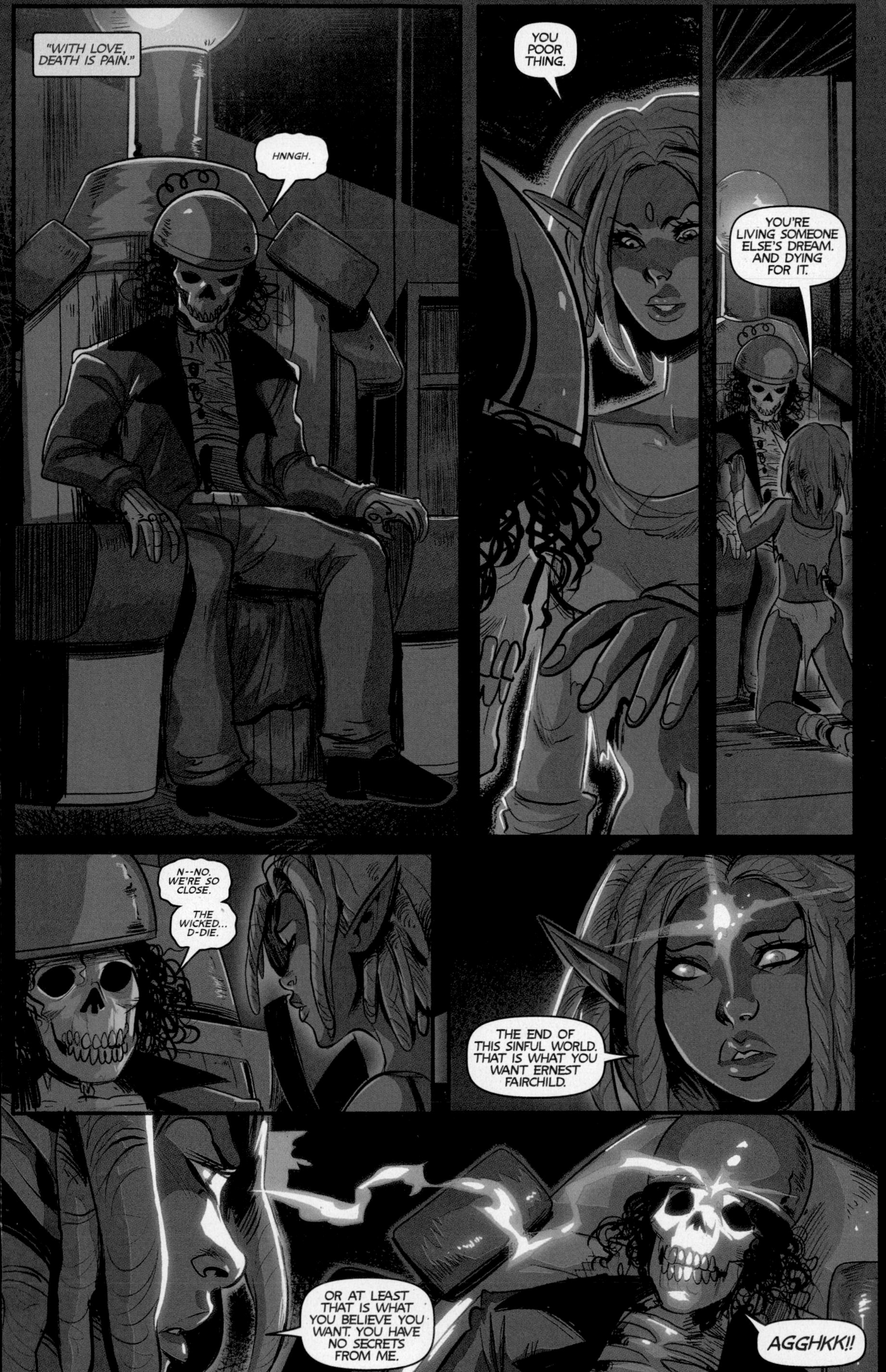
"WITH LOVE, DEATH IS PAIN."
HNNGH.
YOU POOR THING.
YOU'RE LIVING SOMEONE ELSE'S DREAM. AND DYING FOR IT.
N--NO. WE'RE SO CLOSE.
THE WICKED... D-DIE.
THE END OF THIS SINFUL WORLD. THAT IS WHAT YOU WANT ERNEST FAIRCHILD.
OR AT LEAST THAT IS WHAT YOU BELIEVE YOU WANT. YOU HAVE NO SECRETS FROM ME.
AGGHKK!!

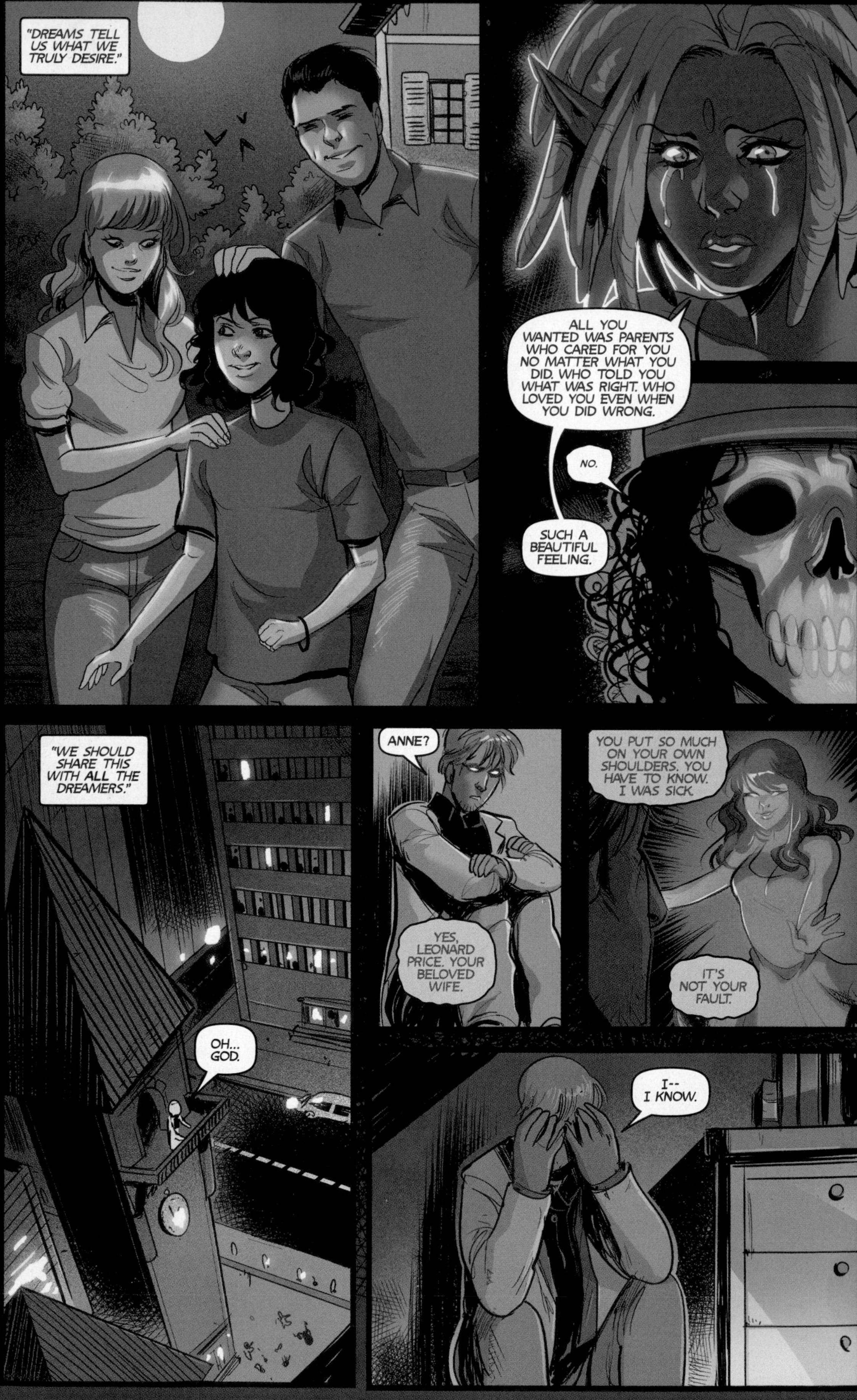
"DREAMS TELL US WHAT WE TRULY DESIRE."
ALL YOU WANTED WAS PARENTS WHO CARED FOR YOU NO MATTER WHAT YOU DID. WHO TOLD YOU WHAT WAS RIGHT. WHO LOVED YOU EVEN WHEN YOU DID WRONG.
NO.
SUCH A BEAUTIFUL FEELING.
"WE SHOULD SHARE THIS WITH ALL THE DREAMERS."
OH... GOD.
ANNE?
YES, LEONARD PRICE. YOUR BELOVED WIFE.
YOU PUT SO MUCH ON YOUR OWN SHOULDERS. YOU HAVE TO KNOW. I WAS SICK.
IT'S NOT YOUR FAULT.
I-- I KNOW.

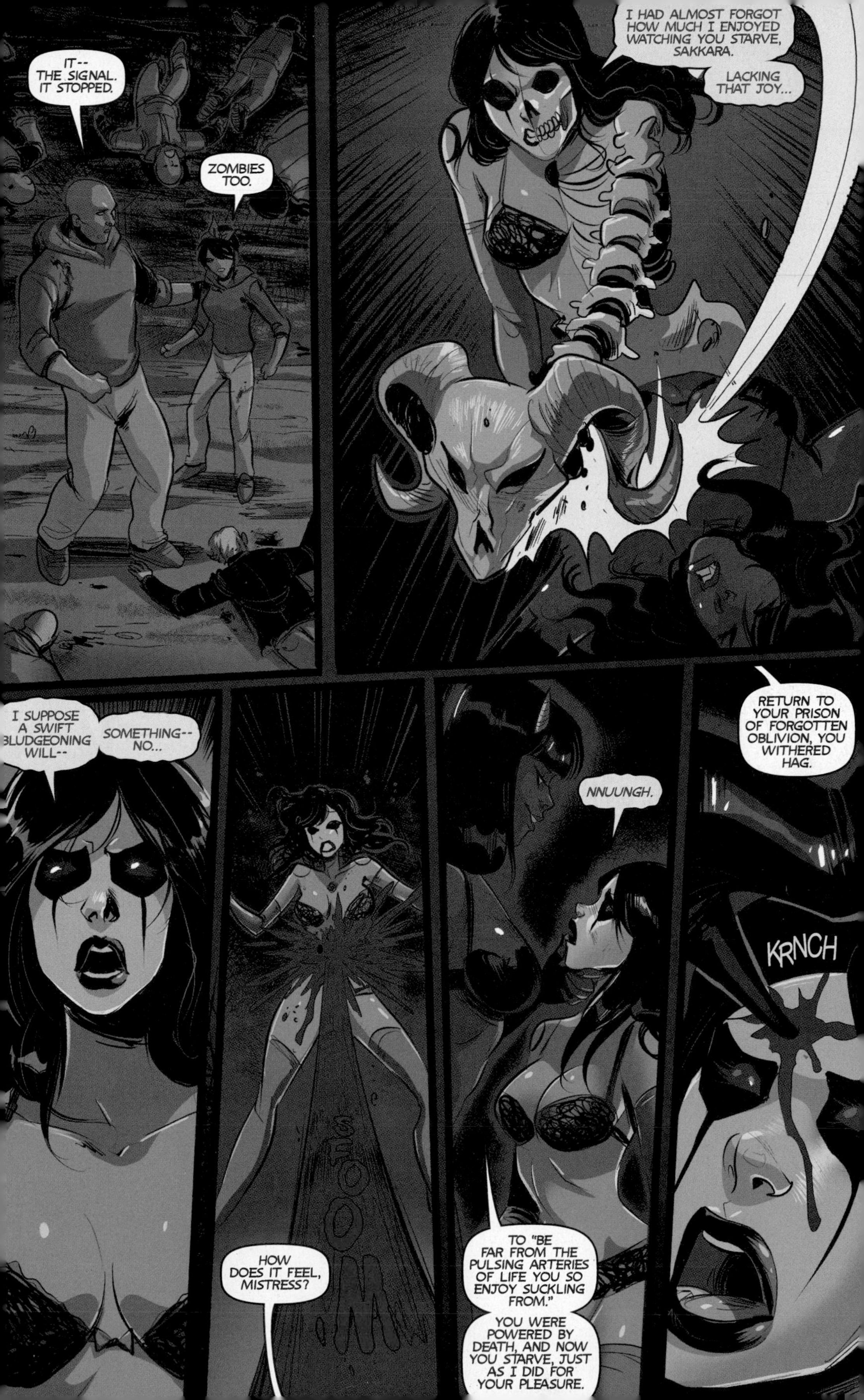
IT-- THE SIGNAL. IT STOPPED.
ZOMBIES TOO.
I HAD ALMOST FORGOT HOW MUCH I ENJOYED WATCHING YOU STARVE, SAKKARA.
LACKING THAT JOY...
I SUPPOSE A SWIFT BLUDGEONING WILL--
SOMETHING-- NO...
HOW DOES IT FEEL, MISTRESS?
NNUUNGH.
TO "BE FAR FROM THE PULSING ARTERIES OF LIFE YOU SO ENJOY SUCKLING FROM."
YOU WERE POWERED BY DEATH, AND NOW YOU STARVE, JUST AS I DID FOR YOUR PLEASURE.
RETURN TO YOUR PRISON OF FORGOTTEN OBLIVION, YOU WITHERED HAG.
KRNCH

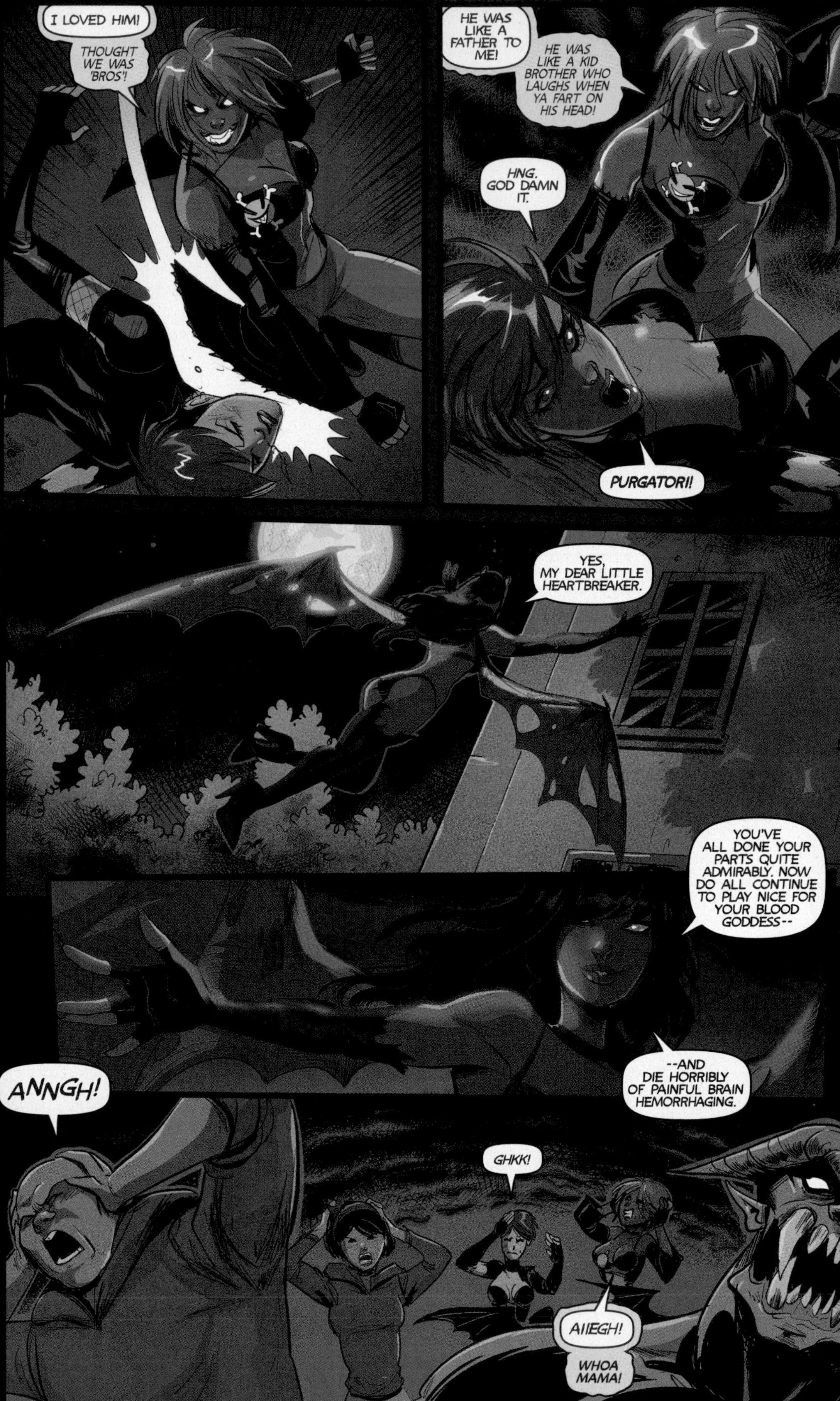

I LOVED HIM!
THOUGHT WE WAS 'BROS'!
HE WAS LIKE A FATHER TO ME!
HE WAS LIKE A KID BROTHER WHO LAUGHS WHEN YA FART ON HIS HEAD!
HNG. GOD DAMN IT.
PURGATORI!
YES, MY DEAR LITTLE HEARTBREAKER.
YOU'VE ALL DONE YOUR PARTS QUITE ADMIRABLY. NOW DO ALL CONTINUE TO PLAY NICE FOR YOUR BLOOD GODDESS--
--AND DIE HORRIBLY OF PAINFUL BRAIN HEMORRHAGING.
ANNGH!
GHKK!
AIIEGH!
WHOA MAMA!

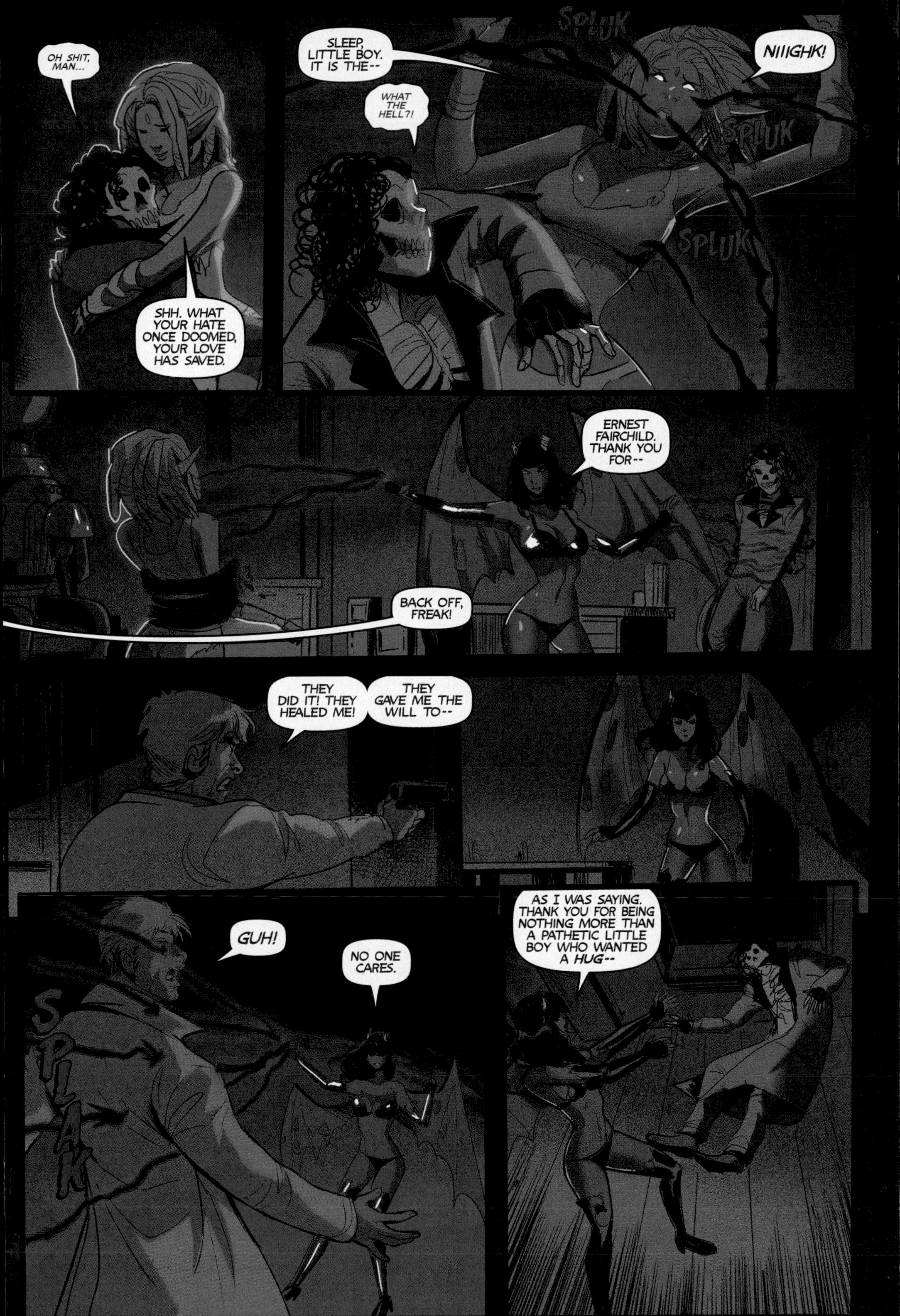

OH SHIT, MAN...
SHH. WHAT YOUR HATE ONCE DOOMED, YOUR LOVE HAS SAVED.
SLEEP, LITTLE BOY. IT IS THE--
WHAT THE HELL?!
SPLUK
NIIIGHK!
SPLUK
SPLUK
ERNEST FAIRCHILD. THANK YOU FOR--
BACK OFF, FREAK!
THEY DID IT! THEY HEALED ME!
THEY GAVE ME THE WILL TO--
GUH!
NO ONE CARES.
SPLAK
AS I WAS SAYING. THANK YOU FOR BEING NOTHING MORE THAN A PATHETIC LITTLE BOY WHO WANTED A HUG--

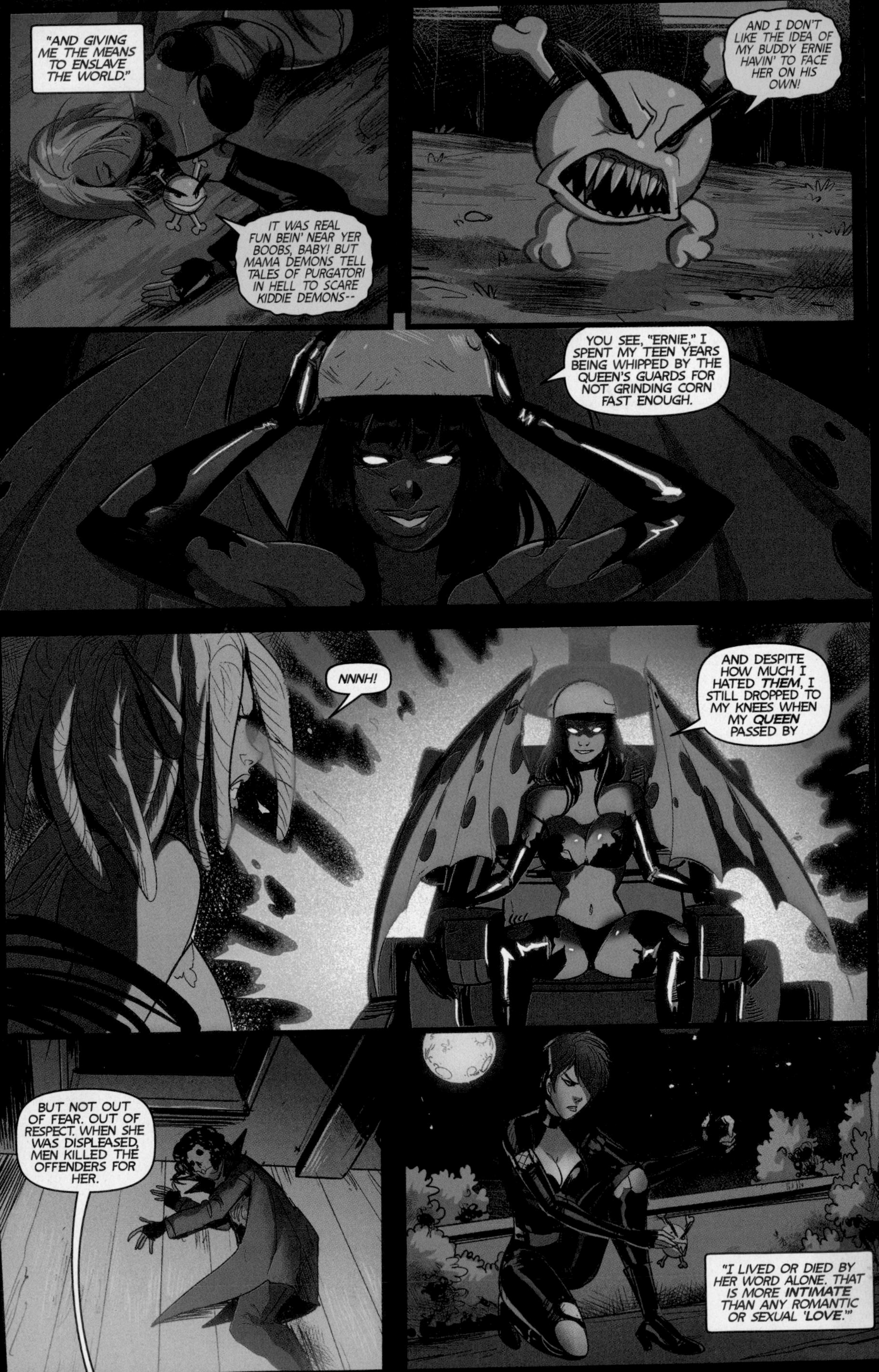
"AND GIVING ME THE MEANS TO ENSLAVE THE WORLD."
IT WAS REAL FUN BEIN' NEAR YER BOOBS, BABY! BUT MAMA DEMONS TELL TALES OF PURGATORI IN HELL TO SCARE KIDDIE DEMONS--
AND I DON'T LIKE THE IDEA OF MY BUDDY ERNIE HAVIN' TO FACE HER ON HIS OWN!
YOU SEE, "ERNIE," I SPENT MY TEEN YEARS BEING WHIPPED BY THE QUEEN'S GUARDS FOR NOT GRINDING CORN FAST ENOUGH.
NNNH!
AND DESPITE HOW MUCH I HATED THEM, I STILL DROPPED TO MY KNEES WHEN MY QUEEN PASSED BY
BUT NOT OUT OF FEAR. OUT OF RESPECT. WHEN SHE WAS DISPLEASED, MEN KILLED THE OFFENDERS FOR HER.
"I LIVED OR DIED BY HER WORD ALONE. THAT IS MORE INTIMATE THAN ANY ROMANTIC OR SEXUAL 'LOVE.'"

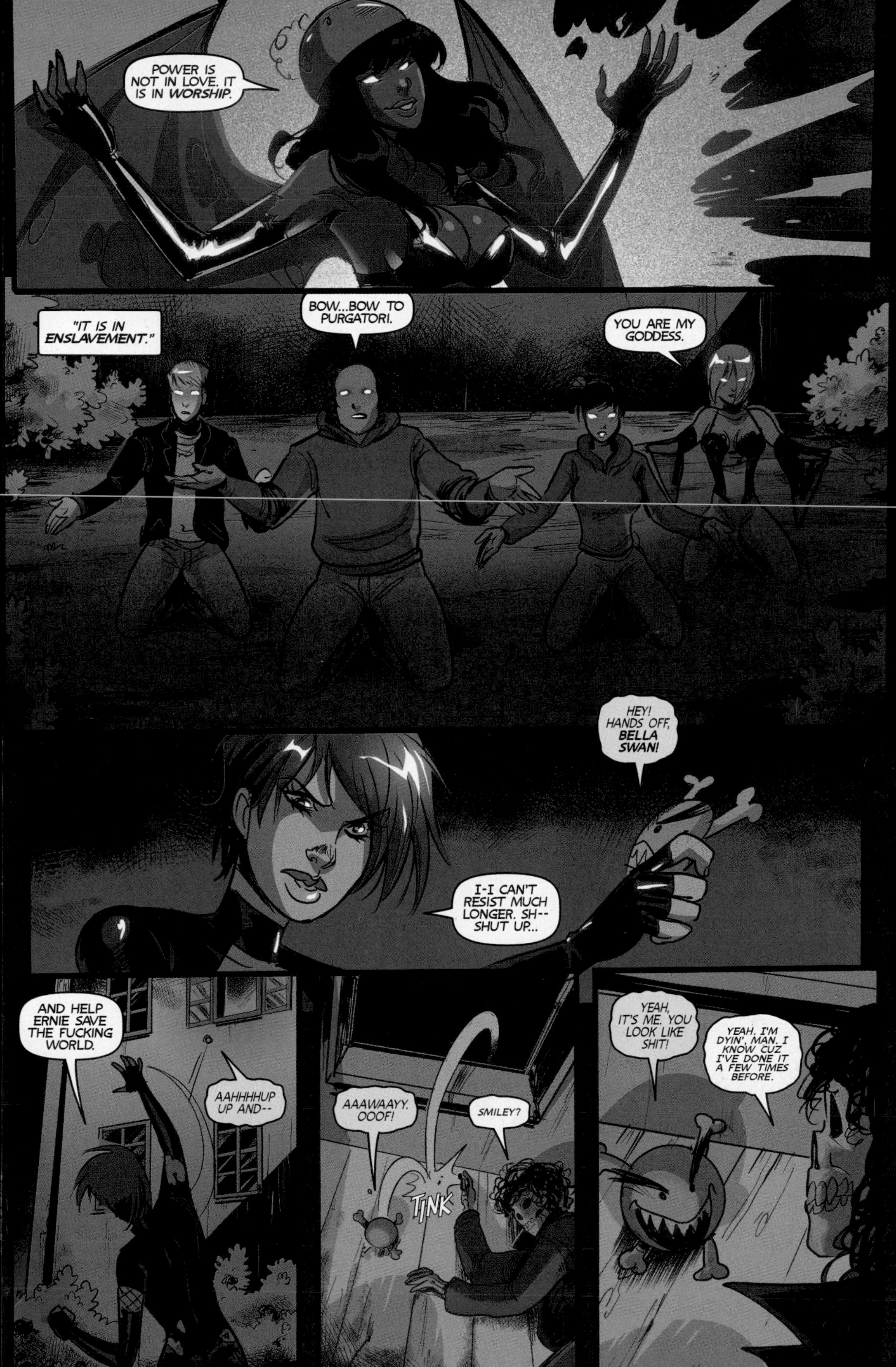
POWER IS NOT IN LOVE. IT IS IN *WORSHIP*.
"IT IS IN *ENSLAVEMENT*."
BOW...BOW TO PURGATORI.
YOU ARE MY GODDESS.
HEY! HANDS OFF, **BELLA SWAN!**
I-I CAN'T RESIST MUCH LONGER. SH-- SHUT UP...
AND HELP ERNIE SAVE THE FUCKING WORLD.
AAHHHHUP UP AND--
AAAWAAYY. OOOF!
TINK
SMILEY?
YEAH, IT'S ME. YOU LOOK LIKE SHIT!
YEAH. I'M DYIN', MAN. I KNOW CUZ I'VE DONE IT A FEW TIMES BEFORE.

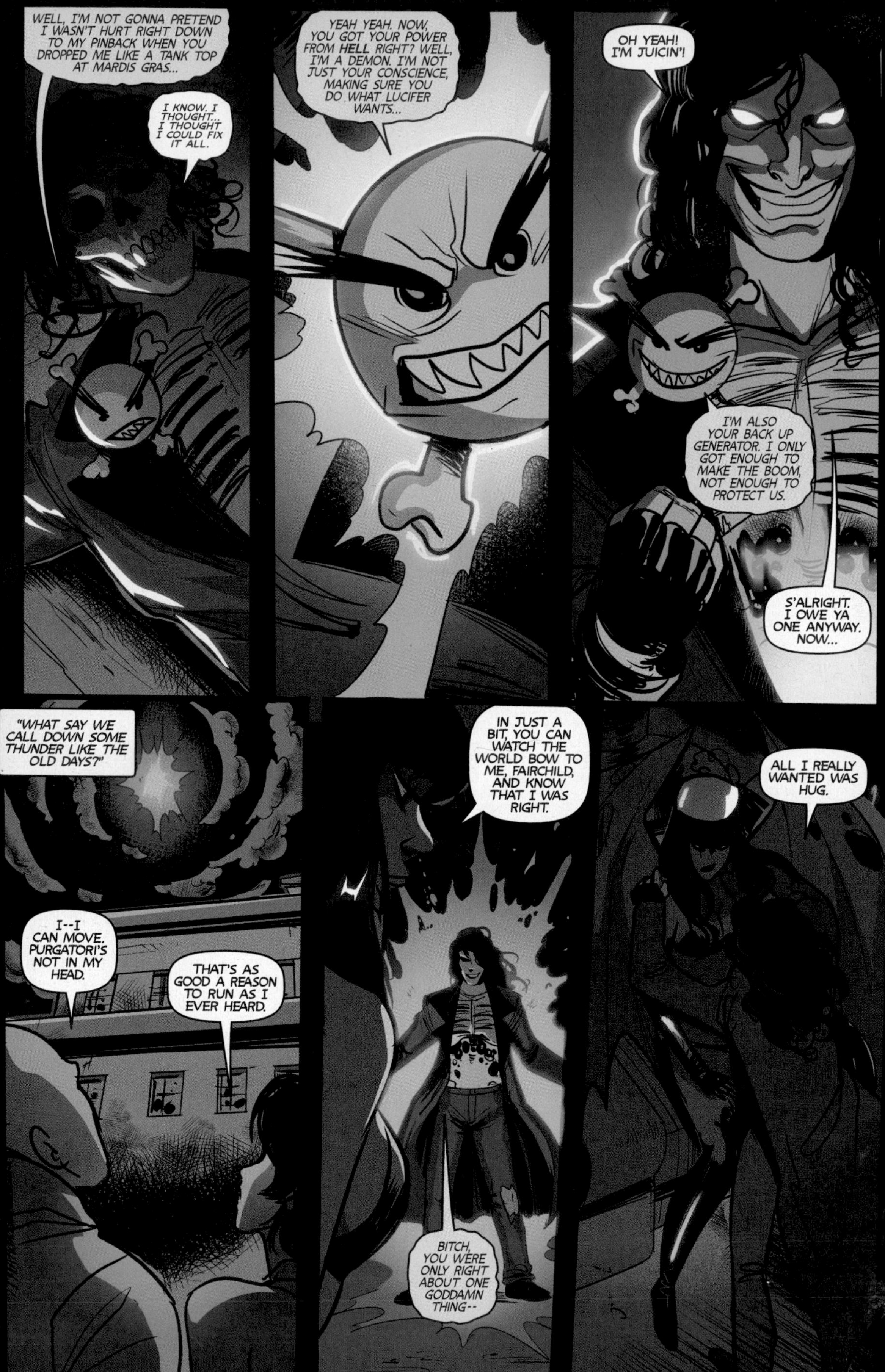
WELL, I'M NOT GONNA PRETEND I WASN'T HURT RIGHT DOWN TO MY PINBACK WHEN YOU DROPPED ME LIKE A TANK TOP AT MARDIS GRAS...
I KNOW. I THOUGHT... I THOUGHT I COULD FIX IT ALL.
YEAH YEAH. NOW, YOU GOT YOUR POWER FROM HELL RIGHT? WELL, I'M A DEMON. I'M NOT JUST YOUR CONSCIENCE, MAKING SURE YOU DO WHAT LUCIFER WANTS...
OH YEAH! I'M JUICIN'!
I'M ALSO YOUR BACK UP GENERATOR. I ONLY GOT ENOUGH TO MAKE THE BOOM, NOT ENOUGH TO PROTECT US.
S'ALRIGHT. I OWE YA ONE ANYWAY. NOW...
"WHAT SAY WE CALL DOWN SOME THUNDER LIKE THE OLD DAYS?"
I--I CAN MOVE. PURGATORI'S NOT IN MY HEAD.
THAT'S AS GOOD A REASON TO RUN AS I EVER HEARD.
IN JUST A BIT, YOU CAN WATCH THE WORLD BOW TO ME, FAIRCHILD, AND KNOW THAT I WAS RIGHT.
BITCH, YOU WERE ONLY RIGHT ABOUT ONE GODDAMN THING--
ALL I REALLY WANTED WAS HUG.

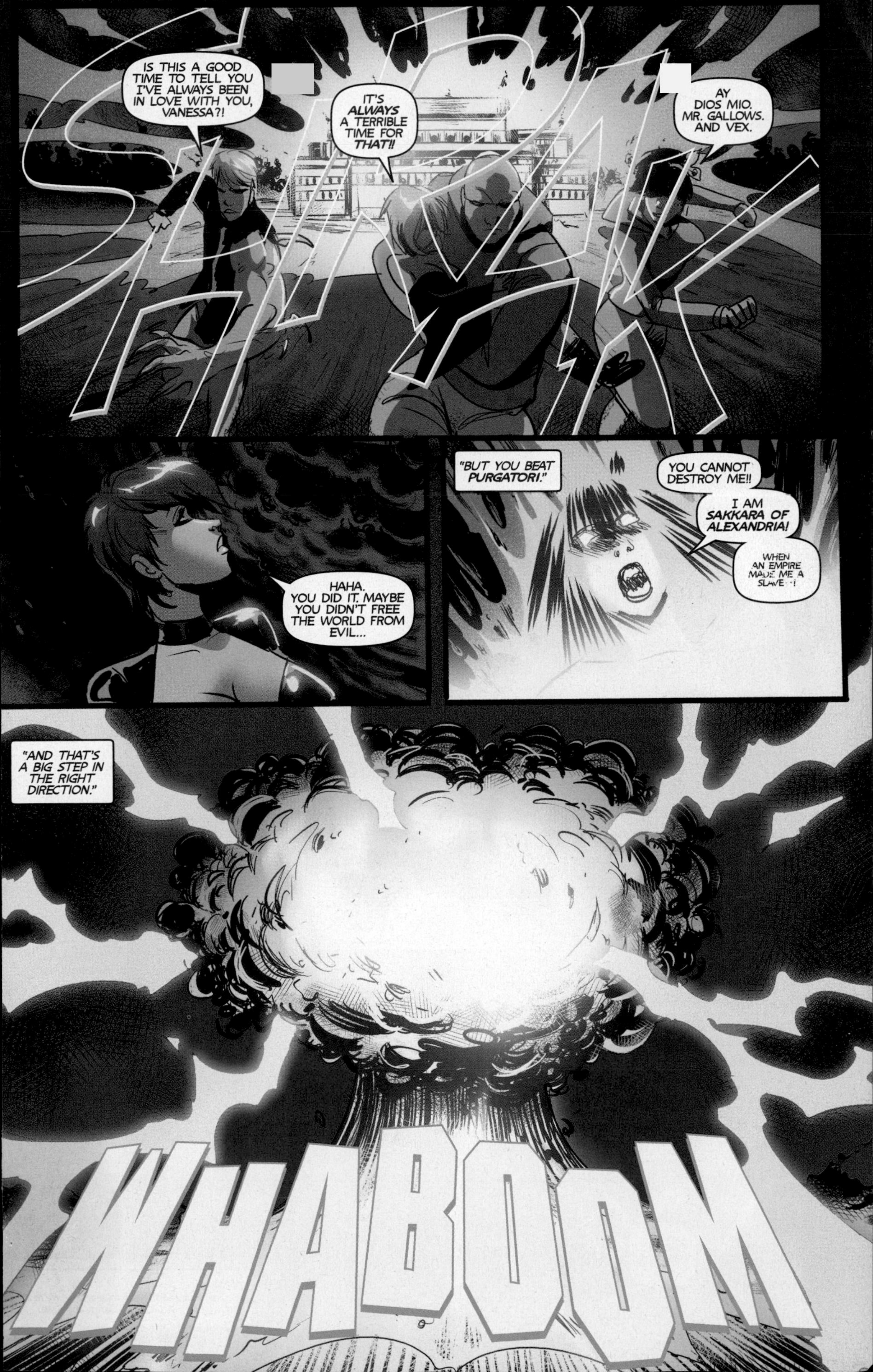
IS THIS A GOOD TIME TO TELL YOU I'VE ALWAYS BEEN IN LOVE WITH YOU, VANESSA?!
IT'S *ALWAYS* A TERRIBLE TIME FOR *THAT!!*
AY DIOS MIO. MR. GALLOWS. AND VEX.
HAHA. YOU DID IT. MAYBE YOU DIDN'T FREE THE WORLD FROM EVIL...
"BUT YOU BEAT *PURGATORI.*"
YOU CANNOT DESTROY ME!!
I AM *SAKKARA OF ALEXANDRIA!*
WHEN AN EMPIRE MADE ME A SLAVE--!
"AND THAT'S A BIG STEP IN THE RIGHT DIRECTION."
WHABOOM

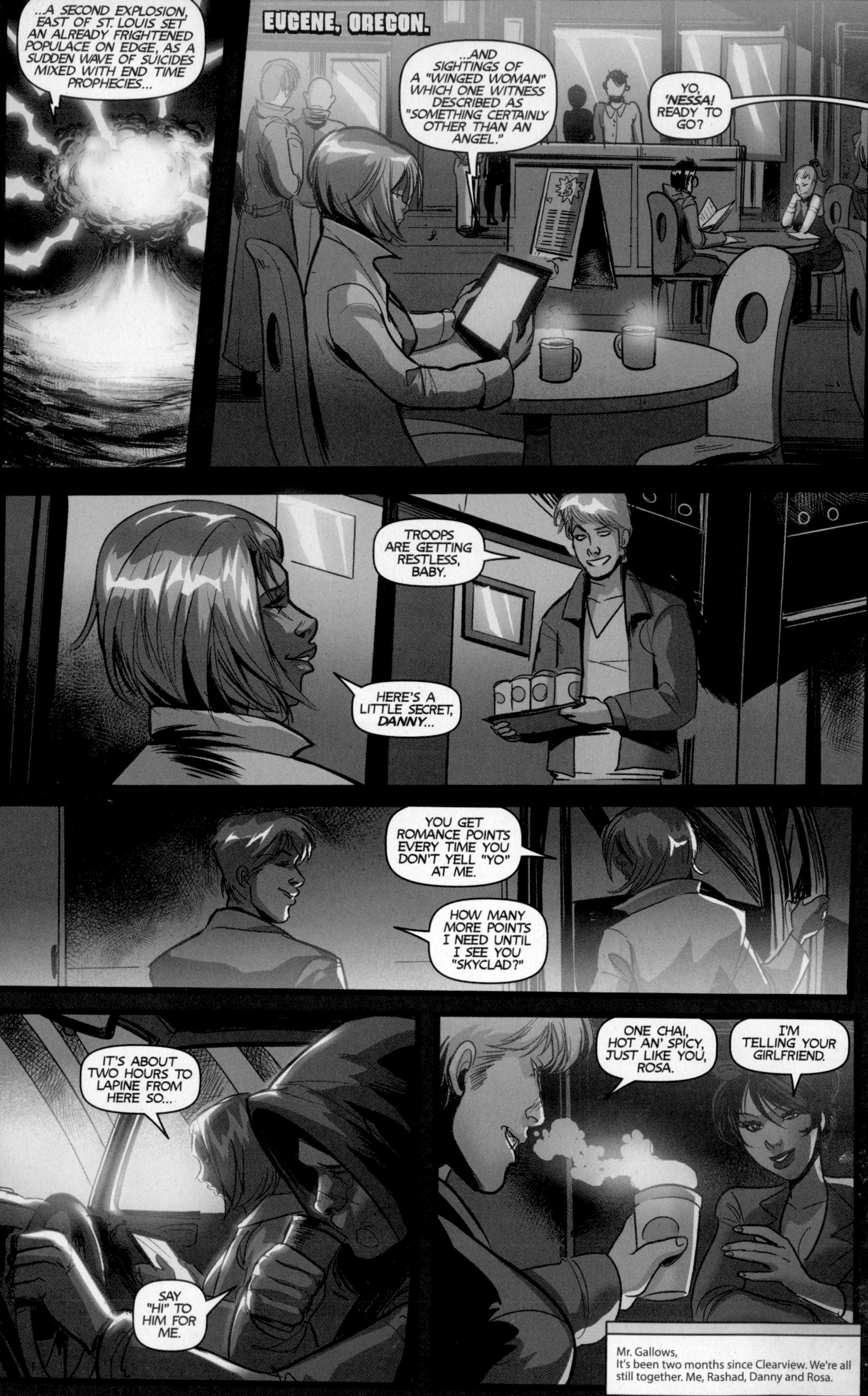
...A SECOND EXPLOSION, EAST OF ST. LOUIS SET AN ALREADY FRIGHTENED POPULACE ON EDGE, AS A SUDDEN WAVE OF SUICIDES MIXED WITH END TIME PROPHECIES...
EUGENE, OREGON.
...AND SIGHTINGS OF A "WINGED WOMAN" WHICH ONE WITNESS DESCRIBED AS "SOMETHING CERTAINLY OTHER THAN AN ANGEL."
YO, 'NESSA! READY TO GO?
TROOPS ARE GETTING RESTLESS, BABY.
HERE'S A LITTLE SECRET, DANNY...
YOU GET ROMANCE POINTS EVERY TIME YOU DON'T YELL "YO" AT ME.
HOW MANY MORE POINTS I NEED UNTIL I SEE YOU "SKYCLAD?"
IT'S ABOUT TWO HOURS TO LAPINE FROM HERE SO...
SAY "HI" TO HIM FOR ME.
ONE CHAI, HOT AN' SPICY, JUST LIKE YOU, ROSA.
I'M TELLING YOUR GIRLFRIEND.
Mr. Gallows,
It's been two months since Clearview. We're all still together. Me, Rashad, Danny and Rosa.

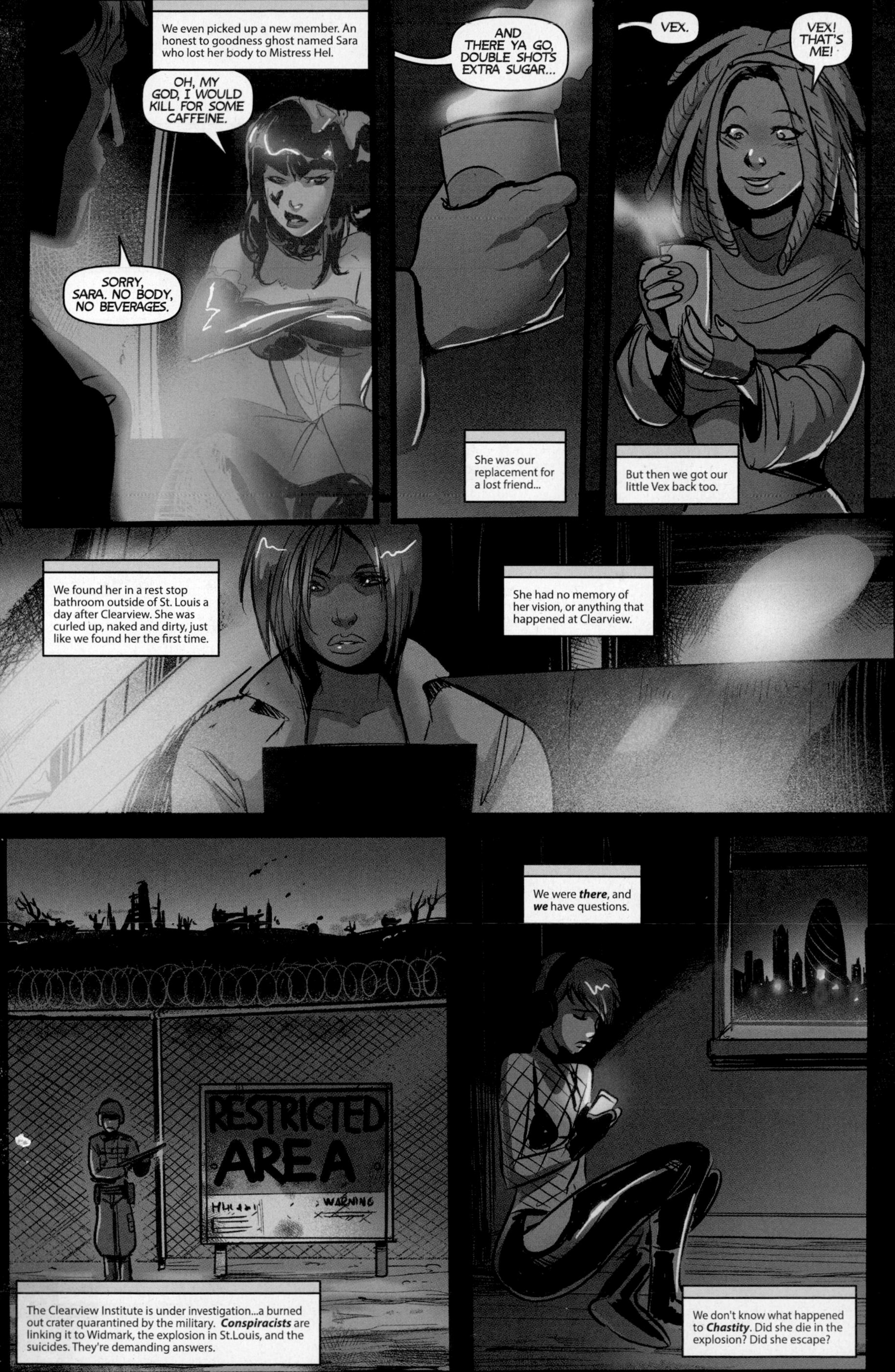
We even picked up a new member. An honest to goodness ghost named Sara who lost her body to Mistress Hel.
OH, MY GOD, I WOULD KILL FOR SOME CAFFEINE.
SORRY, SARA. NO BODY, NO BEVERAGES.
AND THERE YA GO, DOUBLE SHOTS EXTRA SUGAR...
She was our replacement for a lost friend...
VEX.
VEX! THAT'S ME!
But then we got our little Vex back too.
We found her in a rest stop bathroom outside of St. Louis a day after Clearview. She was curled up, naked and dirty, just like we found her the first time.
She had no memory of her vision, or anything that happened at Clearview.
RESTRICTED AREA
WARNING
The Clearview Institute is under investigation...a burned out crater quarantined by the military. Conspiracists are linking it to Widmark, the explosion in St.Louis, and the suicides. They're demanding answers.
We were there, and we have questions.
We don't know what happened to Chastity. Did she die in the explosion? Did she escape?

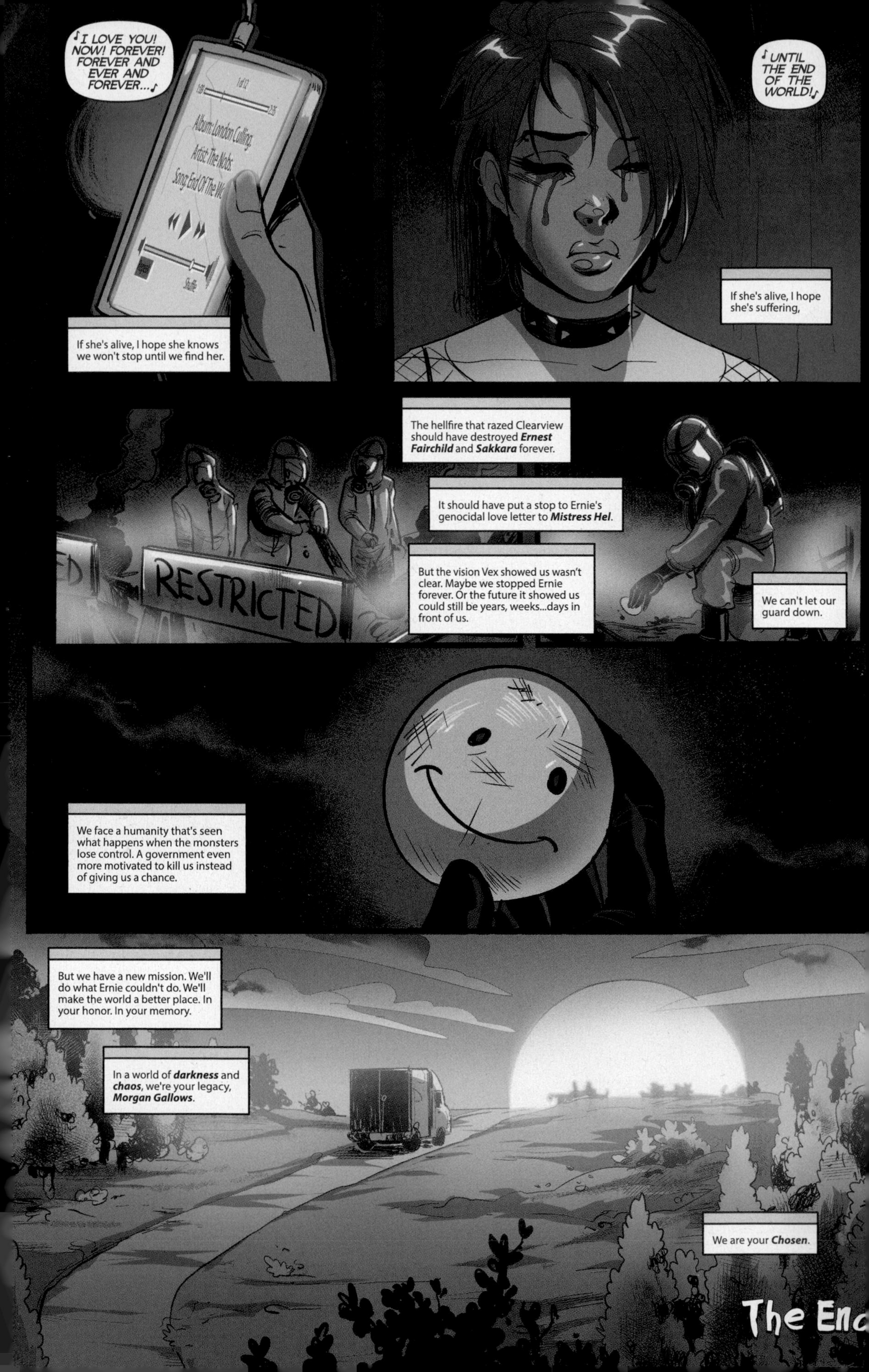

I LOVE YOU! NOW! FOREVER! FOREVER AND EVER AND FOREVER...
1 of 12
Album: London Calling.
Artist: The Nobs.
Song: End Of The W
Shuffle
If she's alive, I hope she knows we won't stop until we find her.
UNTIL THE END OF THE WORLD!
If she's alive, I hope she's suffering,
The hellfire that razed Clearview should have destroyed ***Ernest Fairchild*** and ***Sakkara*** forever.
It should have put a stop to Ernie's genocidal love letter to ***Mistress Hel***.
RESTRICTED
But the vision Vex showed us wasn't clear. Maybe we stopped Ernie forever. Or the future it showed us could still be years, weeks...days in front of us.
We can't let our guard down.
We face a humanity that's seen what happens when the monsters lose control. A government even more motivated to kill us instead of giving us a chance.
But we have a new mission. We'll do what Ernie couldn't do. We'll make the world a better place. In your honor. In your memory.
In a world of ***darkness*** and ***chaos***, we're your legacy, ***Morgan Gallows***.
We are your ***Chosen***.
The End

BONUS MATERIAL

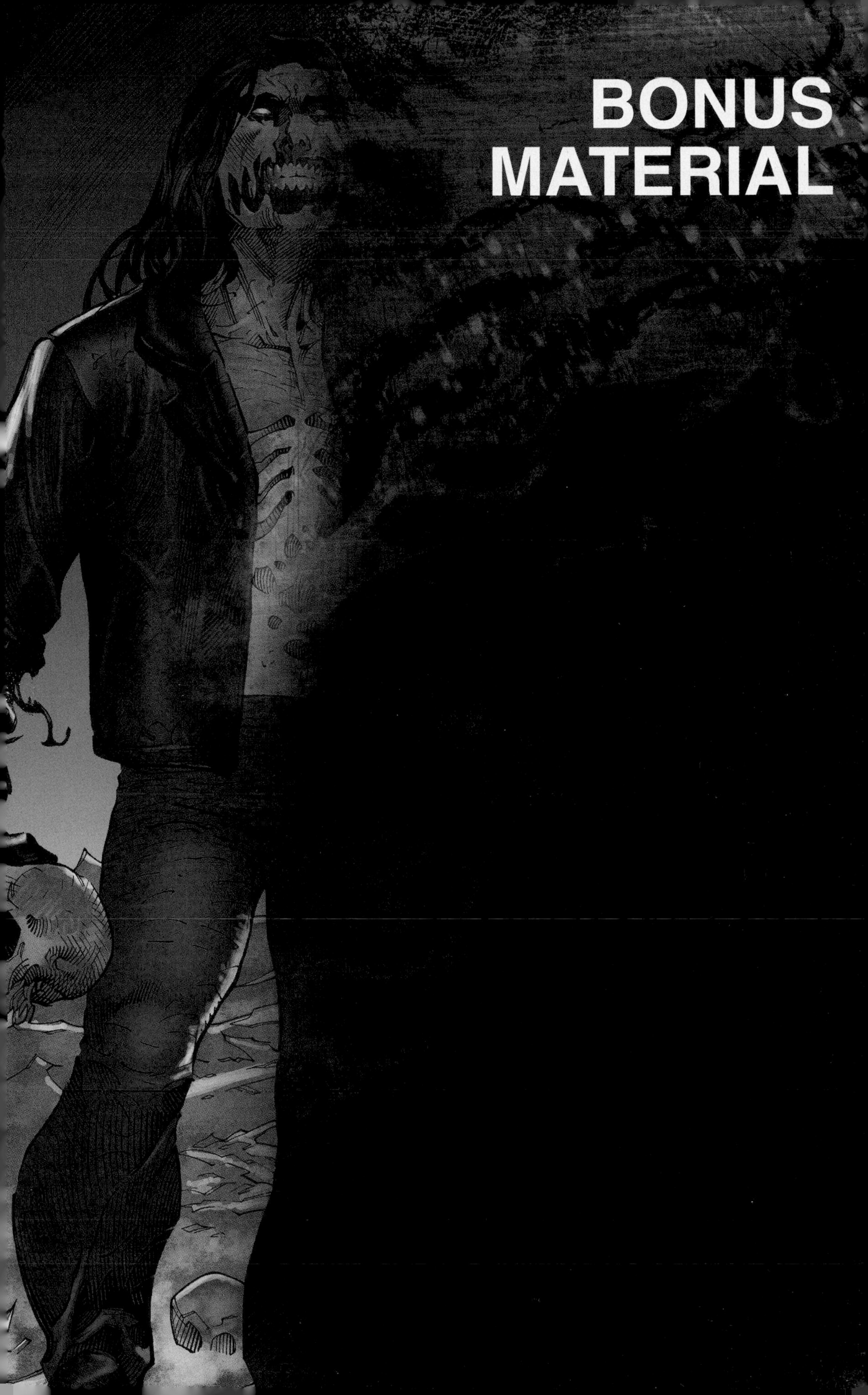

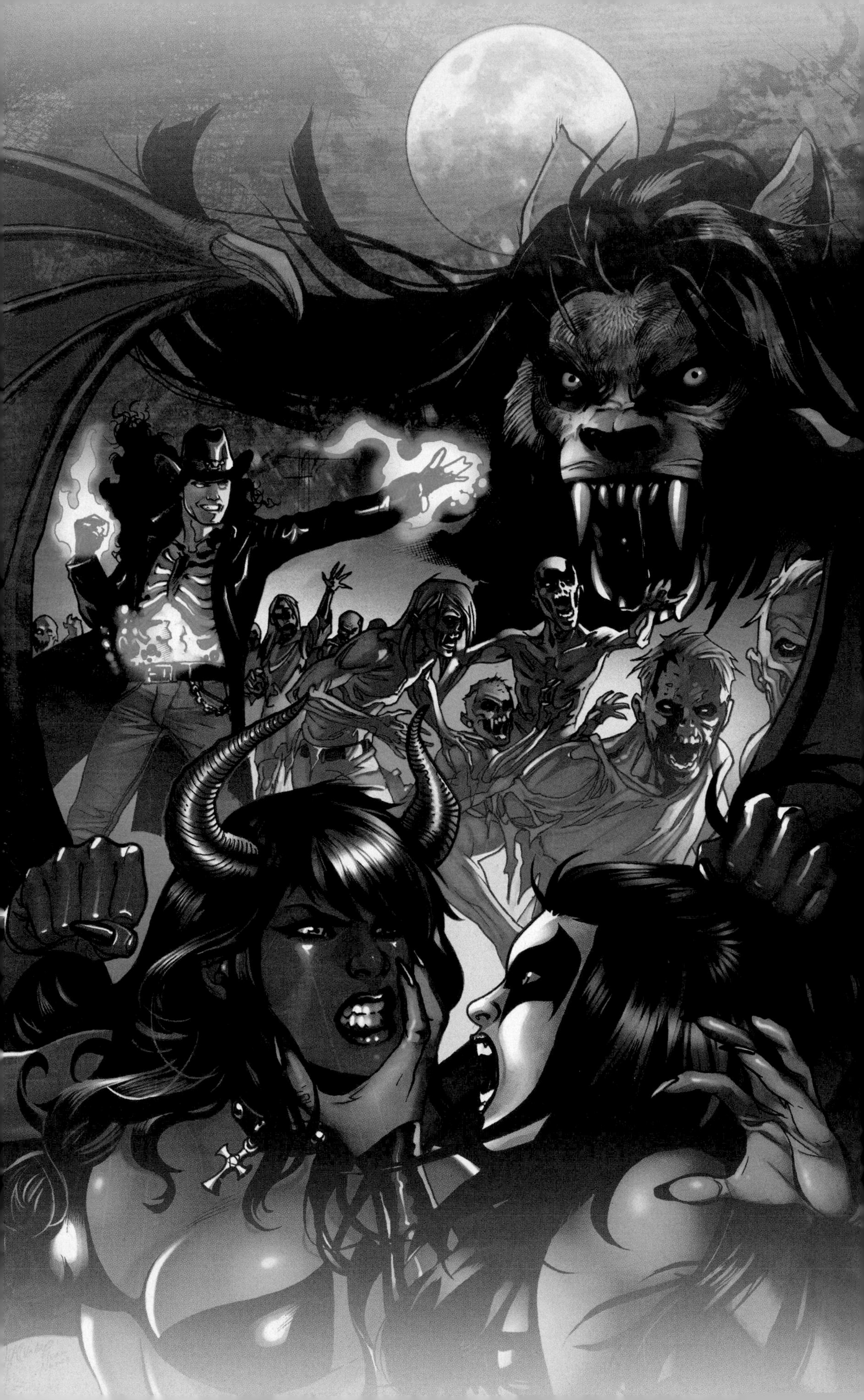

Issue 1
Written by Tim Seeley

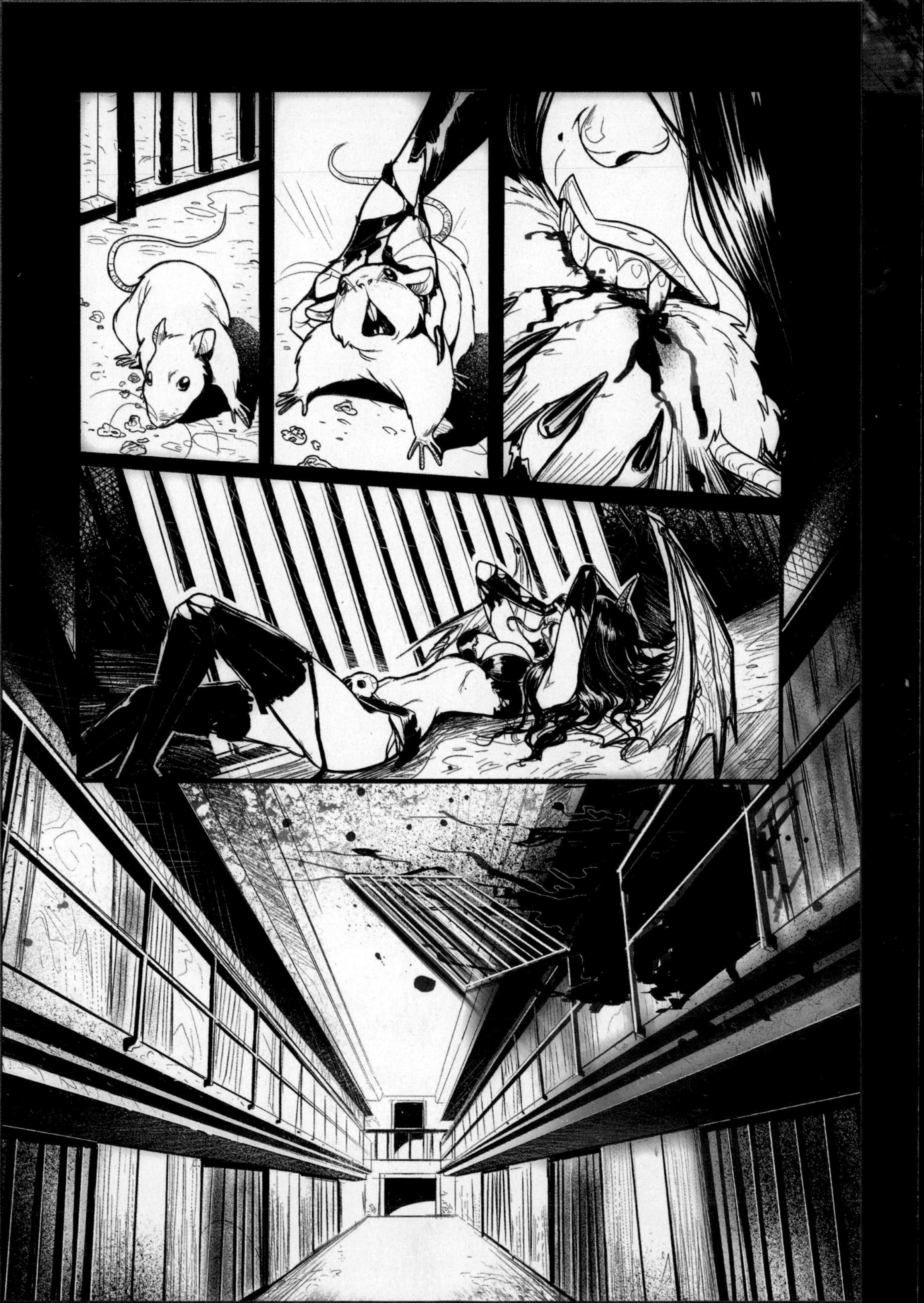

PAGE 1

Panel 1: Open on a shot of a large rat, nibbling its way across a dirty cement prison floor, picking at a trail of small crumbs.

Caption: Then.

Panel 2: Suddenly the red-brown skinned hand of Purgatori grabs the rat. The poor thing shrieks in terror.

Purgatori (weak): yes...

Rat: Shrre!

Panel 3: And, on her fanged mouth as she bites into the rat. Blood sprays out.

SFX: Scrnch!

Panel 4: We pull back now, a dank, dark cell. Purgatori is in tattered remnants of clothing, feeding on the floor of the cell...ecstatically.

Purgatori (weak): The blood...the blood....

Panel 5: from outside the cell...a huge cell block made of black obsidian glass, as the door is blown off its hinges by a **blast of blood!**

Purgatori: **THE BLOOD!**

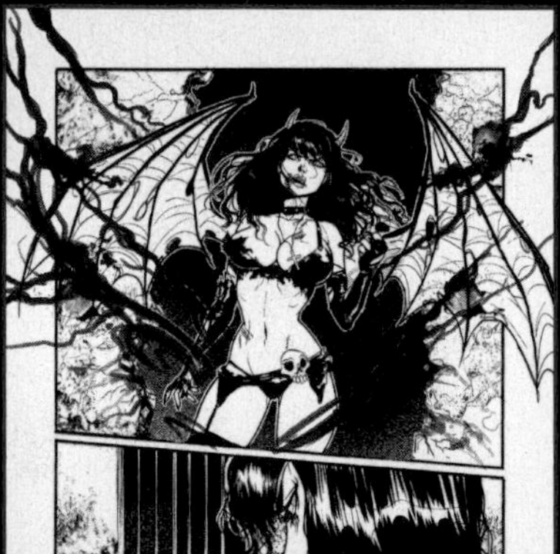

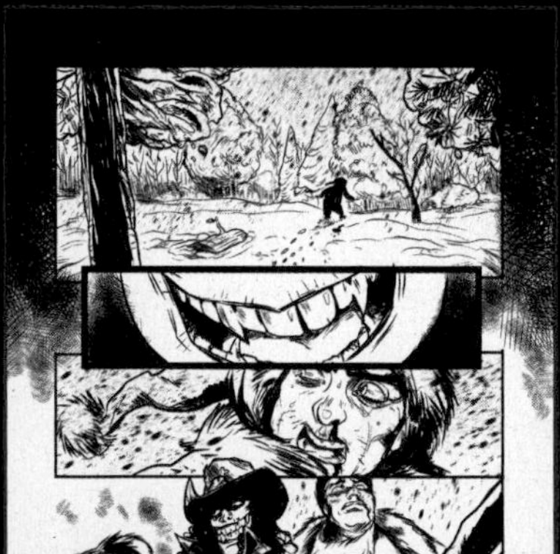

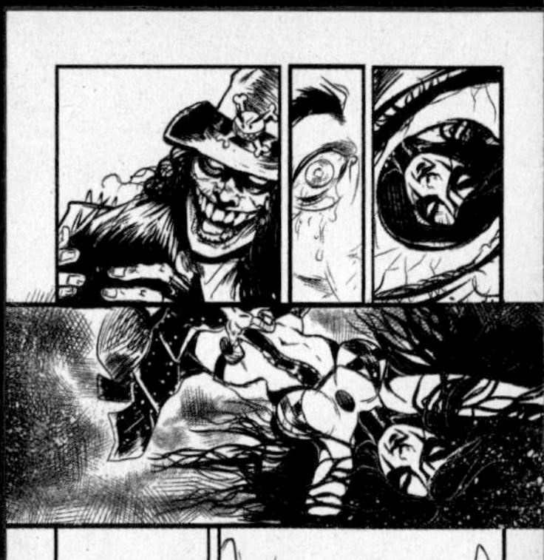

PAGE 2

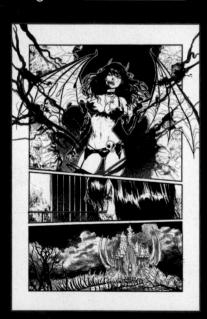

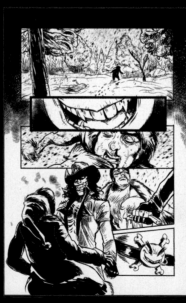

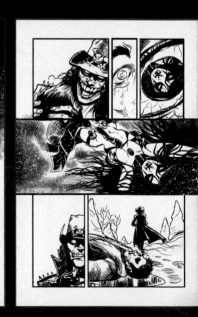

Panel 1: Big shot. PURGATORI in all her glory emerges from the cell, angry as hell. Her clothes are tattered, and her long black hair is dirty and stringy. She still

ooks, y'know, hot though. Whip like tendrils of blood swirl around her, ready to attack anything that gets in her way.

Purgatori: You would make a prisoner out of **ME, Sakkara of Alexandria!?** When an empire made me a slave, I killed slavemasters! Feasted upon kings and queens! Fell nations!

Purgatori: My teeth have torn the throat of the Devil! No **little god** can imprison me! Face me, so you can suffer for my exile in this **Purgatory!**

Panel 2: She looks around...there is no one there...an empty place.

Purgatori: Face me so your poets can write of your suffering!

Panel 3: And, we pull back...Lady Hel's realm (also called Hel) and her giant castle made from the bones of giant and gods, sitting alone in barren blasted landscape....nothing lives, nothing moves...a veritable endless graveyard.

Purgatori: **FACE ME!!!**

PAGE 3

Panel 1: Late afternoon. Rural south Dakota. It's one of those all-white days...the sky and the snow on the ground. Santa Claus is running, with some difficulty, through a snowy forest, terrified for his life. Or at least, that's what it looks like. It's a mall Santa type guy, who has become the target of Evil Ernie. He's clearly already taken a few hits from Ernie, and his fake beard is stained red with blood.

Caption: Marty, South Dakota.

Caption: Yesterday.

Santa: No no no..please...

Smiley (singing, free floating): dashing through the snow...

Panel 2: Close in one Smiley's creepy toothy mouth as he sings...

Smiley(singing): a fat guy we're about to slay, o'er the fields he goes...

Panel 3: Santa looks back over his shoulder, terrified...

Santa: I'm sorry. I couldn't stop myself...

Smiley(singing): his jugular will soon spray...

Panel 4: And he runs right into Evil Ernie, which knocks loose his hat. The costume beard swings to the side. Ernie is wearing a cowboy hat and a long jacket. He looks really scary. Smiley, attached to his hat, sings happily.

Smiley: Take it Ernie!

Santa: Hnf!

Panel 5: Close in at waist level as Ernie plunges a knife into this department store Santa's stomach.

SFX: Sllch!

Santa: Hngh!

Panel 6: On Smiley. He's enthusiastic about murder as per usual.

Smiley: Oooh! right in the bowl full of jelly!

PAGE 4

Panel 1: Ernie is looking into the guy's face. He's in shock, of course, staring back at Ernie...

Ernie: Look at me.

Ernie: This is for the children. You lured them in. You tormented them.

Panel 2: Close in on the guy's eyeball, wide, terrified...

Ernie: Now you owe me...

Panel 3: Same shot, but we see a faint image of Lady Hel there, as the guy dies

NO DIALOGUE

Panel 4: Close in. A dreamy image of Lady Hel, beckoning, flirtatious, beautiful, and spooky.

Lady Hel (whisper): Ernie.

Panel 5: Ernie drops the dead guy on the ground.

Smiley: Boss? Earth to the Ernster! Calling Evil!

Panel 6: Pull back...the snowy, quiet forest, as Ernie turns to leave. The Santa guy bleeds out in the snow.

Smiley: You, uh...lose a contact in that guy's head or something?

Ernie: We need to find more sinners.

Panel 1: It's night off a dusty country road not far from the US/Texas border. We focus on a shot of Morgan Gallows, shouting to his team.

Caption: Ten miles outside of Eagle's Pass, Texas.

Caption: Now.

Morgan Gallows: The trucker's a **groupie*!** Watch out!

Caption: *Groupie-noun, informal. An ardent follower of a vampire....

Panel 2: We open on a shot of a truck driver type guy, in his mid 40s, with a beer gut and a net backed hat, rushing at the "camera" with murderous rage in his eyes. His mouth is frothing with foam spit, and his eyes are bloodshot. He's got a rusty tire iron in his hands. This is one of Purgatori's mind-controlled followers....

Caption: --often to the point of near mindless devotion.

Trucker: Bleed for queen **Sakkara!!** Die for the **blood goddess**, Purg---

Carcass (from off panel): I got him.

Panel 3: And, the guy's head is punched right off his body by the undead teen tough and member of the Chosen, Carcass.

SFX: PLAK!

Panel 4: Pull back, as bit, as we see CARCASS, RIP, and Gallows. Gallows is putting his gun back into the holster at his belt. Carcass looks at his hands a little surprised at his own strength. RIP ribs his buddy, while Gallows is pleased.

Carcass: Daaamn.

Rip: Bitchin'. That was some serious "Zombie-on-Zombie violence," bro.

Gallows: Good catch, **Carcass.**

Panel 5: Focus on Gallows now, addressing his team off panel....

Gallows: Alright, **Chosen.** We've successfully interrupted another one of Sakkara's **shipments.**

PAGE 6

Panel 1: Long panel across the top...
We get introduced now to the current Chosen "team" (Gallows, Oblivia, Rip, Carcass, Vanessa...no Vex yet). They've all obviously just been part of some big action (pulling over these trucks."

Gallows (from off panel): And now, **my little monsters,** the difficult part of this job begins...

Panel 2:
Big shot. Pull back. The Chosen "team" stands near a truck pulled over to the side of the road. The back of the truck is being opened by Oblivia, Gallows, and Carcass, revealing that it's full of terrified Mexican women. 10-15 of them.

The truck: An older model, rusty freight truck, with a large box cab, which would usually contain boxes of food intended for a grocer. "Lil' Devil Snack Cakes" is written on the side of it, and features a cute, cartoony "Devil Girl." A "chibi "version of a "Coop" devil girl, which of course, bears at least a faint resemblance to the buyer of all these poor slave girls, PURGATORI.

The Women: All are in their 20s, and all are very pretty. They've been kidnapped from their small towns or villages, and have been living in a truck for the past several days.

Gallows: Trying not to scare the hell out of the **shipment**.

PAGE 7

Panel 1: Gallows speaks to Vanessa who holds up a voodoo-pentagram necklace charm...(Note, this thing should have "sharp edges" as that'll come in later!)

Gallows: **Childe**. Be on the lookout for curses and charms. Sakkara's devil-blood

...gives her access to some **nasty black juju,** and I don't want to bring any of that crap with us.

Vanessa: Yes, sir, **Mr. Gallows.**

Panel 2: Vanessa and Oblivia help a few frightened women off the back of the truck, as behind them, Gallows gives instructions in Spanish.

Gallows: *Debe andar 2 kiliometers al Oeste. Hay una estación fronteriza allí. Los americanos le ayudarán. No nos mencione.*

Vanessa: I'll say one thing about Purgatori...

Oblivia: Ain't supposed to call her that.

Vanessa. Okay. Then, Sakkara. The thing is...she's definitely got a "type."

Panel 3: The two of them are now on the back of the truck, walking into it. There's a lot of dirty sheets and clothing...Obliva speaks very matter-of-factly. Vanessa gives her a look indicating she definitely thinks that was a strange response.

Oblivia: **AB negative.** It's every vamp's favorite. Real rare. It's like a **delicacy,** you know?

Vanessa: Uh...I was thinking more like "brown skinned, dark-haired, young, and totally terrified."

Panel 4: The pair have reaches the back of the cab. Oblivia looks back at Vanessa. Vanessa 's necklace is glowing red...

Vanessa: **Oblivia**....my necklace. We've got magic.

Oblivia: Yeah. And maybe we got proof...

Panel 5: Above shot. VEX is nestled in the fetal position amongst a pile of rages and boxes. She's nude (but cover up her bare boobs with her arm), and dirty, seemingly sleeping.

Oblivia (from off panel): ...that Purgatori likes to mix it up every once in a while.

PAGE 8

Panel 1: Establishing shot. Saint Louis, Missouri. Night. An abandoned mental health facility on the edge of town. Feel free to base it on aspects of these real life abandoned mental health facilities: http://io9.com/six-abandoned-asylums-with-genuinely-chilling-backstori-512154481

Caption: Clearview Mental Institution.

Caption: Established 1877. Closed 1989.

Dr. Price (free floating): It's 11 PM. December 12th.

Panel 2: In a basement laboratory we see the makeshift laboratory of Dr. Leonard Price. There are racks of sleep monitoring equipment and computers, most of it out of date, but modified to keep it working. There's also a wall of glass cases, filled with rats for animal testing. The whole place is lit by shop lights hastily hung from pipes and collapsing rafters. There's a large table, filled with journals, computer equipment, and empty fast food containers.

In this room, is Dr. Leonard Price, strapped to an upright platform. An IV line runs into a mounted gauntlet at his left wrist. His right hand is holding onto small recorder. He speaks into it.

Dr. Price: This is trial...**fourteen** today, the first time with the 40% **Cesare Solution.** Self-assessment...still at **seven of ten.**

Panel 3: The table has rotated to a horizontal position, and a "helmet" lowers over Price's head. It should look rather homemade, covered in lenses, mirrors and small cameras...very steampunk and a little scary.

Dr. Price: Ahem...This is **Dr. Leonard Price** speaking. For the purposes of this experimental **dream-probe**, I am both scientist...

Panel 4: Small shot. On Price's wrists as a needle stabs into the vein at his left wrist, held tight by the gauntlet. Blood trickles out.

SFX: SHNK!

Dr. Price: Hnh. And **guinea pig.**

Panel 5: Closing in on the helmet as it begins to flash lights, and Dr. Price grits his teeth

Dr. Price: Increase in Cesare has raised parietal lobe activity .9% in **hypnagogia state.**

Dr. Price: Inducing **parahypnagogia...**

PAGE 9

Panel 1: Inside Price's mind. A barrage of images. Dream logic. Clips from Price's life. Some suggested montage images!

• A black and white scene of a thin, black dressed man with a pale face, walking

down a large, empty hallway...a sort of half remembered image form the old silent film "The Cabinet of Dr. Caligari."
A field of skeletal, starving cattle standing in a lush green field with blue skies.
An old porcelain bathtub, with clawed feet, filled to the brim with red water...

Dr. Price (free floating): Beginning of dream activity at 38.4 seconds. Memory distortions...old movies. Frightening images.

Dr. Price (free floating): Visions of neglect...guilt....

Panel 2: And then, an image of a young woman, sitting in an academic looking office, circa the late 90s...she's beautiful, a brunette---Price's former fiancée, Anne. She's talking to Leonard, and we see her from his view.

Dr. Price (free floating): **Anne.**

Dr. Price (free floating): Pre-programmed suggestion implemented---

Anne: Oh Leonard.

Panel 3: Same shot.

Anne: You put so much on your own shoulders. You know it's not your fault.

Anne: Now, let's take a niiice bath---

Panel 4: And, a shot of Anne's hand, as seen from the side of that claw footed porcelain tub, gripping the rim...blood pouring down the sides of the tub from her wrist.

Anne: The blood makes the water so much warmer.

Panel 5: Back to the "real" world as Price tears the helmet/mask off his head.

Dr. Price: Aaagh!

Panel 6: And, on him, hanging his head in the background, as in the foreground, on the table littered with papers and garbage is a small handgun.

Dr. Price: Hnh. Hnh.

Dr. Price: Trial fourteen...unsuccessful. Assessment level: Seven out of ten...

Dr. Price: On a scale of how bad I want to **kill myself.**

Panel 1: An establishing shot of a low rent "tiki-themed" hotel on a roadside in rural Texas. Early evening. The full moon is low in the sky. The place has clearly seen better days, and is pretty rundown. This hasn't stopped them form decorating with garish Christmas decorations, of course, and there's bright red and green lights everywhere. The "Lil' Devil" Truck is parked in the lot, having been appropriated by the Chosen team.

https://lh5.googleusercontent.com/-kiqtOlEazDU/S9BThZ7jfVI/AAAAAAAAAI4/ArITTEKA_S4/s600/kk1.jpg
https://lh6.googleusercontent.com/-uL7ly02DA-s/S9BUS3FScjI/AAAAAAAAAJI/6oFdVgEl3Sc/s553/sign.jpg
http://critiki.com/images/locations/303/3293_medium.JPG

Caption: Kona Mona Tiki Hotel.

Caption: Kilgore, Texas.

Rip (from hotel): We're stuck in this boring hotel room, while Obliva gets to tip a glass with the bossman?

Panel 2: A shot inside the kid's hotel room. Rip is pacing, annoyed and bored as Vanessa sits at the desk calmly reading a spell book. Carcass eats pizza and watches TV.

Carcass: Vanessa, can you exorcise his demon-ass or somethin'? I'm trynna watch **Bridezillas.**

Rip: Naw, man! Ain't fair! I wanna drink! I like lil' umbrellas as much as she does!

Panel 3: Over on Vanessa, as she turns a page in her book. The pages are all filled with strange, occult etchings. She's got a yellow highlighter at her ear for picking out spells and such she wants to get back to. Rip is annoyed.

Vanessa: Rosa's twenty-one. You aren't.

Rip: Sheeit, we run around the country **fighting monsters** and **killin' psychos,** and Gallows is worried about us being the **legal drinking age?** Priorities, man!

Panel 4: Rip looks over at the closed bathroom door, folding his arms. Vanessa rolls her eyes.

Rip: I can't even go in the bathroom to rub one out!

Rip: I mean, you ever heard of a **dirty hippie** taking a shower for this long?

Vanessa: Danny, sit down, and shut up.

Panel 5: Vanessa is at the bathroom door, gently rapping on it

Vanessa: The girl doesn't remember her name or where she comes from.

Vanessa: Who knows what kinda dirt she wants to wash off.

Panel 6: We cut over to inside the bathroom. The shower is on, and the curtain is pulled across the small stall. Vex is sitting in the corner of the shower, looking at the water pooling in her hands with intense wonder and interest.

Vanessa(from outside): Honey, are you okay in there?

Vex: Yes. I just want to be alone for a while...

Vex (small): With my new friend, the **tiny ocean.**

PAGE 11

Panel 1: We cut over to the front of the tiki bar attached to the hotel as Gallows walks out with another man. This is one of his old friends in the government. The guy is in his late 40s, and in a disguise, wearing a t-shirt advertising a BBQ rib joint, cargo shorts and sandals with socks. Gallows has a plastic cup in his hand, decorated with olives and garnishes.

Undercover guy: Thanks for the drink, **Mr. Garou.**

Gallows: Anytime **Bob.** Say hi to Carol for me, would you?

Panel 2: As Gallows walks back towards the guest rooms across the parking lot, Oblivia appears out of the shadows, fading in as is she were made out of the shadows themselves. Gallows doesn't seem surprised or unnerved...

Oblivia: He don't look like no **secret agent.**

Gallows: If he did, he'd be a pretty shitty secret agent.

Panel 3: Gallows passes Oblivia the cup as they walk.

Gallows: Here. One **Bloody Mary** - no garlic. Thanks for covering me. Bob's a good guy, but things have been...**touchy** since **Widmark.**

Oblivia: What'd he say?

Panel 4: On Gallows.

Gallows: Most of the population is content to believe there was a reactor accident near the prison,* but there's been a lot of chatter on the internet about demons and angels, and not just on the nutty sites

Gallows: Been multiple sightings of the **Fairchild kid** too. He's becoming an urban legend. A bogeyman...

Caption: * See Evil Ernie 1-6!

Panel 5: Suddenly Oblivia stops, sniffing the air, dropping her Bloody Mary.
Gallows: He thinks if shit like that keeps scaring the **straights** it could get hairy fo people like us. **Hairier.**

Obliva: Snf.

PAGE 12

Panel 1: Back at the hotel room, Rip is knocking on the bathroom door, impatiently

Rip: Yo, girl! Dreadlocks! I got a serious **pee-boner** here.

Panel 2: Vex is still seated on the floor of the shower, pouring the water between her cupped hands, her face still utterly entranced with something she sees there...

Rip (from off panel): If you could finish, like douching or whatever, I'd be real grateful.

Vex: I think my name is the sound of the tide.

Vex: Or...No, no it's **Vex.**

Panel 3: Back to Gallows and Oblivia. She sprints into motion, surprising Gallows.

Gallows: Rosa! What'd you smell, girl?

Panel 4: Pull back... Vex, in the shower. Behind the curtain, the sexy silhouette shape of the very curvaceous vampire assassin CHASTITY raising a bladed knife to stab poor Vex right through the curtain.

Caption (Oblivia): Vampire.

PAGE 13

Panel 1: Outside, as the running pair of Gallows and Oblivia approach the side of the hotel...the outside wall of the bathroom Vex is in.

Gallows: Oh shit. Sakkara?!

Oblivia: No. Younger. Fresher. But she's got the stink on her...

Panel 2: Oblivia blows through the wall of the bathroom from the outside, and barrels into CHASTITY. Oblivia's mouth is open wide, revealing her own fanged teeth

Chastity should be wearing some kind of sexy punk/goth outfit that's also practical and contains places for her to carry her magical items and weapons. She also should wear gloves of some sort she can handle some of the blessed items she uses.

Note! In the CHAOS! universe, there are different types of vampires. Oblivia is a ahuelpuchi, a Mesoamerican breed. They hale more from the vulture, carrion bird side of vampires, instead of bats, etc, and are born vampiric. Maybe when she "vamps out" she has more "talon" like claws and scary vulture eyes: http://www.wild.uzh.ch/bg/pi/allg/bgauge.jpg
Chastity on the other hand is a European type vampire, and the only effect "vamping out" has on her is fangs, and white "pupiless" eyes.)

FX: KROOM!

Oblivia: She's definitely Purgatori's lily white bitch.

Chastity: Little girl, until you know what you're talking about....

Panel 3: Chastity is a highly experienced fighter, and little Oblivia is no match for her speed and discipline. She dodges away from Oblivia's flailing, angry attack, and reaches into one of her pouches...

Obliva: Hhssssst!

Chastity: You should keep your **trap shut.**

Panel 4: Chastity has retrieved a small spray bottle, once used for expensive perfume. Close in on it as she sprays Oblivia right in the mouth with it.

SFX: FSSST

Chastity: Besides, you never know when someone's going to spray **silver nitrate** into it.

Panel 1: Oblivia shrieks, pawing at her smoking mouth and diving towards the shower where poor confused Vex is, backed against the wall...there's water spraying everywhere.

Vex: oh. Hey, are you, like, a dragon?

Oblivia: Ghhbl!

Panel 2: Chastity turns back as Rip "rips" through the door, his hands now clawed and demonic. His eyes glow green.

SFX:SSHRRK!

Rip (monster voice!): Hhhhk!

Panel 3: Rip, all rage and green flame slashes at Chastity, his claws cutting through the wall near the sink, and the pipes behind it.

Rip (monster voice!): I still gotta pee!!

SFX: SHRRK!

Panel 4: Vex is trying to help Oblivia in the shower. Oblivia's face is still smoking painfully.

Oblivia: Aaaargh!

Vex: Here. The water says you should put some of it in your mouth.

Panel 5: Carcass and Vanessa are through the door. Vanessa has her book in her hand, but rushes to Oblivia. In the background, Chastity and Rip tangle.

Carcass: This what you get for complaining about being bored, **McCarty.**

Vanessa: Rosa!

Panel 6: Obliva looks over her shoulder at Vanessa. He mouth is burned down to the skull. And she looks mad.

Obliva: Thuh 'pell! Thuh un oo oozed on nee--

Vanessa: The spell--? Oh!

PAGE 15

Panel 1: Back to Chastity as she throws Rip right into Carcass.

Carcass: Ah, dude--!

Chastity: Sigh. So young and so dumb. Obsessed with your phones and boy bands.

Panel 2: She raises her blade, about to slash Carcass across the throat.

Chastity: Probably never even heard of the **Buzzcocks.**

Vanessa (from off panel): **Kalfu** of the **Crossroads!**

Panel 3: Close in on Vanessa's hand as she runs her sharp edged pentagram necklace across her palm, making it bleed...

Vanessa: I offer you my **virgin blood!** In exchange I ask...

Panel 4: Pull back as a red crescent moon shaped rune burns into the floor beneath Chastity's feet, as Vanessa reads from the book.

Vanessa: That this child of night be cast from your black paths!

Panel 5: Pull back. Chastity is trying to move, but is frozen in place. She's MAD. Vanessa grips makes a fist to help staunch the bleeding. Her blood drips onto the wet ground. On the ground, not far from her, Vex is kneeling, having just wrapped herself in a towel.

Chastity: Loa! You let me walk or will hunt you to the **Other Side!**

Gallows (from off panel): Not bad, my Chosen.

Panel 6: Gallows enters through the hole on the wall made by Oblivia. He's got a big handgun in his hand, and some other gear he's picked up from the truck outside, most notably a spool of silver wire.

Gallows: But not good enough. It was real nice of her to send us a minor league hitter, but this isn't gonna cut it when it comes to Sakkara....

PAGES 16-17

Panel 1: Vex, kneeling, is looking at the blood-tinted water on the ground. Gallows is walking by in the background, instructing his students.

Gallows (from off panel): Let's move before Johnny Law shows up. Carcass, double knot the redhead in silver chords...

Vex: oh...woah.

Panel 2: On Vex's eyes, wide. She's sees something terrifying in the water on the ground.

Gallows (from off panel): We'll take 'er out to the desert for some impromptu **Vampicide 101**.

Vex: I see.

Panel 3: Vex smashes her hand into the pool of water in complete anguish, surprising everyone around her with the impossible volume of her scream, as waves of energy/electricity strike everyone around using the water as a conduit.

Vex: **I SEE!!**

Panel 4: BIG full bleed MONTAGE, of Vex's vision of the future to come. Make

this an epic and horrifying look at a horror apocalypse that every death metal band wishes they could get on an album cover.
Cities burn. Zombies feasts upon the living. Vampires and werewolves battle each other for the last scraps of meat. The sky is black.

Evil Ernie stands looking over all of this from the shattered remains of the Clearview Mental Institute. The sky is choked with dust and fire. A hooded, cloaked female figure stands just behind him.

Panel 5: We close in on Ernie and the figure, as he holds out a hand for her. She's turned away from him, her hands up at the hood...

Ernie: "Earth shall be riven...and the over-heaven."

Ernie: For you.

Panel 6: And, she turns back, her hood falling away, revealing her beautiful face and a haunting smile. This is **Lady Hel.**

Ernie: For **us.**

PAGE 18

Panel 1: Back to the hotel room...everyone, including Chastity is doubled over from the painfully powerful experience of the end times vision...
Vanessa: all....all the pain...

Rip: No one left, man. No one at all...

Panel 2: Oblivia , who is still lying close to Vex inside the shower stall, looks up at her, tears in her eyes, with a look of almost betrayal.

Oblivia: It was the end of the world. My mother, she said there'd be Jesus... and a place for the good people at his side.

Panel 3: Switch angles, as Chastity, in the foreground, sullenly shakes off what she just saw. The spell-rune is gone... In the background, Oblivia and Vex talking. Vex seems to be taking the whole thing rather well, sort of dreamy and disconnected.

Oblivia: Oblivia: --but there was no good. No one spared.

Oblivia: Quien... quien eres?

Vex: Hm. I'm not wearing pants and I'm surrounded by strangers.

Panel 4: Chastity stumbles towards the hole in the wall in the background. Chastity passes by Gallows, on his hands and knees.

Vex (from off panel): I must be in **History Class.**

Gallows: Uhn. Oh God.

Panel 5: Chastity looks at the knife in her hand. He's basically helpless. She could kill him, but it's clear that she's conflicted...

NO DIALOGUE.

Panel 6: And, she ducks out, leaving him to live, as Oblivia comes to the aid of Gallows.

Gallows: hunh.

Oblivia: Mr. Gallows!

PAGE 19

Panel 1: An establishing shot of the Luxor Hotel in Las Vegas, focusing mostly on the faux Egypt aspects of the place (which are, of course, what Purgatori likes about it so much!). It's late at night.

Caption: Las Vegas, Nevada.

Mook 1 (from building): Another one?

Panel 2: In the hallway of the rooftop suite, we see two Vegas mob/tough guy types carrying a body wrapped in a sheet towards an employee/freight elevator.

Mook 1: The desert got more bodies with her name on 'em than any of our other clients.

Mook 2: Her money spends the same.

Panel 3: We see a beautiful young girl, her eyes filled with tears as Purgatori's's hand gently caresses her face. This is Alla, a thin, pale Russian girl with black hair, an unfortunate victim of Purgatori's affection for keeping some love-slaves/snacks around at all times.

Purgatori (from off panel): Oh, my darling Alla, don't shed a tear for Jon. His time had come.

Alla: Will---will my time come soon?

Panel 4: We pull back to see Purgatory is lounging in a large, luxurious bed with 2 other girls (besides Alla), and 2 guys. All are young (in their early 20s, of various races, all pretty, all with black hair) and quite naked (though cover up the stuff.) Those four are asleep, but Purgatori is paying special attention to Alla. She treats her more like a pet than anything, and the young girl is afraid of her, but knows to act as if she adores the scary winged vampiress. The huge room around them is a high-end suite in the hotel, and it's full of some garish, and some really expensive Egyptian themed decorations.

Purgatori: Little thing...So beautiful and so naive. You remind me of myself... once.

Alla: But, Mistress Purgatori, you always say that Chastity Marks reminds you of yourself.

Panel 5: On Purgatori, a sinister smile on her lips...

Purgatori: Oh, she does. She reminds me of a version myself I hate...someone I killed long ago.

Purgatori: It's why I delight in tormenting her so. It's why crushing her spirit brings me such joy.

Panel 6: We cut to Chastity now, on a Custom Cb350 motorcycle (once owned by Sid Vicious, of course!) down a highway...

REF: http://www.bikeexif.com/wp-content/uploads/2012/09/honda-cb350-custom-2.jpg

Caption (Purgatori): It's also why, no matter the consequences...

Caption (Purgatori): ...she'll do exactly what I ask of her.

PAGE 20

Panel 1: A bit later. The full moon hangs over the desert.

Caption: Later.

Gallows (from off panel): When I worked for the government, I got real good at telling myself that what I was doing was for the greater good.

Panel 2: On Gallows looking up at he full moon. He's shirtless.

Gallows: Sure, some of 'em deserved to die, but most of 'em were just trying to live normal, everyday lives.

Panel 3: On Gallows eye, as it become a golden wolf-like eye...

Gallows: The middle-aged vampire who worked the late shift at 7-11. The demon who couldn't tell his fiancée why they couldn't have their wedding in a church.

Panel 4: From behind, as his back starts to warp and change, black hair sprout across his shoulder blade...

Gallows: When I'd take out one of those types, I'd just tell myself it was only a matter of time

**The next three shots should just be a progression of Gallows hand changing from human into his clawed werewolf form...

Panel 5: On his hand, becoming a claw, phase one.

Gallows: A monster's a monster...

Panel 6: On his hand, becoming a claw, phase two.

Gallows: ...and sooner a later, a monster's going to lose control.

Panel 7: On his hand, becoming a claw, full werewolf phase!

Gallows: Nobody understood that better than me, right?

Panel 1: A big shot of Gallows in his full werewolf form.

Gallows: But then I had a dream...a vision that led me to you all; my **Chosen**-- monsters that could learn to control themselves and do good.

Panel 2: Focus on the "original" Chosen kids, RIP,CARCASS, OBLIVIA, and VANESSA sitting around the Lil' Devil truck, which is parked in the desert, listening to Gallows talk off panel.

Gallows (from off panel): Chosen to destroy the real monsters...like Sakkara. Like a government that would prefer to just kill us, instead of give us a chance.

Gallows (from off panel): That vision was the most important thing that every happened to me. So, I'm not the kind to doubt them...

Panel 3: Vex, now dressed in a collection of mismatched clothes the crew has scrounged for the her.

Gallows (from off panel): Especially not when I can feel the heat from burning cities. Smell the scraps of rotting flesh. Taste the death in the air

SPLASH!

Panel 1: Pull back, dramatic shot of the Chosen team, the full moon behind them....looking like the bad-ass Teen-Titans-by-way-of-a-horror-movie-marathon that they are.

Gallows: We have a new mission, my Chosen. We have to destroy **Ernest Fairchild.**

Gallows: Before he kills the world.

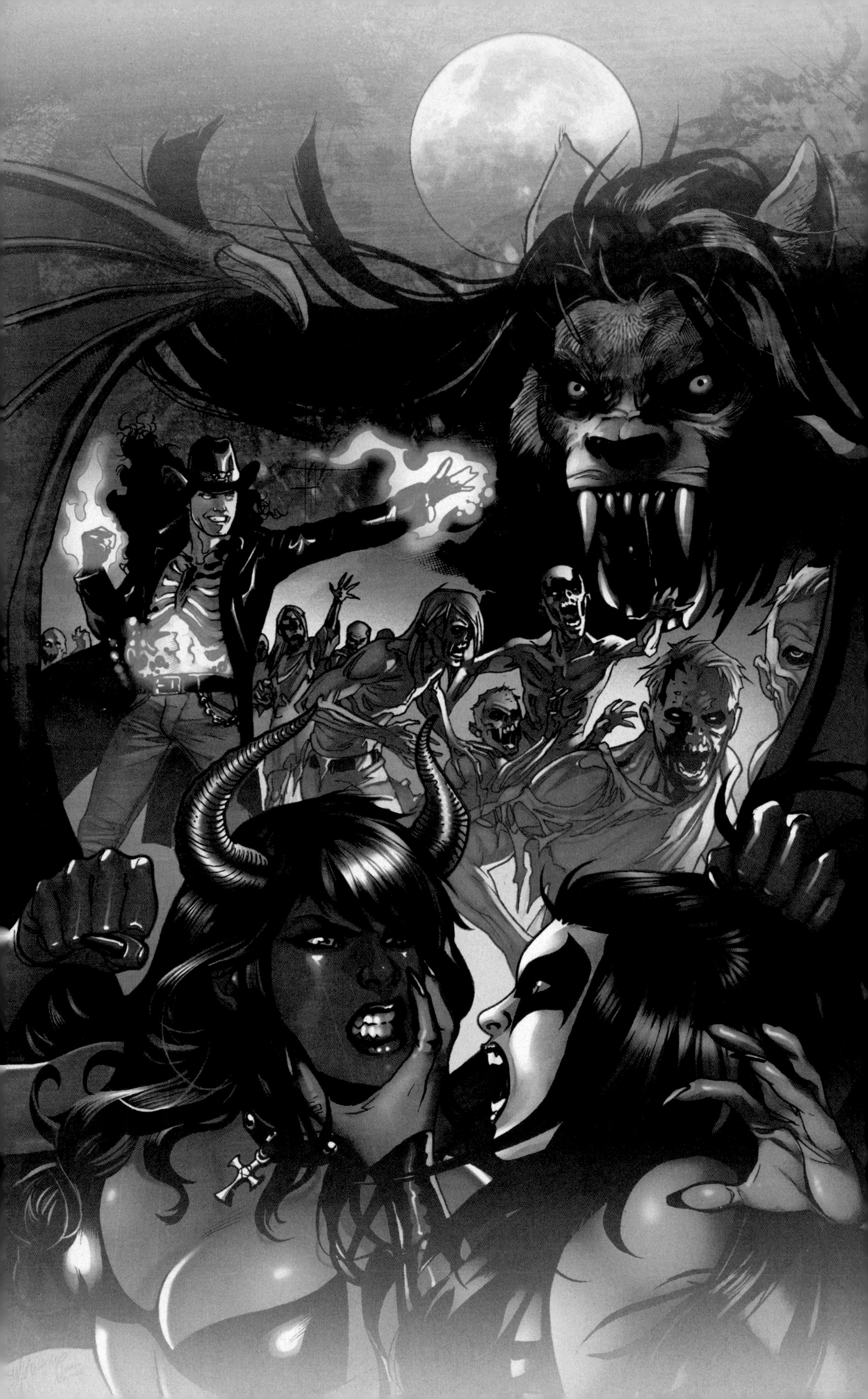

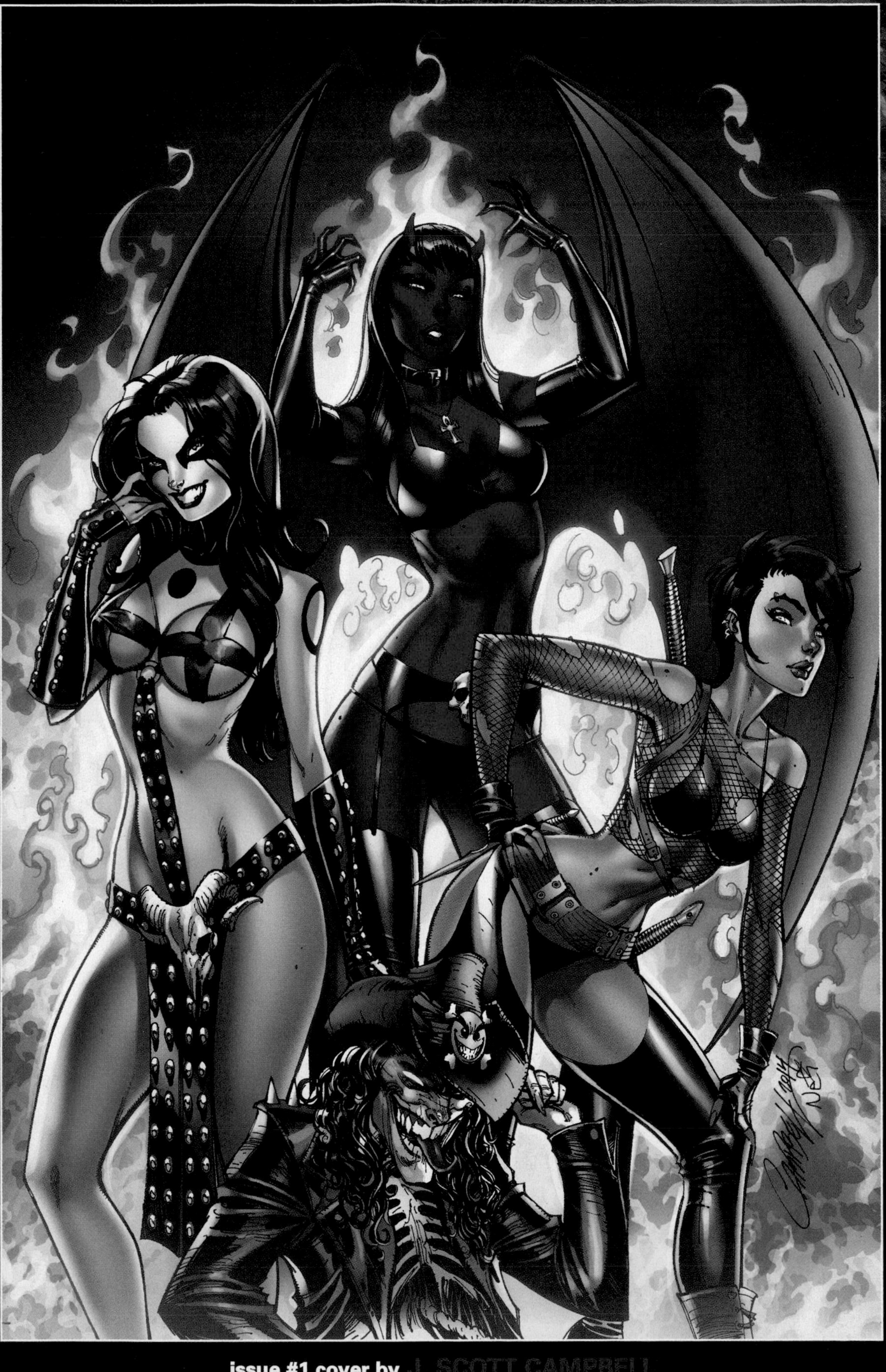

issue #1 cover by J. SCOTT CAMPBELL
colors by NEI RUFFINO

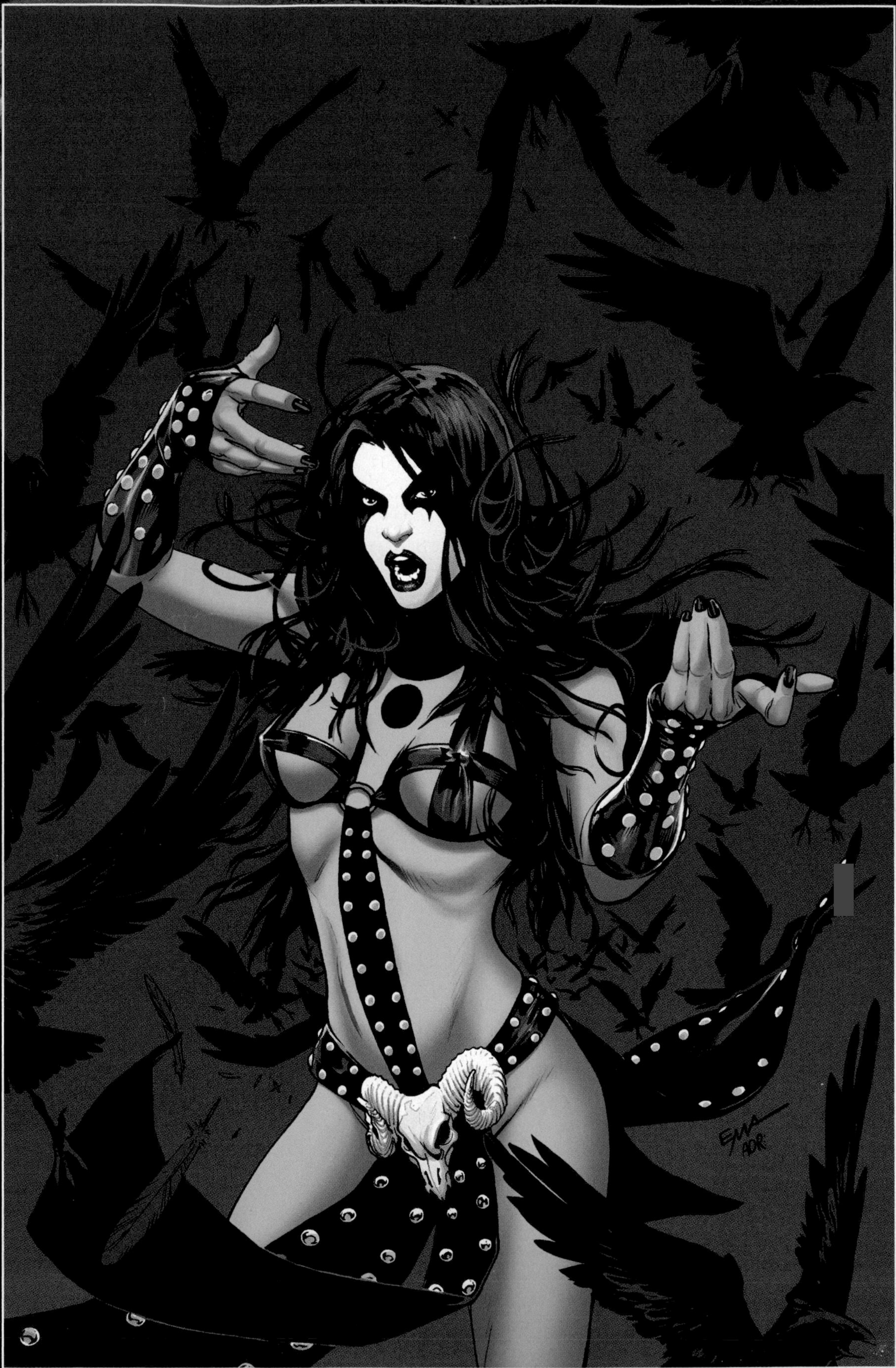

issue #1 cover by EMANUELA LUPACCHINO
colors by IVAN NUNES

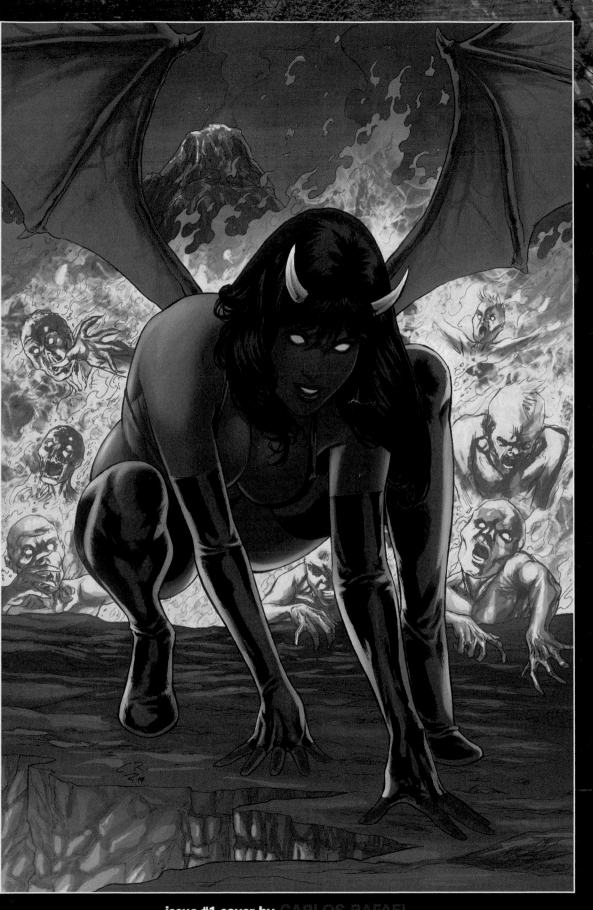

issue #1 cover by CARLOS RAFAEL
colors by ADRIANO LUCAS

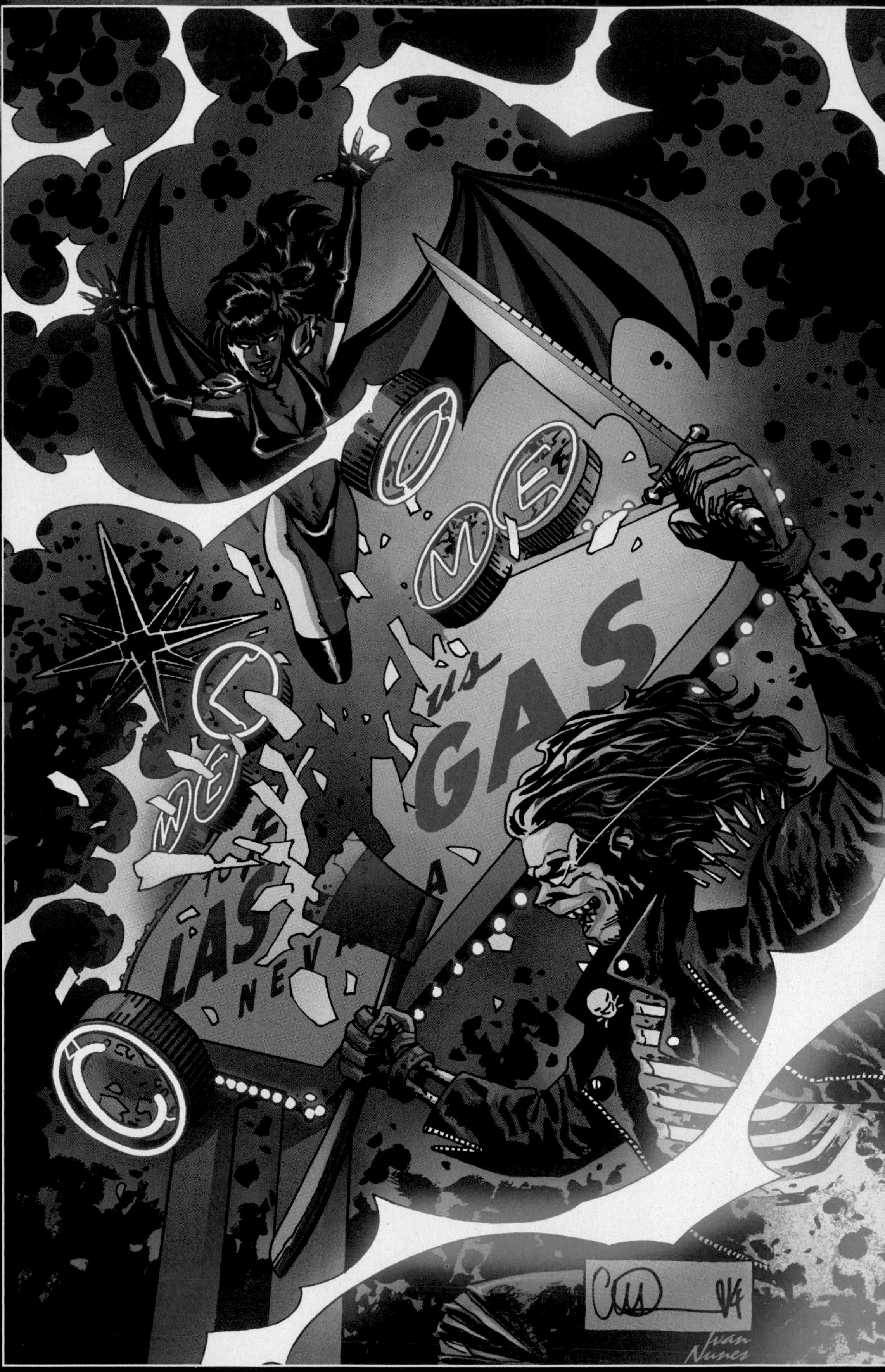
GAS
LAS
NEV
Ivan Nunes

issue #1 cover by CHARLIE ADLARD
colors by IVAN NUNES

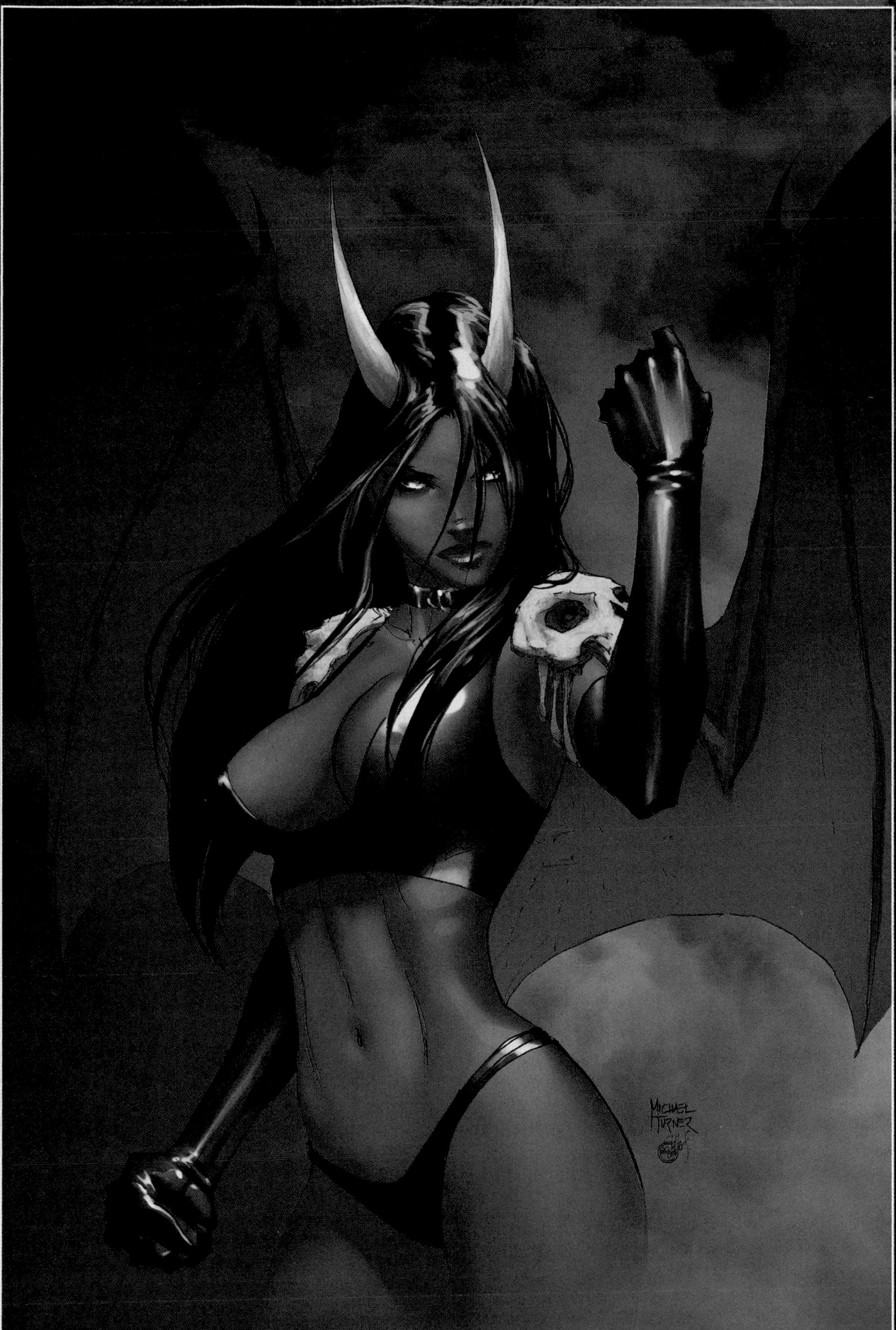
MICHAEL TURNER

issue #1 cover by MICHAEL TURNER
colors by PETER STEIGERWALD

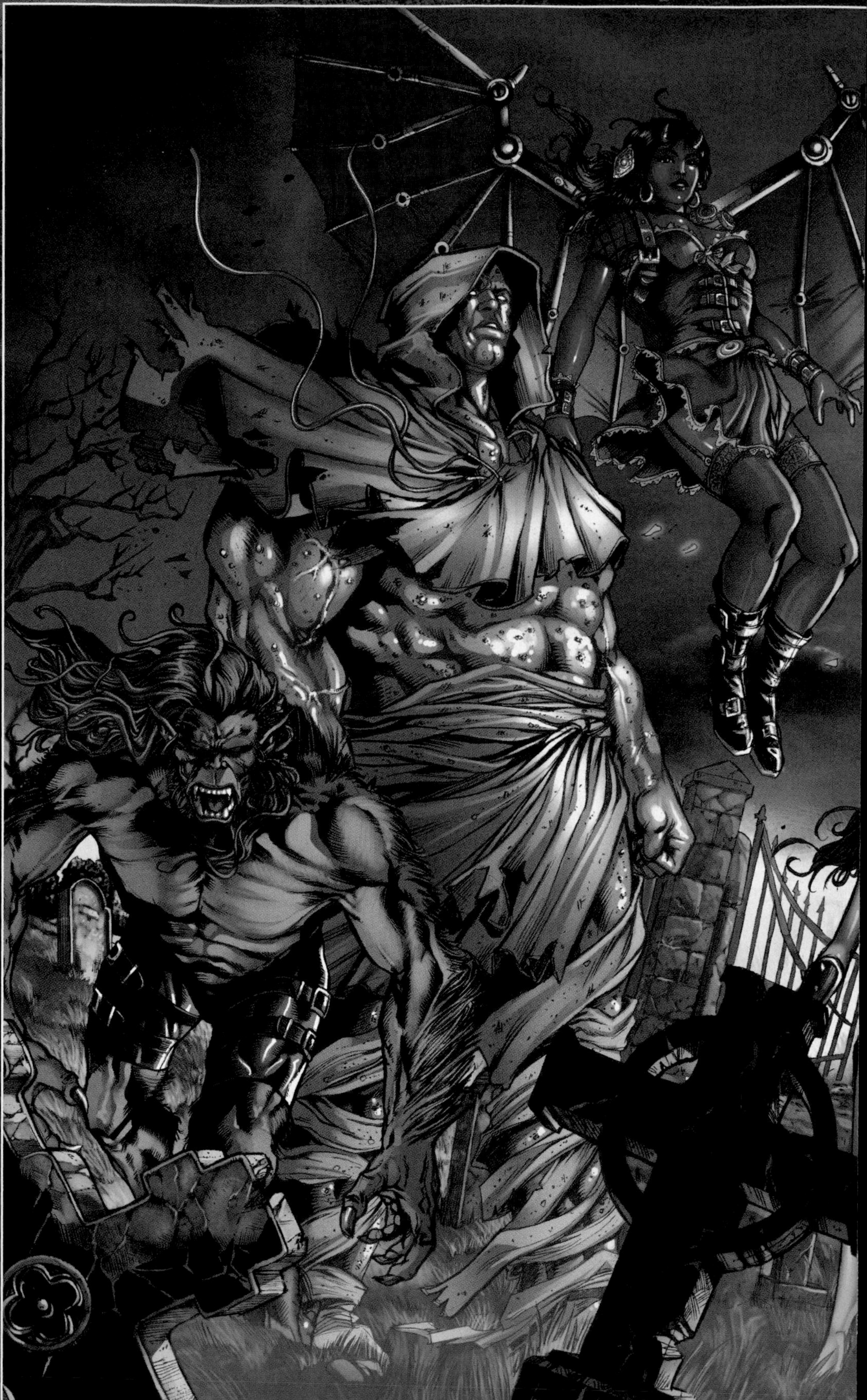

issue #1 cover by SERGIO FERNANDEZ DAVILA

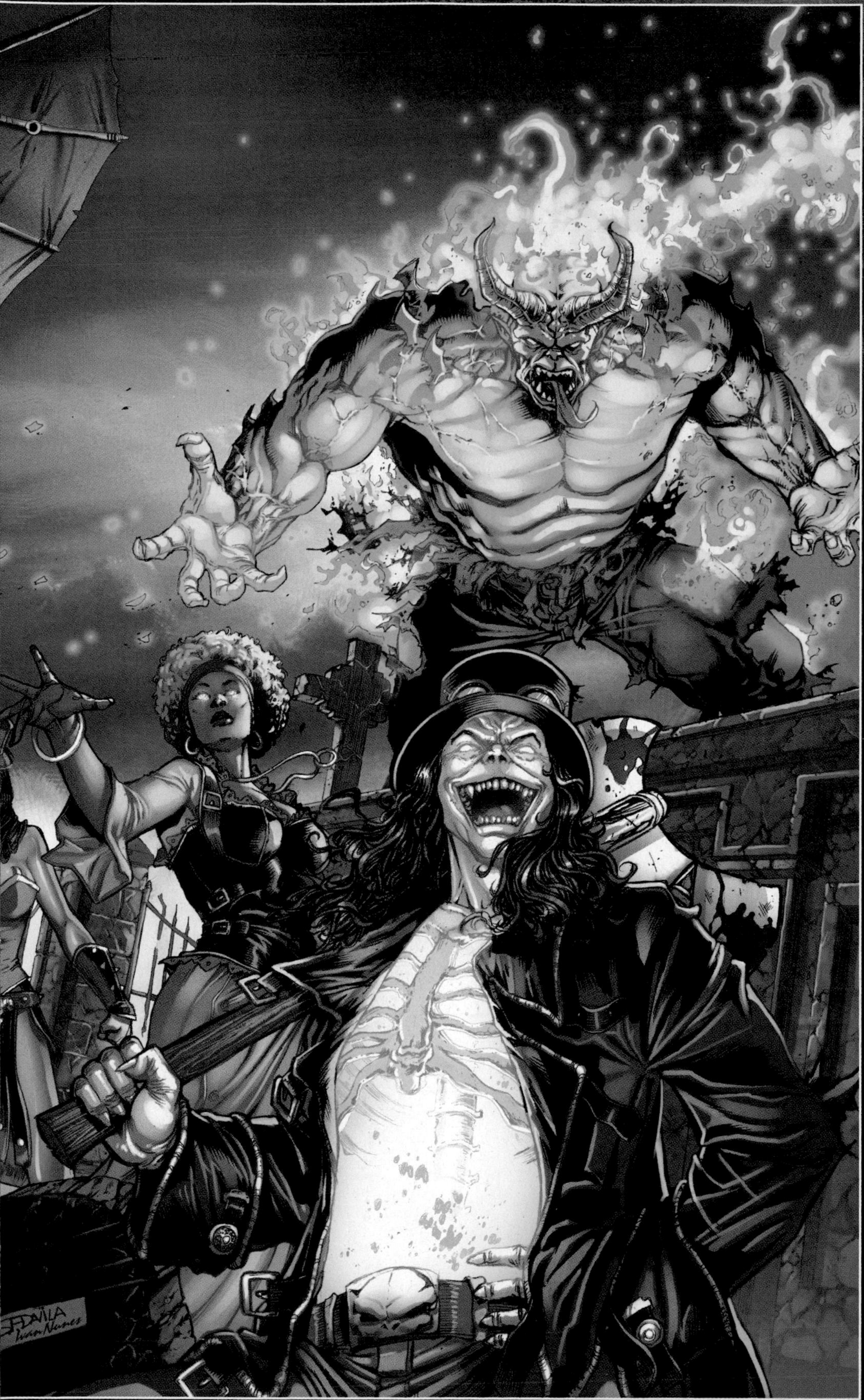

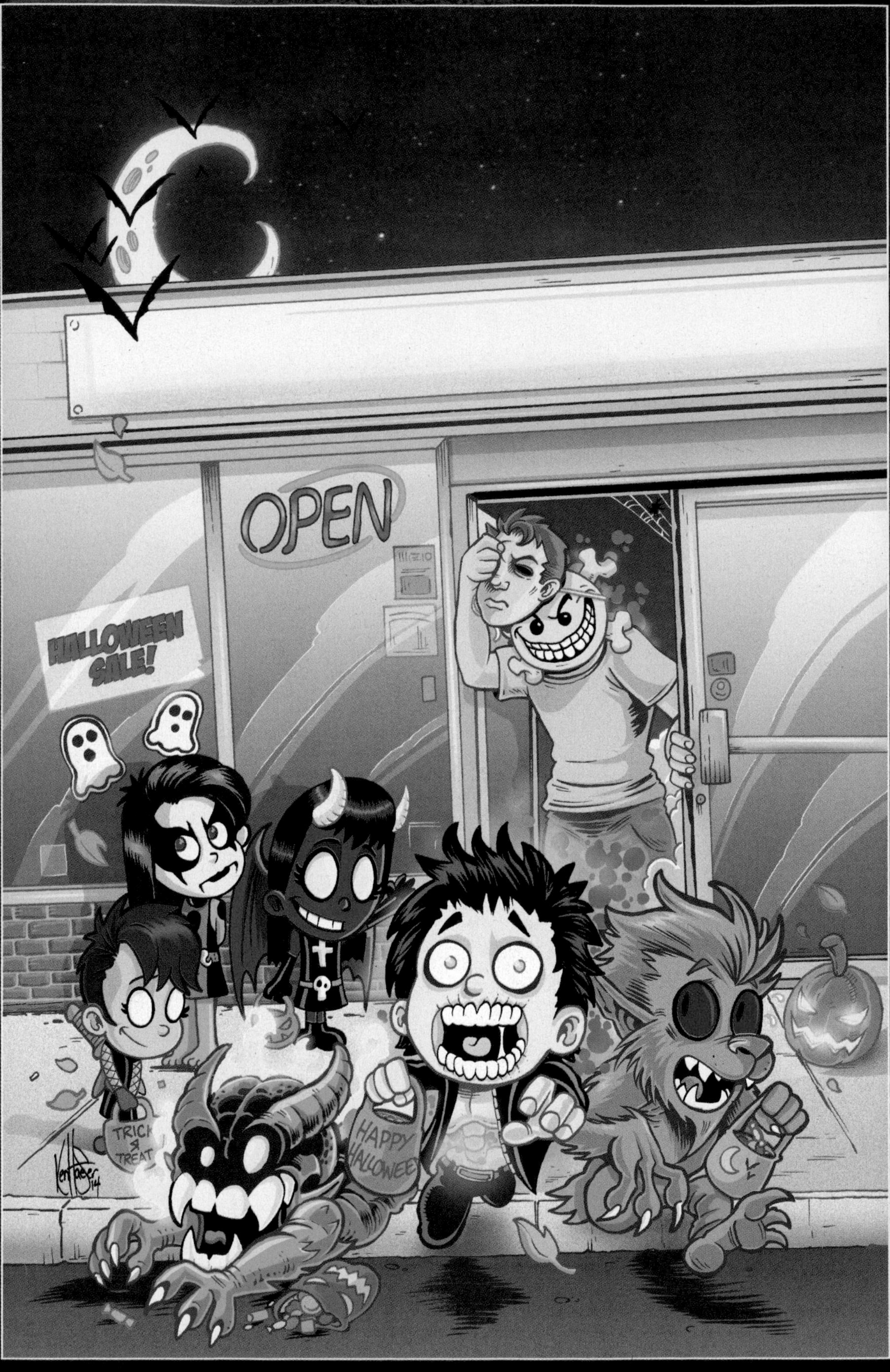
OPEN
HALLOWEEN SALE!
TRICK R TREAT
HAPPY HALLOWEE

issue #1 cover by KEN HAESER

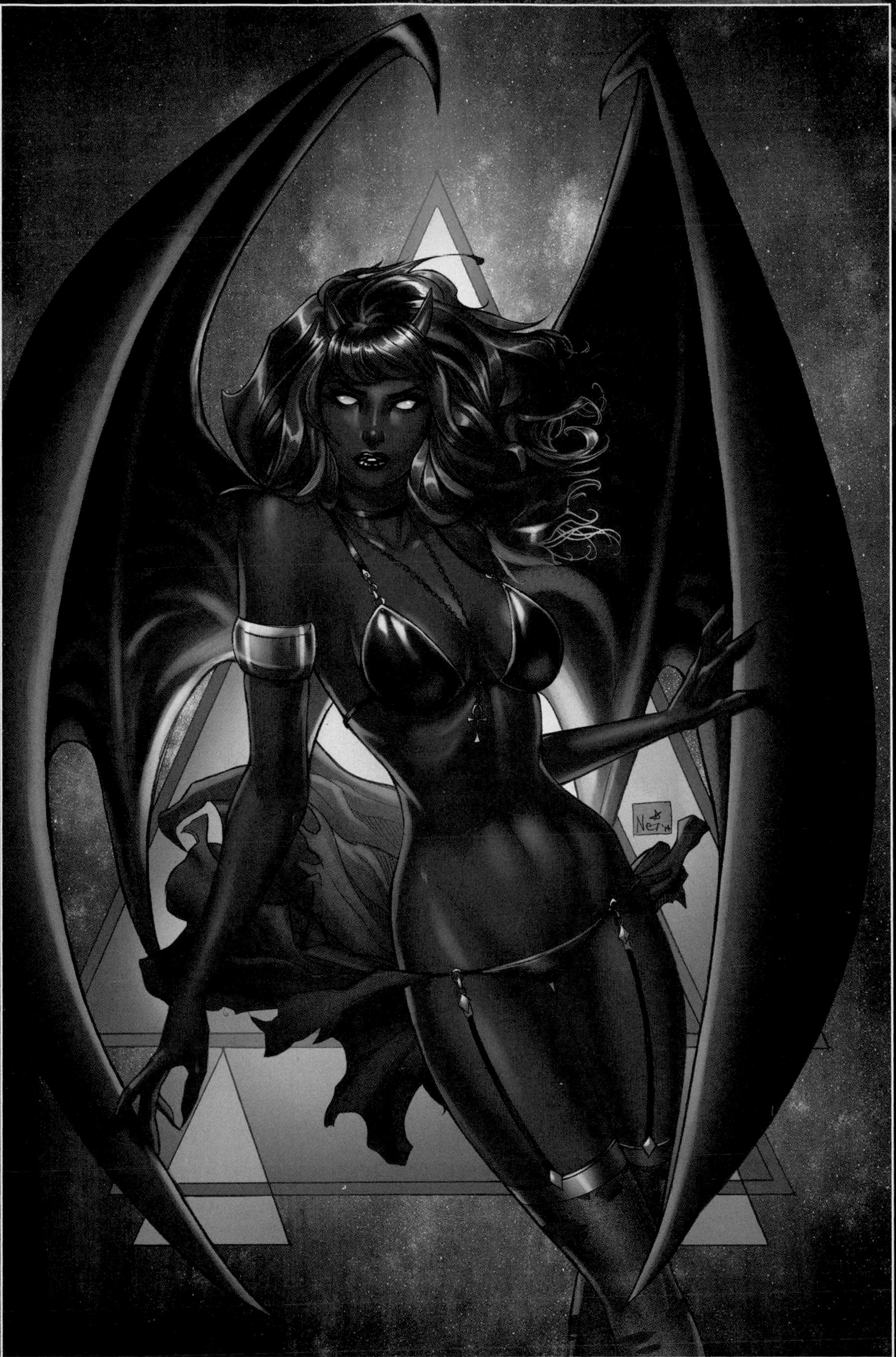

issue #1 cover by NEI RUFFINO

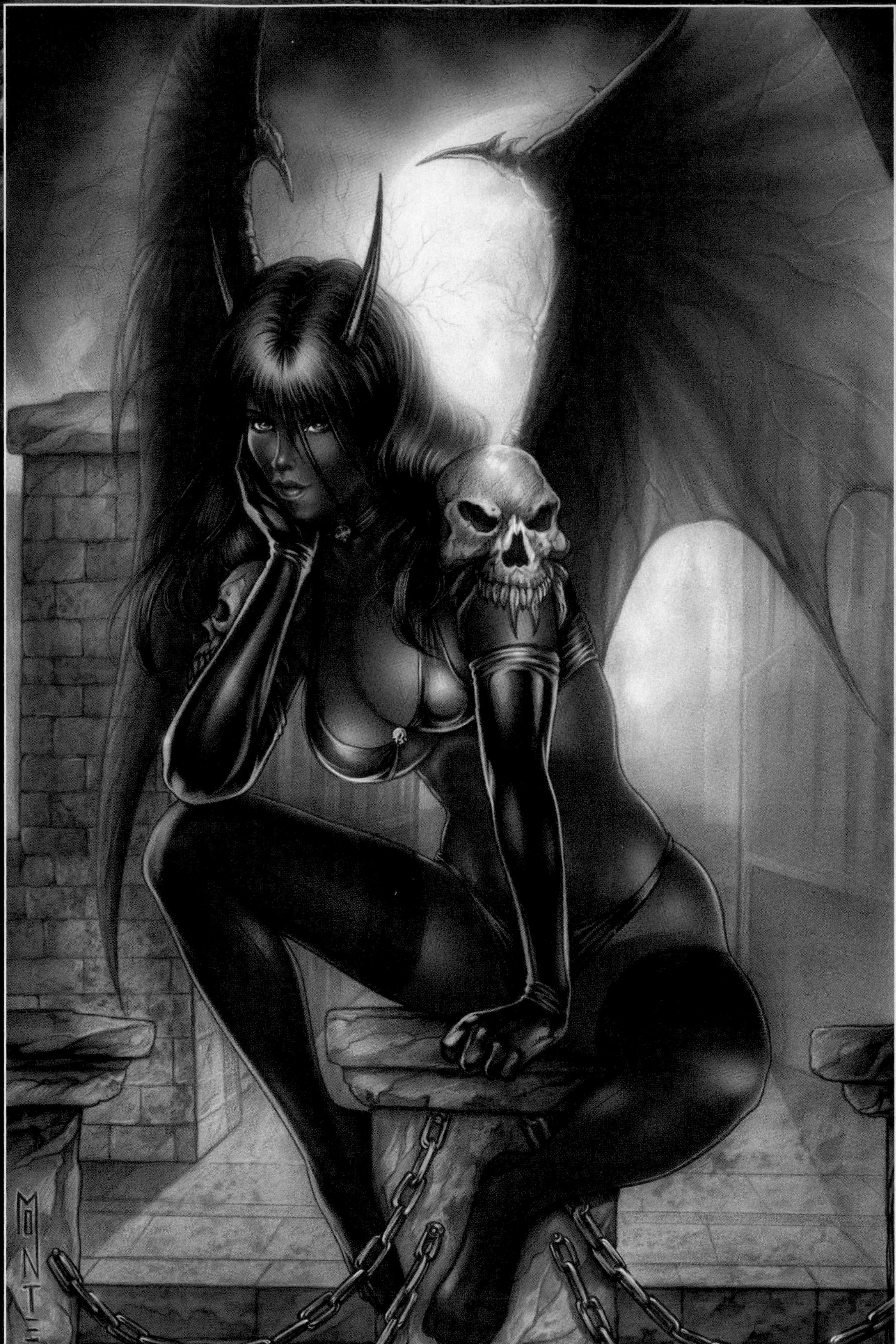

issue #1 cover by MONTE MOORE

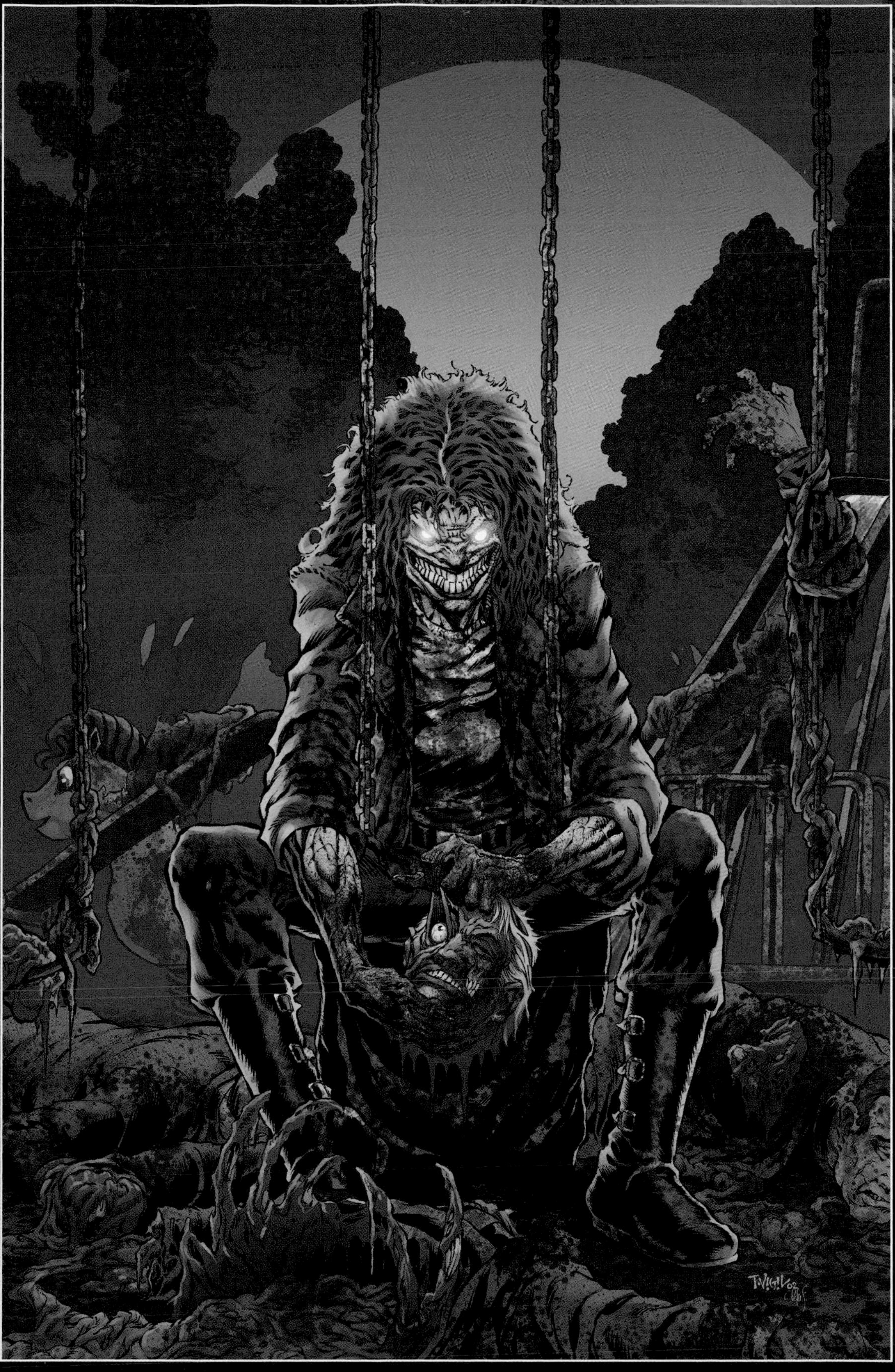

issue #1 cover by TIM VIGIL
colors by PETER STEIGERWALD

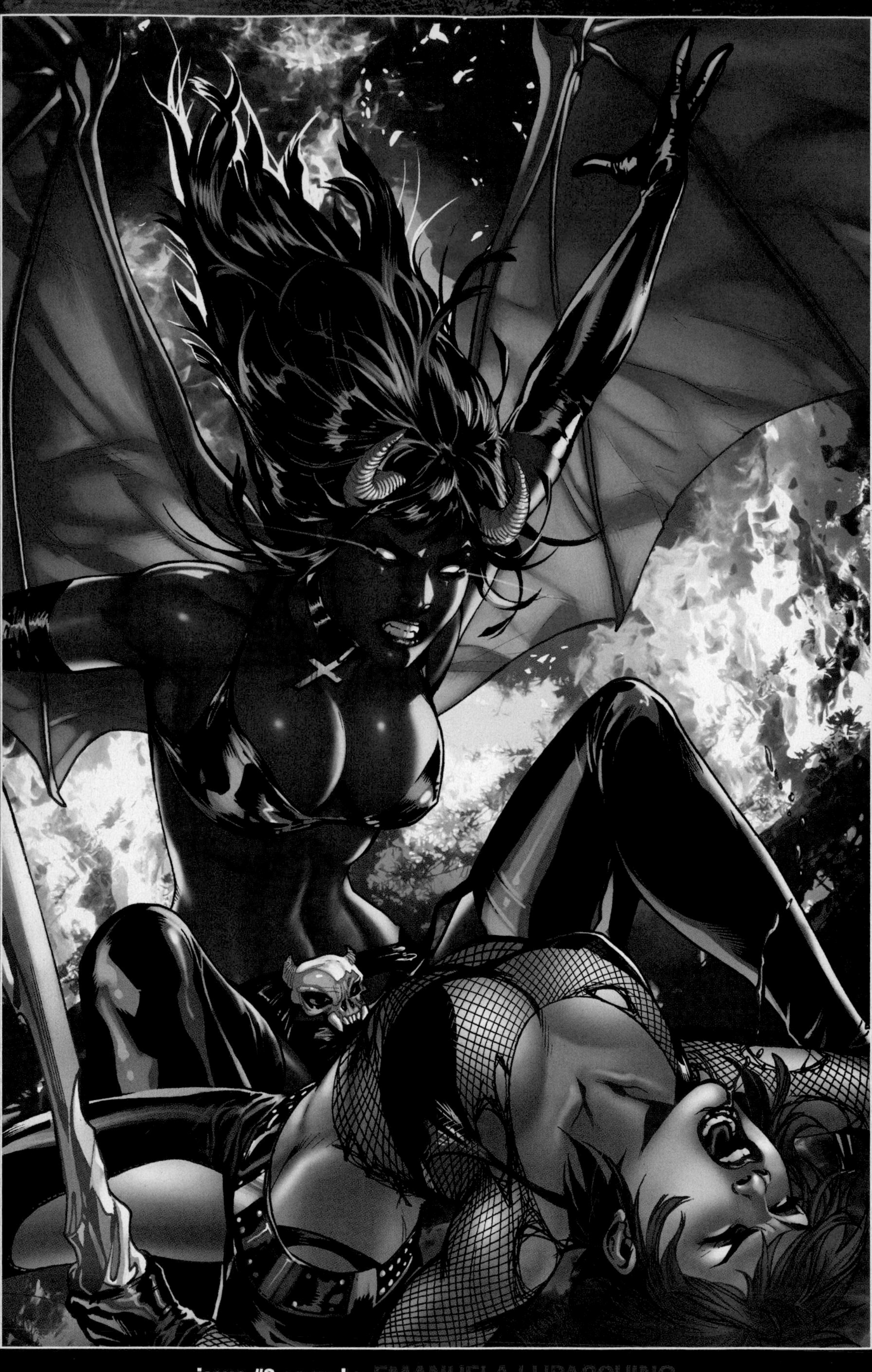

issue #2 cover by EMANUELA LUPACCHINO
colors by IVAN NUNES

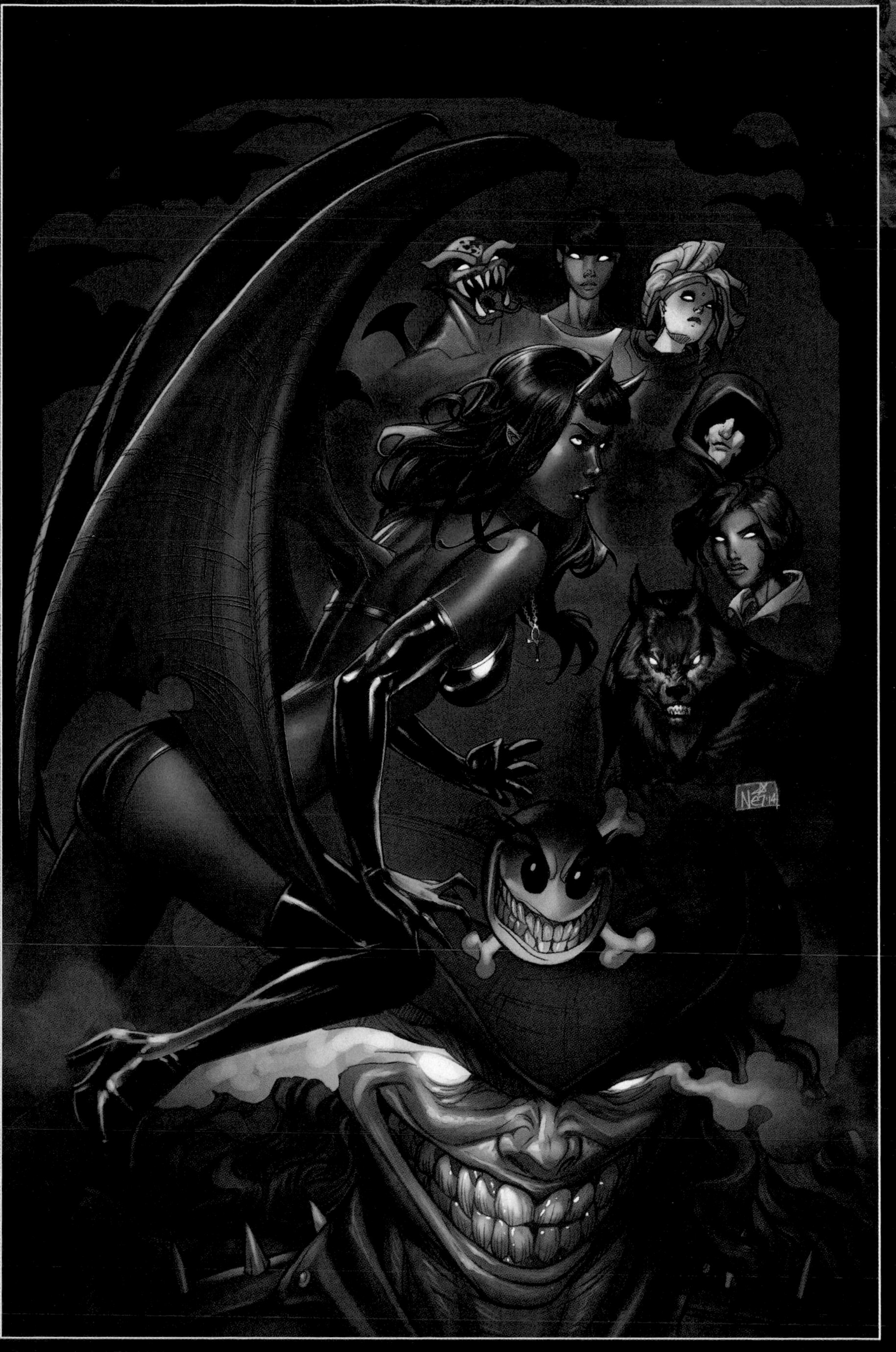

issue #2 cover by NEI RUFFINO

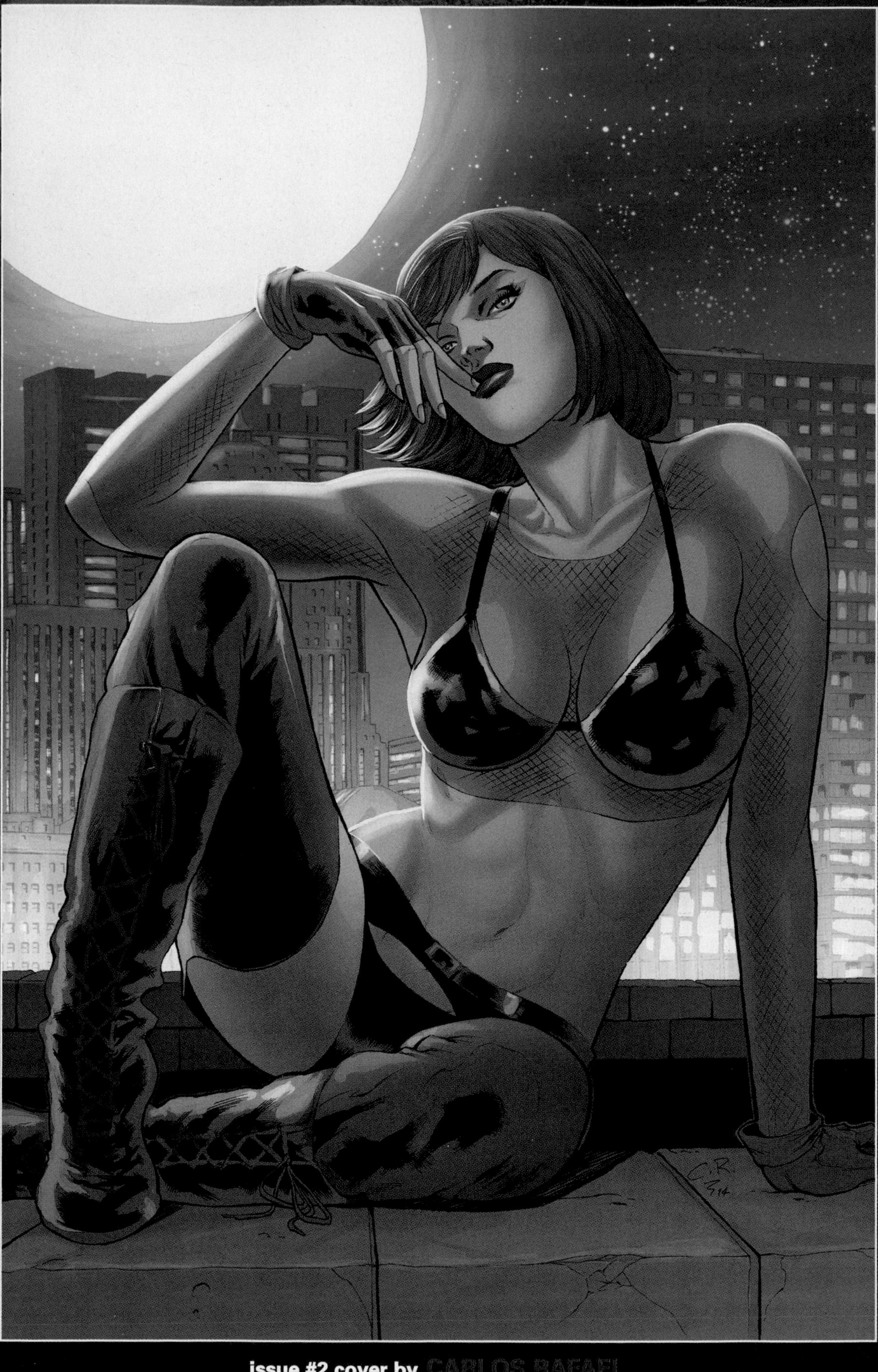

issue #2 cover by CARLOS RAFAEL
colors by ADRIANO LUCAS

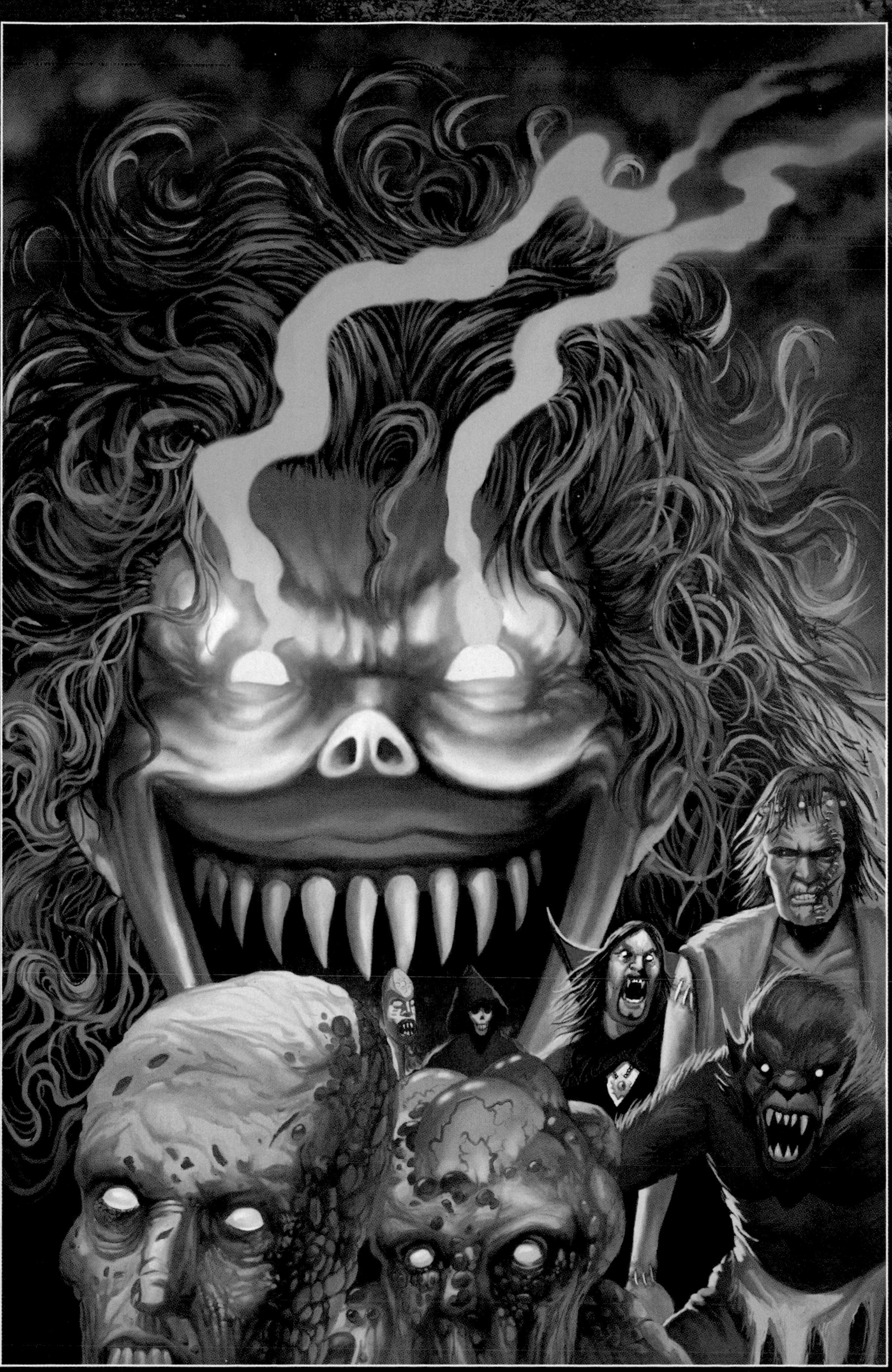

issue #2 cover by WALTER FLANAGAN
colors by WAYNE JANSEN

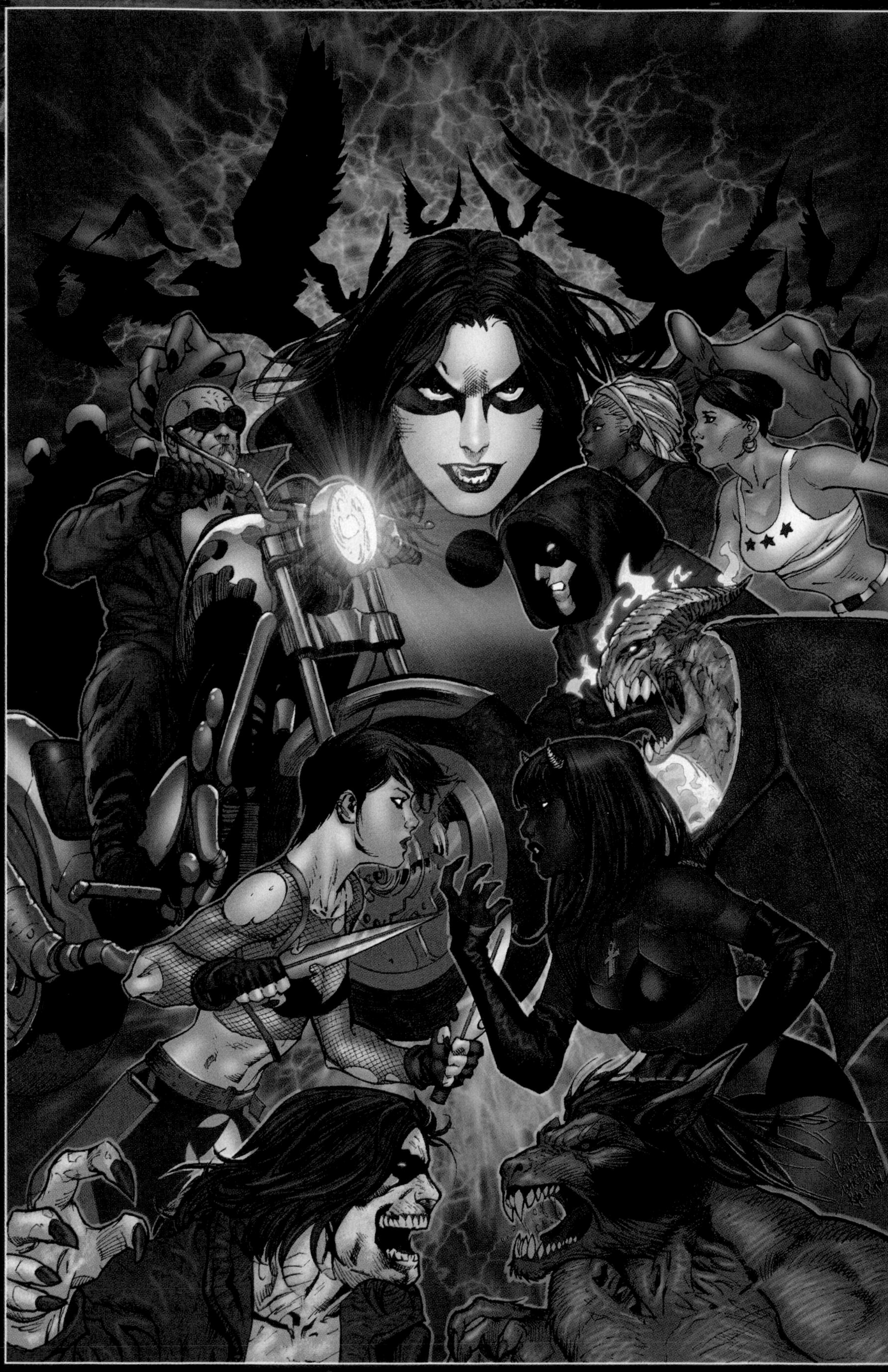

issue #2 second print cover by ARDIAN SYAF

inks by CORAL MARTINEZ colors by KYLE RITTER

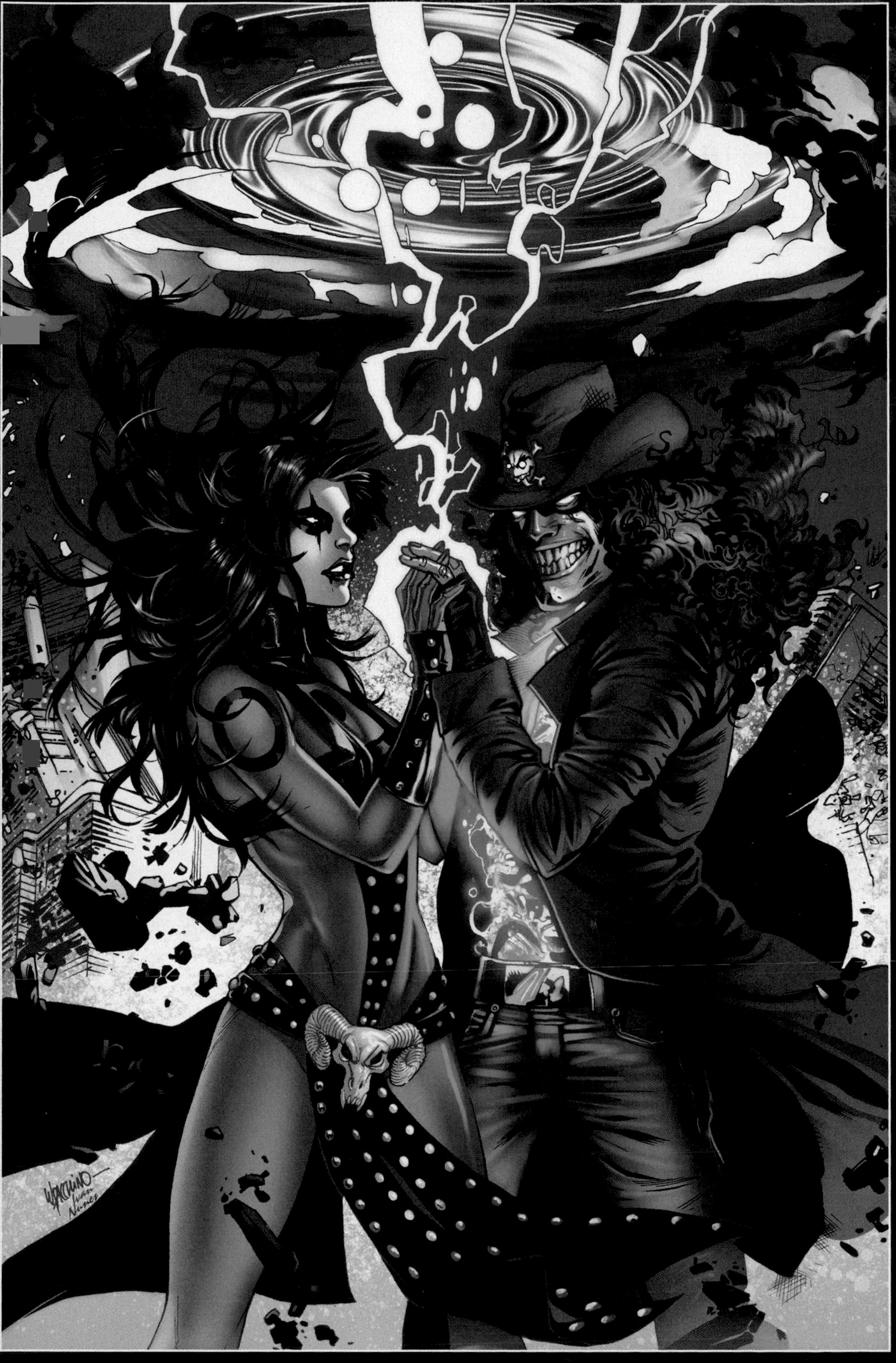

issue #3 cover by EMANUELA LUPACCHINO
colors by IVAN NUNES

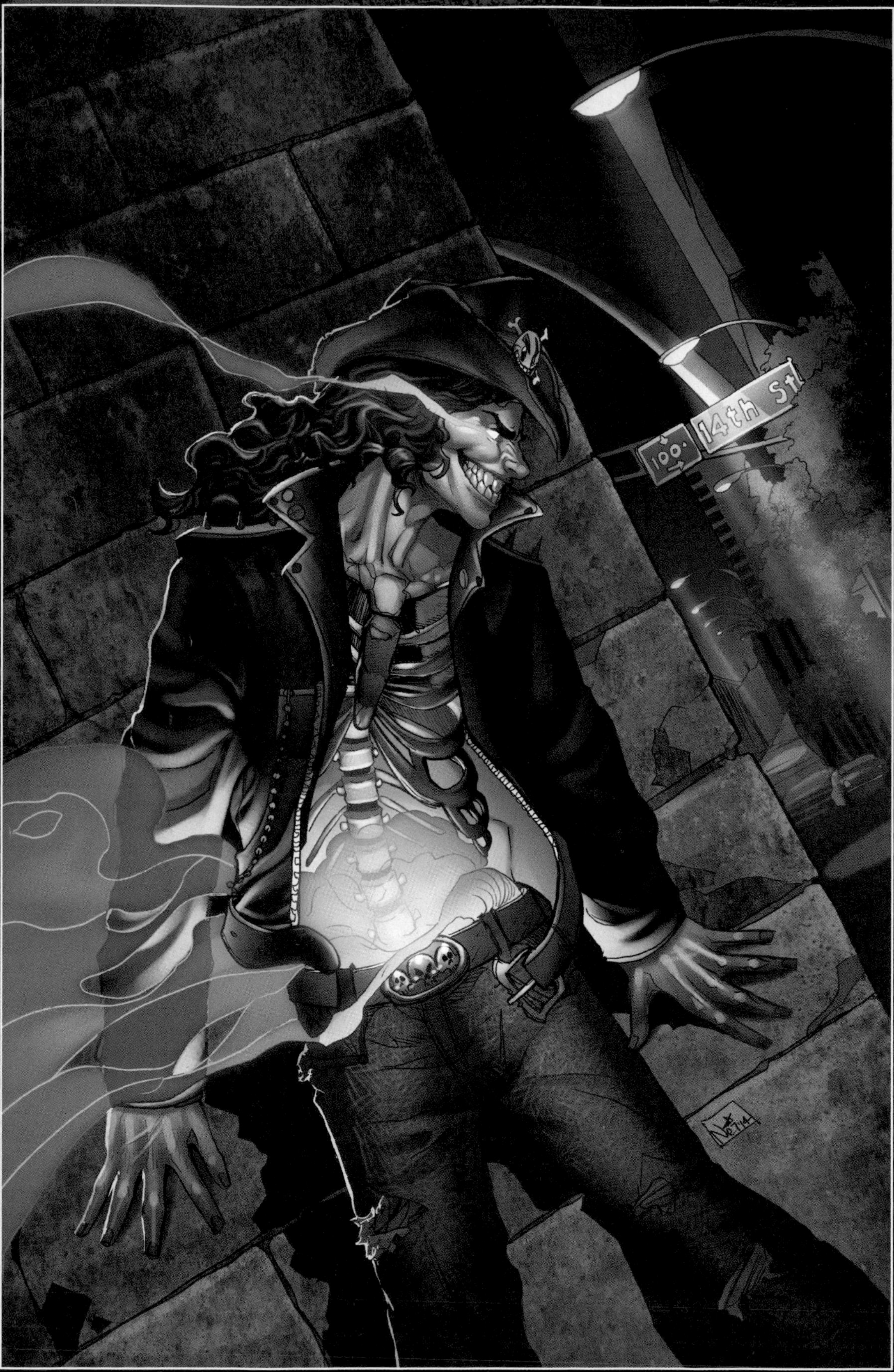
14th St
100

issue #3 cover by NEI RUFFINO

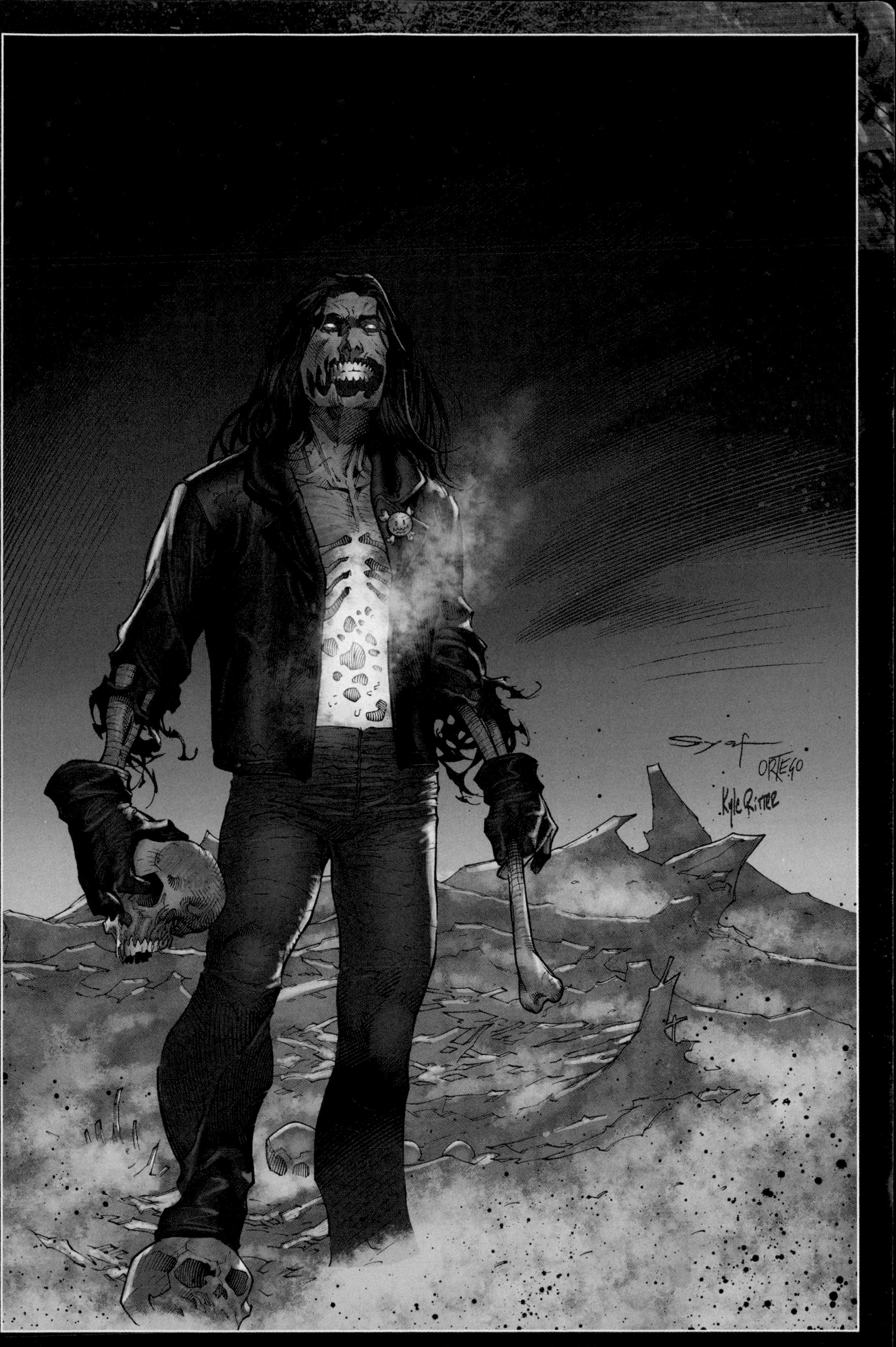
Syaf
ORTEGO
Kyle Ritter

issue #3 cover by ARDIAN SYAF
inks by GUILLERMO ORTEGO colors by KYLE RITTER

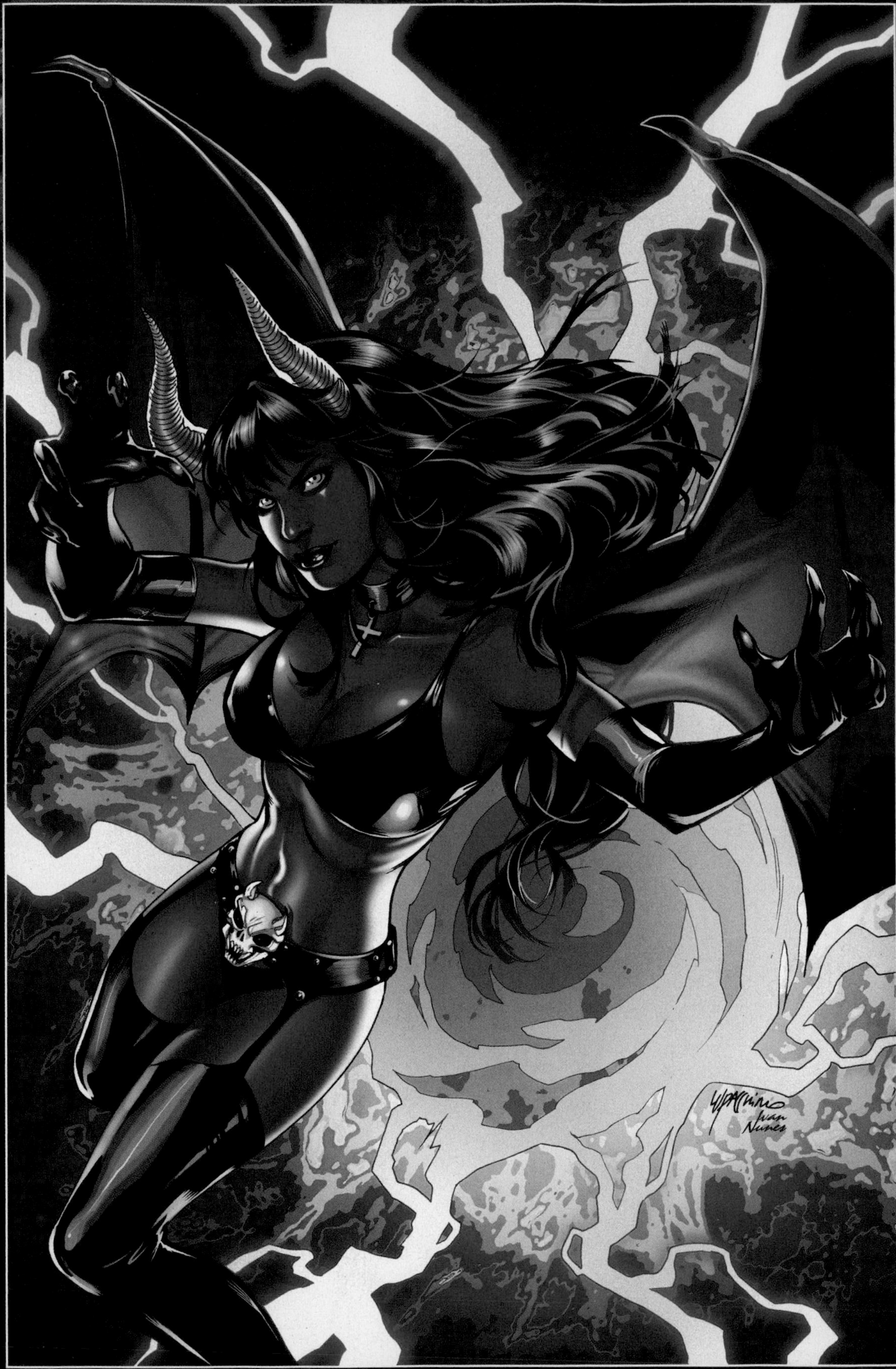

LUPACCHINO
IVAN NUNES

issue #4 cover by EMANUELA LUPACCHINO
colors by IVAN NUNES

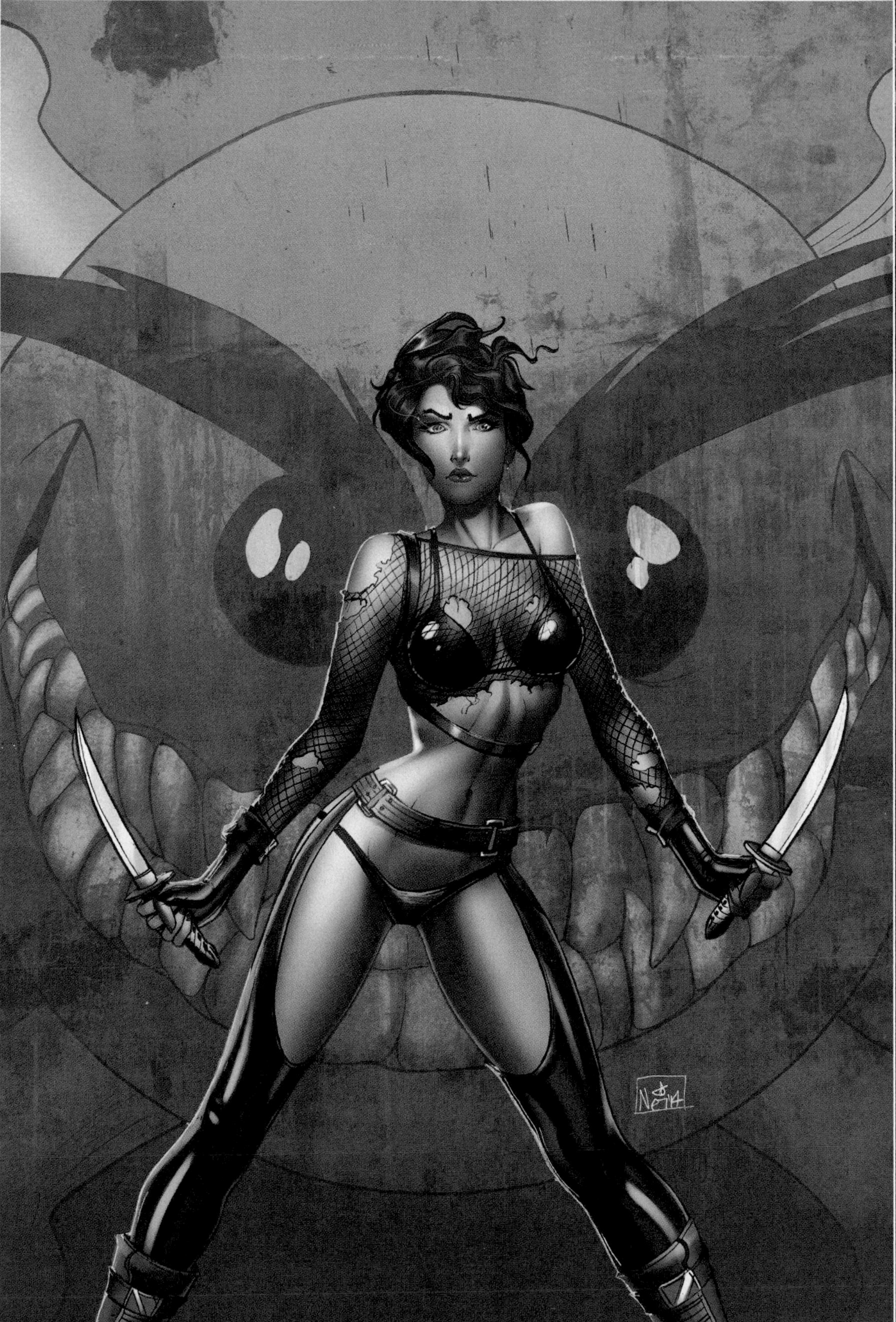

issue #4 cover by NEI RUFFINO

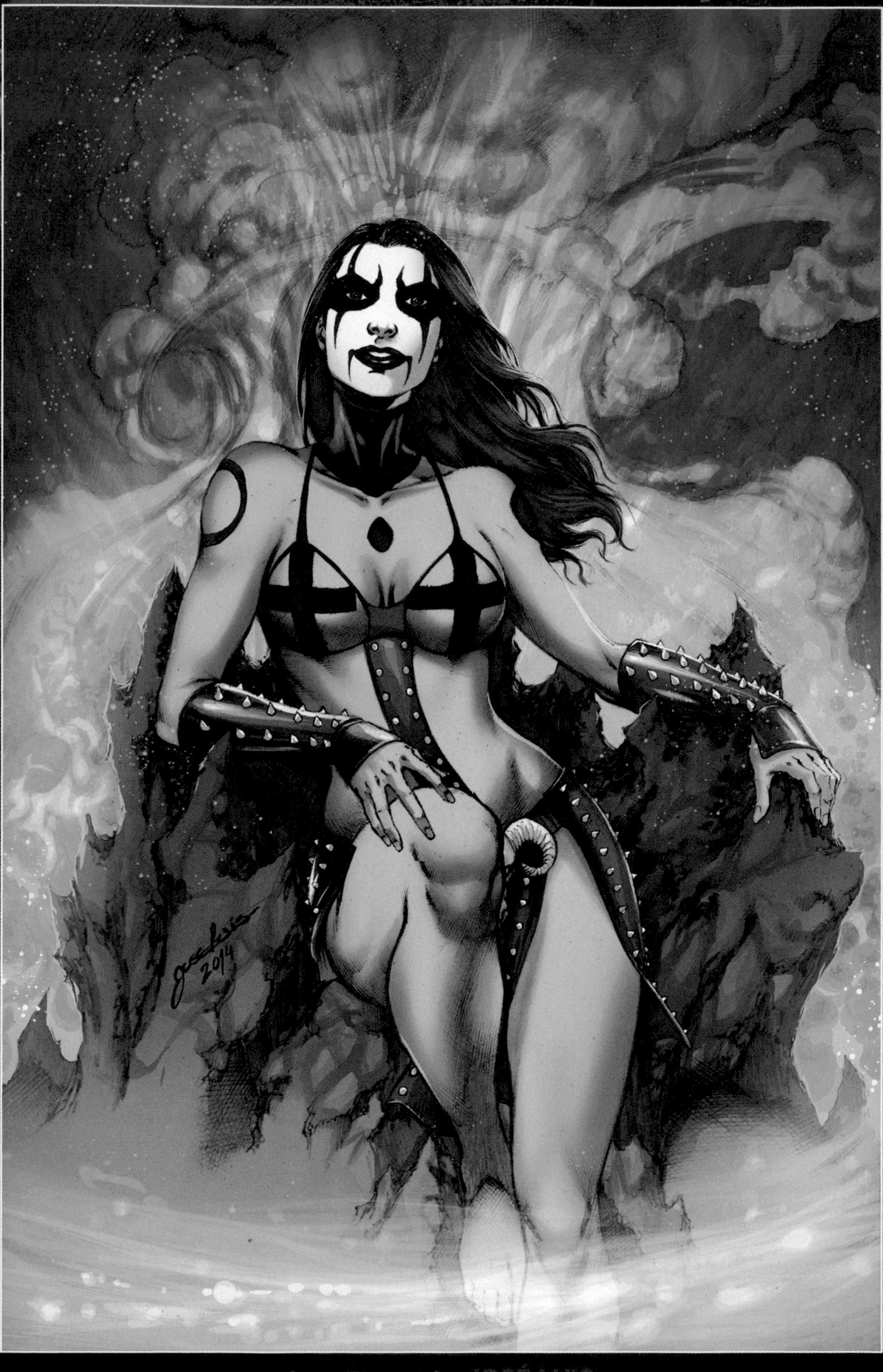
jose luis
2014

issue #4 cover by JOSÉ LUIS
colors by ADRIANO LUCAS

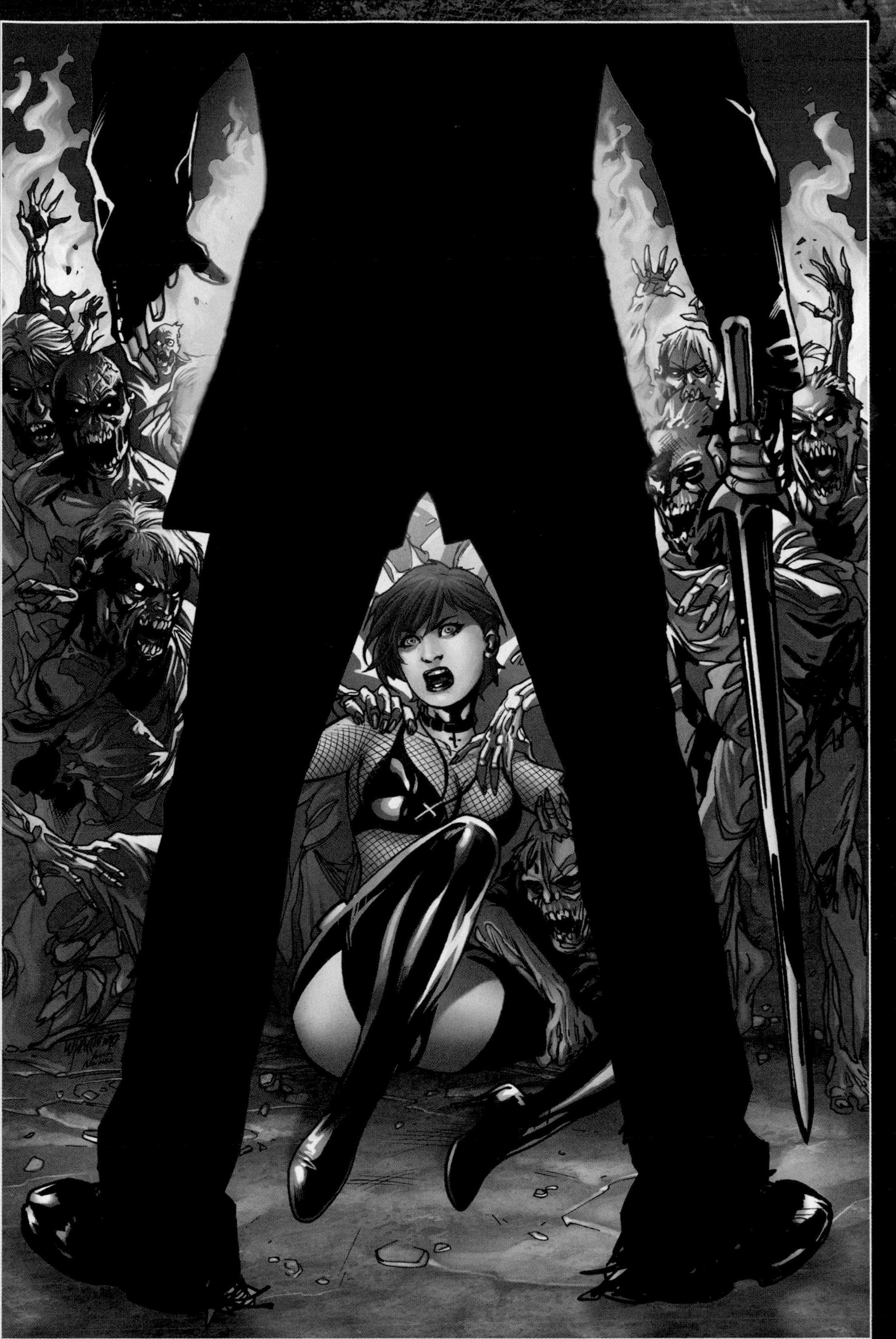

Issue #5 cover by EMANUELA LUPACCHINO

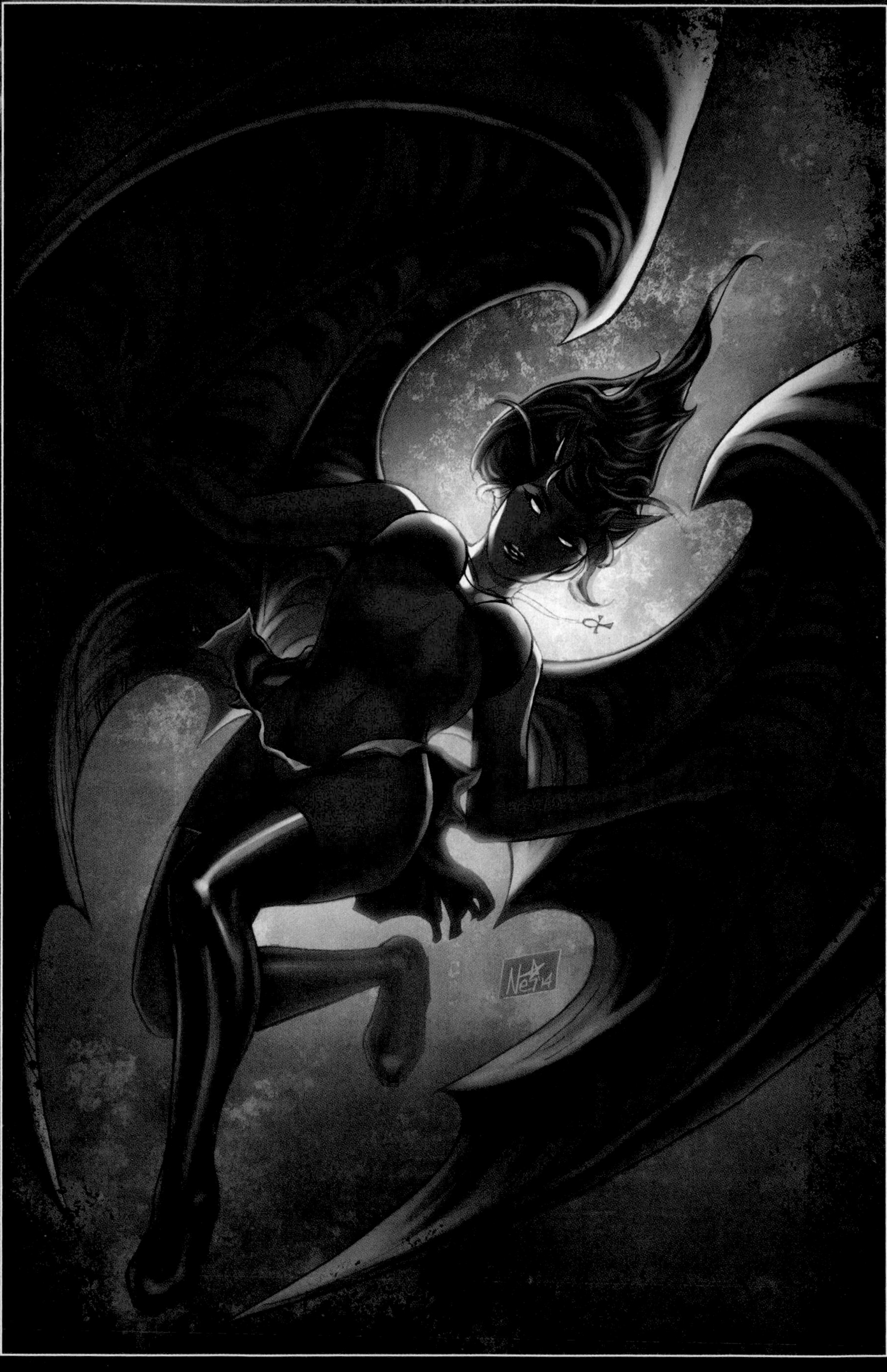

issue #5 cover by NEI RUFFINO

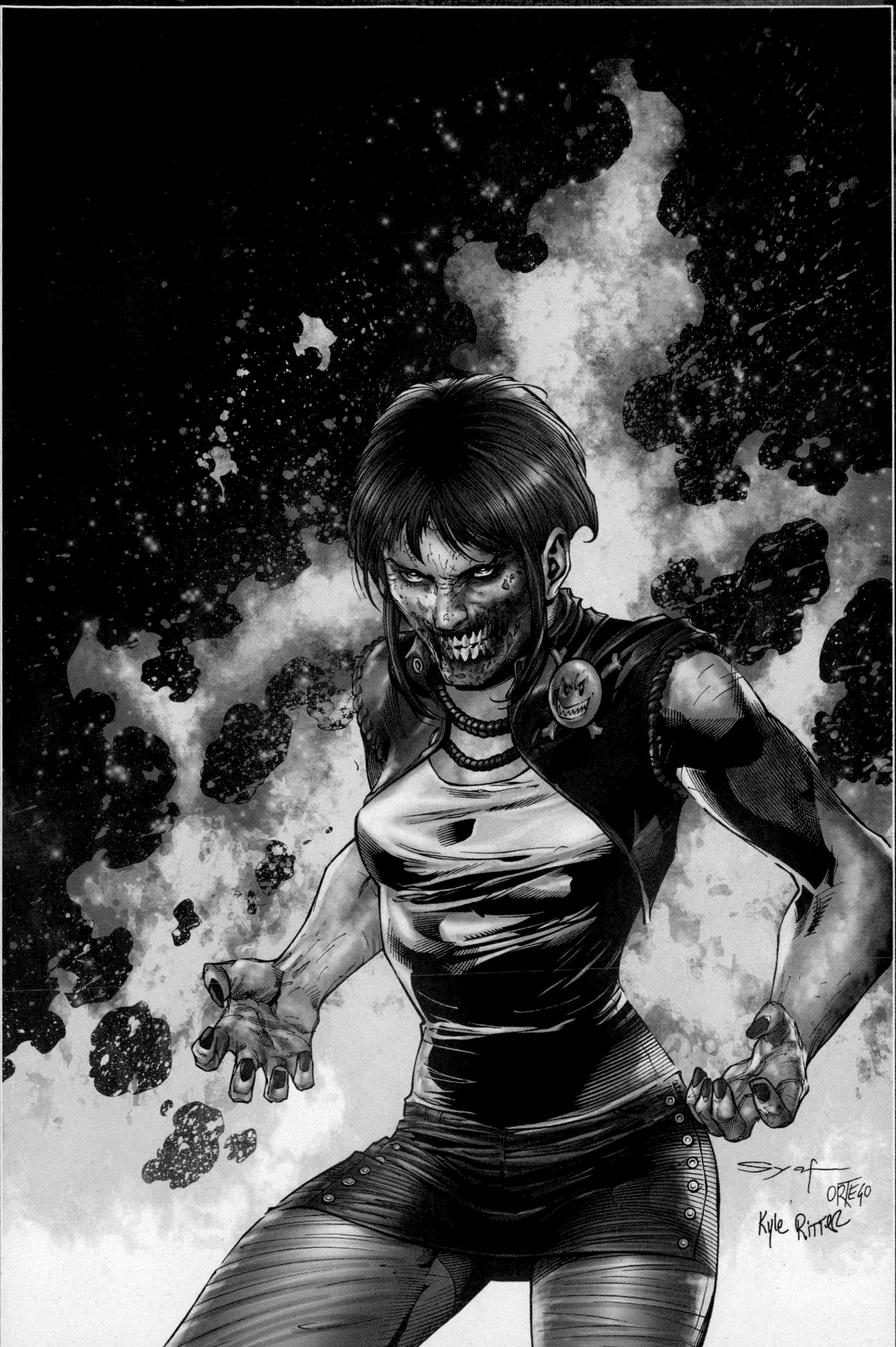
Syaf
ORTEGO
Kyle Ritter

issue #5 cover by ARDIAN SYAF

inks by GUILLERMO ORTEGO colors by KYLE RITTER

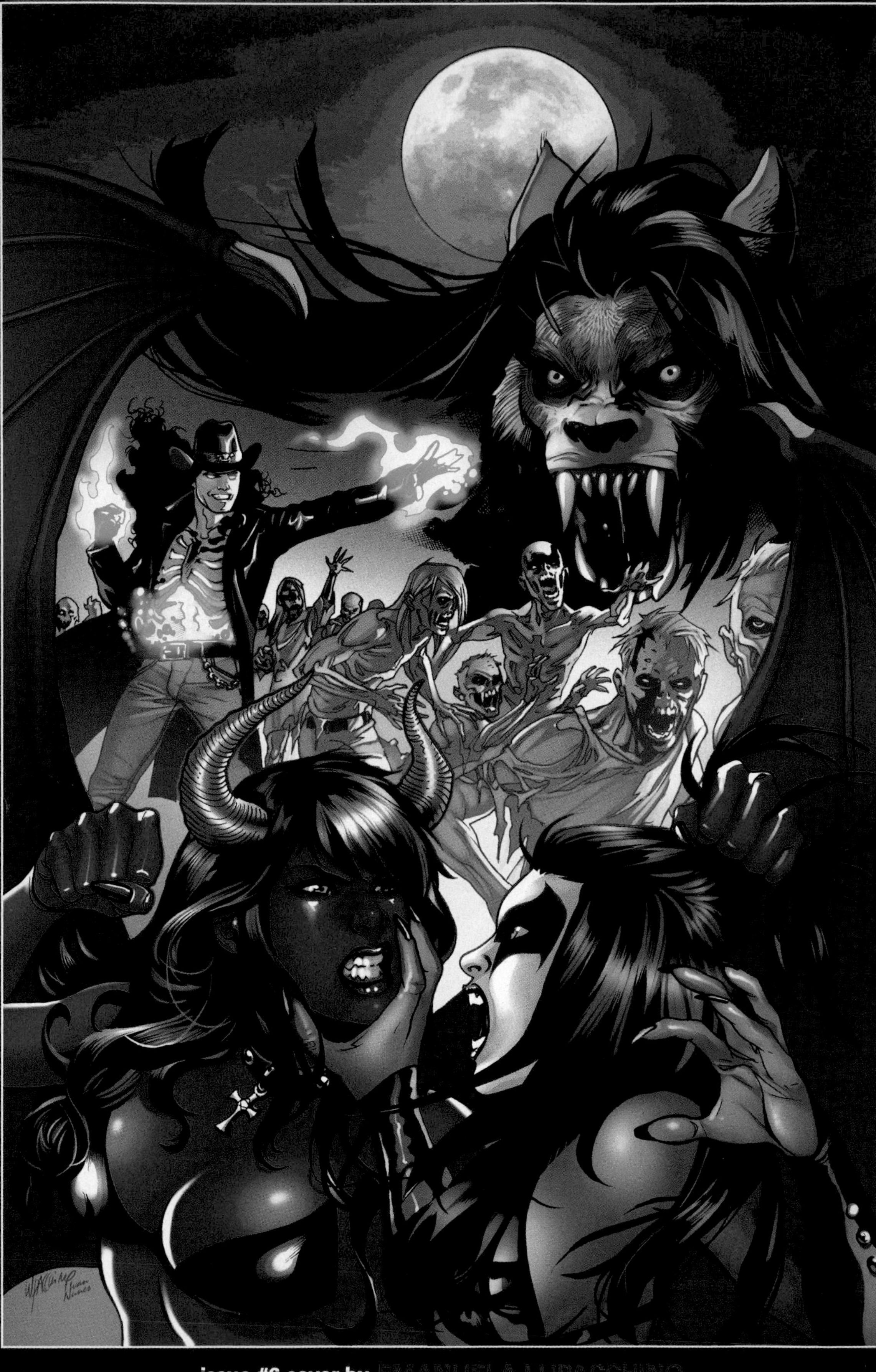

issue #6 cover by EMANUELA LUPACCHINO
colors by IVAN NUNES

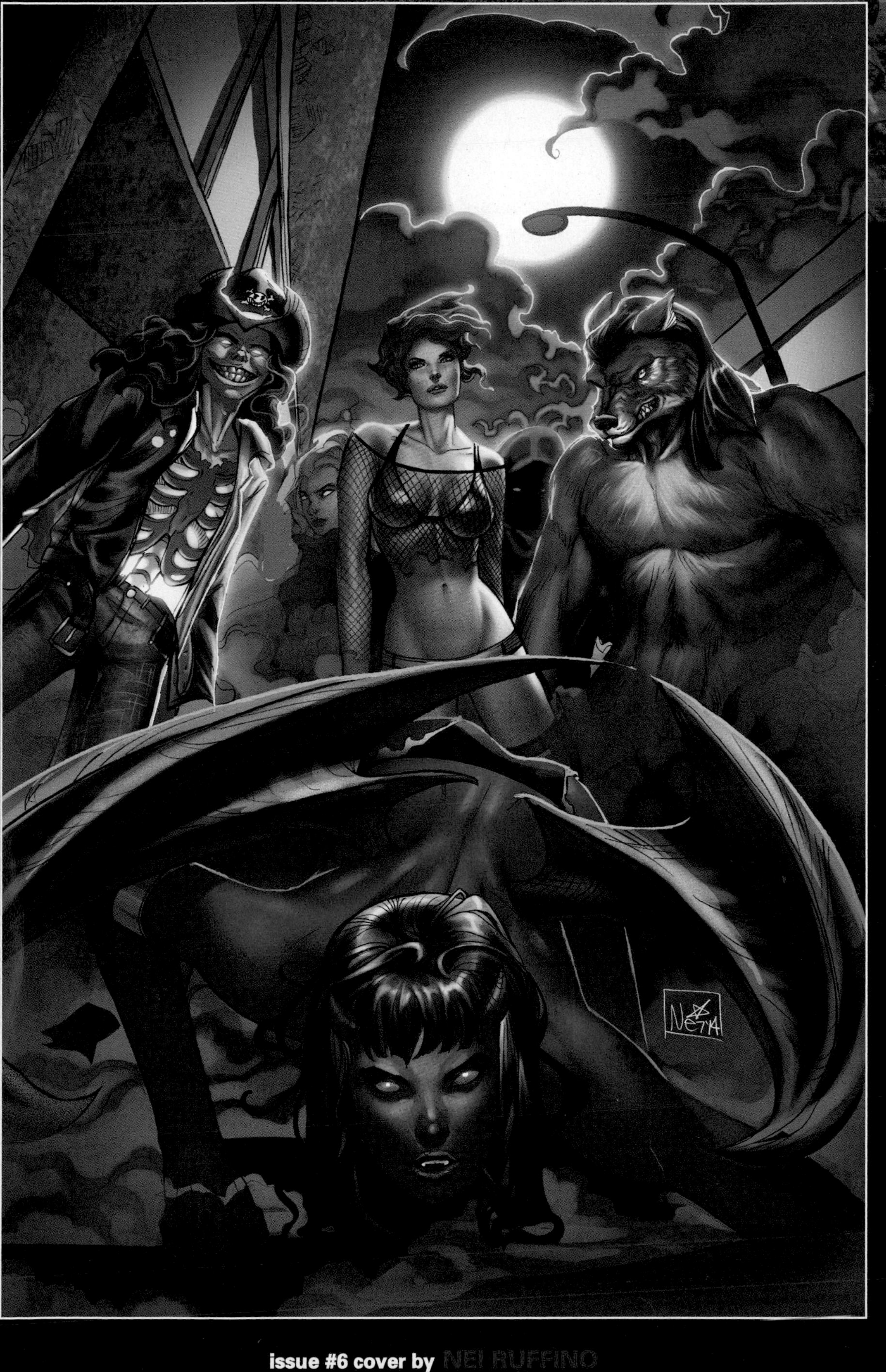
NEI 14

issue #6 cover by NEI RUFFINO

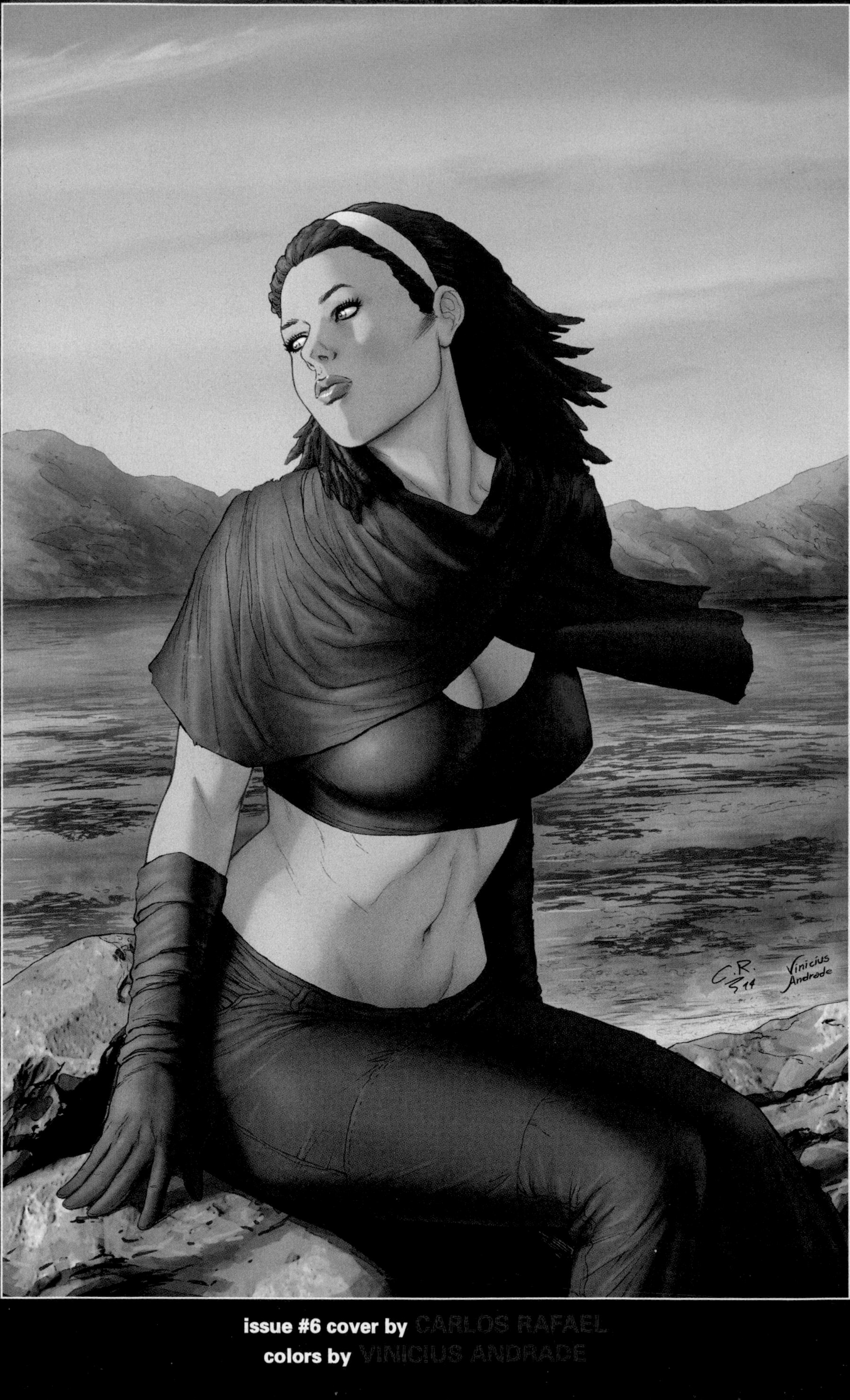
C.R.
Vinicius Andrade

issue #6 cover by CARLOS RAFAEL
colors by VINICIUS ANDRADE